Health and Work Productivity

The John D. and Catherine T. MacArthur Foundation

Series on Mental Health and Development

HEALTH & WORK PRODUCTIVITY

Making the Business Case for Quality Health Care

RONALD C. KESSLER
AND PAUL E. STANG, EDITORS

THE UNIVERSITY OF CHICAGO PRESS • Chicago & London

RONALD C. KESSLER is professor in the Department
of Health Care Policy at Harvard Medical School. He is the coeditor
of several volumes, including, most recently, *How Healthy Are We?
A National Study of Well-Being at Midlife*, also published by
the University of Chicago Press.
PAUL E. STANG is associate professor in the College of Health Sciences
at the West Chester University of Pennsylvania and executive vice president
and chief scientific officer at Galt Associates, a medical risk management
consulting firm.

The University of Chicago Press, Chicago 60637
The University of Chicago Press, Ltd., London
© 2006 by The University of Chicago
All rights reserved. Published 2006
Printed in the United States of America

15 14 13 12 11 10 09 08 07 06   1 2 3 4 5

ISBN: 0-226-43212-2 (cloth)

Library of Congress Cataloging-in-Publication Data

Health & work productivity : making the business case for quality health care /
Ronald C. Kessler and Paul E. Stang, editors.
    p. ; cm. — (The John D. and Catherine T. MacArthur Foundation series on
mental health and development)
    Includes bibliographical references and index.
    ISBN 0-226-43212-2 (cloth : alk. paper)
    1. Health—Social aspects. 2. Social medicine. 3. Industrial hygiene. 4. Labor
productivity. [DNLM: 1. Cost of Illness—Congresses. 2. Occupational Health—
Congresses. 3. Efficiency, Organizational—economics—Congresses.
4. Employer Health Costs—Congresses. 5. Health Benefit Plans, Employee—
economics—Congresses. 6. Health Policy—Congresses. WA 400 H43445 2006]
I. Title: Health and work productivity. II. Kessler, Ronald C. III. Stang, Paul E.
IV. Series.

RC963.H43 2006
362.1—dc22   2005024583

⊗ The paper used in this publication meets the minimum
requirements of the American National Standard for Information
Sciences—Permanence of Paper for Printed Library Materials,
ANSI Z39.48-1992.

Contents

Acknowledgments

ix

Chapter 1
Intersecting Issues in the Evaluation of Health and Work Productivity
RONALD C. KESSLER AND PAUL E. STANG

I

PART ONE
APPROACHES TO STUDYING THE EFFECTS OF
HEALTH ON WORKER PRODUCTIVITY

Chapter 2
Linking Administrative Claim Data with Archival
Productivity Measures to Inform Employer Decision-Making
PAUL E. GREENBERG AND HOWARD G. BIRNBAUM

29

Chapter 3
Simulation for Measurement of Occupational Performance
JONATHAN HOWLAND, THOMAS W. MANGIONE, AND ANGELA LARAMIE

54

Chapter 4
Measuring Health-Related Work Productivity with Self-Reports
DEBRA J. LERNER AND JENNIFER LEE

66

Chapter 5
Use of the Experience Sampling Method in Studies
of Illness and Work Performance
PHILIP S. WANG AND NANCY A. NICOLSON
88

Chapter 6
Estimating the Dollar Costs of Productivity Losses Due to Illness:
An Application of O*NET
LANCE ANDERSON, SCOTT H. OPPLER, AND ANDREW ROSE
120

Chapter 7
Labor-Market Consequences of Health Impairments
THOMAS DELEIRE AND WILLARD G. MANNING
142

PART TWO
STAKEHOLDER PERSPECTIVES

Chapter 8
Overcoming Barriers to Managing Health and Productivity in the Workplace
DENNIS P. SCANLON
165

Chapter 9
Investing in Health to Boost Employee Productivity:
The Employer's Perspective
JAMES F. MURRAY, SEAN NICHOLSON, MARK PAULY, AND MARC L. BERGER
185

Chapter 10
The Role of Health Plans in Linking Quality of Care to Labor Outcomes:
Challenges and Opportunities
ARNE BECK
207

Chapter 11
The Pharmaceutical Industry and Productivity Research
CHRISTOPHER J. EVANS
224

Chapter 12
A Regulatory Perspective on Productivity Claims:
Implications for Future Productivity Research
PAUL E. STANG, PAUL E. GREENBERG, HOWARD G. BIRNBAUM,
RONALD C. KESSLER, LYNN HOFFMAN, AND MEI-SHENG DUH
242

Chapter 13
Investing in Health to Promote Human Capital in Developing Countries:
The Importance of Productivity and Health to the World Bank
HARVEY WHITEFORD
253

PART THREE
CONCLUSION

Chapter 14
Future Directions in Health and Work Productivity Research
RONALD C. KESSLER AND PAUL E. STANG
271

Contributors
287

Author Index
289

Subject Index
297

Acknowledgments

This volume is the product of a conference that was held with support from the John D. and Catherine T. MacArthur Foundation as part of its larger support of the Harvard Health and Work Performance Initiative. The purpose of the conference was to bring together researchers and policy stakeholders who have an interest in the relationship between worker health and job performance in order to build a consensus about the best ways to conceptualize and measure work performance. Such a consensus could aid in evaluating the effects of ill health on work performance and the ameliorative effects of guideline-based treatment on reversing these effects.

The idea for the conference came from our impression, based on a review of the health-and-productivity literature and discussions with stakeholders, that there was a mismatch between the measures and designs of researchers, which were geared primarily to communicating with colleagues in scientific journals, and the needs of stakeholders for practical measures and research designs that could be implemented and used to make real-world health care purchasing decisions. Academic research was not having much effect on practice, we felt, because academic researchers were focused too much on talking to each other and not enough on talking to the people who make health care purchasing decisions. The idea to bring the two groups together and to publish the results of the meeting was a natural extension of this thinking.

The conference and the work that went into preparing the chapters presented there would not have been possible without the vision of Bob Rose, who was at the time of the conference the director of the Health Program at the John D. and Catherine T. MacArthur Foundation. We thank him for his thoughtful guidance and intellectual support of our work. Other colleagues who played an important part in shaping our ideas about health and productivity include Janna Crittendon, Alison Keith, Dennis Richling, Sean Sullivan, and Bill Whitmer, all of whom will see their influences in the organization and focus of this volume. Finally, we would like to thank the staff of the

Harvard Health and Work Performance Initiative for their excellent work organizing the conference, editing the papers, and preparing the manuscript for publication. Special thanks go to Eric Bourke, Jerry Garcia, Alison Hoffnagle, Josh Kendall, Lisa Pfeiffer, Emily Phares, and Todd Strauss, as productive a crew as any boss could ever hope to have work for him.

CHAPTER 1

Intersecting Issues in the Evaluation of Health and Work Productivity

RONALD C. KESSLER AND PAUL E. STANG

INTRODUCTION

Interest in the social consequences of illness has broadened in the past decade as policy analysts have joined health economists and health services researchers to devise methods that rationalize the allocation of health care resources (Gold et al. 1996; Sloan 1996). Research showing that untreated and undertreated health problems exact substantial personal costs from the individuals who experience them as well as from their families, employers, and communities has been a central part of this work (Patrick and Erickson 1993; Tarlov et al. 1989). Among the most important of these results have been those concerning the workplace costs of illness from the perspective of the employer (Kessler, Davis, et al. 2001; Pauly et al. 2002). There are enormous implications for the economy. For example, a recent study estimated that depression causes an annual loss of $33 billion in work absenteeism in the United States (Greenberg et al. 1996). Given the low rate of depression treatment (Kessler, Zhao, et al. 1999) and the fact that treatment substantially improves role functioning among people with depression (Coulehan et al. 1997; Wells et al. 2000), such data suggest that it might be cost-effective for employers to increase the proportion of depressed workers who receive treatment (Kessler, Barber, et al. 1999). Similar arguments have been made for a number of other illnesses (Boonen et al. 2002; Kessler, Almeida, et al. 2001; Reginster and Khaltaev 2002).

The underlying notion in these arguments is that expansion of employee health care benefits might represent an investment opportunity for employers. This assertion is presumably most true for interventions aimed at commonly occurring health problems that have substantial effects on work performance, that are undertreated, and that can be treated in a cost-effective manner. Indeed, reallocation of existing health care benefits to focus more heavily on costly conditions for which effective interventions exist would presumably be a way to enhance the benefits of employer-sponsored health care to employers in the absence of additional investment. Epidemiological surveys document the existence of a number of undertreated conditions that have substantial effects on work performance (Kessler 2001). Controlled evaluations document the cost-effectiveness of interventions for a number of these conditions that focus either on prevention (Serxner et al. 2001), treatment quality improvement (Lucas et al. 2001), or disability management (Atcheson 2001). Yet, only a small minority of employers has embraced the notion that reallocation of existing health care resources to focus on these conditions or expanded health care benefits to include more of these conditions can be cost-effective. Why has this uptake been so low?

There has been much speculation among health care researchers and policy advocates about this question. A number of factors are doubtlessly involved. One of the most important is that employers have traditionally thought of health care as a benefit, not an investment. The responsibility for health care purchasing has consequently been delegated to benefit managers rather than to investment managers, with the result that health care investment decisions have been divorced from the line functions of the company. Health care benefit managers have therefore typically been rewarded for minimizing costs rather than for maximizing profits. This reward structure, in turn, has encouraged a silo mentality, in which positive effects of expanded health care outside of the medical department, such as effects on increased productivity, have been devalued or ignored completely by benefits managers.

But things are changing. There has been a dramatic increase in empirical research on the association between poor health and low work productivity over the past decade (Brandt-Rauf, Burton, and McCunney 2001). This research strongly suggests that interventions aimed at prevention, early detection, and best-practices treatment of workers with targeted health problems can promote substantial productivity gains for employers. Such evidence comes at a time when corporate America is experiencing dramatic changes due to an unprecedented series of mergers, acquisitions, and associated downsizing (Carter 1999). Corporate belt-tightening caused by these changes now requires workers to perform increasingly complex tasks and to produce much more per worker than their predecessors (Marks and DeMeuse 2002). These requirements, in turn, lead to substantial increases in per-worker training investments. As training investments grow and the base of workers on which they are made narrows, employers will inevitably come to realize that corporate success hinges more than ever on the strength of human capital (Fitz-Enz 2000). They will begin thinking of employee health care as not only an employee benefit, but also a human capital investment opportunity that needs to be optimized. Even in times of shrinking resources this way of thinking will be important, because the negative impact on work performance of the need to cut benefits can presumably be muted by targeted reductions in treatments that are known not to have positive effects on work performance.

Based on this new mind-set, a number of corporations have moved to an integrated model of health and productivity management in an effort to break down the silo mentality that has hampered the rationalization of health and productivity management in the past (McGrail et al. 2002; Watson and Huban 1997). A practical impediment, though, is the lack of data and systems to capture and measure information about the relationship between employee health and productivity (Miller 2001). In the absence of such information, it is impossible to implement a rational program of integrated benefit management. Although most corporations have access to anonymous employee health claims and pharmacy data through third-party vendors, information on untreated health problems is usually nonexistent, making it impossible to evaluate the potential effects of expanded outreach and treatment programs. Similarly, productivity data are usually unavailable at the individual level. Even basic data on short-term sickness absence are collected in many companies only for blue-collar and pink-collar workers, not for white-collar workers. Work-performance data, furthermore, are often nonexistent, superficial, or very difficult to obtain in machine-readable form.

Recognizing the need for such data, health service researchers have developed measurement tools that can be used to collect self-report data on health and work performance in employee surveys. Lynch and Riedel (2001) and Loeppke and colleagues (2003) reviewed the most widely used of these tools. The self-report data collected in this way are clearly inferior to objective archival data about health from physical examinations and about productivity from either payroll records or objective performance audits. Unlike archival data, though, self-report data can easily be obtained for an entire workforce by administering a simple self-report (Kessler et al. 2003). As a result, the developers of these methods argue that self-report measures could be of great value to facilitate integrated benefit management. Judging from the high interest in the self-report tools on the part of corporate human resource professionals and management consultants, employer-consumers seem to agree. However, none of the existing self-report measures has emerged as the preferred tool for integrated-benefit-management research. Nor has a consensus yet emerged about a data collection and analysis paradigm for the use of such a measure.

The institutionalization of a consistent measurement-and-analysis approach is clearly a critical next step in the evolution of integrated benefit management. This volume is the outgrowth of a conference sponsored by the John D. and Catherine T. MacArthur Foundation to work toward the development of such an approach. Rather than start with the assumption that self-report assessment is the preferred methodology, the conference brought together experts in all three of the main approaches to individual-level productivity measurement that are currently in wide use among health services researchers: archival measurement of actual objective productivity indicators (e.g., days worked, units produced); simulation of performance in hypothetical situations (e.g., flight simulators for airline pilots, standardized typing tests for clerical workers); and self-report. The experts were asked to review the methodological state of the art in their areas of measurement, to discuss the substantive health and productivity research questions that they envisioned this measurement approach as being best suited to answer, and to present the research designs that they considered optimal for answering these research questions. Our organizing assumption in making this request, which was confirmed in the discussions that followed each presentation at the conference, was that the three measurement approaches were oriented toward answering somewhat different kinds of research questions and that choosing the best measurement approach depends on the question being asked.

The conference also included representatives of stakeholders who have an interest in using the results of health and productivity research for practical decision-making. We asked each stakeholder to begin by telling us the kinds of research questions they would like to see answered by health and productivity research, setting forth the standards of proof that they would find convincing, and describing the gaps that exist between the perspectives of the measurement experts and the realities of the decision-making situations faced by stakeholders. Although our initial focus was on employer-purchasers, it quickly became clear as we began planning the conference that the number of stakeholders is actually much broader than we originally envisioned. We came to see that within the corporate environment, the perspective of benefit managers, who attempt to maximize value for fixed resources, is quite different from the perspective of the senior corporate decision-makers, who determine the volume of resources to invest in employee benefits, and that both of these differ from the perspective of the labor economists, whose focus is more on the functioning of markets than on the performance of individual companies within those markets. As a result, a separate panel of experts was invited to a subsequent conference to present the perspectives of human resource managers, senior management, and the labor market.

The markets in which employer-purchasers operate are regulated by entities that have different perspectives from those of the market actors. The two most relevant groups of market actors in the United States for health and productivity management are the agencies that monitor occupational health and safety and the agencies that regulate the research-based claims of health plans and pharmaceutical companies about the effects of their products and services on work performance. We consequently included experts at the conference who discussed the perspectives of the National Institute for Occupational Safety and Health (NIOSH) and the Federal Drug Administration (FDA). In addition, experts affiliated with the International Labor Organization discussed health and productivity from the employee perspective. Finally, experts from the World Bank considered health care as a human-capital investment in developing countries based on a societal perspective.

The give and take among conference participants made it clear that researchers who work with each of the three main measurement approaches differ in the research questions they address and that these questions are not always the same as the ones posed by stakeholders. This mismatch has almost certainly slowed the development of agreement about the best approach to take in health and productivity data collection and data analysis in the integrated-benefit-management arena. Although the conference did not resolve these discrepancies, it did sensitize participants to the existence of the discrepancies and, in this way, resolved some previous confusion. We hope that the sharing of perspectives among participants at the conference, and now among readers of this volume, will be helpful to health service researchers in their ongoing efforts to carry out research that captures the interest of employer-purchasers.

PART 1 OF THE BOOK

Part i presents a review of the three main productivity-measurement approaches now being used in health and productivity research. We begin with a discussion by Paul Greenberg and Howard Birnbaum about the use of objective archival performance data. The ideal data-availability situation for integrated benefit management is for a company to offer annual physical examinations to all its employees and to link the results with archival data on health claims, pharmacy claims, work-related accidents and injuries, sickness absence, and work performance. These data would make it possible to describe the associations between untreated illness and work performance, to evaluate before-after changes in employee health and productivity based on interventions that are aimed at increasing the rate of treatment or the quality of treatment, and to monitor ongoing trends in these patterns in a quality-assurance framework. If all companies possessed integrated data of this sort, there would be no need for the current volume. However, most companies lack such a full collection of data, and therefore it is necessary to develop special measurement and data-analysis procedures to support integrated health and productivity management. Greenberg and Birnbaum discuss one set of such procedures: to work with objective archival data for some of the elements we would ideally like to study in a segment of the workforce. The particular case they consider is one in which good short-term trend data are available on individual-level worker productivity linked to medical claim data. Greenberg and Birnbaum show that partial linked databases of this sort can be very useful in drawing inferences both about the adverse effects of illness on work performance and about the effects of medical interventions.

It is important to recognize that the data considered by Greenberg and Birnbaum are usually available only for a small number of occupations within any one company. This limitation would not greatly detract from the ability to develop rational integrated-benefit-management strategies in those cases where specific occupations dominate a company workforce (e.g., delivery truck drivers in a large nationwide delivery company). In the more typical scenario, however, objective data on productivity are not available for the majority of the workforce. If decision-makers are willing to assume that the patterns found in a restricted set of work units apply, at least in part, to the remainder of the workforce, then focused archival data analyses on these units can be very useful. One would think that such an extrapolation would be most secure for inferences about the effects of new medical interventions. For example, if the introduction of nonsedating antihistamines into the company drug formulary leads both to increased treatment of seasonal allergies in the medical claim database for the entire company and to substantially increased productivity among the workers who receive such treatment in the segment of the workforce where archival productivity data exist, then a good indirect case could be made that this is a cost-effective innovation. The case would be stronger yet if the company had, say, three or four different types of workers for whom archival productivity data were available and this kind of analysis could be carried out, each using a different type of productivity measure (e.g., number of claims resolved per week among claims processors, number of new sales among salespeople, supervisor ratings of performance quality among telephone customer-service representatives).

In addition to presenting data to illustrate how such data can be used to make practical employer-purchaser decisions, Greenberg and Birnbaum discuss future expansions of research using archival records that link such records across a variety of different sources (e.g., clinical trials and archival administrative claims files) in novel ways to answer particular research questions. One of the most interesting possibilities here would be to blend objective archival data collected in the segments of the workforce where such data are available with self-report data collected in the entire workforce in an effort to increase the external validity of archival data analysis. For example, archival medical claim data could be merged with self-report productivity data obtained from all workers in an annual health risk appraisal survey, and this combined data file could be used to carry out analyses identical to those described by Greenberg and Birnbaum in the entire workforce. The objective archival work-performance data available for workers in a small number of occupations could then be merged into this integrated data file in order to validate self-reports of performance and to compare the estimated effects of health problems on performance using objective versus self-report data. Confirmation of consistency of results, using both archival productivity data in the restricted sample and self-report productivity data in the entire workforce, would substantially increase confidence in extrapolating results based on the archival data from the restricted sample to the entire workforce.

Jonathan Howland, Thomas Mangione, and Angela Laramie discuss a second commonly used approach to performance assessment: simulation. Simulations are tests that allow researchers to get a total picture of performance on a job by collecting data for standardized tasks in controlled settings. The authors note that even though occupational simulation has been used since the early years of the last century, opportunities for applying this method have greatly expanded since the development of personal computers. Simulation is not suited to all types of jobs. It would be difficult, for example, to devise a simulation to assess the work performance of a lawyer—but not so much because of the complexity of the work. It would be much easier to use simulation to assess the performance of a heart surgeon, even though heart surgery is an extremely complex type of work. The point is that valid simulations become more difficult to devise as the variety and interpersonal complexity of the work increases. In situations where formal simulations are not possible, naturalistic quasi-simulation equivalents are often possible. A common method of evaluating the performance of workers who interact with the public is the "mystery-customer" method (Johnson and Gustafsson 2000). In this naturalistic equivalent of a simulation, a company that offers consumer services either recruits someone from the community or uses an actor to play the part of a difficult customer in an effort to evaluate the performance of customer-service personnel in dealing with the public. The evaluation can be based either on a tape recording of interactions (e.g., when bogus customers call an airline reservations 800 number to see how well the telephone sales agents do their job) or on ratings of worker performance made by the mystery customer at the end of the interaction (e.g., when bogus customers visit stores in a convenience store chain to check on store staff performance). Large corporations with a strong customer-service orientation often use the mystery-customer method as one core determinant of store managers' quarterly bonuses. A similar approach has been employed to evaluate the performance of physicians in dealing with complex complaints presented by bogus patients (Lawrie, Parsons, and Patrick 1996).

An important limitation of simulation and quasi-simulation methods is that they can be expensive to develop and implement. It is not uncommon for some simulations to take a full day to complete, and quasi-simulations using the mystery-customer approach usually require a number of replications for each individual or unit being evaluated during each evaluation time period. These requirements can result in substantial per-unit assessment costs that have limited the use of simulation as a routine aspect of performance evaluation. Therefore, routine use of simulation is generally limited to four types of situations. One involves safety-sensitive jobs in which it is important to have training and evaluation of response to crises. The simulated drills that are routine in situations of this sort are sometimes very expensive; the extreme case is "war games" that can cost tens of millions of dollars, used by the military to simulate actual battle situations. Because readiness in safety-sensitive jobs is so crucial for public safety, simulations are carried out despite their financial burden. A second situation in which simulation is commonplace involves cases wherein the costs of in vivo training and evaluation (e.g., with actual flight experience) are themselves high and the costs of developing complex simulations are offset by the cost savings of substituting simulation for some aspects of in vivo training. In the third type of situation the number of workers is so large that the cost of developing a complicated simulation (e.g., fork-lift-operator performance simulation) can be justified. For the fourth situation simulations can quite easily be developed, implemented, and evaluated for a large number of workers (e.g., computer-based clerical worker simulations).

A great advantage of simulations over other methods of performance evaluation is that they can be used to explore the limits of performance in ways that would not be either practical or ethical with in vivo evaluation. It is interesting to note, with regard to this feature, that health and productivity studies based on simulations often include experimental manipulations of exposure to drugs that might have adverse effects on work performance (e.g., the effects of alcohol on motor control). A variant on this approach is the experimental manipulation of exposure to allergens in a pollen chamber to simulate the effects of seasonal allergy on work performance (Howarth 1999). Although studies of this sort tell us nothing definitive about work performance in any real workforce, they generate useful information about likely effects in settings that do not create dangers for the participants or inefficiencies in real work processes.

Simulations yield data that are similar in this respect to the limited archival data described in chapter 2 by Greenberg and Birnbaum. Indeed, performance audits, one of the most common ways in which archival productivity data of the sort described by Greenberg and Birnbaum are generated (Harbour 1997), can be thought of as in vivo equivalents of simulations. Perhaps the most important similarity for our purposes is that both limited archival evaluation and simulation generate unique evaluations for workers in one, or at most a few, occupations rather than broad-based evaluations of all workers in a company. Thus our earlier discussion about the possibility of blending self-report work-performance assessments obtained for an entire workforce with archival assessments that focus on a more limited subset of workers applies equally well to the potential blending of self-report with simulation data.

Debra Lerner and Jennifer Lee, in chapter 4, review recent methodological advances in the development of self-report work-productivity measures. Although acknowledging that self-reports are inferior to objective measures, the authors correctly note that self-reports are often the only feasible measures of work productivity. It is therefore important to evaluate the limits of accuracy of self-report measures, as well as to consider ways in which accuracy can be improved. Recent calibration studies have shown that self-reports can be surprisingly accurate. Two recent studies, for example, indicate that self-reports about sickness-absence days in the past week and the past month are very strongly related to official payroll record data on sickness absence (Kessler et al. 2003; Revecki et al. 1994). This result is very encouraging in light of the fact, noted earlier in this introduction, that data on short-term sickness absence is not available for white-collar workers in many major corporations. Lerner and Lee also review evidence that some self-report measures about quantity and quality of work performance are significantly related to archival productivity records.

Despite this encouraging evidence, self-reports are likely to be such a critical aspect of health and productivity management in the future that test developers should continue to explore strategies to improve the accuracy of these reports. It is useful to begin such an exploration by noting that self-reports of factual information are all subject to three types of errors: lack of understanding on the part of the respondent about how to answer the question; unwillingness to provide an accurate response; and inability to provide an accurate response. Survey methodologists have developed ways to deal with all three types of errors (Sudman, Bradburn, and Schwarz 1996). Lerner and Lee focus on the first of the three, emphasizing the importance of rigorous pilot testing and debriefing to guarantee that self-report questions make sense to respondents. But the other two types of error can be equally, if not more, damaging.

Regarding the second source of error, workers might be reluctant to give honest answers about their work productivity for fear that their responses will have adverse effects on their job conditions. However, there is clear evidence from experimental studies that improvements in explanations of the rationale of the data-collection, increases in the perceived integrity of the auspices of the data collection, and improvements in confidentiality guarantees can all substantially improve workers' willingness to give honest responses (Turner et al. 1998). More research is needed on the effects of these enhancements on self-reports in employee health and productivity research.

Regarding the third source of error, methodological studies demonstrate that surveys about factual reports, such as those concerning self-reported productivity, often ask respondents about things that they are unable to report accurately, even if they are willing, because of the limits of encoding and memory (Clark and Schober 1992). Surveys that ask respondents to tell more than they know indirectly encourage guessing (Tourangeau, Rips, and Rasinski 2000). It is consequently important, in developing self-report surveys about health and work productivity, to recognize the limits of memory and to tailor questions to ask only about factual details that respondents are able to report. In doing this, though, one must also appreciate that people often know more than they think they know and that the accuracy of factual reports can be improved by using questioning strategies that help respondents recover memories through thoughtful cognitive search strategies. A good deal of research has been done to develop such strategies for purposes of obtaining accurate retrospective reports in surveys (Schwarz and

Oyserman 2001). It would be useful to explore the possibility of using some of these same strategies to improve the accuracy of self-reports in health and productivity research.

Philip Wang and Nancy Nicolson, in chapter 5, describe a special kind of self-report measurement technique that is designed to minimize the problem of recall bias. This method, called the Experience Sampling Method (ESM), uses a signaling device (such as a pager) to prompt respondents at randomly chosen times to record moment-in-time experiences in an ESM diary. The data collection typically continues for a period of days or weeks so that a representative sample of moments-in-time is built up to characterize either the individual (if a large enough sample of time points is available) or the population (based on a two-stage clustered sample of random moments-in-time among randomly selected individuals in the population). Unlike more typical self-reports that require recall over a week or a month, ESM asks respondents to report on experiences more or less as they are happening, thus eliminating recall bias. In addition, since ESM produces multiple "snapshots" of the experiences of respondents, it can enable researchers to study events that are rapidly changing, such as a respondent's improved work performance as he recovers from an episode of depression. Wang and Nicolson, in their description of ways in which ESM has been used to study chronic illnesses, state that most such studies have to date focused on contextual variables that affect symptoms rather than on the impact of illness on work performance. However, Wang and Nicolson note, ESM could be a very good method for studying the connection between illness and work productivity.

Because of the data-collection demands of ESM, it is not realistic to think that this method will ever be widely used to carry out ongoing audits of work performance in large workforces. However, it might be possible to use ESM to calibrate more conventional self-report measures in situations where objective archival measures are not available. For example, ESM was used in methodological studies of the World Health Organization Health and Work Performance Questionnaire (HPQ) (Kessler et al. 2003). The HPQ includes retrospective self-report questions about such things as time off-task and concentration at work over the past week. Responses to those questions were calibrated by comparing them with ESM reports obtained from the same respondents about these experiences at random moments over the previous work week. ESM can also be used to gain insights into the mechanisms involved in the effects of specific illnesses on more global measures of productivity, whether based on objective or self-report assessment methods, by decomposing these effects into separate assessments of time, such as length of work breaks, time off-task while ostensibly working, and concentrating versus daydreaming while performing work tasks. Such decompositions, in turn, might be useful in designing interventions aimed at reducing the performance decrements associated with target health problems.

The four chapters reviewed up to this point differ not only in the kinds of measurement approaches they espouse, but also in the extent to which they focus on component versus aggregate performance outcomes. Greenberg and Birnbaum concern themselves largely with aggregate measures of performance, such as number of claims processed by a claims processor over a two-week period. Their focus is clearly on the task of monetizing these performance measures as a first step in the calculation of return on investment of medical interventions for target conditions. Lerner and Lee, in comparison, emphasize separate measures of the core component activities that go into performance (e.g., difficulties with such things as lifting, walking, and concentrating). Their rationale for doing so is a reasonable one: that self-reports about more abstract global outcomes, such as self-rated overall work performance, are likely to be much less accurate than separate self-reports about more concrete activity limitations. However, if this disaggregation is intended to improve measurement quality, we have to consider the measurement implications of subsequently recombining responses to arrive at an aggregate assessment of overall work performance. Lerner and Lee do not do this. This task is nontrivial, as the importance of individual component activities to overall work performance doubtlessly varies enormously across occupations. Difficulty in lifting because of a bad back, for example, is presumably much more disruptive to the work of a manual laborer than to that of a white-collar worker, while the reverse is probably true of difficulty in concentration. One cannot simply add up reports of difficulties across these different domains to arrive at an assessment of overall difficulty in work performance without taking differences in relevance into account.

Lerner and Lee do not grapple with this problem because they implicitly approach the study of health and work performance from a quality-of-life perspective rather than from a cost-of-illness perspective. In the quality-of-life perspective, the researcher attempts to create a profile of the many ways in which health problems affect the lives of the people who suffer from them by evaluating functioning across a wide range of life domains (Patrick and Erickson 1993). The purpose is to demonstrate that the effects of illness are multidimensional; no effort is made to aggregate the separate effects into a summary score. Documenting that particular illnesses have adverse effects in many different areas of life and that particular treatments help restore functioning in these same areas is enough in itself from this perspective. Researchers with a cost-of-illness perspective, in comparison, favor self-report work-performance measures that are global rather than disaggregated because an assessment of overall work performance is needed to estimate the cost of illness.

Another perspective that favors disaggregated assessment of work performance is the pharmacoepidemiological perspective, which is illustrated by Howland and coauthors' description of the use of simulation to study drug effects. From this perspective, the researcher studies the effects of a particular drug by profiling the effects of the drug (both positive and negative) on a wide range of dimensions of behavioral, cognitive, and emotional functioning. Simulation is ideal for studying the behavioral aspects of these effects by experimentally manipulating exposures to a drug and then evaluating the effects on subtle aspects of behavioral functioning that can be measured much more accurately in simulations than in naturalistic settings. As the focus is on multidimensional assessment, no attempt is made to aggregate the different measures of outcomes into a global measure of overall work performance. Because of this orientation, Howland and his colleagues, like Lerner and Lee, do not discuss ways in which the detailed measurements of performance effects in simulations can be combined to create global assessments of overall work performance.

The same favoring of disaggregated to global assessment can be found in the discussion of ESM methods by Wang and Nicolson. The strength of ESM, like that of simulation, is the ability to obtain detailed assessments that disaggregate global measures into components. In the case of simulation, the disaggregation is substantive, while in ESM the disaggregation is temporal. The focus in ESM is on sampling randomly selected moments-in-time to assess thoughts, behaviors, and emotions that are occurring at the immediate moment of assessment. Sampling theory is then used to make accurate inferences from this sample to all moments throughout the entire workweek. Unlike simulation, though, the substantive assessment is no more disaggregated in ESM than in any other self-report measures. As a result, ESM can be used to ask substantively disaggregated self-report questions (e.g., about difficulty with lifting or concentrating), more global questions (e.g., overall rating of job performance), or both, about the particular moment-in-time that is being assessed. ESM is, in this way, the self-report equivalent of conventional objective work-performance audits. In the latter, a randomly selected set of work products is selected for detailed evaluation and used to estimate the overall performance of the worker. Random audit of this sort is a routine part of classical quality-control methodology (Holloway, Lewis, and Mallory 1995). For example, insurance claim processors routinely have a random sample of their completed claims audited, whereas telephone sales representatives routinely have a random sample of their calls tape-recorded and reviewed by their supervisors. The aggregation of the audited cases is used to assign a performance score to each worker. ESM can be employed logically in the same way. And as with other audits, a question can be asked about whether the criteria being used to evaluate quality of work are objective. It is important to recognize that ESM has no advantage over other types of self-report assessment in answering this question other than in addressing the problem of recall bias.

It is useful to make a distinction between the moment-in-time equivalent of the assessment of absenteeism and the assessment of work performance. Conventional self-report assessment is generally found to do an excellent job of assessing absenteeism because workers can accurately recall and report the number of days they were out sick over the past week or past month (Revecki et al. 1994). Concerns about the validity of self-report are limited to the evaluation of work performance. If the same logic is applied to ESM, we might say that ESM is on the firmest ground in evaluating time-on-task—whether or not the worker is, in fact, working at any randomly selected moment-in-time. Being on-task is certainly not the only measure of work performance one would like to have. In addition, there is probably a nonlinear relationship between percent of time-on-task and global work performance that would have to be taken into account when interpreting results regarding this measure of performance (Galinsky et al. 2000). Nonetheless, time-on-task is certainly a core measure of work performance that has broad meaning across many different occupations. It is consequently worth noting that time-on-task is a measure that ESM is ideally suited to assess. We are not aware of any published methodological research on the accuracy of more conventional retrospective time-on-task self-reports. However, unpublished preliminary analyses of our own methodological studies that compared one-week ESM data with retrospective reports at the end of the week about time-off-task during the preceding week show substantial underestimation of time-off-task in conventional self-reports compared to ESM. As a result, time-on-task might be a dimension that ESM, among self-report measures, is uniquely able to assess.

In chapter 6, Lance Anderson, Scott Oppler, and Andrew Rose address the issue of recombining disaggregated work-performance measures to arrive at an accurate assessment of overall work performance by using the O*NET occupational information system. O*NET was developed by the Department of Labor (DOL) as a resource to identify and develop the skills needed in the U.S. workforce. O*NET classifies each of the thousands of jobs in the workforce in terms of its required knowledge, skill, and ability (KSA) and its general work activities (GWAs) based on systematic observations of day-to-day work performance in each occupation by DOL employees. This system has been put online (www.onetcenter.org) and links are provided to other sites with information on jobs, educational opportunities, and labor-market needs. The system is set up to help job-seekers search for occupations that fit their skill set, to help employers develop job descriptions using a standardized vocabulary, to help educators design curricula that address current workplace needs, and to help educational policymakers forecast future workplace human resource needs.

As noted by Anderson and colleagues, the KSA and GWA ratings for individual occupations could be used to solve the problem of aggregating disaggregated measures of job performance into a global measure of overall performance by providing importance weights. Difficulty in lifting heavy objects, for example, might be down-weighted in the evaluation of the job performance of a white-collar worker because the ability to lift heavy objects has low relevance in the O*NET profile for that occupation. An accurate global work-performance score could be created using this logic by combining disaggregated performance measures with an O*NET occupation-specific vector of relevance weights. An impediment to using this approach is that currently available disaggregated self-report and simulation measures of work performance do not cover all the relevant KSA and GWA dimensions in the O*NET system. An additional obstacle is that there is a large number of these O*NET dimensions. As a result, the amount of time needed to carry out an assessment of job performance (either with self-report or simulation methods) that maps onto all O*NET dimensions would be prohibitive. This problem could be overcome if a small number of higher-order O*NET dimensions could be isolated empirically. Encouraging evidence that such dimensions might exist was reported years ago in a psychometric analysis of an earlier version of the DOL occupational information system (Miller et al. 1980). We are aware of no comparable work with the O*NET system, but this is certainly a needed area of further research.

In the final chapter in part 1, Thomas DeLeire and Willard Manning go beyond valuation of the level of the individual workers to consider the market-level effects of aggregate shifts in health and productivity. Their microeconomic analysis has implications for both policymakers who want to assess the social cost of illness and individual firms interested in rationally allocating scarce health care dollars. By delineating a series of microeconomic models based on supply-and-demand curves for labor, DeLeire and Manning add an important new dimension to the cost-of-illness literature. To date, policy analysts have typically ignored the impact that worker illness has on labor-market equilibrium and have assumed, incorrectly, that the social cost of illness can be defined by the sum of the productivity loss of all workers in the market with the illness. DeLeire and Manning's analysis shows that this is not the case and that any shift in the behavior of workers (such as a decline in productivity caused by a high level of health-related work impairment) has ripple effects through market forces. For example, they argue that if a high rate of illness reduces the labor supply, wages will go down by an amount that is less than the decline in productivity per individual worker because some workers will leave the labor force. This subtle microeconomic analysis leads the authors to conclude that the usual methods by which policy analysts value the market-level costs of illness typically underestimate both the social costs of commonly occurring diseases and the marketwide benefits of medical treatments that improve work productivity.

PART 2 OF THE BOOK

In part 2 the emphasis shifts from research methodology to the specific needs of stakeholders. Dennis Scanlon begins the section by discussing health and productivity from the perspective of the human resource manager. He notes that a number of barriers account for the fact that few human resource managers aggressively engage in health and productivity management even though sophisticated methods now exist to measure the relationship between health and productivity and even though effective health interventions exist for early detection and treatment of many workplace health problems. The key barriers that Scanlon identifies include lack of insight into the general workplace health and productivity issues on the part of employer-purchaser decision-makers, the silo mentality in managing health care programs in large corporations, and the absence of integrated data in the decision process.

An intriguing remedy proposed by Scanlon is for employers to adopt a population-health approach that links insurance programs and views them as health care programs. This model makes the employer not a purchaser of health care but an active population health care manager. It would, of course, change the employer-vendor relationship significantly and would require active coordination and planning for the care of the designated population on the part of the employer. Because the employer does not have control over medical practice, the efficient implementation of Scanlon's model would depend in large part on the willingness of practitioners and patients to be actively committed to the model. Physician autonomy, difficulties with incentives, and the emerging power of the patient threaten the success of such an approach.

Scanlon also argues that advancement of the health and productivity agenda will eventually require formal analysis of return on investment in health care and payment of vendors based on performance. As a practical matter, this will be feasible for any other than the largest employers only if a consortium of employers in a given market agree to pool health and productivity information and tie it to common payment incentives. Such data pooling will require a new level of coordination across employers in the collection of health and productivity data. Market-level coordination like this is currently being attempted in several market-level business groups on health associated with the National Business Coalition on Health (NBCH) by carrying out market-level health and productivity surveys using the HPQ. (See www.hpq.org for more information on this initiative.)

Even if coordinated data of this sort become available, as they are in several NBCH markets, most human resource departments lack the information technology infrastructure and analytic expertise to undertake analyses of these data. The new Health Insurance Portability and Accountability Act (HIPAA) regulations also present challenges for employers who seek to create pooled databases of this sort. A number of employer membership organizations that support the health and productivity agenda, such as the NBCH and the Integrated Benefits Institute, are attempting to create tools that will help local employers deal with these problems. An innovative program recently launched by the Midwest Business Group on Health (MBGH) under the aegis of the NBCH is attempting to develop a strategy for integrated market-level analysis of health and productivity survey data, claims data, and data collected from a standardized analysis of provider resources to improve the rationality and cost-effectiveness of contracts between employers and health care providers.

Clearly, as the costs of health care to employers continue to rise, economic considerations will force employers to make increasingly difficult decisions about restriction of health care expenditures. Managed care organizations and disease management programs, recognizing the inevitability of cost-effectiveness considerations playing a key role in these decisions, are more and more appealing to employer-purchasers to invest in disease management programs designed to improve productivity, but without the existence of an independent audit capacity that would allow their productivity claims to be verified. Integrated market-level audits of the kind being developed by the MBGH might hold the key to rationalizing decision-making in response to these marketing efforts.

James Murray, Sean Nicholson, Mark Pauly, and Marc Berger discuss the employer's perspective on health and productivity in chapter 9. They begin by noting that although businesses take an investment approach when considering most major expenditures, they rarely do so when purchasing health benefits. There are two obvious reasons. The first is that employers, like HR professionals, tend to see health care expenditures as benefits to be managed rather than as opportunities for investment. The second is that employers lack the empirical data needed to develop rational health care investment strategies. Would widespread implementation of the data-collection and analysis approaches described in part 1 remove these barriers by providing the evidence needed to make a business case for investment in employee health care? Murray and his coauthors offer a sobering assessment of this question by observing that employers are interested in more highly aggregated outcomes than the individual-level measures discussed in part 1. Overall company profitability is the outcome of ultimate interest, with more proximate outcomes being overall productivity and stability in the wage rate. The methods of measuring the productivity of individual workers are of limited help in evaluating these more highly aggregated outcomes.

Because of this mismatch, translation rules are needed to capture the attention of employers with data on health and productivity. Murray and co-workers propose a theoretical model for the purpose by using information about individual-level work productivity to make inferences about more highly aggregated company outcomes. Their model implies that monetizing the workplace costs of illness based on sickness absence alone usually leads to an underestimation of the effect of health on company-wide productivity: the group production requires teamwork, and the temporary absence of an individual (one who cannot be easily replaced) slows down the entire production process. The authors argue that firm-specific models are needed to calculate benchmark monetary cost-benefit ratios for reducing lost productivity. They say that only on the basis of these estimates can rational evaluations be made about the cost-effectiveness of specific health care interventions aimed at increasing worker productivity. Given how little we currently know about the effects of such interventions on productivity, the authors recommend that companies consider implementing annual employee surveys to help assess these effects in the context of preexisting benchmark cost-benefit calculations.

Chapter 10, by Arne Beck, provides a health care organization's perspective on health and productivity management. Beck's discussion of the role of health plans as stakeholders in health and productivity management focuses on the gaps between health plans, employers, and researchers that contribute to the current tension regarding the measurement of health care quality and the incorporation of this measurement into value-based health care purchasing decisions.

Beck explains that for two reasons health plans are in a unique position to quantify information on the effects of treatment. First, researchers who work for health plans have access to large, well-organized electronic medical record databases that can be used to estimate statistical models of health care treatment outcomes and the cost-effectiveness of treatments. Second, health plans have the critical mass to carry out such analyses in ways that individual employer-purchasers cannot. Because of these two facts, health plans have increasingly come to be the source for data on treatment quality.

Yet, health plans have not effectively translated these data into actionable information that is sufficiently compelling to employers to make a business case for investment in evidence-based health services. Beck argues that a main reason for this failure is that health plans have not considered costs of illness from the employer perspective. Indeed, health plan quality indicator assessment (report cards) currently focuses largely on the measurement of treatment process and short-term health outcomes rather than on information about work productivity. The result is that the value-based purchasing movement has stalled, since the outcomes of greatest value to employers-purchasers have not been measured.

Consistent with Scanlon's comments in chapter 8, Beck notes that at least part of the blame for this mismatch has to be laid at the feet of health care purchasers, who generally view the provision of health care as a cost of doing business rather than as a human capital investment. Because of this emphasis, the audit questions that employer-purchasers pose to health plans have to do largely with resource management. It is little wonder, then, that the data systems set up by health plans to provide feedback to purchasers focus on processes of treatment aimed at helping a small group of human resource personnel in employer-purchaser organizations manage health care benefits.

Beck finds that some currently available health plan performance measures do address the value question, but that they do so mainly with regard to the value of investing in a given health care delivery system instead of a competitor system. As Beck notes, health plans see little evidence that currently available performance measures influence contract decision-making and equally scant evidence that Health Plan Employer Data and Information Set (HEDIS) quality measures lead to membership growth. Health plans consequently see a challenge in expanding existing measures to make them more relevant to and actionable for employers.

Beck suggests that the way forward is to develop a common language and understanding of evidence-based medicine and research techniques, to organize stakeholders around benefit design based on value-based purchasing with a health and productivity management orientation, and to integrate measurement of productivity into the value assessment of health care delivery. Beck sees the health care organization as the logical stakeholder to take the lead in the creation of these new kinds of databases, based on the research infrastructure and resources available to the health care delivery system, its inherent research and evidence-based approach, its ability to measure and articulate a return on investment, and its ability to integrate new measurements and applications.

A major challenge in developing an innovative approach of the sort proposed by Beck is that many employer clients either fail to grasp the vision or fail to accept the legitimacy of the data generated in this approach. It is impossible to sustain a market geared toward value-based purchasing unless there is agreement on the integrity of the underlying measurement system. As a result, Beck argues that ground-up agreement on the details of a health and productivity measurement system is integral to his proposed agenda. One might also ask whether independent auspices of the measurement approach are also critical. In other industries where payment is based on value assessment (e.g., the television industry, where the costs of advertisement are based on overnight Nielsen ratings), measurement is, in effect, an audit that is carried out by an independent organization that functions as an auditing company. It is likely that the same model will need to be implemented in health care if value-based purchasing is to become a larger reality than it is presently. In the process health plans will undoubtedly be required to generate data, but it is likely that these data will have to be audited and independently verified by a separate data-aggregation organization.

The first three chapters in part 2 focus on health and productivity from the perspective of individual employer-purchasers, but there is also a larger way of looking at the relationship between health and productivity from various market-level perspectives. Christopher Evans takes this broader view in chapter 11 as he considers the importance of health productivity research for the pharmaceutical industry. Pharmaceutical companies are the focus of a great deal of interest because the costs of medication are rising more rapidly than other health care costs. Attempts to control these costs in the United States have taken the form of group purchasing through formularies that often have a tiered structure with increasing copayments associated with higher tiers. Pharmaceutical companies have responded with a two-part approach that combines efforts at the organizational level to influence formulary decisions and at the direct-to-consumer level to influence brand recognition and patient demand for particular products. Evidence regarding the effects of specific health problems on productivity and of particular pharmaceutical products on recovering productivity has obvious value in both types of communications.

Evans points out that pharmaceutical companies are, in some ways, interested in the same kinds of health and productivity research as health plans are. Specifically, both want to begin with a foundation of research documenting the workplace costs of illness, but to move on from there with experimental or quasi-experimental research to document the cost-effectiveness of a given intervention in recovering lost productivity. In the case of health plans, it might also be important to document superiority in relation to competitor plans, although current research carried out by health plans largely focuses on documenting the cost-effectiveness of the services provided by the plan itself rather than making between-plan comparisons. In a similar way, pharmaceutical companies sometimes find it important to document the equivalence (in relation to more expensive competitive products) or superiority (in relation to less expensive competitor products) of their product to a competitor product in experimental studies, although the majority of the clinical-trial research carried out by the pharmaceutical industry uses placebo controls rather than comparisons with other active agents.

The pharmaceutical industry is faced with several important methodological challenges in carrying out health and productivity research (measurement selection, integration into the clinical trial paradigm) as well as the challenge of translating results into marketing opportunities. The design decisions involved here are of special importance because of the federal requirements for promotion of these findings, which is strongly regulated by the Food and Drug Administration (FDA). Evans reviews existing measures and research paradigms in order to evaluate currently available options in those measures as they relate to feasible research designs that might answer the kinds of research questions that are relevant to pharmaceutical company stakeholders.

In chapter 12, Paul Stang, Paul Greenberg, Howard Birnbaum, Ronald Kessler, Lynn Hoffman, and Mei-Sheng Duh look at productivity research from the perspective of another market-level stakeholder, the FDA. The FDA has the job of regulating claims made by pharmaceutical marketers and other marketed health care interventions. The regulatory perspective of the FDA has become involved in health and work productivity research because a number of pharmaceutical companies have sought permission to make claims about the effects of their products on work performance. The FDA Office of Medical Policy's Division of Drug Marketing, Advertising and Communications (DDMAC) is responsible for assessing such claims. The mandate of DDMAC is to protect public health and safety by preventing the spread of misinformation and by verifying the accuracy of all pharmaceutical marketing and advertising claims. Claims regarding the effects of pharmaceuticals on work performance are of increasing interest to pharmaceutical companies because these companies have come to realize that employers, as the primary purchasers of health care in the United States, have enormous power to influence health plan drug formularies. Since it must evaluate such claims rigorously, DDMAC has an interest in the accuracy of research on health and work productivity. As Stang and coauthors explain, there are two types of productivity claims: those involving clinical information and those involving economic information. Under FDA regulations, each type must adhere to specific evidentiary standards. The authors review recent shifts in these regulations and address the limitations of currently existing measures in helping regulatory stakeholders such as the FDA obtain adequate data to assess productivity claims. Stang and colleagues argue that a productivity-measurement gold standard needs to be developed, one that is applicable across occupational and organizational categories. Based on their evaluation of the alternatives reviewed in part 1, they suggest that a validated self-report measure holds out the most hope of becoming this kind of gold standard.

In chapter 13, Harvey Whiteford takes an even broader view of health and productivity research by discussing the World Bank's international perspective on health and work productivity in developing countries. Whiteford says economists have traditionally assumed that the best way to improve the health of people in developing countries is to increase the gross national product (GNP). He argues, though, that the association between health and GNP is reciprocal—a healthier workforce can lead to a more productive economy just as economic growth can improve the health of a nation's population. Based on this perspective, Whiteford asserts that human capital investments aimed at improving the health of the workforce should be a public policy priority for the leaders of developing countries. A healthy and educated workforce, in this view, can have value in attracting international capital. Indeed, Whiteford argues persuasively that low human capital (i.e., poor health and low education of the labor force) has been a major restraint on development in Third World countries. He calls for empirical research using the procedures described in part 1 in order to help key stakeholders, including international agencies and governments in developing countries, target their health care investments.

PART 3 OF THE BOOK

The volume closes with a review of the main ideas that emerged at the conference about using health and productivity measurement to rationalize employer investments in health care. The final chapter also describes the Harvard Health and Work Productivity Initiative, a research program established by the John D. and Catherine T. MacArthur Foundation for the purpose of developing a survey system to aid in the process of rationalizing employer investments in health care. This system uses annual workplace health and productivity self-report tracking surveys to estimate the separate workplace costs of a wide variety of health problems, to evaluate the cost-effectiveness of health care intervention aimed at reducing these costs, and to provide ongoing quality assurance for these programs once they are implemented.

It is unclear whether the Harvard system will eventually emerge as the one that health and productivity researchers embrace. However, it is clear that the originally disparate researchers who have become involved in this new area of research over the past decade are beginning to consolidate their ideas, goals, and procedures for measurement and analysis. A number of nonprofit interdisciplinary organizations have emerged to facilitate this consolidation, among them the Integrated Benefits Institute (www.ibiweb.org) and the Institute for Health and Productivity Management (IHPM) (www.ihpm.org). A new journal, *Health and Productivity Management,* was recently launched by IHPM to create a forum for sharing new information about research, practice, and policy analysis.

Agreement on methods will almost certainly bring with it a rapid accumulation of replicated case studies of the workplace costs of particular illnesses and the return on investment (ROI) of particular health care interventions. The synthesis of this information will create a foundation for the rationalization of employer investments in worker health care, whether they are increases in investments or decreases brought on by the need to stem the tide of rising health care costs. With this rationalization will inevitably come new demands on the part of employer-purchasers for data documenting health care quality assurance similar to the types of data used by corporations to evaluate the ROI of other business investments. An important shift is likely to occur in the relationship between employer-purchasers and health care organizations at this juncture, as ROI evaluations focus on workplace outcomes rather than on the treatment-process measures that are the preferred quality assurance targets of health care professionals (National Committee 2002). The inevitable disagreement about process and outcome quality assurance standards that will occur between purchaser organizations and provider organizations is likely to be resolved in favor of the purchasers. This outcome, in turn, is likely to lead to a deeper and more sustained interest among employers in quality-based purchasing of health care services. Employers may become more eager to invest or less so, depending on the results of cost-effective studies that remain to be carried out.

REFERENCES

Atcheson, S. G. 2001. Paying doctors more: Use of musculoskeletal specialists and increased physician pay to decrease workers' compensation costs. *Journal of Occupational and Environmental Medicine* 43 (8): 672–79.

Boonen, A., D. van der Heijde, R. Landewe, A. Spoorenberg, H. Schouten, M. Rutten-van Molken, F. Guillemin, M. Dougados, H. Mielants, K. de Vlam, H. van der Tempel, and S. van der Linden. 2002. Work status and productivity costs due to ankylosing spondylitis: Comparison of three European countries. *Annals of the Rheumatic Diseases* 61 (5): 429–37.

Brandt-Rauf, P., W. N. Burton, and R. J. McCunney. 2001. Health, productivity, and occupational medicine. *Journal of Occupational and Environmental Medicine* 43 (1): 1.

Carter, T. 1999. *The aftermath of reengineering: Downsizing and corporate performance*. New York: Haworth.

Clark, H. H., and M. F. Schober. 1992. Asking questions and influencing answers. In *Questions about questions: Inquiries into the cognitive bases of surveys*, ed. J. M. Tanur, 15–48. New York: Russell Sage Foundation.

Coulehan, J. L., H. C. Schulberg, M. R. Block, M. J. Madonia, and E. Rodriguez. 1997. Treating depressed primary care patients improves their physical, mental, and social functioning. *Archives of Internal Medicine* 157 (10): 1113–20.

Fitz-Enz, J. 2000. *The ROI of human capital: Measuring the economic value of employee performance*. New York: American Management Association.

Galinsky, T. L., N. G. Swanson, S. L. Sauter, J. J. Hurrell, and L. M. Schleifer. 2000. A field study of supplementary rest breaks for data-entry operators. *Ergonomics* 43 (5): 622–38.

Gold, M. R., J. E. Siegel, L. B. Russell, and M. C. Weinstein. 1996. *Cost-effectiveness in health and medicine*. New York: Oxford University Press.

Greenberg, P. E., R. C. Kessler, T. L. Nells, S. N. Finkelstein, and E. R. Berndt. 1996. Depression in the workplace: An economic perspective. In *Selective serotonin reuptake inhibitors: Advances in basic research and clinical practice*, 2nd ed., ed. J. P. Feighner and W. F. Boyer, 327–63. New York: John Wiley.

Harbour, J. L. 1997. *The basics of performance measurement*. Selton, CT: Productivity Press.

Holloway, J., J. Lewis, and G. Mallory. 1995. *Performance measurement and evaluation*. Thousand Oaks, CA: Sage Publications.

Howarth, P. H. 1999. Assessment of antihistamine efficiency and potency. *Clinical and Experimental Allergy* 29 (suppl. 3): 87–97.

Johnson, M. D., and A. Gustafsson. 2000. *Improving customer satisfaction, loyalty, and profit: An integrated measurement and management system*. San Francisco: Jossey-Bass.

Kessler, R. C. 2001. The effects of chronic medical conditions on work loss and work cutback. *Journal of Occupational and Environmental Medicine* 43:218–25.

Kessler, R. C., D. M. Almeida, P. A. Berglund, and P. Stang. 2001. Pollen and mold exposure impairs the work performance of employees with allergic rhinitis. *Annals of Allergy, Asthma, and Asthma Immunology* 87:289–95.

Kessler, R. C., C. Barber, A. Beck, P. A. Berglund, P. D. Cleary, D. McKenas, N. Pronk, G. Simon, P. Stang, T. B. Üstün, and P. S. Wang. 2003. The World Health Organization health and work performance questionnaire (HPQ). *Journal of Occupational and Environmental Medicine* 45 (2): 156–74.

Kessler, R. C., C. B. Barber, H. G. Birnbaum, R. G. Frank, P. E. Greenberg, R. M. Rose, G. E. Simon, and P. S. Wang. 1999. Depression in the workplace: Effects on short-term disability. *Health Affairs* 18 (5): 163–71.

Kessler, R. C., R. B. Davis, D. F. Foster, M. I. Van Rompay, E. E. Walters, S. A. Wilkey, T. J. Kaptchuk, and D. M. Eisenberg. 2001. Long-term trends in the use of complementary and alternative medical therapies in the United States. *Annals of Internal Medicine* 135 (4): 262–68.

Kessler, R. C., S. Zhao, S. J. Katz, A. C. Kouzis, R. G. Frank, M. J. Edlund, and P. J. Leaf. 1999. Past-year use of outpatient services for psychiatric problems in the National Comorbidity Survey. *American Journal of Psychiatry* 156 (1): 115–23.

Lawrie, S. M., C. Parsons, and J. Patrick. 1996. A controlled trial of general practitioners' attitudes to patients with schizophrenia. *Health Bulletin* 54:201–3.

Loeppke, R., P. A. Hymel, J. H. Lofland, L. T. Pizzi, D. L. Konicki, G. W. Anstadt, C. Baase, J. Fortuna, and T. Scharf. 2003. Health-related workplace productivity measurement: General and migraine-specific recommendations from the ACOEM Expert Panel. *Journal of Occupational and Environmental Medicine* 45 (4): 349–59.

Lucas, D. O., L. O. Zimmer, J. E. Paul, D. Jones, G. Slatko, W. Liao, and J. Lashley. 2001. Two-year results from the asthma self-management program: Long-term impact on health care services, costs, functional status, and productivity. *Journal of Asthma* 38:321–30.

Lynch, W., and J. E. Riedel. 2001. *Measuring employee productivity: A guide to self-assessment tools.* Denver: Institute for Health and Productivity Management.

Marks, M. L., and K. P. DeMeuse. 2002. *Resizing the organization, managing layoffs, divestitures, and closings: Maximizing gain while minimizing pain.* J-B Siop Professional Practice series. San Francisco: Jossey-Bass.

McGrail, M. P., Jr., M. Calasanz, J. Christianson, C. Cortez, B. Dowd, R. Gorman, W. H. Lohman, D. Parker, D. M. Radosevich, and G. Westman. 2002. The Minnesota health partnership and coordinated health care and disability prevention: The implementation of an integrated benefits and medical care model. *Journal of Occupational Rehabilitation* 12:43–54.

Miller, A. R., D. J. Treiman, P. S. Cain, and P. A. Roos, eds. 1980. An assessment of the Dictionary of Occupational Titles as a source of occupational information. In *Work, jobs, and occupations: A critical review of the dictionary of occupational titles,* 148–95. Washington, DC: National Academy Press.

Miller, W. 2001. Promising strategies help employers integrate pharmacy and medical programs—and reap cost, quality advantages. *Employee Benefits Journal* 26 (3): 23–27.

National Committee for Quality Assurance. 2002. *Disease management standards and guidelines for accreditation and certification.* Washington, DC: National Committee for Quality Assurance.

Patrick, D. L., and P. Erickson. 1993. *Health status and health policy: Quality of life in health care evaluation and resource allocation.* New York: Oxford University Press.

Pauly, M. V., S. Nicholson, J. Xu, D. Polsky, P. M. Danzon, J. F. Murray, and M. L. Berger. 2002. A general model of the impact of absenteeism on employers and employees. *Health Economics* 11 (3): 221–31.

Reginster, J. Y., and N. G. Khaltaev. 2002. Introduction and WHO perspective on the global burden of musculoskeletal conditions. *Rheumatology* 41 (Suppl. 1): 1–2.

Revecki, D. A., D. Irwin, J. Reblando, and G. E. Simon. 1994. The accuracy of self-reported disability days. *Medical Care* 32 (4): 401–4.

Schwarz, N., and D. Oyserman. 2001. Asking questions about behavior: Cognition, communication, and questionnaire construction. *American Journal of Evaluation* 22 (2): 127–60.

Serxner, S., D. Gold, D. Anderson, and D. Williams. 2001. The impact of a worksite health promotion program on short-term disability usage. *Journal of Occupational and Environmental Medicine* 43 (1): 25–29.

Sloan, F. A. 1996. *Valuing health care: Costs, benefits, and effectiveness of pharmaceuticals and other medical technologies.* New York: Cambridge University Press.

Sudman, S., N. M. Bradburn, and N. Schwarz. 1996. *Thinking about answers: The applications of cognitive processes to survey methodology.* San Francisco: Jossey-Bass.

Tarlov, A. R., J. E. Ware Jr., S. Greenfield, E. C. Nelson, E. Perrin, and M. Zubkoff. 1989. The Medical Outcomes Study: An application of methods for monitoring the results of medical care. *Journal of the American Medical Association* 262 (7): 925–30.

Tourangeau, R., L. J. Rips, and K. Rasinski. 2000. *The psychology of survey response.* New York: Cambridge University Press.

Turner, C. F., L. Ku, S. M. Rogers, L. D. Lindberg, J. H. Pleck, and F. L. Sonenstein. 1998. Adolescent sexual behavior, drug use, and violence: Increased reporting with computer survey technology. *Science* 280 (5365): 867–73.

Watson, R. M., and S. P. Huban. 1997. Managing disabilities in an integrated health environment: The experience of Aetna. *Benefits Quarterly* 13:65–71.

Wells, K. B., C. Sherbourne, M. Schoenbaum, N. Duan, L. Meredith, J. Unutzer, J. Miranda, M. F. Carney, and L. V. Rubenstein. 2000. Impact of disseminating quality improvement programs for depression in managed primary care: A randomized controlled trial. *Journal of the American Medical Association* 283 (2): 212–20.

PART ONE

*Approaches to Studying the Effects
of Health on Worker Productivity*

CHAPTER 2

Linking Administrative Claim Data with Archival Productivity Measures to Inform Employer Decision-Making

PAUL E. GREENBERG AND HOWARD G. BIRNBAUM

> That men in general should work better when they are ill fed than when they are well fed, when they are disheartened than when they are in good spirits, when they are frequently sick than when they are generally in good health, seems not very probable. Years of dearth, it is to be observed, are generally among the common people years of sickness and mortality which cannot fail to diminish the produce of their industry.
> —Adam Smith, *Wealth of Nations*, 1776

INTRODUCTION

Well over two hundred years ago, Adam Smith warned that employee illness is likely to manifest itself in the form of reduced productivity in the workplace. Smith was also ahead of his time in understanding the importance of mental health, noting that being "disheartened" rather than "in good spirits" was unlikely to be associated with improved work performance. Unfortunately, even today, corporate America largely ignores Smith's wise observations.

Most employers still do not address, in health care benefit design, the burden of employee illness on productivity. One key impediment to action may be that productivity research has not been sufficiently compelling. Although the vast cost-of-illness literature features estimates of lost productivity, these results are often framed in terms that are not relevant to employers. For example, Rice's cost-of-illness approach (1966), which distinguishes direct from indirect costs, takes a societal view. The same is true for the friction cost method of valuing forgone productive capacity (Koopmanschap and Rutten 1996; Koopmanschap et al. 1995). Furthermore, the estimates obtained by simulation models based on expert judgment (Greenberg et al. 2003; Greenberg et al. 1993; Stoudemire et al. 1986) also do not reflect actual patterns of employee behavior, the variable that matters most to corporate decision-makers. In other words, there is currently a mismatch between the kind of evidence corporate managers require to make benefit-design decisions and the type of research results that have been disseminated about various illnesses. Without empirical findings that speak to their specific concerns, employers can hardly be expected to tailor health care programs to improve productivity.

Two research strategies can provide relevant information for employers. The first approach, called self-report, which uses interview-based data to relate health status to work performance, incorporates disease-specific information regardless of whether the individual is currently being treated for that illness. As a result, self-report has the advantage of permitting productivity comparisons based not only on clinical but also on treatment status information. This method is especially useful for disorders that often go untreated (e.g., depression, migraine) (Kessler, Zhao, et al. 1999). Furthermore, broad-based surveys of this type often tend to be more representative of the entire population and more readily available than objective measures of employee behavior.

In contrast, the second approach, sometimes referred to as "archival data," relies on retrospective administrative data to infer the clinical status of the patient. Unfortunately, since there is no marker in an administrative claims data set to identify a sufferer of a particular disease unless a diagnosis is recorded or treatment is provided, this approach is unable to identify all patients who could potentially benefit from a given form of treatment. In addition, since there are usually no explicit severity markers for each treated patient contained in such a data set, it can be difficult to relate changes in the severity of disease status to changes in resource utilization over time. Furthermore, because these studies tend to focus on a few individual employers, research based on archival data may not yield generalizable results.

Despite these drawbacks, objective evidence from a company's own administrative systems can show productivity effects by documenting, for example, increases in sick days among particular employees due to illness, or decreases in sick days following treatment. For many corporate decision-makers, self-report measures of work performance (i.e., employee recollections about their absenteeism patterns in relation to the timing of symptoms of illness), obtained using a survey-based research design, may prove to be inadequate for their needs. However, if researchers also incorporate archival data into the analysis, benefits managers may well be more receptive to the findings.

Many large companies routinely keep archival productivity measures, even though the data are recorded primarily for administrative reasons (e.g., benefit management, reimbursement) rather than for health outcomes research. In this sense, their use for pharmacoeconomic investigation usually involves a retrofit of sorts, requiring an explicit linking of disparate data sets at the employee level. For example, since different corporate information technology systems may record data concerning an individual's medical, pharmaceutical, disability, worker's compensation, and sick-leave history, the required linkages for health service research may be quite intricate. Nonetheless, despite the potential difficulty associated with bridging these different information systems, such links can provide meaningful results to employers, while still preserving the anonymity of the employees whose treatment and work-performance records are being studied in detail (Birnbaum, Cremieux, et al. 1999).

In this chapter we provide a survey of the medical, health-economics, and managed-care literature concerning the linking of disparate data sets to measure the consequences of illness and its treatment on employee productivity. To date, only a limited number of initiatives using linked archival data have been documented. However, this approach offers the promise of showing exactly how health care benefit design affects productivity. Therefore, it can be a powerful tool to convince potentially skeptical employers that worker productivity is an important health outcome over which they have some control.

Besides offering this literature review, we also describe a categorical framework for grouping the different research strategies that have been used to analyze the relationship between employee productivity, on the one hand, and illness and its treatment, on the other. Since the value of linked data sets is greatest with respect to archival measures of workplace productivity, we highlight the studies using these measures. We conclude with suggestions for future research.

FRAMEWORK FOR ASSESSING THE PRODUCTIVITY IMPACT OF ILLNESS AND ITS TREATMENT

At the outset, it is important to clarify what is meant by productivity in this review. Our primary focus is on two particular categories: (1) *work cutback* or *presenteeism* during episodes of illness, when employees show up at work but are unable to contribute at their usual level of performance because of either the symptoms of illness or the side effects of treatments, and (2) *absenteeism* that is either sporadic (e.g., periodic sick leave) or chronic in nature (e.g., short- or long-term disability as well as worker's compensation claims).

Four different research strategies can be used to examine these workplace productivity impacts of illness and its treatment, depending upon the productivity and clinical data available. As noted above, there are two common approaches to gathering productivity data:[1]

> *Self-report,* in which respondents with a broad range of employment experiences complete surveys concerning their individual level of work cutback or work absence in a recent period, and
> *Archival,* involving targeted groups of individuals in employment settings where employee performance or absenteeism is recorded by the company.

Similarly, clinical status measures have been gathered using two different strategies:

> *Retrospective,* often using administrative claims data to infer health status at various milestones or survey data to assess it at a specific moment in time, and
> *Prospective,* typically involving very careful monitoring of patient health status in a clinical trial setting or through health risk assessments (e.g., where laboratory values are collected concerning a variety of health status indicators such as blood pressure, cholesterol, and body-mass index).

Table 2.1 illustrates how these alternative data sources permit different kinds of analyses of the relationships among workplace productivity, clinical status, and health care service utilization. In this chapter, we focus primarily on two of these types of studies. *Self-report* productivity measures, often used in epidemiological surveys, typically consist of questions about both work impairment (e.g., "How many days in the past month did you miss work due to health problems?") and health status (e.g., "Are you currently suffering from any health problems?"). In this sense, the approaches described in Quadrant 1 do not require any linking of data sets, as both economic and clinical data are obtained from the very same source.[2]

In contrast, approaches in Quadrant 3 focus on the link between *archival* productivity data and retrospective clinical status measured at the individual worker level. Here, researchers rely on linkable administrative data systems (e.g., medical, pharmaceutical, sick leave, and disability data as well as on-the-job performance records) to analyze the relationship between

1. Another approach to productivity measurement in health outcomes analysis, which falls between the subjective nature of self-report data and the more objective quality of archival records, involves the use of beepers to prompt employees concerning the precise nature of their performance at random moments during the workday. See chapter 5.

2. Chapter 4, by Debra Lerner and Jennifer Lee, considers *self-report* productivity measures gathered in clinical trial case report forms along with much more detailed clinical status measures than are generally compiled in survey research (i.e., Quadrant 4).

TABLE 2.I.

APPROACHES TO ASSESSING PRODUCTIVITY IMPACT OF ILLNESS

AND ITS TREATMENT

PRODUCTIVITY DATA (E.G., CUTBACK AT WORK, TIME MISSED FROM WORK)	PATIENT-SPECIFIC CLINICAL STATUS DATA	
	RETROSPECTIVE	PROSPECTIVE
SELF-REPORT WORK MEASURES ("ASK")	(1) Both cross-sectional and longitudinal epidemiological/ naturalistic surveys assessing *respondent's clinical status* In relation to his/her recollection of work impairment level in the recent past	(2) Controlled and uncontrolled clinical trials, including effectiveness trials in HMO settings, documenting *differential responses to alternative interventions* In relation to patient or clinician replies to series of questions concerning work performance and resource utilization
ARCHIVAL WORK MEASURES ("COUNT")	(3) Company-specific studies showing *administrative claims data documenting patient clinical status and patterns of resource utilization* In relation to actual patterns of work cutback and/or time missed and (possibly) also in relation to lifestyle data (e.g., smoking behavior) from health risk assessments	(4) Workplace-based clinical trials permitting analysis of *disease-related severity over time (e.g., following an intervention)* In relation to well-defined, worker-specific productivity measures

objective measures of employee performance and illness.[3] Until recently, impediments to data availability, coupled with prohibitive computing costs, precluded the creation of comprehensive data warehouses capable of linking health status with work productivity. However, several recent research initia-

3. A promising area for future research involves gathering archival productivity measures in workplace-based clinical trials, and linking them to clinical trial or health risk assessment data on a prospective basis (i.e., Quadrant 4).

tives have combined relevant records derived from distinct parts of the corporate benefits and personnel systems concerning the same individuals.[4] While the primary purpose of this chapter is to summarize the health outcomes literature that relies on these archival productivity measures, we will first discuss key findings that use a self-report approach.

Self-Report Measures of Productivity Gathered in Retrospective Studies

A number of recent epidemiological surveys use self-report measures of the impact of illness and its treatment on productivity. For example, based on the Midlife Development in the United States Survey (MIDUS), researchers have identified the five most impairing chronic conditions in the United States in terms of work loss and work cutback as follows (with the average number of *extra* days missed per month noted in parentheses):

panic disorders	(1.8 days)
ulcers	(1.7 days)
chronic sleep problems	(1.6 days)
autoimmune diseases	(1.5 days)
major depression	(1.4 days) (Kessler et al. 2001)

Figure 2.1 presents a range of findings for numerous physical and mental health disorders derived from survey data in MIDUS. These results compare the prevalence rate of each illness with the typical number of accompanying impairment days. As shown in the figure, the majority of these conditions either have a relatively low prevalence rate coupled with a substantial number of impairment days among those affected (e.g., autoimmune disease, hernia), or a relatively high prevalence rate coupled with a limited degree of impairment (e.g., hay fever, skin problems). However, for some conditions in the workplace (e.g., major depression, arthritis), many people suffer a significant level of work impairment. In contrast, several relatively nonimpairing conditions (e.g., thyroid disease, gum problems) affect a small minority of people and have a limited impact on work loss.

From an employer's perspective, these results point to critical distinctions

---

4. We used a computer search to find published reports on the cost of illness that included the key words *absenteeism, work loss, productivity, sick leave, employment,* and *earnings,* and we also contacted researchers who were actively investigating related issues. While only a limited number of published studies were found, more are actively under way or in the planning phase, and others have reportedly been conducted for private employer clients.

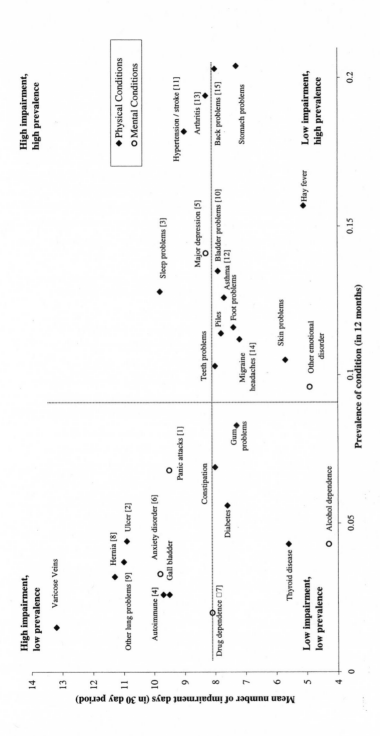

Figure 2.1. Prevalence and mean number of impairment days for selected physical and mental conditions

Notes: (1) Impairment days are defined as a weighted sum of work loss days plus 50% of work cutback days accumulated during the preceding month by respondents who reported at least one work loss or work cutback day during that time. (2) Numbers in brackets reflect rank order of per capita number of impairment days, for a reduced set of chronic conditions, adjusted for sociodemographic influences and to account for persons with multiple conditions. Quadrants are determined by mean prevalence and impairment.

Source: 1997 MIDUS survey data reported in Kessler et al. 2001.

among diseases. Since productivity effects depend on the prevalence and degree of work impairment associated with a given condition, it is possible to create a hierarchy regarding how to manage workplace illnesses. The visual basis for such a ranking is presented in figure 2.1. If the analysis ignores productivity costs, then one ranking of conditions in terms of costs and benefits would result. However, if the analysis incorporates productivity costs, a different ranking would result. To the extent that productivity offsets affect net treatment costs differently across diseases, a reranking of relative resources devoted to each illness is justified compared with the status quo. Coupled with data concerning the demographic distribution of a particular company's workforce, these results can provide a useful tool for enhancing the sophistication of benefit plan design.

Because administering most surveys is relatively straightforward, this research design can be undertaken and replicated in different populations for a variety of diseases. One illness that has been studied very closely in this context is major depression. For example, using data from MIDUS as well as the National Comorbidity Survey (NCS), research has shown that depressed workers experience between 1.5 and 3.2 more work-absence days in a 30-day period than nondepressed workers. This result implies a salary-equivalent productivity loss averaging between $182 and $395 during such periods of time. Thus, since the cost of achieving 30 depression-free days approaches $400, there is a large potential productivity offset (Kessler, Barber, et al. 1999). Several other survey findings also document that depressed workers tend to experience substantially more disability when compared with asymptomatic workers (Broadhead et al. 1990; French and Zarkin 1998; Kessler and Frank 1997; Kouzis and Eaton 1994, 1997; Ormel et al. 1993; Von Korff, Ormel, Katon, and Lin 1992), and that treatment of depression is associated with reductions in missed work (Katzelnick et al. 1997).

Migraine is another chronic condition for which survey-based data on productivity are widely reported in the literature. A number of studies document that the indirect cost burden in terms of work absenteeism exceeds the direct costs of medical treatment (Legg et al. 1997; Osterhaus, Gutterman, and Plachetka 1992; Rasmussen et al. 1991; Solomon and Price 1997; Stang and Osterhaus 1993; Stang, Von Korff, and Galer 1998; Stewart and Lipton 1996; Van Roijen et al. 1995). In addition, research suggests that there is an unequal distribution of work impairment, such that 90% of recorded work loss results from only half of all migraineurs (Lipton, Stewart, and Von Korff 1997). Furthermore, as noted by these researchers, two-thirds of this productivity loss is attributable to impaired performance on the job as opposed to days missed from work.

Similar results on the workplace impact of illness and offsets from treatment have been found for other conditions (e.g., diabetes) (Mayfield, Deb, and Whitecotton 1999; Testa and Simonson 1998) and health promotion programs (Warner et al. 1988; Bertera 1991). By describing the mechanism by which specific illnesses exact economic burdens in the workplace, these self-report findings can also spur employers to redesign health benefits.

Likewise, a study that relied on the National Medical Expenditure Survey (Rizzo, Abbott, and Pashko 1996) estimated the workplace costs and benefits associated with drugs prescribed to treat a number of chronic conditions. As the researchers noted, the increased productivity gained from prescription medications taken for hypertension, heart disease, depression, and diabetes more than offset the added costs of the medications themselves. The annual net benefit (in 1987 dollars) to employers from pharmaceutical intervention was as follows:

diabetes	$1,475 (16.1 days saved)
depression	$ 822 (9.1 days saved)
heart disease	$ 633 (7.3 days saved)
hypertension	$ 286 (3.5 days saved)

Some of these findings are consistent with those reported in figure 2.1. For example, in both studies, major depression looms as a significant employer concern. However, whereas diabetes is characterized in figure 2.1 as a low-prevalence–low-impairment condition that may not merit much employer attention, here it ranks as the condition for which drug treatment can bring about the biggest productivity gain. These findings are not necessarily inconsistent, since the beneficial effects of drug treatment may already be reflected in figure 2.1. Methodological differences between the studies (e.g., in terms of how each controlled for the comorbid conditions) also may play a role in these discrepancies, since reliance on responder recall to assess productivity impacts of illness and treatment can sometimes yield invalid results.[5] In any case, complementing such results with findings from archival data can undoubtedly increase the credibility of this approach and thus motivate employers to develop better ways to manage indirect costs.

Archival Productivity Measures Gathered in Retrospective Studies

Table 2.2 presents the studies using archival measures to examine the impact of illness and treatment on productivity. These studies are targeted to specific

5. However, at least one validation study of employee recall of work-loss time due to illness found that survey data, in fact, corresponded relatively closely to archival data regarding sick leave. See Revicki et al 1994. The extensive literature on the use and quality of self-reported absence data is described by Johns (1994).

TABLE 2.2.

IMPACTS OF ILLNESS ON PRODUCTIVITY: SELECTED STUDIES USING OBJECTIVE MEASURES

ARTICLE	ILLNESS CONDITION	PRODUCTIVITY MEASURE	ESTIMATED PRODUCTIVITY IMPACT
BERNDT ET AL. 2000	Mental illness	Objective measure of actual at-work performance linked to employer medical claims records	Work performance (i.e., daily output of claims processed by insurance claims processors): "Over an extended time period of up to thirty months, the average daily productivity of employees diagnosed with and receiving treatment for one or more mental disorders is no different from that of employees with no mental disorders" (p. 255).
BIRNBAUM, BARTON, ET AL. 2000	Rheumatoid arthritis	Employer disability and medical claims records	Work loss (i.e., short-term disability [STD] and long-term disability [LTD]): • 44% prevalence of disability among employees treated for rheumatoid arthritis (RA), equivalent to 2 times that of employees overall • Disability accounts for 54% of average total cost (i.e., medical plus disability) for employees treated for RA.
BIRNBAUM, GREENBERG, ET AL. 1999	Depression	Employer disability and medical claims records	Work loss (i.e., STD and LTD): • Among depressed patients, monthly disability days were: 1–1.5 days/10-day period prior to treatment; increased to 3.5–4.5 days per 10-day period during

Study	Conditions	Data source	Findings
			period when treatment was initiated; and then decreased to 2 days per 10-day period. • Decreased disability payments by $93 per depressed patient in first 30 days following initial treatment.
BURTON AND CONTI 1999	Asthma Depression Diabetes Hypertension Ulcers	Employer disability and medical claims records	Work loss (i.e., STD): • Depression: 43 days/STD episode • Diabetes: 33 days/STD episode • Hypertension: 25 days /STD episode • Ulcers: 24 days/STD episode • Asthma:19 days/STD episode
BURTON ET AL. 1999	Mental health Respiratory illness Injury Digestive disorder Musculoskeletal disorder Cancer Other	Measures of actual at-work performance linked to employer disability and medical claims records	Work loss (sick leave and disability plus time lost due to failure to maintain productivity standard): The average worker lost 4 hours/week, compared to time lost of employees with • Mental health disorders: 13 hours lost/week • Digestive disorders: 16 hours lost/week Time lost associated with selected health risks: • Perception: distress, 5 hours lost/week • Biological risks: diabetes, 11 hours lost/week; BMI at risk, 6 hours lost/week

TABLE 2.2. (CONTINUED)

ARTICLE	ILLNESS CONDITION	PRODUCTIVITY MEASURE	ESTIMATED PRODUCTIVITY IMPACT
CLAXTON, CHAWLA, AND KENNEDY 1999	Depression	Employer disability and medical claims records	Work loss (i.e., sick leave and disability): • Among depressed patients, monthly work loss was: 2–4 days/month prior to treatment; increased to 5–7 days/month during month when treatment was initiated; and then decreased to 2–4 days per month, following initial treatment
COCKBURN ET AL. 1999A, 1999B	Allergies	Objective measure of actual at-work performance linked to employer medical claims records	Work performance (i.e., daily output of claims processed by insurance claims processors): • Productivity of claims processors taking sedating antihistamines was 12% less than employees taking nonsedating antihistamines • The incremental cost to an employer of claims processors taking nonsedating antihistamines rather than sedating medications is less (at $1.50/day) than the benefit in terms of reduced lost output (at $9/day).
GREENBERG ET AL. 1999	Mental illness Back sprains/strains Nonback sprains/strains Substance abuse	Employer disability and medical claims records	Work loss (i.e., STD) annual costs/FTE (STD as % of medical plus disability costs): • Mental illness: $80 (40%) • Back sprains/strains $76 (68%)

Cancer

Musculoskeletal

Cerebrovascular

Chest pain

Heart attack

Ischemic heart

- Nonback sprains/strains $39 (70%)
- Substance abuse $17 (20%)
- Cancer $16 (8%)
- Musculoskeletal disorders $15 (17%)
- Cerebrovascular disorders $12 (19%)
- Chest pain $10 (10%)
- Heart attacks $8 (10%)
- Ischemic heart disease $8 (4%)

ROSENHECK ET AL. 1999   Mental health

Employer disability and medical claims records

Work loss (i.e., sick leave):

- Over a 3-year period in which a corporation's mental health services were cut back by 1/3: sick days increased by 21% among employees who used mental health services and sick days declined by 10% among employees not using mental health services.

employers, in contrast to the ones using the self-report approach described above. In addition, this approach enables researchers to combine records obtained from distinct parts of the corporate benefit system concerning the same individuals and thus to perform simultaneous analysis of productivity and health utilization data.

One study of the economic impact of depression based on an integrated health and disability data-management system found that both the average length of disability and the disability relapse rate for depressive disorders were greater than for comparison conditions (Conti and Burton 1994).[6] Subsequent research using an expanded data set for the same employer examined five common chronic conditions—asthma, depression, diabetes, hypertension, and ulcers—and showed how a health data warehouse can be used to integrate an employer's personnel, medical claim, disability, absenteeism, and health-risk appraisal information systems at the employee level (Burton and Conti 1999). Distinct measures were developed for on-the-job productivity and sickness-absence costs (e.g., sick time, disability). Work absences per illness event and rates of recidivism varied substantially on a disease-by-disease basis. For example, asthma resulted in relatively brief absences from work but a high rate of recidivism, while depression had the longest average duration absence but a lower rate of recidivism. These illness-specific patterns underscore the importance of disease-management strategies that are tailored to the particular workplace characteristics of each disorder.

A descriptive analysis of the direct and indirect burden of the ten most costly medical conditions facing a large manufacturing company revealed that three key factors drive disability costs for any specific illness: (1) the number of medical claimants for that condition, (2) the percentage of medical claimants that subsequently become disability claimants, and (3) the average duration of disability per claimant (Greenberg et al. 1999). For example, cancer and stroke caused extended absences from work but occurred rather infrequently, while mental illness was especially costly because of its high prevalence. Since these categories are inherently intertwined, when companies try to address medical and disability costs separately, substantial inefficiencies can result. To allocate their benefit dollars optimally, employers need to evaluate systemwide expenses by linking administrative data.

Figure 2.2 recasts these results to permit more direct comparison with the findings in figure 2.1. Despite fundamental differences in research

6. The comparison disorders were diabetes, high blood pressure, low back pain, and heart disease.

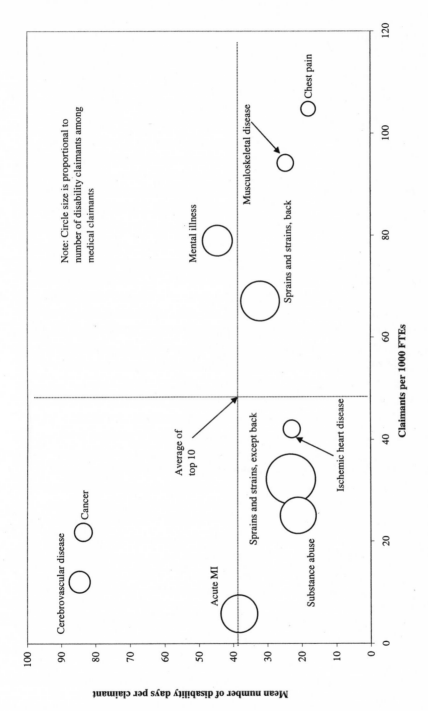

Figure 2.2. Short-term disability cost components to an employer for most costly diseases, 1995–1997
Source: Greenberg et al. 1999.

design, many of the common illness categories are similarly situated on these two charts.

The linking of administrative claims data concerning direct and indirect cost categories can provide other useful insights. One common question relevant to employers concerns the full extent of disease-specific costs such as, for example, the burden of depression on chronic absenteeism. Unfortunately, since ICD-9 (International Classification of Diseases, 9th ed.) diagnostic coding in the disability claims system often is either incomplete or inaccurate, a simple tabulation of the diagnostic codes on these claims would identify only those depressed patients who were already identified as disabled for that reason. However, linking ICD-9 diagnostic information from medical claims files with these disability records allows for a more thorough assessment of the disability burden of a specific illness.

One study used this approach with linked data to show that 45% of the employees of a national employer diagnosed with major depression were disabled specifically because of depression, and that these employees incurred three times more in disability costs than the average employee. Furthermore, 69% of eligible employees had a disability claim for any reason and incurred almost five times more in disability costs per worker than the company average (Birnbaum, Greenberg, et al. 1999). In this case, simply identifying patients with disability claims for depression would have missed half of the employer's depression-related disability problem.[7] Similar studies document the workplace burden for other conditions, including pneumonia (Birnbaum et al. 2001), diabetes (Ramsey et al. 2002), rheumatoid arthritis (Birnbaum, Barton, et al. 2000) and treatment-resistant depression (Birnbaum et al. 2004).

Two separate studies examined the large contribution of indirect costs to the total costs of depression as well as the impact of treatment. In an analysis that used medical and prescription claims in addition to employee work-loss data (i.e., sick leave as well as short-term disability) from a group of employers, average monthly absenteeism was compared before and after the initiation of antidepressant treatment. Absenteeism increased before treatment initiation, peaked shortly afterward, and then declined. Moreover, these patterns varied by type of antidepressant prescribed (Claxton, Chawla, and Kennedy 1999).

Using a different data source that contained the medical, pharmaceu-

---

7. Productivity loss estimates reported here are conservative since they omit the additional costs of overtime pay to healthy workers to maintain production and administrative and training expenses for replacement workers.

tical, and disability claims (i.e., both short- and long-term) of a national employer, a methodologically equivalent investigation reported the extent of disability before and after initial treatment for major depression. A similar pattern of work absence emerged, with work loss increasing just before the onset of treatment, peaking shortly afterward, and then declining substantially. According to this study, the value to the employer of reduced disability payments in the first 30 days following initial treatment amounted to $93 per depressed patient (Birnbaum, Cremieux, et al. 2000). Both studies using this approach concluded that treatment is associated with a substantial reduction in the workplace burden of depression. Not all conditions exhibit such a pattern. For example, while work loss for cancer patients also peaks around the time of initial treatment, the reduction in days missed from work is far less following the start date than for patients treated for depression (Birnbaum, Cremieux, and Greenberg 2000).

Whereas the studies described above used archival data to assess burden of illness and impact of treatment decisions, one recent study used this approach to analyze the workplace impact of changes in benefit design. Drawing on employee claims data at a company that experienced a substantial reduction in mental health benefits, the researchers found that "reducing mental health care was associated with potentially adverse consequences for employees with mental health problems, with no gain for the employer's 'bottom line'" (Rosenheck et al. 1999, 200). In fact, while the company was successful in achieving a 38% reduction in mental health spending per user, non–mental health service use and days missed from work both increased by a comparable amount among employees.

The majority of studies that link archival measures of productivity with health status information focus on time missed from work, but one research initiative focused on an archival measure of at-work productivity and examined units of output per hour and time spent at work by claims processors at a large health insurer (Berndt et al. 1997). In a series of analyses that involved several disease-specific investigations, on-the-job performance was linked to patterns of health care utilization, as recorded in retrospective medical and pharmaceutical claims files. One analysis revealed that not only do the symptoms of illness result in adverse productivity consequences to employees, but so do the side effects of treatment. In fact, the productivity of claims processors who took nonsedating antihistamines exceeded that of workers prescribed sedating antihistamines by approximately 13% (Cockburn et al. 1999a). Moreover, the productivity benefits from treatment with the more costly, nonsedating antihistamines more than offset the higher treatment costs of these prescription drugs themselves. Whereas the value of the

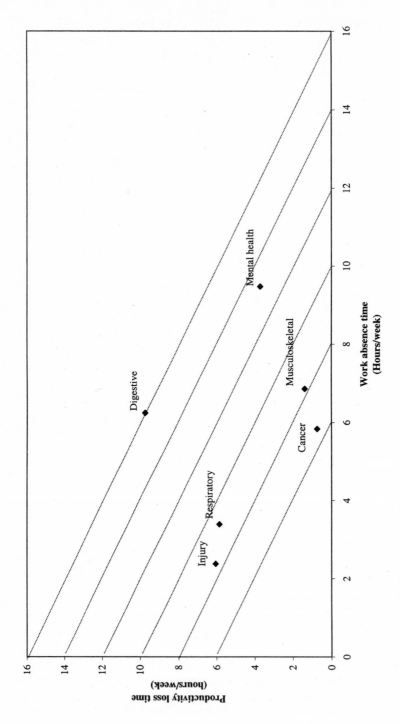

Figure 2.3. Components of indirect cost, by condition

Notes: Points along each dotted line represent the same total work-loss time. Total work-loss time is the sum of productivity loss plus work absence loss.

Source: Burton et al. 1999.

incremental output associated with taking nonsedating antihistamines averaged $9.00 per day, the incremental cost of these medications was approximately $1.50 per day (Cockburn et al. 1999b). While such findings demonstrate the value of archival measures of productivity linked to treatment choice, a second analysis of the same data set did not find a link between illness and productivity. In this separate analysis of mental disorders, the authors conclude that "although medical care use differs considerably among employees with no, one, or several treated mental disorders, in most cases their annual average absenteeism and average at-work productivity performance do not differ" (Berndt et al. 2000, 244). In this particular study, sample size and dilution of impact over time raise questions about the inferences drawn by the authors.

Finally, a recent study brings together both at-work productivity and absenteeism data with medical claims records, thereby providing a detailed look at this relationship at the employee level (Burton et al. 1999). In addition, it relates these data to health risk assessments, which have produced useful insights about employee productivity patterns in previous research (Bertera 1991; Yen, Edington, and Witting 1992).

For the job categories considered here, both the magnitude of productivity loss and the components of work loss varied by condition (see fig. 2.3). Although mental illness and digestive disorders were associated with the greatest lost productivity, mental illnesses were associated with substantial time missed from work, while digestive disorders resulted in significantly reduced productivity while at work. Moreover, among the risk factors noted on the health risk assessment, diabetes, a high general distress score, and a high body-mass index were associated with reduced at-work productivity as well as elevated absenteeism from work. Furthermore, productivity declined as the number of health risk factors increased.

FUTURE DIRECTIONS FOR PRODUCTIVITY-BASED HEALTH OUTCOME RESEARCH

It is not surprising that many diseases have an adverse impact on workplace performance. To estimate the differential impairment in employee productivity, researchers can ask those suffering from the illness how they are performing at work when experiencing different health states. In addition, supervisors, co-workers, friends, and family caregivers can describe changes in patterns of at-work contribution and absenteeism during the time surrounding particular episodes of adverse health. A recent goal in some productivity research has involved measuring the hidden costs of illness in the workplace in creative new ways.[8] This chapter has focused on studies that have linked archival records of productivity changes over time with health status measures. However, the field of health outcome research is still developing. In the future, new kinds of data-linking approaches should address deficiencies in this first wave of research designs. For example, while productivity data have been successfully linked with administrative claims records, these data are only imperfect indicators of health status. Far better clinical measures emerge from prospective studies that either compare the effects of treatment versus placebo, or assess health outcomes in an observational setting. By gathering information about changes in clinical status, such prospective studies can both help to establish the impact of treatment on productivity and provide more clinically accurate and detailed data than those obtained from retrospective claims.

Thus, the ideal study design might take elements of all four approaches described in table 2.1 and blend them together in a novel manner. A workplace-based clinical trial design could be very illuminating if it included the opportunity to link patient-specific self-report and clinical status records with archival employee-productivity data. At the same time, administrative claims data would add value in documenting patterns of resource utilization and employer medical expenditures. In other words, the most compelling research studies might link elements from all of these different data sources (clinical trial, archival productivity, and administrative claims). Indeed, it may be possible to use data from multiple sources to develop and validate a "gold standard" measure of workplace performance (Greenberg et al. 2001). (See chapter 12 of this book for a more complete discussion of this gold-standard measure.)

In this review, we have illustrated how the information gleaned from archival data can be valuable in thinking about corporate benefit design. In addition to the work-loss categories considered here, impairment due to illness also has an aggregate cost. Many people with illnesses are forced to limit their hours of work, quit their jobs, or refrain from even entering the labor force. When illness impedes workforce participation in meaningful ways, a loss of productive capacity is borne by society, even though no individual employer necessarily incurs the resulting cost.

Similarly, although significant improvements in labor-market outcomes typically result from successful treatment, health outcome researchers have not examined this phenomenon. These outcomes include, for example,

8. For example, several employee health care coalitions are investigating the productivity impact of workplace illnesses (Shinkman 1999).

moving from part-time to full-time employment status, switching to a job that is more consistent with an employee's educational and professional experience, being promoted regularly, and being rewarded more routinely with salary increases. Each of these outcomes is highly relevant to understanding the long-term impact of illness and treatment. Perhaps because of the time frames required for analysis, however, these categories are only infrequently linked back to changes in health status, particularly from an employer's perspective (Von Korff, Ormel, Keefe, and Dworkin 1992; Jackson et al. 1998).

It also is important to recognize that current measures of productivity focus on workers as stand-alone contributors to the production process, even though most work situations actually involve significant interdependencies among employees. As a result, accomplishments of employees during a specific period of time may not be accurately reflected in the 0% to 100% scale that is used in most productivity-based health outcome research. At times, employees suffering from any number of debilitating health disorders may contribute negatively to the production process. For example, even though co-workers may be able to "pick up the slack" in the short run, eventually, the entire team's output can be undermined by an unusually high error rate. In fact, the health problems of some workers can cause productivity to fall below 0% on a given day. In other words, when employees are part of a team, absenteeism may be less disruptive to productivity than presenteeism.

Linking productivity data to health care claims also can provide insights into the nature of health care expenditures. For example, one study that linked disability and health care claims data found that while approximately 20% of employees of a national corporation had a disability claim, these employees accounted for approximately 60% of the overall health care costs of employees (Auerbach and Lucas 1997). This concentration of cost is not surprising since the most costly health care events typically involve inpatient hospital admissions that are frequently associated with substantial work loss. Auerbach and Lucas's study underlines the close relationship between successful treatment and improvements in labor-market outcomes.

By carefully measuring the productivity consequences of illness and treatment, research can provide a clearer picture of the value of specific health care benefits. However, a productivity offset, on its own, is an incomplete basis for deciding whether and in what way to make treatments available to those affected by health disorders. Not only would a required 100% cost offset in the workplace be an insurmountable threshold for all but the rare intervention; even in such an extreme situation, productivity improvements would constitute only one piece of the equation. The purpose of linking administrative claims with archival data for pharmacoeconomic investigation is not to replace clinical criteria with economic ones, but rather to allow economic insights to inform and ultimately refine clinical reasoning to the benefit of the patient, the payer, and the provider.

REFERENCES

Auerbach, R., and B. Lucas. 1997. Linking health plan performance with disability outcomes. *Benefits Quarterly* 13:46–56.

Berndt, E. R., H. L. Bailit, M. B. Keller, J. C. Verner, and S. N. Finkelstein. 2000. Health care use and at-work productivity among employees with mental disorders. *Health Affairs* 19:244–56.

Berndt, E. R., S. N. Finkelstein, P. E. Greenberg, A. Keith, and H. Bailit. 1997. Illness and productivity: Objective workplace evidence. Working Paper 42-97, MIT Program on the Pharmaceutical Industry, Cambridge, MA.

Bertera, R. L. 1991. The effects of behavioral risks on absenteeism and health-care costs in the workplace. *Journal of Occupational Medicine* 33:1119–24.

Birnbaum, H. G., M. Barton, P. E. Greenberg, T. Sisitsky, R. Auerbach, L. A. Wanke, and M. C. Buatti. 2000. Direct and indirect costs of rheumatoid arthritis to an employer. *Journal of Occupational and Environmental Medicine* 42:588–96.

Birnbaum, H. G., P. Y. Cremieux, and P. E. Greenberg. 2000. Understanding the pharmacoeconomic profile of cancer. *ONE: Oncology Economics* 1:36–9.

Birnbaum, H. G., P. Y. Cremieux, P. E. Greenberg, and R. C. Kessler. 2000. Management of major depression in the workplace: Impact on employee work loss. *Disease Management and Health Outcomes* 7:163–71.

Birnbaum, H. G., P. Y. Cremieux, P. E. Greenberg, J. LeLorier, J. Ostrander, and L. Venditti. 1999. Using healthcare claims data for outcomes research and pharmacoeconomic analyses. *PharmacoEconomics* 16:1–8.

Birnbaum, H. G., P. E. Greenberg, M. Barton, R. C. Kessler, C. R. Rowland, and T. E. Williamson. 1999. Workplace burden of depression: Case study in social functioning using employer claims data. *Drug Benefit Trends* 11, no. 8: 6–12.

Birnbaum, H. G., P. E. Greenberg, P. Corey-Lisle, M. Marynchenko, and A. Claxton. 2004. Economic implications of treatment-resistant depression among employees. *PharmacoEconomics*, 22 (6): 363–73.

Birnbaum, H. G., M. Morley, P. E. Greenberg, M. Cifaldi, and G. L. Colice. 2001. Economic burden of pneumonia in an employed population. *Archives of Internal Medicine* 161:2725–31.

Broadhead, W. E., D. G. Blazer, L. K George, and C. K. Tse. 1990. Depression, disability days, and days lost from work in a prospective epidemiologic survey. *Journal of the American Medical Association* 264:2524–28.

Burton, W. N., and D. J. Conti. 1999. Use of an integrated health data warehouse to measure the employer costs of five chronic disease states. *Disease Management* 1:17–26.

Burton, W. N., D. J. Conti, C. Y. Chen, A. B. Schultz, and D. W. Edington. 1999. The role of health risk factors and disease on worker productivity. *Journal of Occupational and Environmental Medicine* 41:863–77.

Claxton, A. J., A. J. Chawla, and S. Kennedy. 1999. Absenteeism among employees treated for depression. *Journal of Occupational and Environmental Medicine* 41: 605–11.

Cockburn, I. M., H. L. Bailit, E. R. Berndt, and S. N. Finkelstein. 1999a. Loss of work productivity due to illness and medical treatment. *Journal of Occupational and Environmental Medicine* 41:948–53.

Cockburn, I. M., H. L. Bailit, E. R. Berndt, and S. N. Finkelstein. 1999b. When antihistamines go to work. *Business and Health* 17:49–50.

Conti, D. J., and W. N. Burton. 1994. The economic impact of depression in a workplace. *Journal of Occupational Medicine* 36:983–88.

French, M. T., and G. A. Zarkin. 1998. Mental health, absenteeism, and earnings at a large manufacturing worksite. *Journal of Mental Health Policy and Economics* 1: 161–72.

Greenberg, P. E., M. Barton, H. G. Birnbaum, P. Cremieux, M. Slavin, F. D'Souza, and B. Auerbach. 1999. Tackling costs one disease at a time. *Business and Health* 17: 31–2.

Greenberg, P. E., H. G. Birnbaum, R. C. Kessler, M. Morgan, and P. Stang. 2001. Impact of illness and its treatment on workplace costs: Regulatory and measurement issues. *Journal of Occupational and Environmental Medicine* 43:56–63.

Greenberg, P. E., R. C. Kessler, H. G. Birnbaum, S. Leong, and S. Lowe. 2003. The economic burden of depression in the United States: How did it change between 1990 and 2000? *Journal of Clinical Psychiatry* 64 (12): 1465–75.

Greenberg, P. E., L. E. Stiglin, S. N. Finkelstein, and E. R. Berndt. 1993. The economic burden of depression in 1990. Journal of Clinical Psychiatry 54:405–18.

Jackson, T., A. Iezzi, K. Lafreniere, and K. Narduzzi. 1998. Relations of employment status to emotional distress among chronic pain patients: A path analysis. *Clinical Journal of Pain* 14:55–60.

Johns, G. 1994. How often were you absent? A review of the use of self-reported absence data. *Journal of Applied Psychology* 79 (4): 574–91.

Katzelnick, D. J., K. A. Kobak, J. H. Greist, J. W. Jefferson, and H. J. Henk. 1997. Effect of primary care treatment of depression on service use by patients with high medical expenditures. *Psychiatric Services* 48:59–64.

Kessler, R. C., C. B. Barber, H. G. Birnbaum, R. G. Frank, P. E. Greenberg, R. M. Rose, G. E. Simon, and P. S. Wang. 1999. Depression in the workplace: Effects on short-term disability. *Health Affairs* 18:163–71.

Kessler, R. C., and R. G. Frank. 1997. The impact of psychiatric disorders on work loss days. *Psychological Medicine* 27:861–73.

Kessler, R. C., K. D. Mickelson, C. Barber, and P. Wang. 2001. The association between chronic medical conditions and work impairment. In *Caring and doing for others: social responsibility in the domains of family, work, and community*, ed. A. S. Ross, 403–26. Chicago: University of Chicago Press.

Kessler, R. C., S. Zhao, S. J. Katz, A. C. Kouzis, R. G. Frank, M. Edlund, and P. Leaf. 1999. Past-year use of outpatient services for psychiatric problems in the National Comorbidity Survey. *American Journal of Psychiatry* 156:115–23.

Koopmanschap, M. A., and F. F. Rutten. 1996. A practical guide for calculating indirect costs of disease. *PharmacoEconomics* 10:460–6.

Koopmanschap, M. A., F. F. Rutten, B. M. van Ineveld, and L. van Roijen. 1995. The friction cost method for measuring the indirect costs of disease. *Journal of Health Economics* 14:171–89.

Kouzis, A. C., and W. W. Eaton. 1994. Emotional disability days: Prevalence and predictors. *American Journal of Public Health* 84:1304–7.

Kouzis, A. C., and W. W. Eaton. 1997. Psychopathology and the development of disability. *Social Psychiatry Epidemiology* 32:379–86.

Legg, R. F., D. A. Sclar, N. L. Nemec, J. Tarnai, and J. I. Mackowiak. 1997. Cost benefit of sumatriptan to an employer. *Journal of Occupational and Environmental Medicine* 39:652–57.

Lipton, R. B., W. F. Stewart, and M. von Korff. 1997. Burden of migraine: Societal costs and therapeutic opportunities. *Neurology* 48:S4–S9.

Mayfield, J. A., P. Deb, and L. Whitecotton. 1999. Work disability and diabetes. *Diabetes Care* 22:1105–9.

Ormel, J., M. Von Korff, W. Van Den Brink, W. Katon, E. Brilman, and T. Oldehinkel. 1993. Depression, anxiety, and social disability show synchrony of change in primary care patients. *American Journal of Public Health* 83:358–90.

Osterhaus, J. T., D. L. Gutterman, and J. R. Plachetka. 1992. Healthcare resource and lost labour costs of migraine headache in the U.S. *PharmaceoEconomics* 2:67–76.

Ramsey, S., K. H. Summers, S. A. Leong, G. H. Birnbaum, J. E. Kemner, and P. E. Greenberg. 2002. Productivity and medical costs of diabetes in a large employer population. *Diabetes Care* 25:23–29.

Rasmussen, B. K., R. Jensen, M. Schroll, and J. Olesen. 1991. Epidemiology of headache in a general population: A prevalence study. *Journal of Clinical Epidemiology* 44:1147–57.

Revicki, D. A., D. Irwin, J. Reblando, and G. E. Simon. 1994. The accuracy of self-reported disability days. *Medical Care* 32 (4): 401–4.

Rice, D. P. 1966. *Estimating the cost of illness.* U.S. Public Health Service Publication no. 947–6. Washington, DC: Government Printing Office.

Rizzo, J. A., T. A. Abbott, and S. Pashko. 1996. Labour productivity effects of prescribed medicines for chronically ill workers. *Health Economics* 5:249–65.

Rosenheck, R. A., B. Druss, M. Stolar, D. Leslie, and W. Sledge. 1999. Effect of declining mental health service use on employees of a large corporation. *Health Affairs* 18:193–203.

Shinkman, R. 1999. Report cards target hidden cost of illness. *Modern Health Care* 29 (42): 76–79.

Solomon, G. D., and K. L. Price. 1997. Burden of migraine: A review of its socioeconomic impact. *PharmacoEconomics* 2:1–10.

Stang, P. E., and J. T. Osterhaus. 1993. Impact of migraine in the United States: Data from the National Health Interview Study. *Headache* 33:29–35.

Stang, P., M. Von Korff, and B. S. Galer. 1998. Reduced labor force participation among primary care patients with headache. *Journal of General Internal Medicine* 13: 296–302.

Stewart, W. F., and R. B. Lipton. 1996. Work-related disability: Results from the American Migraine Study. *Cephalagia* 16:231–38.

Stoudemire, A., R. Frank, N. Hedemark, M. Kamlet, and D. Blazer. 1986. The economic burden of depression. *General Hospital Psychiatry* 8:387–94.

Testa, M. A., and D. S. Simonson. 1998. Health economic benefits and quality of life during improved glycemic control in patients with type 2 diabetes mellitus: A randomized, controlled, double-blind trial. *Journal of the American Medical Association* 280:1490–96.

Van Roijen, L., M.-L. Essink-Bot, M. A. Koopmanschap, B. C. Michel, and F. F. Rutten. 1995. Societal perspective on the burden of migraine in the Netherlands. *PharmacoEconomics* 7:170–79.

Von Korff, M., J. Ormel, W. Katon, and E. H. Lin. 1992. Disability and depression among high utilizers of health care. *Archives of General Psychiatry* 49:91–100.

Von Korff, M., J. Ormel, F. Keefe, and S. F. Dworkin. 1992. Grading the severity of chronic pain. *Pain* 50:133–49.

Warner, K. E., T. M. Wickizer, R. A. Wolfe, J. E. Schildroth, and M. H. Samuelson. 1988. Economic implications of workplace health promotion program: Review of the literature. *Journal of Occupational Medicine* 30:106–12.

CHAPTER 3

Simulation for Measurement of Occupational Performance

JONATHAN HOWLAND,
THOMAS W. MANGIONE, AND ANGELA LARAMIE

INTRODUCTION

By clarifying the relationship between health status and performance, valid
and reliable measures of occupational performance can be instrumental in
boosting worker productivity. Accurate measurement is important for (1) understanding the impact of specific health conditions on performance, (2) estimating the cost-effectiveness of interventions, and (3) comparing the performance benefits of different intervention strategies. Even though benefit
managers and human resource personnel in most production systems (e.g.,
corporations and nonprofit organizations) could benefit enormously from
greater access to data linking health status and performance, research in this
area has been scant. A major problem has been that developing valid and reliable measures of occupational performance is difficult, both conceptually
and technically. The merits and problems of various approaches to performance measurement are reviewed throughout this volume. The purpose of
this chapter is to raise awareness of the potential of occupational simulation
as a method for performance assessment.

We begin by defining simulation and providing a brief overview of how
simulation has evolved over the past century. We then discuss the advantages
and disadvantages of simulation as compared to other measurement approaches such as self-report and archival data. We also give examples of studies using simulation to assess occupational performance, including our own
research on the effect of low-dose alcohol use on performance. After exam-

ining issues of validity and licensing, we conclude by highlighting how simulation can be used in future studies.

DEFINING SIMULATION

Within the context of occupational performance assessment, we define *simulation* as a representation that approximates the actual operating conditions
of a job. A *scenario* is the representation of a specific set of conditions, usually developed for the purpose of training for, or assessing, a discrete set of
skills. A *simulator* is a device that generates simulation (National Research
Council 1996).

In essence, a simulation is a particular kind of test, one that enables researchers to assess overall job performance. In comparison, the Department
of Labor's new database called O*NET, as discussed in chapter 6, allows for a
micro approach to assessing job performance, whereas simulation represents a macro approach. O*NET breaks down any particular job into component parts or abilities such as reaction time or selective attention; simulation
provides a snapshot of the "big picture." To illustrate the two approaches, one
could rate New York City taxi drivers by testing either specific skills (such as
their knowledge of the city's geography) or their performance in a simulation
chamber designed to approximate actual driving conditions in the city.

There are several reasons why simulation is likely to emerge as an important method for occupational performance measurement. On the supply
side, sophisticated, computer-based interactive simulators are increasingly
available for training and performance assessment across a growing range of
industries. The capacity of the technology that drives these simulators is constantly expanding, while the costs decrease. There is every reason to believe
these trends will continue. On the demand side, globalization of the economy and the emergence of new free market economies have increased both
corporate concern for productivity and methods for measuring occupational
performance. From a research perspective, simulation allows for testing hypotheses about occupational performance in ways that were hitherto infea-
sible, unethical, or both. For example, associations observed in cross-sectional
employee surveys or in studies using archival data can be assessed using rigorous experimental designs when nonsimulated performance would pose a
risk to individuals and/or property.

Although simulators are typically initially adopted as training devices,
they logically evolve as tools for assessing skills for educational or formal
certification purposes. Consequently, simulators may become, de facto, the

gold standard for performance measurement within an increasing number of industries.

THE HISTORY OF SIMULATION

The use of mechanical or electrical simulators for occupational training and performance evaluation dates back to the beginning of the twentieth century. As early as 1910, bus and trolley simulators were developed to assess the competence and skills of public transit operators. Initially, stimuli mounted on a moving belt tested driver response and reaction time. Later, full-scale model vehicles were mounted on conveyor belts, which were painted to simulate roadways (National Highway Traffic Safety Administration 1996). In 1913 crude aircraft simulators were developed to familiarize student pilots with the mechanics of flight control. Some of the early devices were mounted on pivots so that the simulator pitched or banked in response to movements of stick and pedal. By the 1930s, Link Trainers were available for teaching blind flying. Although these devices provided no view, simulated or real, of the outside world, they gave trainees the sensations typically associated with flying, enabling instructors to teach instrument flying. Pneumatic pistons drove the pitch, yaw, and roll of the simulator "box" in which the pilot was seated.

Occupational simulation today is predominately computer-based, allowing for interaction between the operator and the simulated environment. In some occupations, the use of simulation for training and evaluation may even be mandated by regulation. For example, in commercial aviation, simulator training is now used extensively, and simulator time is, by regulation, interchangeable with actual flight time. Likewise, the maritime industry makes extensive use of simulators for training merchant mariners and naval officers. Applications include bridge simulators, replicating the movement of a vessel in and out of ports or docking facilities; engine simulators, replicating the operation of steam, diesel, or gas turbine power plants; and liquid cargo-loading simulators, replicating the loading and unloading of tankers. The International Maritime Organization, of which the United States is a member, is developing standards for simulator training and evaluation (International Maritime Organization 1978). Furthermore, each nuclear power facility in the United States includes a plant-specific simulator used to train and assess employees on the site (Lewins and Becker 1986).

Current medical applications include anesthesiology simulators that feature a full-scale mock-up of an operating room and a mechanical patient with vital signs that respond interactively to the actions of physicians in training (Henson and Lee 1998). Ultrasound simulators, surgery simulators for specific procedures (e.g., laparoscopy), and dental simulators that allow students to practice oral examinations and procedures using simulated patients are also in use.

Simulation is being increasingly employed in the military for training and evaluation across a range of procedures, from target practice with gunnery simulators to decision-making in complex war-game simulations. The U.S. Department of Defense has recently funded a major simulation center at the University of Southern California to assist in the development of new simulation systems with military applications.

ADVANTAGES OF SIMULATION

Approaches to studying worker productivity tend to fall into two categories: objective approaches and subjective approaches. Simulation is in the first category along with the Experience Sampling Method (ESM) (described in chapter 5) and employer archival data on workplace behavior (described in chapter 2). In contrast, the self-report method (described in chapter 4) relies on respondents' reconstructions of past events (e.g., work absences).

Unlike these other approaches, simulation can be used only for a small group of occupations. As noted above, over the past century, the application of simulation has been restricted largely to measuring workers' ability to use machinery or drive vehicles. For professionals such as scientists, legislators, or corporate managers, simulation cannot accurately assess job performance because the tasks are so varied and complex. However, where simulation is applicable, it can offer several unique advantages over other assessment methods.

Safety

Safety is perhaps the most important advantage of the use of simulation for occupational training and assessment. Simulation allows participants to perform job functions under a range of circumstances without risk of injury or property loss. Accordingly, simulation allows for training and assessment in a range not feasible in the real world. Under actual operating conditions, a given training/assessment exercise must conclude at the point where risk becomes unacceptable. Depending upon the situation, this point may be reached well before a given scenario evolves to catastrophe. Thus, real-world training/assessment has a risk ceiling that leaves an experiential blind spot. Simulation, however, permits an exercise to approach or reach catastrophe.

The exercise can be repeated until the remedial procedures are learned. Furthermore, the participant is able to have sole command over the exercise, experiencing responsibility for the consequences of decisions in a safe learning environment. To cite a concrete example, simulation could readily assess the performance of bus drivers who are taking sedating antihistamines under highly stressful conditions (e.g., inclement weather) without endangering people or property. A simulation replicating normal working conditions, moreover, might be able to pick up subtle effects of these drugs that would not show up in other assessment methods.

Objectivity

Simulation can be preferable to self-report because it provides objective data. For example, suppose researchers assessed the performance of 3,000 pilots who had arthritis and 3,000 without the illness using a flight simulator. As opposed to a self-report survey, the data would not be vulnerable to the recall bias of the pilots. (The precise extent of this advantage would depend on the face validity of the simulator; however, as noted below, face validity is usually high in simulation).

Replication

Simulation allows for replication of training/assessment scenarios. From a training perspective, the same exercise can be performed as many times as required to meet didactic objectives. From an assessment perspective, replication allows for measurement of scenario reliability, an important characteristic of any performance measurement method.

Consistency

Simulation can provide consistency in training/assessment procedures, which, in turn, allows for the comparison of performance across individuals or worksites or for the comparison of individuals or groups measured repeatedly over time.

Recording and Playback

A simulated training/assessment exercise can be recorded and played back. This provides an opportunity for participants to repeatedly observe their own performance within the context of a given scenario. In addition to the didactic value of exercise playback, the ability to record performance allows for comparison over time and facilitates interpretation by multiple assessors.

Creation of Rare Events

For some occupations, the true measure of employee performance may lie in response to rare events. For example, researchers might want to assess how pilots would respond to a terrorist on board the plane. By definition, these events have a low probability of occurring under real-world circumstances, and even less probability of occurring during a training exercise. Nonetheless, response to rare events may be critical to overall system safety and performance. Simulation allows for the creation of rare but potentially important events and, as noted above, for unlimited replication of these scenarios until appropriate response procedures are learned.

Multiple Task Loading

Employee performance can vary as a function of demand load. The ability to effectively and appropriately prioritize multiple tasks is an important measure of performance capacity. With simulated training/assessment exercises, complexity and difficulty can be altered with great precision, while keeping a core task constant. Thus, the same basic scenario can be run under a range of conditions, from routine operation to emergency situations.

Cost-Effectiveness

Although sophisticated simulators can be expensive, for a number of reasons they can also be cost-effective. Simulators not only prevent training-related injury or property damage; they also allow for training and assessment without tying up real equipment that would otherwise be directly involved with production. Simulators can function 24 hours per day, regardless of season or weather conditions. Depending upon the industry and the simulator capacity, day can be simulated at night or night simulated during the day. Fair or poor weather can also be simulated, as needed. There is minimal downtime between simulations.

LIMITATIONS OF SIMULATION

With regard to capturing the feel of the workplace, performance assessment using simulators falls somewhere in between the two "extremes" or "poles" of testing in the laboratory and testing in the actual workplace setting itself. The laboratory experimental/assessment environment, which usually has a feel and look that is much different from that of the workplace itself, is better suited to measuring specific skills and abilities than measuring overall performance. Obviously, research/performance assessment that takes place while work is actually performed is well suited to measuring overall performance in the workplace environment. However, this option can be problematic because the process of measurement often intrudes on or changes the normal workplace atmosphere. Although it is clear that job performance expressed in a simulator is not "real," researchers typically are successful in making the trainee/research subjects feel as if they were operating under "real" conditions and in getting them to behave in ways that capture their normal performance.

Nevertheless, in some cases, even though simulation may be easy to implement, it has some significant limitations when compared with other methods. For example, the laboratory setting offers a much greater degree of control over confounding variables, since laboratory tests provide a precise measurement of specific functions such as cognition, reaction time, divided attention, and memory, rather than a gross measure of overall job performance. Likewise, because simulators try to incorporate more of the workplace context, they are vulnerable to unknown confounding due to these contextual representations. An example of such a confounding variable is motivation. By definition, subjects in a simulation know they are being tested and thus may be more highly motivated to do a good job than under other normal working conditions.

Let's assume we are trying to test the performance of airline pilots who take antihistamines; we might test two groups of pilots using a flight simulator, one group taking first-generation sedating antihistamines and one group taking nonsedating antihistamines. This study might underestimate the sedating impact of the first-generation antihistamines because the pilots who took them might be able to force themselves to concentrate for the duration of the test even if they could not be expected to maintain this level of concentration throughout a normal workday.

Furthermore, conducting performance assessment in the workplace also offers the advantage of both maximizing ecological validity and overcoming any "artificiality" that may remain in a simulator environment. Assessments in the workplace are better able to incorporate measurement of such abstract notions as *group norms* or *history of work procedures* that would be difficult or impossible to include when using a simulator. What is lost in the simulator is the richness of the real world, the infinite number of variables that impinge upon the worker and, in varying degrees, affect performance.

In addition, simulation is simply unnecessary in those cases where the real world allows easy, efficient, and safe performance measurement. To assess performance in word processing or data entry, simulation is redundant since assessment can be carried out easily in the actual workplace.

EXAMPLES OF USING SIMULATORS TO ASSESS PERFORMANCE-RELATED FACTORS

Although the use of simulation in measuring occupational performance is in its early stages, the literature is growing rapidly. Without attempting a comprehensive review, we can illustrate with several examples the usefulness of simulation for examining factors thought to affect occupational performance. A common avenue of investigation is to observe the effects of an illness (e.g., depression or substance abuse) on job performance. For example, automobile and truck simulators have been used in randomized studies to assess the effects of various doses of alcohol (Laurell 1977; Liguori et al. 1999; Tornos and Laurell 1991). Similar studies have been conducted using flight simulators (Morrow, Leirer, and Yesavage 1990; Morrow et al. 1991; Ross and Mundt 1988; Yesavage, Dolhert, and Taylor 1994; Yesavage and Leirer 1986). In addition, flight simulators have been used to assess the effects of marijuana, nicotine (Mumenthaler et al. 1998), and various mixtures of breathing atmospheres (Collins 1980). A randomized trial was recently conducted on the effects of sleep deprivation on surgical performance. Performance was measured using a simulator for laparoscopic surgery (Taffinder et al. 1998).

Our own research on the effects of low-dose sedation on occupational performance illustrates the interplay of cross-sectional and simulator-based experimental studies. We conducted a large employee survey with more than 6,500 respondents at work sites belonging to seven major U.S. corporations (Mangione et al. 1999). The survey included questions on drinking practices. Questions on work-performance problems (e.g., producing lower-quality work) were also asked. Respondents were not asked to attribute their work problems to any particular cause. We observed a linear relationship between average daily volume of alcohol and the frequency of reported work problems. We also observed that respondents who reported drinking during the workday (usually at lunch) reported more work problems, even when the analysis was stratified by alcohol dependence. Using regression analysis, we determined that average daily volume and drinking during lunch were independently significant in predicting frequency of work-performance problems. We hypothesized that average daily volume affected work performance through residual effects of heavy drinking (e.g., hangovers), while drinking at lunch reflected the impact of low-dose sedation on performance. Other obvious explanations were also possible. Poor work performance could cause alcohol use or some third factor (e.g., personality characteristics) could cause both drinking and performance problems. The cross-sectional nature of our study did not allow us to disentangle these interpretations.

Using maritime simulators that replicate merchant ship operation, we were able to test our hypotheses using randomized trials. To test the effects of low-dose alcohol exposure on work performance, we randomly dosed maritime cadets to a level of 0.04 g% BAC (the equivalent of 2–3 drinks) and measured their performance using ship simulators (Howland et al. 2001). In separate trials, significant effects were found for low-dose alcohol exposure on simulated power plant operation (Howland et al. 2000) and simulated piloting (Howland et al. 2001). We are also testing simulated ship operation the day after random dosing at 0.10 g% BAC. Thus, experimental studies using a single occupational model were able to confirm the causal interpretation of associations derived from a large-scale cross-sectional survey. In this case, simulation picked up subtle effects (of low-dose alcohol sedation on work performance) that were not visible in surveys. Needless to say, the merchant-ship experiments could not have been conducted without the use of simulators.

Another common use of simulation has been to assess the effect of treatment on performance. For example, numerous studies have employed simulation to test the effect of sedating medications (e.g., first-generation antihistamines) on driver performance (Vermeeren and O'Hanlon 1998; Weiler et al. 2000).

VALIDITY

There are several types of validity characterizing any measure. *Face validity* is the extent to which a measure plausibly reflects the concept it assesses. As opposed to more abstract measures of cognitive or physical function, simulators tend to have high face validity because they are designed precisely to replicate a given occupational task in a real-world setting. The extent to which simulators achieve this goal is often a function of the sophistication of the mathematical modeling employed. The difference, for instance, between a computer game and a FAA certified flight simulator depends on the quality of graphic imaging and, more important, on the extent to which the aerodynamic modeling of a particular aircraft replicates the behavior of the actual plane under a variety of circumstances. In contrast to traditional measures of cognition and neurological function, findings from simulation can provide persuasive evidence to policymakers. Industry representatives and regulators are likely to find performance data from simulation more convincing than performance data derived from abstract tests of reaction time, signal recognition, and divided attention.

Internal validity reflects the extent to which a performance measure translates to actual performance in real-world settings. Internal validity is possible regardless of face validity. With the exception of commercial flight simulation, there is relatively little research on the validity of most occupational simulators. The problem of internal validity varies according to the type of task simulated. A word-processing or data-entry simulation will have both high face and internal validity because the task simulations are essentially identical to real-world operations. A ship, flight, or driving simulator cannot replicate real-world circumstances to the same degree.

External validity refers to the extent to which findings for a sample of a given population can be generalized to all members of that population. As with any experimental finding, external validity can be assessed only through repeated trials using different samples of the population to which inference is drawn.

SIMULATION AND REGULATION/LICENSING

The role of simulation in the training and certification of commercial airline pilots has been mentioned above. Simulation is also a part of the International Maritime Organization recommendations for training and certification of merchant mariners (International Maritime Organization 1978). The National Highway Traffic Safety Administration (NHTSA) has conducted at least one study on the value of simulation for driver training. At the University of Iowa, construction of NHTSA's national driving simulator is under way (Gabriel 1995). Although this simulator will be used for research, it will advance the technology of driving simulation. It is likely that within the next decade, simulators will be routinely used for licensing and recertifying commercial and private drivers. We expect that the government will increasingly depend on simulation for certification in occupations subject to public regulation. This example, in turn, will increase the use of simulation for training purposes among nongovernment entities and further establish simulation as a method for assessing occupational performance.

CONCLUSION

Simulation is a powerful tool for measuring occupational performance in general and for studying the relationship between productivity and health status in particular. Although it may be difficult to use for some professions, simulation has several advantages over other assessment methods, including its cost-effectiveness and its ability to test rare events. Researchers may also want to combine simulation with other research approaches, as we did in our study showing the effect of low doses of alcohol on work performance. Simulators can be used to measure the impact of medical conditions, such as depression, migraine headaches, or allergies, on productivity and can assess the relative benefits of various therapeutic interventions for employee performance.

However, despite the numerous advantages of simulation, researchers continue to underutilize this valuable option. For example, in a recent research report on road safety that discussed the link between over-the-counter (OTC) medications (e.g., antihistamines) and unwanted sleepiness, British researchers (Horne and Barrett 2001) stress the need for more simulator studies on the effects of OTC medications on driving performance, lamenting that only a few have been conducted to date.

Finally, simulation can assess prospectively the performance impacts of environmental or organizational changes to the workplace. With better data on the contribution of human factors to occupational performance, managers can make more informed decisions about resource allocation and investment in human capital.

REFERENCES

Collins, W. E. 1980. Performance effects of alcohol intoxication and hangover at ground level and at simulated altitude. *Aviation Space and Environmental Medicine* 51:327–35.

Gabriel, L. H. 1995. *Estimating demand for the National Advanced Driving Simulator.* Washington, DC: Transportation Research Board.

Henson, L. C., and A. C. Lee. 1998. *Simulators in anesthesiology education.* New York: Plenum Press.

Horne, J. A., and P. R. Barrett. 2001. Over-the-counter medicines and the potential for unwanted sleepiness in drivers: A review. London: Department for Transport.

Howland, J., D. J. Rohsenow, J. Cote, B. Gomez, T. W. Mangione, and A. K. Laramie. 2001. Effects of low-dose alcohol exposure on simulated merchant ship piloting by maritime cadets. *Accident Analysis and Prevention* 33:257–65.

Howland, J., D. J. Rohsenow, J. Cote, M. Siegel, and T. W. Mangione. 2000. Effects of low-dose alcohol exposure on simulated merchant ship handling power plant operation by maritime cadets. *Addiction* 95:719–26.

International Maritime Organization. 1978. STCW 1978. International Convention on Standards of Training, Certification, and Watchkeeping, London, Eng.

Laurell, H. 1977. Effects of small doses of alcohol on driver performance in emergency traffic. *Accident Analysis and Prevention* 9:191–201.

Lewins, J., and M. Becker. 1986. *Advances in nuclear science and technology: Simulators for nuclear power*. Vol. 17. New York: Plenum Press.

Liguori, A., R. B. D'Agostino, S. Dworkin, D. Edwards, and J. H. Robinson. 1999. Alcohol effects on mood, equilibrium, and simulated driving. *Alcoholism: Clinical and Experimental Research* 23:815–21.

Mangione, T. W., J. Howland, B. Amick, J. Cote, M. Lee, N. Bell, and S. Levine. 1999. Employee drinking practices and work performance. *Journal of Studies on Alcohol* 60:261–70.

Morrow, D., V. Leirer, and J. Yesavage. 1990. The influence of alcohol and aging on radio communication during flight. *Aviation Space and Environmental Medicine* 61:12–20.

Morrow, D., V. Leirer, J. Yesavage, and J. Tinklenberg. 1991. Alcohol, age, and piloting: Judgement, mood, and actual performance. *International Journal of the Addictions* 26:669–83.

Mumenthaler, M. S., J. L. Taylor, R. O'Hara, and J. A. Yesavage. 1998. Influence of nicotine on simulator flight performance in non-smokers. *Psychopharmacologia* 140:38–41.

National Highway Traffic Safety Administration. 1996. Feasibility of new simulation technology to train novice drivers. In *DOT HS 808548*. Washington, DC: U.S. Department of Transportation.

National Research Council. 1996. *Simulated voyages: Using simulation technology to train and license mariners*. Washington, DC: National Academy Press.

Ross, L. E., and J. C. Mundt. 1988. Multiattribute modeling analysis of the effects of a low blood alcohol level on pilot performance. *Human Factors* 30:293–304.

Taffinder, N. J., I. C. McManus, Y. Gul, R. C. Russell, and A. Darzi. 1998. Effect of sleep deprivation on surgeons' dexterity on laparoscopy simulator. *Lancet* 352:1191.

Tornos, J., and H. Laurell. 1991. Acute and hangover effects of alcohol on simulated driving performance. *Blutalkohol* 28:24–30.

Vermeeren, A., and J. F. O'Hanlon. 1998. Fexofenadine's effects, alone and with alcohol, on actual driving and psychomotor performance. *Journal of Allergy and Clinical Immunology* 101:306–11.

Weiler, J. M., J. R. Bloomfield, G. G. Woodworth, A. R. Grant, T. A. Layton, T. L. Brown, D. R. McKenzie, T. W. Baker, and G. S. Watson. 2000. Effects of fexofenadine, diphenhydramine, and alcohol on driving performance: A randomized, placebo-controlled trial in the Iowa driving simulator. *Annals of Internal Medicine* 132:354–63.

Yesavage, J. A., N. Dolhert, and J. L. Taylor. 1994. Flight simulator performance of younger and older aircraft pilots: Effects of age and alcohol. *Journal of the American Geriatrics Society* 42:577–82.

Yesavage, J. A., and V. O. Leirer. 1986. Hangover effects on aircraft pilots 14 hours after alcohol ingestion: A preliminary report. *American Journal of Psychiatry* 143:1546–50.

CHAPTER 4

Measuring Health-Related
Work Productivity with Self-Reports

DEBRA J. LERNER AND JENNIFER LEE

INTRODUCTION

Work productivity is increasingly regarded as a critical barometer for measuring success in managing the health problems of working-age adults (Pope and Tarlov 1991). This perspective reflects the influence of three important trends: an increased prevalence of chronic health problems among the adult population, intensified concerns about the quality-of-life and cost implications associated with these health problems, and the desire of some employers to play a proactive role in reducing the economic burden of illness and medical care.

Work productivity is already an important endpoint within several fields of research. In health-economics and health-policy research, work-productivity variables are used to estimate the portion of total health care costs attributable to lost productivity (Grabowski and Hansen 1996). In clinical research, work productivity is regarded as a marker of functional effectiveness, a key component of a person's or a population's total health status (Fries and Spingh 1996). Work productivity is also related to the concept of disability.

A standard approach to measuring work productivity in health studies is to obtain data by means of self-report. Self-reported data (information that individuals provide about themselves) are typically obtained from questionnaires or interviews. Self-reports can be elicited from respondents using single-item questions or multi-item scales and batteries.

Self-report methods have been used for many years within psychology, education, public-opinion polling, and market research. In the past decade, the health care industry also has increasingly turned to patient self-reports for information about the outcomes of patients' illnesses and treatments and their satisfaction with medical services (Patrick and Erickson 1993). As self-reports have achieved a high degree of acceptance in health care, physicians, administrators, policymakers, and scientists have had to overcome the prevalent misconception that "self-report" necessarily implies "inaccurate" or "biased."

However, establishing the credibility of the self-report health measures has not been easy. This process has involved years of refining survey research methods, testing new questionnaires, and documenting test results in peer-reviewed journals. The actual use of self-reports in studies of health and work productivity is a relatively new idea. Thus, both health service researchers and stakeholders need assurances that self-reports are valuable.

This chapter describes the state-of-the-art methods of asking individuals about the impact of their health problems and treatments on work productivity (referred to as *health-related work productivity*). The presentation focuses on productivity in paid employment (thus excluding household work and other forms of unpaid productivity).

Among the topics we cover are the rationale for asking people about their health and its impact on work, the criteria for "good" self-report data, and specific issues that threaten data accuracy. We also discuss available indicators and scales and assess their strengths and weaknesses. After examining the self-report method in detail, we briefly allude to some other measurement alternatives, such as employer archival data.

WHY USE SELF-REPORT

Generally, self-report measures are chosen over other data-collection methods for one of three reasons. First, the questionnaire respondent may be the best available information source. This is often the premise of studies aimed at eliciting opinions, attitudes, values, and/or perceptions with regard to specific events or experiences. Likewise in some situations, the respondent functions as a source of "objective" data. For example, patients are frequently asked to complete health status questionnaires because they are regarded as the most accurate source of information about their own functional performance. In these situations, self-reports constitute the gold standard.

Second, self-reports may be chosen over other data sources because they are a practical substitute for gold-standard data. In this case, self-reports are shortcuts to collecting information that otherwise would be cumbersome, costly, or even potentially unethical to obtain. For example, self-report chronic disease checklists are frequently used in population health surveys because physical examinations would be too costly and time-consuming.

Finally, self-report methods may be chosen over other approaches because objective data simply are unavailable or inaccessible. This is frequently the situation for work-productivity data.

PERFORMANCE CRITERIA FOR SELF-REPORT SURVEY METHODS

When evaluating a measure for use in a study or project, researchers need to keep in mind four criteria: the measure must provide valid, reliable, and meaningful data, and it must be practical to administer. In recent years, important advances have been made in developing self-report survey measures. Familiarity with research methods and performance criteria is necessary in order to choose among the different measures. Several excellent texts are available to guide the novice through the process of developing, assessing, and administering self-report questions (Fowler 1988; Streiner and Norman 1995).

The *validity* of a single item or a scale refers to the degree to which it has accurately captured the concept or phenomenon its authors intended to measure. According to Hays, three main types of validity are "content" (the degree to which attributes of a concept are sampled in a measure); "construct" (the relationship of one measure to another measuring a parallel concept); and "criterion" (a survey instrument's relationship to a gold-standard measure) (Hays, Anderson, and Revicki 1998). Another property of validity is "responsiveness," or the degree to which a measure varies in response to true change.

Reliability refers to the reproducibility of the data or the degree to which survey responses remain stable, when no change has occurred. Reliability has an additional meaning when applied to multi-item scales. In this case, it is the degree to which items within a scale measure a homogeneous or cohesive concept. After all, a measurement tool can generate responses that are highly reliable but not valid—such as a scale that consistently misreads weight by five pounds.

A numerical score based on a self-report survey has three components: the true value, random error, and errors known as biases (Hays, Anderson, and Revicki 1998). The true value refers to how people would score on a test if it were administered to the entire population in exactly the same manner. Random error occurs as a result of differences between the true value within a population and the value observed within a study sample. The magnitude of this type of error is estimated using statistical techniques. Biases are reporting inaccuracies that occur because of problems associated with the survey instrument itself, the survey context and mode of administration, and/or the respondent. A questionnaire should be reasonably free of bias before it is used in research, or the user should determine how to adjust the data for biases that cannot be eliminated in advance.

Even if a questionnaire or an interview produces valid and reliable data, the results may not be *meaningful*. A necessary property of all survey data is that scores derived from responses must be easily interpreted. Two approaches to interpreting data are normative and criterion-based (Ware and Keller 1996). The normative approach involves obtaining data from an appropriate reference population. In industry, this practice is known as benchmarking. The criterion-based approach establishes the meaning of survey responses by calibrating the data against an externally measured criterion, the meaning of which is known (e.g., self-reported weight as compared to weight measured by a physician's scale). Interpretation is frequently facilitated by standardized measurement; repeated usage encourages the accumulation of comparative data.

Practicality in administration is an important feature of questionnaires and interviews. Practicality is influenced by the amount of time it takes to answer a survey's questions as well as the degree of difficulty involved (sometimes referred to as response burden). Practicality may also be determined by features such as a measure's availability in different formats (e.g., telephone, mail, Web, and interviewer-administered) and its cost per administration.

Choosing a measurement method typically involves certain trade-offs such as the choice between questionnaire length and data reliability. Longer questionnaires containing more items potentially are more likely to offer reliable, valid data as compared to shorter versions with fewer items. Similarly, the researcher may have to decide whether the benefits of a costly interviewer-administered version of a questionnaire are substantially greater than a less expensive phone or Web version. The marginal improvement in accuracy may not be worthwhile when both respondent burden and cost are factored in.

SOURCES OF ERROR IN SELF-REPORT

Fowler and Cannell wrote, "survey research measurement rests on a model that assumes that a consistently understood set of questions is posed that respondents are willing and able to answer" (1996, 15). All self-reports are vulnerable to several types of reporting errors.

Recall Error

According to Tourangeau, answering survey questions is a process that requires respondents to perform four tasks (2000). The first is interpreting a question's meaning. The second is retrieving information from memory to provide an answer about the event or topic in question. The third is formulating information into an integrated judgment. The fourth is giving an answer to the question, such as by marking a response option on a pencil-and-paper questionnaire, or giving a verbal response to an interviewer.

The accuracy of self-report depends in part on each respondent's ability to understand the meaning and intent of a survey question. However, if we asked the question, "In the past four weeks, has your health affected your work productivity?" we would be likely to find that a major barrier to answering this question accurately is that the term *work productivity* is ambiguous. Like the word *freedom*, its meaning will vary among different individuals. (*Health* may also be a confusing term, but it has been defined relatively consistently in surveys.)

The significance of the ambiguity problem was demonstrated in a series of focus groups we conducted. Focus-group participants included employed adults with one or more chronic illnesses (e.g., angina, asthma, migraine headache, and other selected conditions). When asked how health had affected their work productivity, many participants answered by drawing comparisons (e.g., "Compared to x, who is healthy, I would say I was productive"; "Considering how I was feeling last week . . ."; and "Compared to how I used to be able to work . . ."). These remarks illustrate that productivity was perceived as a relative concept that is highly dependent upon context and point of view. Moreover, we found that responses to questions about productivity differed according to whether the chronically ill person was comparing his or her current productivity to his or her own usual productivity or to co-worker productivity. The "current self to usual self" comparison yielded reports of more productivity loss than "current self to co-worker" comparisons.

Avoiding confusion around key terms is critical to obtaining accurate self-report data. This can be accomplished in a variety of ways. The survey form (or interviewer) might start with a brief statement introducing the topic, stating concisely what the survey is about, and giving examples of events that are to be included or excluded. Another approach, using the current example, is to omit the term *work productivity* in favor of questions that use productivity proxies or indicators. For example, instead of asking respondents "Has your health affected your work productivity?" the item might ask about a specific productivity criterion, such as meeting deadlines. Operationalizing key terms and concepts is valuable, but researchers need to be cautious because questions can become too narrowly focused and no longer applicable to certain respondents.

Next, assuming that the question is interpreted correctly, the respondent must be capable of remembering, with varying degrees of precision, the details of past or present events to which the question refers. Using cognitive interview techniques, survey researchers have found that several variables exert an influence on recall accuracy. For example, research has shown that memory of events is influenced by the amount of elapsed time between the events in question and the administration of a survey. According to Bradburn (2000), when asked to remember events within a defined period or to report on the timing of events, respondents frequently make the mistake of "telescoping" (regarding events as occurring more recently than they actually did). However, respondents may also err by omitting events. At present, questions about health-related work productivity vary in the length of the time on which respondents are expected to report, and there is no consensus about the optimal reporting period.

Cognitive research has also demonstrated that recall accuracy in surveys depends partly on respondent knowledge of an event (how clearly it is stored in memory), the salience of the events to the respondent, and the emotions surrounding memories of a particular event (Bradburn 2000; Kihlstrom et al. 2000). Answering questions about the impact that health has had on work productivity is a relatively complicated response task. Without concerted efforts to enhance reporting accuracy, the quality of self-reports is likely to be highly variable among different respondents. For example, there are wide variations in the regularity with which employees obtain feedback about their work productivity and the amount of feedback received.

Some respondents will be relatively well informed about their job performance, while other respondents may have only a vague recollection of it. Cognitive studies also have demonstrated that events we remember as pleasant are more accessible in memory than events we associate with negative emotions. Similarly, events that are associated with a more emotionally intense response are remembered better. Consequently, events in the workplace remembered as signifying "good" performance may be overreported, and/or those remembered as productivity problems may be underreported.

Finally, recall accuracy is influenced by the mental state of the respondent. Kihlstrom and colleagues focus on respondent perception as a source of error, influencing both the process of encoding information about events into memory, and the process of forming judgments about those events (Kihlstrom et al. 2000). This is an important issue because a variety of common health problems (e.g., depression and other mental disorders) can impair memory and judgment. Efforts to improve the accuracy of self-report from mentally impaired populations have been discussed at length in several articles (e.g., Kessler et al. 2000).

Sensitivity of the Questions and Data

Prevailing social norms and values tend to characterize productivity as good and virtuous and lack of productivity as negative or bad. Because many people regard lack of productivity as socially unacceptable, questions about a person's work productivity are frequently perceived as threatening. Threatening questions can seriously decrease reporting accuracy (Sudman and Bradburn 1982).

In the focus groups mentioned previously, our questions about health and work productivity frequently elicited strong reactions. Some participants expressed feelings of sadness and despair over having lost certain job-performance abilities. Some reacted by indicating the questions were offensive.

Sensitivity to answering questions about work productivity also is related to the fear among some employed respondents that survey information will find its way into their employers' hands. Respondents frequently are concerned about confidentiality; some worry that the information they provide could be used against them. Similarly, some employers are concerned that the information employees provide in surveys could be used in litigation against them.

When information is perceived as sensitive, or when there is fear of disclosure, individuals may refuse to participate in studies or may participate but underreport productivity losses. Conceivably, there are also situations in which the respondent perceives that some secondary gain will come out of overreporting productivity losses (e.g., to qualify for benefits). However, in general, underreporting is more common when topics are perceived as sensitive. Reducing the real and/or perceived threat to the respondent and/or the employer is essential. Sensitivity can be reduced by paying careful attention to question wording, for example avoiding emotionally charged terms such as *productive* and *unproductive*. Question order can also neutralize sensitive items. Alternating positively worded and negatively worded questions throughout a survey, embedding questions about productivity within those asking about other work or health topics, and including carefully composed introductory remarks (e.g., "People sometimes find it hard to judge how well they have performed at work.") are techniques that can improve reporting accuracy. Additional suggestions can be found in Sudman and Bradburn 1982. Self-administration may produce more valid data than interviewer-administration. Collecting data in a private location such as the respondent's home or a health clinic is sometimes more effective than collecting data at the workplace. Finally, this research should not be undertaken unless genuine measures for effectively guaranteeing respondent anonymity and/or confidentiality can be instituted. Pilot work is strongly recommended to determine if the proposed methods of data collection are viewed by prospective respondents as acceptable.

CURRENT STATUS OF MEASUREMENT

To move from the general to the specific, we now describe particular health-related work-productivity items and scales that have been used and identify their various strengths and weaknesses.

Labor-Market Participation

The productivity consequences of illness and treatment have been measured by asking individuals to report on the degree to which they have participated in the labor market during a defined period of time. Labor-market participation variables include employment status (e.g., employed full-time, employed part-time, unemployed, retired, disabled, and so on), job loss, and/or return to work (Stoudemire et al. 1986). Since labor-market participation variables are strong, unambiguous indicators of work productivity (e.g., not working implies a total loss of paid work productivity), they are regarded by economists as valuable for estimating productivity costs. Adding to the value of these measures is the large amount of normative and comparative data available on employment status, job loss, and return to work.

In the work-productivity and health literature, there is little evidence to evaluate the prevalent assumption that self-reports of employment status are unbiased within and among different population groups. However, because employment status and change in employment status are both highly salient issues for many adults, they are likely to be remembered relatively easily and accurately (though the exact dates of employment events may be erroneously reported).

Two other potential sources of error are relevant to this discussion. First, employment states are not necessarily discrete, though many questionnaires ask respondents to choose a single response. For example, people over age 65 may engage in part-time work after retirement and thus could be correctly classified in two response categories. Likewise, the distinction between "unemployed" and "disabled" is not always clear-cut. This problem can be addressed by giving respondents clear instructions for choosing a response.

Error may also occur because the relationship between a person's health status and her or his work productivity is usually inferred by comparing work status before and after illness. It is usually not measured directly by asking, for example, "Did your health cause you to lose your job?" Inferring cause from the data can lead to error.

Labor-market participation variables apply to both working and non-working populations. However, they are not useful for studies in which the illness or treatment under investigation is not expected to lead to work exits or entrances (such as job loss, job entry, and job turnover), periods of disability, and/or occupational changes.

Sickness Absences

A common way to measure productivity loss among employed individuals is to obtain self-reports of work absences due to illness or medical care. Self-reported sickness absences have been measured in study populations with migraine headache, angina pectoris, depression, anxiety, and other conditions. This information usually has been reported retrospectively for the previous four weeks or three months and measured by asking respondents to report on the number of whole days and partial days missed because of health problems or medical care. In clinical trials of migraine headache medications, where rapid relief of symptoms is a key outcome indicator, investigators have assessed time loss according to the number of hours missed from work.

Sickness-absence items, which usually are decomposed into full and partial days missed, are used to indicate total and partial productivity loss (Pauly et al. 2002). This method of asking questions facilitates the economic evaluation of productivity loss. Time missed from work is converted into wages; a whole day missed constitutes an entire day's wages, and a partial day missed a portion of a day's wages. Decomposing a topic into component parts and separate items also serves an additional purpose of improving response accuracy for difficult-to-remember information.

Within the work-productivity literature, there have been several applications of sickness-absence measurement. In addition to asking about whole days missed, Broadhead and colleagues ascertained the number of days respondents were late for work or left work early because of illness (1990). Both Broadhead and Marcus have employed the National Health Interview Survey approach for measuring self-reported disability days (Broadhead et al. 1990; Marcus et al. 1997). Items ask about whole or partial days spent in bed because of a condition. Kessler and Frank (1997) utilized two variables: "work loss" days and "work cut back" days. Work-loss days were measured by asking the respondent to report the number of days (in the past 30) that he or she was completely unable to carry out normal activities. Work-cutback-day items asked for the number of days on which the respondent was partially productive (the individual was able to work but either had to cut back on work activities or did not accomplish as much as usual).

Sickness-absence measures have content validity for many occupations, but these variables are especially useful when a work absence translates directly into a productivity loss (e.g., a gas station attendant who is absent cannot pump gas). They also facilitate economic analyses because lost work hours have a relatively direct translation into expenditures (e.g., hourly wages paid to the absent employee). However, sickness-absence measures are vulnerable to recall error and to occupational bias.

The data regarding recall accuracy/error within patient and employee populations are mixed. Johns has demonstrated that employees tend to underestimate their absences (1994). In a small pilot study, Revicki compared self-reported absences for three- and four-month intervals to employer records and found that they met reliability criteria (Revicki et al. 1994).

Using data from a sample of employees within a New England firm, we compared survey reports of sickness absences in the prior two weeks to employer records covering the same period. Employer records were based on electronic time cards. Within the group of employees who were not absent according to employer records ($n = 1,382$), 88% reported that they had not been absent from work. However, among the employees who were on record as having been absent from work in the prior two weeks, only 48% remembered their absences. These results suggest that estimates of time loss based on employee self-reports will err on the side of underestimation.

Some options for reducing recall bias include using absence diaries or shorter survey recall periods. Diaries tend to eliminate the recall problem, but they increase response burden and their administration is labor-intensive and expensive (respondents usually have to be reminded repeatedly to complete them). Unfortunately, the use of relatively short recall periods, such as weekly or biweekly reporting intervals, can sometimes produce data that are skewed toward the minimum value of zero absences.

Sickness-absence data can be confounded by occupation. Both occupations and work organizations vary widely in their formal sickness-absence policies and informal (normative) absence practices. These differences can contribute to error in estimating the effects of health on the work productivity of different groups. For example, in jobs where safety and precision are critical (e.g., ambulance driver and airline pilot), employees may be obligated to stay home from work whenever job performance is impaired, whereas the same will not be true of other occupations.

Perceived Effectiveness

Subjective assessments of effectiveness in performing work activities have been used in studies of depression and migraine headache. Osterhaus and colleagues, as well as Reilly, have proposed self-ratings of on-the-job effectiveness in performing work activities as a means for assessing partial productivity loss (Osterhaus, Gutterman, and Plachetka 1992; Reilly, Zbrozek, and Dukes 1993). Effectiveness questions ask respondents to rate their effectiveness on the job on days they were symptomatic (e.g., during a migraine headache episode). Rating scales run from 0% (not at all effective) to 100% (completely effective). Responses are subtracted from 100% and then multiplied by the number of days the person worked to provide an estimate of diminished productivity on days worked. This information frequently is combined with time-loss data (sickness-absence and/or job-loss data) to estimate total productivity loss. A dollar amount is obtained by converting time loss to wages.

Other investigators have based assessments of impaired work productivity on work-adjustment items from psychological adjustment and depression rating scales (Berndt et al. 1997; Finkelstein et al. 1996; Mintz et al. 1992). These assessments are conceptually similar to the effectiveness ratings.

While psychometric tests have shown encouraging results, the tests have been very limited. Specific biases such as underreporting have not been researched adequately. Moreover, studies documenting the relationship of self-reported effectiveness to archival/objective productivity measures have not been published. Criterion-validity tests, examining the relationship of self-reports to other objective productivity measures, would determine whether effectiveness ratings are related substantially to actual output.

Social-Role Disability Scales

A variety of questionnaires, which fall under the rubric of health status and/or health-related quality-assessment tools, include items that ask respondents to report on limitations in performing work roles because of health problems. Several scales are embedded in generic health-status assessment questionnaires (e.g., the SF-36, the Sickness Impact Profile, and the Quality of Well-Being Scale) (Bergner 1984; Kaplan et al. 1989; Ware and Sherbourne 1992) and thus were intended to be valid and reliable across a range of different patient and demographic groups. Another group of scales is included in condition-specific questionnaires, which have been tailored to measure the impact of certain conditions (e.g., the Health Assessment Questionnaire for arthritis and the Sheehan for depression) (Fries, Spitz, and Young 1982; Leon et al. 1992). A third group focuses mainly on measuring the concept of *handicap* (e.g., the Groningen Disability Schedule and the London Handicap Scale) (Harwood et al. 1994; Wiersma, DeJong, and Ormel 1988). These are not intended to measure work productivity specifically, and we exclude them from the present discussion.

The role-disability scales contained in some of the leading health-status questionnaires have a high degree of validity and reliability for a variety of different population groups and applications. In addition, several are associated with a large body of comparative data, which can be tremendously advantageous in research. Most scales are easy to use and have been adapted for different modes of administration (e.g., phone, mail survey, etc.) and populations.

However, most of the role-disability scales were intended to capture disability in employment and other activities and use a single set of items to accomplish this. (One exception is the Sickness Impact Profile, which has a separate employment battery.) Consequently, many of the role-disability scales include global work-activity indicators (e.g., questions such as "Were [you] limited in the kind of work or other activities . . . ?"). While several of these scales make it possible to compare the impact of an illness or a treatment on different population groups (e.g., employed and unemployed), their global character can make it difficult to distinguish gradations in levels of work activity (e.g., mild, moderate, and severe). When used in employee populations, for example, the frequency with which responses such as "unable to work" are endorsed can be very low and responses will be skewed toward high levels of functioning. Another issue relates to the fact that many individuals perform multiple roles such as paid work and housework. If respondents are not asked to differentiate the job roles from household roles, responses may include consideration of both. Additionally, some employers have found it difficult to generalize from studies using these measures because the questions do not ask that employees specifically identify the work tasks that they can or cannot perform.

The relationship between most of the available scales and objective work criteria has not been established. However, the scales were not initially intended to be used in work-productivity studies but for purposes of assessing specific components of health status.

Work-Productivity Scales

Recent developments in this field of research include the release of new survey instruments that focus specifically on measuring health-related job-performance deficits and productivity loss within the paid work domain (Lynch and Riedel 2001; Loeppke et al. 2003; Hemp 2004; Mayne, Howard, and Brandt-Rauf 2004). Like the social-role disability scales within the health-status assessment surveys, several of the new forms are condition-specific (e.g., the Endicott for depression, the Migraine Work Loss and Productivity Questionnaire, the Angina Work Limitations Questionnaire) (Endicott and Nee 1997; Lerner et al. 1998, 1999). We focus on two new questionnaires, which were designed to apply to a broad range of different patient and demographic groups.

The Health and Labor Questionnaire consists of four modules that address work absences, reduced on-the-job performance (literally, the number of hours needed to compensate for production losses on days respondents lost productivity due to illness), productivity in unpaid work indicated by number of hours spent in these activities (e.g., housework), and degree of trouble performing paid work (van Roijen et al. 1996). This questionnaire attempts to provide a comprehensive method for evaluating health-related productivity loss. Tests of its performance, which have been limited to relatively small samples in the Netherlands, have shown encouraging results.

The Work Limitations Questionnaire (WLQ) is a 25-item, self-administered, self-report questionnaire measuring (1) the degree to which employed individuals have experienced health-related deficits in job performance in the prior two weeks and (2) health-related work-productivity loss or presenteeism (Lerner et al. 2001). The WLQ attempts to portray the specific difficulties individuals with chronic health problems encounter in the course of managing their jobs. Developed with the economic user in mind, it is designed to provide information for estimating productivity costs. The WLQ measures on-the-job performance and productivity. A WLQ module captures sickness absences. To capture additional components of work productivity (e.g., job loss), it should be used in conjunction with other measures.

The WLQ's four scales were developed empirically and reflect the multidimensional character of work demands. The Time Management scale contains five items addressing difficulty in handling time and scheduling demands. The six-item Physical Demands scale covers ability to perform job tasks that involve bodily strength, movement, endurance, coordination, and flexibility. The Mental-Interpersonal Demands Scale has nine items addressing cognitively demanding tasks and on-the-job social interactions. The fourth scale is the Output Demands scale, and it contains five items concerning diminished work productivity. Scale scores range from 0 (limited none of the time) to 100 (limited all of the time) and represent the reported amount of time in the past two weeks that respondents had job-performance limitations. An empirically derived algorithm enables WLQ users to convert work-limitation data into a productivity-loss score.

The WLQ has been tested in both patient and employee settings. Its four scales demonstrate a strong association with physical and mental health indicators. Figures 4.1 and 4.2 demonstrate the construct validity of the WLQ scales, using relative validity as the standard.

Relative validity was computed as the ratio of F-statistics derived from multiple linear regression. The numerator was the F-statistic depicting the relationship of a scale score to health status, measured by the SF-36. The denominator was the F-statistic obtained for the best-performing scale in the comparison. The WLQ Physical Demands scale has the best validity for predicting variation in physical health. The Mental-Interpersonal and Output Demands scales performed best in terms of predicting mental health. These scales outperformed either effectiveness ratings or self-reported time loss.

In addition, the relationship of self-reported WLQ data to objectively measured criteria has been reported (Lerner et al. 2003; Amick et al. 2000; Allen and Bunn 2003). For instance, its relationship to work productivity was

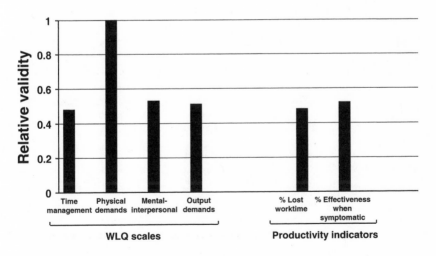

Figure 4.1. Relative validity test: Predicting physical health status measured by the SF-36 physical functioning scale
Notes: F-values from regressions are adjusted for age and gender ($N = 121$). A value of 1 indicates the maximum (best) validity.

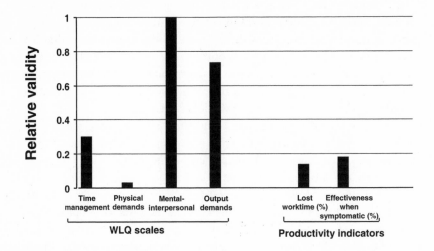

Figure 4.2. Relative validity test: Predicting mental health measured by the SF-36 mental health scale
Notes: F-values from regressions are adjusted for age and gender (N = 121). A value of 1 indicates the maximum (best) validity.

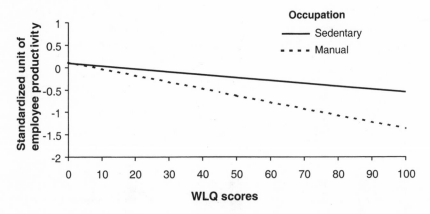

Figure 4.3. Predicted productivity based on WLQ responses
Notes: Employee productivity in the sedentary occupation was number of calls/hour, and in manual occupation it was merchandise units processed per hour. Each productivity criterion was standardized using its mean and standard deviation.

established in a criterion-validity test. This study included two samples from a single employer: approximately 800 telephone-order operators working from two large call centers, and 120 warehouse personnel who repaired and handled returned mail-ordered merchandise. WLQ scores were consistently related to work productivity of employees within each of the two jobs (fig. 4.3).

The WLQ is currently being used by employers, service providers, insurers, pharmaceutical firms, and academic scientists. It is available in more than 20 languages, a short-form version, and various administration modalities (mail, telephone, and Web). As usage continues to increase, the next challenge is to help users interpret and communicate results easily and effectively.

ALTERNATIVES TO SELF-REPORT

For those who remain wary of relying exclusively on self-report to capture work productivity, two alternatives are to collect data by trained "objective" observers in the workplace and to access data collected by employers. The expert-observer approach is used in fields such as ergonomics. Its advantages include an ability to obtain data in real time (thus avoiding recall error), using relatively objective criteria. However, workplace observation is relatively intrusive, labor-intensive, and expensive. As a result, it is frequently not a feasible option for research.

Employer data can be extremely useful in some circumstances, but employers vary a great deal in terms of the range of productivity indicators they collect, the quality of the data they keep, and the accessibility of their data for research purposes. While it is frequently assumed that employer archival data is the gold standard of accuracy for measuring worker productivity, employer data sets were not designed for studies aimed at assessing the effects on productivity of health status and/or medical care.

Comprehensiveness

Employer archival data will not capture the effects of illness or treatment on the work productivity of individuals who are not employed at a study's baseline. This can be a problem when it is necessary to track patient transitions back into the labor market. Employer databases are potentially useful only for studying individuals who are employed at the time a study begins.

Level of Analysis

Productivity analysis in the workplace has been around since the 1880s, but traditionally it has not been done at the level of the individual work unit (Brinkerhoff and Dressler 1990). Many employers measure productivity objectively only at the departmental, plant, and/or organizational levels. Aggregate data are usually inappropriate for health-outcomes research, which is focused mainly on the impact of an illness or a treatment on smaller groups of

individuals, or on populations defined according to one or more health variables (e.g., a treatment group). Moreover, the output criteria measured by
some firms, especially those engaged in team-based work, may be only distally
related to the actions of any one individual. Thus, the available productivity indicators are likely to lack sensitivity to the effects of illness or treatment.

Generalizability

Employers tend to use productivity indicators that are relevant only to the
firm or to the industry in which they operate (Brinkerhoff and Dressler 1990).
For example, a hospital's productivity criteria are likely to differ from those
used by an airline. If a project aim is to study one firm or one industry, generalizability is not a problem. However, if an aim is to make broader state-
ments about the effects of illness or treatment on a population, or to compare
populations, generalizable indicators are necessary.

Intangibility of Certain Outputs

Some industries have a great deal of difficulty in translating their outputs into
measurable terms. The task has become more challenging for some industries as they attempt to rate productivity in terms of quality. Ironically, these
challenges have led some firms to incorporate more self-reported productivity data from employees and consumers into their ongoing productivity
analyses.

Data Quality

Employer data often will not meet the standards for accuracy and complete-
ness that research requires. Frequently substantial efforts are required to
clean and organize the databases.

   Job-performance ratings by an employee's supervisor represent a special
case because they are frequently considered to be the industry standard for
measuring employee performance. But although supervisor ratings are based
on "objective" rating criteria, they still can be highly vulnerable to bias. More
often than not, these biases go unmeasured and cannot be adjusted statistically.

Access and Practicality

It is also important not to overlook the sometimes substantial barriers to
accessing employer data. Many employers consider their productivity data-

bases to be proprietary and/or sensitive and are unwilling to make them available to external parties. In our experience, this has meant engaging in lengthy, time-consuming negotiations for access.

Furthermore, in health and medical care research, study subjects may be recruited from the health care system, not the work site. Thus, the investigator will be forced to collect productivity data from many different firms rather than one central source. In one study, we enrolled 150 disability insurance claimants from a single insurer who were employed by 145 different employers.

Finally, the institutional review boards of many health care institutions may be reluctant to permit investigators to contact patients' employers because of the presumed risk of patient job loss and the institution's exposure to liability.

CONCLUSION

There is little doubt as to the value of asking patients or employees about the impact of their health on their ability to work. The question is, in doing so, what sort of information are we getting? A great deal is known about developing sound survey measurement tools and conducting good survey research. This knowledge is now being applied to the measurement of health-related work productivity.

The accumulating evidence suggests that self-report methods meet many of the basic criteria for validity, reliability, meaningfulness, and practicality. However, certain questions remain. For example, is it feasible to develop a "generic" questionnaire that is accurate across different occupational and clinical populations? Additional testing within and across a range of occupations and industries will be needed to specify the advantages and disadvantages of the different measures. And as the number of applications increases, relevant normative and/or comparative data will be needed. Questionnaire users are likely to influence the direction of these future efforts.

Research will also benefit from understanding how self-reports actually compare with other data sources and knowing in which situations one approach may be preferable to another. Different methods have not been compared head-to-head. However, it is often neither necessary nor desirable from a research standpoint to collect data using a single approach. The best information may be obtained by using multimethod approaches that triangulate self-reports by employees, supervisor or co-worker ratings, and employer records. Multiple sources of data, which may reveal conflicts and consistencies in measurement, are also extremely useful for capturing the intricacies of complex phenomena.

In only a few short years, measurement methods have advanced considerably, and the community of users is expanding. At present, there are several good measurement options available.

REFERENCES

Allen, H. M., and W. B. Bunn III. 2003. Validating self-reported measures of productivity at work: A case for their credibility in a heavy manufacturing setting. *Journal of Occupational and Environmental Medicine* 45 (9): 926–40.

Amick, B. C., III, D. Lerner, W. H. Rogers, T. Rooney, and J. N. Katz. 2000. A review of health-related work outcome measures and their uses, and recommended measures. *Spine* 25 (24): 3152–60.

Bergner, M. 1984. The sickness impact profile. In *Assessment of quality of life in clinical trials of cardiovascular therapies,* ed. J. Elinson, 152–59. New York: LeJacq.

Berndt, E. R., S. N. Finkelstein, P. E. Greenberg, A. Keith, and H. Bailit. 1997. Illness and productivity: Objective workplace evidence. Working Paper 42-97, MIT Program on the Pharmaceutical Industry, Cambridge, MA.

Bradburn, N. M. 2000. Temporal representation and event dating. In *The science of self-report: Implications for research and practice,* ed. V. S. Cain, 49–62. Mahwah, NJ: Lawrence Erlbaum Associates.

Brinkerhoff, R. O., and D. E. Dressler. 1990. *Productivity measurement: A guide for managers and evaluators.* Newbury Park, CA: Sage Publications.

Broadhead, W. E., D. G. Blazer, L. K. George, and C. K. Tse. 1990. Depression, disability days, and days lost from work in a prospective epidemiologic survey. *Journal of the American Medical Association* 264:2524–28.

Endicott, J., and J. Nee. 1997. Endicott Work Productivity Scale (EWPS): A new measure to assess treatment effects. *Psychopharmacology Bulletin* 33:13–16.

Finkelstein, S. N., E. R. Berndt, P. E. Greenberg, R. A. Parsley, J. M. Russell, and M. B. Keller. 1996. Improvement in subjective work performance after treatment of chronic depression: Some preliminary results. Chronic Depression Study Group. *Psychopharmacology Bulletin* 32:33–40.

Fowler, F. J., Jr. 1988. *Survey research methods.* Rev. ed. Newbury Park, CA: Sage Publications.

Fowler, F. J., Jr., and C. F. Cannell. 1996. Using behavioral coding to identify cognitive problems with survey questions. In *Answering questions: Methodology for determining cognitive and communicative processes in survey research,* ed. S. Sudman, 15–36. San Francisco: Jossey-Bass.

Fries, J. F., and G. Spingh. 1996. The hierarchy of patient outcomes. In *Quality of life and pharmacoeconomics in clinical trials,* ed. B. Spilker, 33–40. New York: Lippincott-Raven.

Fries, J. F., P. W. Spitz, and D. Y. Young. 1982. The dimensions of health outcomes: The health assessment questionnaire, disability, and pain scales. *Journal of Rheumatology* 9:789–93.

Grabowski, H. G., and R. W. Hansen. 1996. Economic scales and tests. In *Quality of life and pharmacoeconomics in clinical trials,* ed. B. Spilker, 79–84. New York: Lippincott-Raven.

Harwood, R. H., A. Rogers, E. Dickinson, and S. Ebrahim. 1994. Measuring handicap: The London Handicap Scale, a new outcome measure for chronic disease. *Quality in Health Care* 3:11–16.

Hays, R. D., R. T. Anderson, and D. Revicki. 1998. Assessing reliability and validity of measurement in clinical trials. In *Quality of life assessments in clinical trials: Methods and practice,* ed. P. M. Fayers, 169–82. New York: Oxford University Press.

Hemp, P. Presenteeism: At work—but out of it. 2004. *Harvard Business Review,* October, 49–58.

Johns, G. 1994. How often were you absent? A review of the use of self-reported absence data. *Journal of Applied Psychology* 79:574–91.

Kaplan, R. M., J. P. Anderson, A. W. Wu, W. C. Mathews, F. Kozin, and D. Orenstein. 1989. The Quality of Well-Being Scale: Applications in AIDS, cystic fibrosis, and arthritis. *Medical Care* 27:S27–43.

Kessler, R. C., and R. G. Frank. 1997. The impact of psychiatric disorders on work loss days. *Psychological Medicine* 24:861–73.

Kessler, R. C., H. U. Wittchen, J. Abelson, and S. Zhao. 2000. Methodological issues in assessing psychiatric disorders with self-reports. In *The science of self-report: Implications for research and practice,* ed. V. S. Cain, 229–56. Mahwah, NJ: Lawrence Erlbaum Associates.

Kihlstrom, J. F., E. Eich, D. Sandbrand, and B. A. Tobias. 2000. Emotion and memory: Implications for self-report. In *The science of self-report: Implications for research and practice,* ed. V. S. Cain, 81–100. Mahwah, NJ: Lawrence Erlbaum Associates.

Leon, A. C., M. K. Shear, L. Portera, and G. L. Klerman. 1992. Assessing impairment in patients with panic disorder: The Sheehan Disability Scale. *Social Psychiatry and Psychiatric Epidemiology* 27:78–82.

Lerner D., B. C. Amick III, J. C. Lee, T. Rooney, W. H. Rogers, H. Chang, and E. R. Berndt. 2003. Relationship of employee-reported work limitations to work productivity. *Medical Care* 41 (5): 649–59.

Lerner, D. J., B. C. Amick III, S. Malspeis, W. H. Rogers, D. R. Gomes, and D. N. Salem. 1998. The Angina-related Limitations at Work Questionnaire. *Quality of Life Research* 7:23–32.

Lerner, D. J., B. C. Amick III, S. Malspeis, W. H. Rogers, N. C. Santanello, W. C. Gerth, and R. B. Lipton. 1999. The Migraine Work and Productivity Loss Questionnaire: Concepts and design. *Quality of Life Research* 8:699–710.

Lerner, D., B. C. Amick III, W. H. Rogers, S. Malspeis, K. Bungay, and D. Cynn. 2001. The Work Limitations Questionnaire. *Medical Care* 39 (1):72–85.

Loeppke R., P. A. Hymel, J. H. Lofland, L. T. Pizzi, D. L. Konicki, G. W. Anstadt, C. Baase,

J. Fortuna, and T. Scharf. 2003. Health-related workplace productivity measurement: General and migraine-specific recommendations from the ACOEM Expert Panel. *Journal of Occupational and Environmental Medicine* 45 (4): 349–59.

Lynch, W., and J. E. Riedel. 2001. *Measuring employee productivity: A guide to self-assessment tools.* Denver: Institute for Health and Productivity Management.

Marcus, S. C., M. Olfson, H. A. Pincus, M. K. Shear, and D. A. Zarin. 1997. Self-reported anxiety, general medical conditions, and disability bed days. *American Journal of Psychiatry* 154:1766–68.

Mayne, T. J., K. Howard, and P. W. Brandt-Rauf. 2004. Measuring and evaluating the effects of disease on workplace productivity. *Journal of Occupational and Environmental Medicine* 46 (6): S1–S2 (June 2004 suppl.)

Mintz, J., L. I. Mintz, M. J. Arruda, and S. S. Hwang. 1992. Treatments of depression and the functional capacity to work. *Archives of General Psychiatry* 49:761–68.

Osterhaus, J. T., D. L. Gutterman, and J. R. Plachetka. 1992. Healthcare resource and lost labour costs of migraine headache in the U.S. *PharmacoEconomics* 2:67–76.

Patrick, D. L., and P. Erickson. 1993. Health status and health decisions. In *Health status and health policy*, ed. D. L. Patrick and P. Erickson, 3–26. New York: Oxford University Press.

Pauly, M. V., S. Nicholson, J. Xu, D. Polsky, P. M. Danzon, J. F. Murray, and M. L. Berger. 2002. A general model of the impact of absenteeism on employers and employees. *Health Economics* 11, no. 3: 221–31.

Pope, A. M., and A. R. Tarlov. 1991. *Disability in America: Toward a national agenda for prevention.* Washington, DC: National Academy Press.

Reilly, M. C., A. S. Zbrozek, and E. M. Dukes. 1993. The validity and reproducibility of a work productivity and activity impairment instrument. *PharmacoEconomics* 4:353–65.

Revicki, D. A., D. Irwin, J. Reblando, and G. E. Simon. 1994. The accuracy of self-reported disability days. *Medical Care* 32:401–4.

Stoudemire, A., R. Frank, N. Hedemark, M. Kamlet, and D. Blazer. 1986. The economic burden of depression. *General Hospital Psychiatry* 8:387–94.

Streiner, D. L., and G. R. Norman. 1995. *Health measurement scales: A practical guide to their development and use.* 2nd ed. New York: Oxford University Press.

Sudman, S., and N. M. Bradburn. 1982. Asking nonthreatening questions about behavior. In *Asking questions: A practical guide to questionnaire design*, ed. N. M. Bradburn, 2–53. San Francisco: Jossey-Bass.

Tourangeau, R. 2000. Remembering what happened: Memory errors and survey reports. In *The science of self-report: Implications for research and practice*, ed. V. S. Cain, 29–48. Mahwah, NJ: Lawrence Erlbaum Associates.

Van Roijen, L., M. L. Essink-Bot, M. A. Koopmanschap, G. Bonsel, and F. F. Rutten. 1996. Labor and health status in economic evaluation of health care: The Health and Labor Questionnaire. *International Journal of Technology Assessment in Health Care* 12:405–15.

Ware, J. E., Jr., and S. D. Keller. 1996. Interpreting general health measures. In *Quality of life and pharmacoeconomics in clinical trials,* ed. B. Spilker, 445–60. New York: Lippincott-Raven.

Ware, J. E., Jr., and C. D. Sherbourne. 1992. The MOS 36-Item Short-Form Health Survey (SF-36). I. Conceptual framework and item selection. *Medical Care* 30: 473–83.

Wiersma, D., A. DeJong, and J. Ormel. 1988. The Groningen Social Disabilities Schedule: Development, relationship with I.C.I.D.H., and psychometric properties. *International Journal of Rehabilitation Research* 11:213–24.

CHAPTER 5

Use of the Experience Sampling Method
in Studies of Illness and Work Performance

PHILIP S. WANG AND NANCY A. NICOLSON

RATIONALE AND OVERVIEW

There is growing interest among employers, employee groups, insurers, occupational medicine clinicians, health services researchers, and public policymakers in studying both the productivity of workers in "real-world" settings and the effects of chronic diseases on workplace performance. To collect productivity data, researchers have increasingly relied on self-report surveys in which workers report on their own behavior such as absences from work. (For a thorough review of self-report, see chapter 4). In most cases, workers are asked to provide a single retrospective self-report.

Unfortunately, the accuracy of single reports of recalled events and experiences may be questionable. Recalling remote events and summarizing over extended periods can lead to both errors and biases (Bradburn, Rips, and Shevell 1987; Ross 1989). For example, more recent phenomena tend to be recalled more accurately and in more detail than more remote ones; in summaries over extended periods, respondents are more likely to recall dramatic experiences (Eisenhower, Mathiowetz, and Morganstein 1991).

In addition, summaries of experiences through single retrospective self-reports may be inadequate when studying experiences or events that are rapidly changing. For example, self-reported summaries of work performance may be unable to shed light on how work performance covaries with symptom severity changes among patients with rapidly fluctuating diseases. Similarly, using single summarized self-reports may make it impossible to understand how productivity is correlated with stress among workers in highly changeable work environments.

Fortunately, a family of related techniques has been developed that enables investigators to avoid these methodological problems with self-report. These techniques, which produce multiple "snapshots" of the experience of respondents, have been called by different investigators the Experience Sampling Method (ESM) (Csikszentmihalyi and Larson 1987; deVries 1992b) and Ecological Momentary Assessment (Shiffman and Stone 1998). For the purposes of this chapter, we will refer to all these techniques as ESM. ESM employs repeated assessments over time rather than a single assessment at the end of a study period, making it ideal for the study of rapidly changing phenomena. In addition, since ESM requires respondents to report on immediately experienced phenomena, it can eliminate recall bias.

ESM is easy to implement and leads to the collection of reliable and valid data. It may also be especially advantageous for particular types of investigations of the effects of chronic disease on work performance. At the level of the person, ESM can be useful for describing patterns of work experiences and behaviors over time, including their range and frequency. The effect of illness on work performance can be studied by examining the covariance of illness severity scores reported by individuals with momentary assessments of their productivity (e.g., the covariance between depressive symptom severity and performance). At the level of populations, ESM can be useful for identifying and comparing the distribution of work-related experiences, behaviors, and performance over time in groups of interest, such as groups with and without a particular chronic disease. For example, ESM can enable researchers to compare the percentages of time spent on-task by employees with asthma and those without.

In this chapter we provide an overview of ESM, highlighting applications that are relevant to studies of work performance and the effect of illness on productivity. After discussing how ESM methods can be implemented in studies, we provide examples of how ESM has been used to assess constructs similar to work productivity and to assess the overall impact of chronic illness on daily life. Other reviews of ESM are available and should be consulted by readers interested in more comprehensive, detailed, or technical coverage of aspects of ESM (deVries 1992b; Reis and Gable 2000; Schwartz and Stone 1998; Stone, Kessler, and Haythornthwaite 1991; Stone, Shiffman, and deVries 1999).

REVIEW OF ESM METHODS

The methods used in ESM are the results of pioneering efforts by psychologists and social scientists, such as Csikszentmihalyi and colleagues at the University of Chicago (Csikszentmihalyi, Larson, and Prescott 1977), as well as more recent studies by investigators such as deVries and co-workers in Maastricht (deVries 1992b). These methods have largely grown out of the need to obtain accurate measurements of the daily emotional experiences and activities of individuals in their natural environments. As a result of research over the past quarter of a century, ESM now encompasses a wide variety of techniques for scheduling reports, signaling respondents, and recording data.

Determining a Schedule for Recording Information

One of the first tasks of ESM studies is to decide what schedule will be used to sample a respondent's experience or behavior. Researchers need to determine during what periods of the day information will be collected as well as how frequently and over how long a period (e.g., number of days or weeks). These decisions depend on who is being studied, the type of question being investigated, and the statistical power that is needed to answer study questions (Stone, Kessler, and Haythornthwaite 1991).

With regard to the period(s) during the day when information will be collected, researchers typically have four options. Perhaps the simplest strategy is to have participants record information only when a particular phenomenon has occurred (e.g., a mishap or argument at work). Unfortunately, this strategy will not yield information on the experiences of workers under other circumstances. A second strategy is to require that participants report on experiences or behavior at a specific time during the day (e.g., at 10:00 a.m.). This approach may be useful if there are particular times in the workday that are of interest to the investigator; however, the information generated may not allow for a complete description of the experiences and behavior of the population under study. A third approach is to divide the daily time period of interest (e.g., an eight-hour work shift) into uniform periods, such as four two-hour periods. A random-number generator can then be used to determine when in each time block a person is sampled. A fourth strategy is a hybrid of the fixed-interval and systematic sampling approaches in which investigators systematically sample over particular time periods of interest (Reis and Gable 2000; Shiffman and Stone 1998).

In prior studies, the frequency with which information is collected during daily periods of interest has varied widely—from less than once per day to as often as every 30 minutes. A typical frequency is approximately once per 1–2 hours. The frequency of observations in ESM studies often depends upon the periodicity and duration of phenomena that the investigator is trying to measure. Another important consideration is the need for statistical power—with a greater frequency leading to more observations and generally enhanced power. However, the advantages of increased frequency must be balanced against the disadvantages, including diminished study participation and cooperation by subjects. A wide range of study durations has also been used (e.g., several days to several months) in previous ESM studies, although a typical duration is one week.

Signaling and Data-Collection Instruments

ESM studies require the use of a signaling device to alert participants when to record information. To collect information that is representative across time periods of interest, the device must be capable of signaling according to a random schedule. The stimuli emitted from signaling devices are usually either sounds (e.g., beeps) or vibrations.

Several types of signaling devices can be used. Earlier ESM studies often relied on random timers such as programmable wristwatches. Unfortunately, such timers often do not have a means for recording whether participants actually responded to signals. In addition, investigators are unable to reprogram the timers to change the scheduling of signals once they have been given to participants. Another type, pagers, can both record whether study subjects responded to the signal and alter the schedule of signals at any time. However, respondents carrying pagers may need to remain within a limited area in order to receive the transmitted signals. Likewise, handheld computers also have some drawbacks, including their fragility under physically demanding working conditions (e.g., construction sites), the expense, the complexity of programming devices, and the potential effects of low computer literacy on their acceptability and the reliability of data.

The ways respondents record information in ESM studies have also been varied. With paper-and-pencil techniques, respondents write down their experiences in a diary. Handheld computers offer several advantages, including the ability to record data that is relatively free of transcription and data-entry errors. Computers also provide an accurate means of recording the time of a response (Hormuth 1986; Shiffman 2000).

Regardless of the recording instrument chosen, researchers using ESM must also decide on the degree to which questions asked of respondents are highly structured (e.g., asking a subject to choose among fixed options) or open-ended (e.g., allowing a subject to spontaneously describe phenomena). While free-form responses can capture information on unanticipated experiences, they also require extra time and effort both by respondents and by investigators (Csikszentmihalyi and Larson 1992). In addition to the information gathered from respondents at each sampled time period, summaries over the day or week are usually collected. One purpose of these daily or weekly summaries is to "debrief" individuals, gauge data quality, and identify issues that need improvement (Hormuth 1986). (Those interested in techniques that are available for data aggregation and analysis in ESM studies are advised to see Affleck et al. 1999; Larson and Delespaul 1992; Schwartz and Stone 1998.)

Recruiting and Training Study Participants

Researchers conducting ESM studies must also decide how many and what type of subjects to include. Statistical techniques (i.e., clustered probability and iterative estimation) for simultaneously determining the optimal study sample size and the frequency and duration of observations are generally used, but these go beyond the scope of this chapter (Cochran 1963).

Strategies to decrease sample size, frequency of observations, and duration of the study should also be considered. For example, one might choose to employ study populations that are "enriched" with persons likely to have outcomes of interest (e.g., selecting subjects with a history of asthma to increase the likelihood that one will observe acute asthmatic episodes).

Recruitment in ESM studies can be difficult because of actual or perceived demands on individuals in terms of time, intrusiveness, or potential disruption to work activities. In fact, some investigators have found participation rates to be as low as 20% (Hormuth 1986). Since subjects often overestimate the burdens of study participation, they may benefit from an accurate portrayal of the demands on their time. Offering incentives for participation may also be critical. After the study participants have been selected, researchers need to familiarize them with the ESM techniques employed in the study, including the signaling device and recording instruments. Without such training, subjects may not adhere to the study protocol and thus the reliability and validity of collected data will be limited.

Potential Methodological Problems and Solutions

ESM researchers face several common methodological problems, some of which tend to arise specifically in studies of productivity or the effects of chronic disease on work performance.

RELIABILITY AND VALIDITY OF DATA COLLECTED WITH ESM

Productivity researchers using ESM need to make sure that they collect accurate data. For example, it is important to demonstrate reliability (i.e., consistency in the measurements of a construct over time). However, this can be difficult when what is being measured is changing rapidly in quality or quantity. Attempts to demonstrate reliability through the internal consistency of a subject's responses across items in the survey instrument may also be problematic, since phenomena assessed by one item may be totally independent of phenomena assessed by another item (Stone, Kessler, and Haythornthwaite 1991). Comparing the consistency of ESM responses by multiple raters is possible, but only for observable events.

Standard strategies to evaluate validity may not always be effective for ESM data. For example, it may not be possible to compare reports of phenomena provided by subjects using ESM with objective measures (e.g., archival data), because it is not clear which source should be regarded as the gold standard. In fact, some studies comparing ESM information on daily activities with other assessments have shown discrepancies, such as the greater reporting of idle time in ESM records (Robinson 1977; Szalai et al. 1972). Clearly, such discrepancies may provide evidence not of the inaccuracy of ESM data, but of the greater sensitivity of ESM methods (Csikszentmihalyi and Larson 1992). Another indirect means of judging the validity of ESM data has been to examine the extent to which subjects actually responded when signaled or the degree of lag between signal and subject response (Csikszentmihalyi and Figurski 1982; Savon-Williams and Demo 1983). Although such assessments give some indication of the quality of reported ESM data, they should be considered markers of validity rather than direct measures.

Additional work is needed to allow investigators to evaluate the accuracy of data collected through ESM. Some promising developments include using innovative interview methods to verify observable phenomena (Brown and Harris 1978) and comparing ESM reports to information arrived at by consensus among observers (Stone and Neale 1982). Regardless of how limitations in evaluating the reliability and validity of ESM data are addressed, investigators can increase the accuracy of their ESM data by providing adequate instruction in the use of tools to participants, as well as by encouraging subjects to respond promptly to all signals and minimizing the burdens associated with filling out the response instruments.

TYPES OF NONRESPONSE IN ESM STUDIES

Participants in ESM studies may fail to respond properly to signals in a variety of ways. First, subjects may fail to respond to all signals or fail to respond to some signals. This type of nonresponse usually occurs because subjects have technical difficulties with the signaling device, forget about the signaling or response instruments, or are engaged in an activity that makes a response inconvenient or impossible (Csikszentmihalyi and Larson 1992). Both complete and partial nonresponse can introduce a response bias if study participation is related to the phenomena of interest. When the characteristics of nonrespondents and respondents are available, weighting schemes can be employed to adjust for the differential probability of response among study subjects; alternatively, control variables can be used in statistical models to correct for response bias (Stone, Kessler, and Haythornthwaite 1991).

Alternatively, subjects may respond to signals but fail to complete all items on the response instrument. A simple solution to this problem is to restrict analyses to responses with complete data. But this approach can seriously diminish study power and introduce bias, especially if the failure to complete all items is related to the phenomena being studied (Stone, Kessler, and Haythornthwaite 1991). (For information on a more sophisticated approach involving the use of statistical techniques that have been developed for imputing values in item-missing data, see Little and Rubin 1987; Rubin 1987.)

In addition, study participants may respond to signals but only after a delay, because they are engaged in tasks that make it inconvenient to respond. Fortunately, researchers (Csikszentmihalyi and Larson 1992; Hormuth 1986) have found that such delays are generally quite short. However, it may be necessary to eliminate responses that are not made within a set amount of time (e.g., 20 minutes from the time of signaling).

Regardless of the specific measures taken to address particular types of nonresponse, investigators using ESM techniques should also follow some general principles to enhance participant compliance. First, they need to make it easy for subjects to fill out responses by keeping the frequency of signals as low as possible and the duration of data-collection periods as short as possible. Second, all subjects should be adequately instructed in the use of ESM tools and strongly encouraged to respond promptly to all signals.

PROBLEMS SPECIFIC TO ESM STUDIES OF THE EFFECTS OF ILLNESS

Sometimes patients have physical or cognitive disabilities that prevent them from responding properly to signals. In addition to recognizing obvious conditions (e.g., dementia) that may prevent subjects from participating in ESM studies, researchers should consider whether the illnesses under study can exert subtle effects on the quantity and quality of data. For example, investigators interested in studying the effects of depression on productivity should be aware of the possibility of a pessimism bias in reports of work performance from depressed workers (Morgado et al. 1989).

Researchers using ESM also need to take into account the subjects' need for privacy and confidentiality, especially when the illness being studied is stigmatizing (e.g., a mental illness) or has a poor prognosis. Subjects wearing signaling devices (such as beepers) or filling out diaries could be noticed by colleagues and supervisors, thus increasing the likelihood that information on their health status will become known to others. A simple strategy is to design inconspicuous signaling devices (e.g., hidden vibrating signalers as opposed to visible sounding beepers). A second approach is to avoid revealing what disease is being studied; however, this approach may not be possible or ethical in many circumstances. Investigators should also consider using a large control group (i.e., subjects without the illness) or studying multiple illness groups simultaneously to decrease the likelihood that patients with a particular illness are identified. Finally, ESM itself may affect the disease under study because frequent self-examination and self-focus by patients may affect their symptoms, disability, and/or quality of life (Hormuth 1986).

PROBLEMS SPECIFIC TO ESM STUDIES OF WORK PERFORMANCE

Just as certain illnesses preclude patients from participating in ESM studies, certain work environments are not amenable to ESM. For example, workers who drive vehicles or operate potentially dangerous machinery may not be able to fill out diaries immediately after being signaled. Researchers should also anticipate that the type of worker or occupation being studied can have subtle, but important, effects on the quantity and quality of ESM data collected. For example, workers who spend a large proportion of their time talking with clients may have long delays before responding to signals.

When conducting ESM studies among workers, researchers need to have the support of supervisors so that workers who take time to fill out diaries are not penalized. Likewise, since respondents may fear negative consequences for reporting poor productivity (and may thus "game" their responses), researchers need to emphasize that all data are confidential and will be presented only in aggregate form.

EXAMPLES OF THE USE OF ESM IN STUDIES OF CHRONIC DISEASE AND PRODUCTIVITY

ESM Studies of Work Performance

Table 5.1 provides an overview of ESM studies that have been conducted in the workplace.[1] The occupational groups and work settings in which studies have successfully been carried out (shown in the second column of the table) range from blue-collar manufacturing workers through top management, including jobs with high task demands. This information should allay fears that ESM is too disruptive to be used by workers whose jobs entail time pressure, precision, frequent social interaction, or rapid decision-making.

PARTICIPANTS

Sample sizes for ESM workplace studies have ranged from 7 to more than 100 subjects, recruited through employers, professional organizations, institutions in the community (e.g., daycare centers) (Williams et al. 1991), advertisements, or referral by other participants. Data concerning the willingness of employers or professional organizations to cooperate in obtaining samples for ESM studies or the willingness of individuals to participate as subjects are rarely included in published reports.

Employers may be unwilling to work with ESM researchers for a variety of reasons including, for example, their concern about work disruption or increased risk of error, which typically depends on the type of work performed. Such hesitation might be most likely if the work requires speed, physical effort, or contacts with clients. In addition, employers may be reluctant to become involved if there are high expected costs in terms of time, money, and effort. For example, employers may balk at the prospect of distributing information about the study (or questionnaires to identify subsamples of employees), making rooms available for briefing and debriefing subjects, or granting employees free time to participate in these aspects of the

1. Whereas all ESM studies of employed individuals have sampled participants in work as well as in nonwork settings, the studies highlighted here specifically investigated hypotheses related to the subjective experience of work. Although relevant to understanding individual and contextual influences on performance, ESM investigations of students in the classroom and doing homework have also been omitted from table 5.1 (Massimini and Carli 1988; Moneta and Csikszentmihalyi 1996; Schiefele and Csikszentmihalyi 1995; Wong and Csikszentmihalyi 1991).

research. Concerns about the sensitivity of the hypotheses to be tested, the possibility of bad publicity, confidentiality of results, and the possible burden to employees can present further obstacles. All of these issues arose during our discussions with directors of the companies or agencies we approached to participate in an ESM study of daily stress (van Eck 1996); three of the nine organizations eventually declined. Determining the likely reasons for employer refusal is difficult. (Unfortunately, if organizational characteristics are responsible for a bias in the sample, the findings may not be generalizable.)

Compliance can be improved by providing realistic information about the potential disruptiveness of the study, helping to cover any costs to the employer, and stressing the benefits of participation such as good public relations or the prestige associated with scientific research. Ideally, the organization will have some stake in the topics being investigated. For example, the employer may be interested in learning more about employee task performance or satisfaction, or the effects of shift schedules or of interventions intended to improve productivity. In some cases, it may be possible to incorporate a specific interest of the employer into the design without compromising the scientific integrity of the study or the privacy of the participants. Success in recruiting subjects may also depend on obtaining support from a professional organization or a union. Here, issues such as the perceived burden on subjects, confidentiality of results, and anticipated benefit of the study to employees as a group will need to be addressed.

In theory, ESM can be used with all individuals who can read, write, and respond to the signaling device. Assuming that the employer or supervisor has approved employee participation, how many individuals are likely to agree to be subjects in an ESM study? And are these volunteers likely to represent an unbiased sample of the working population? Few data are available to answer these questions, and it is not clear whether recruitment for an ESM study is more difficult than for a conventional survey in the workplace. For example, van Eck, Nicolson, and Berkhof (1998) reported that 30% to 40% of the white-collar males who received an initial screening questionnaire completed it; of this group, more than 80% were willing to take part in an ESM study. Education often plays a role. In an ESM study in which 44% of 1,026 workers in five large Chicago-area companies expressed willingness to take part, for example, volunteers were much more highly represented among skilled workers (75% of the eligible population) than among unskilled workers (only 12%) (Csikszentmihalyi and LeFevre 1989). There is some evidence that females are more willing to participate in ESM studies than males (Csikszentmihalyi and Larson 1987).

TABLE 5.1.
ESM STUDIES CONDUCTED IN WORK SETTINGS

STUDY	SAMPLE CHARACTERISTICS	ESM (D × B)[a]	MEASURES USED IN THE ANALYSIS		
			BEEP LEVEL	SUBJECT LEVEL	NOTES
CSIKSZENTMIHALYI & LEFEVRE 1989; KUBEY & CSIKSZENTMIHALYI 1990	107 assembly-line, clerical, and managerial employees	7 × 8	Activity, location, challenge, skills, enjoyment, motivation, mood, ability to concentrate	Occupational level	Compared work vs. leisure times
LARSON & RICHARDS 1994	110 working parents (community sample)	7 × 8	Anger, frustration, competition, ability to concentrate, negative events (solitary and social)	Gender, occupational level, hours worked	Compared at home vs. at work
WILLIAMS ET AL. 1991	20 professional, clerical, and service (working mothers participants)	8 × 8	Activity checklist, positive and negative affect, task enjoyment, role-juggling	Neuroticism, extraversion	Compared role contexts: work, family, or other
ALLIGER & WILLIAMS 1993	41 professional and clerical workers	7 × 8	Goal progress, skill at task, enjoyment, mood	Job satisfaction, involvement, competence	Only beeps at workplace included in the analysis
HAWORTH & EVANS 1995	57 vocational trainees	7 × 8	Activity, challenge, interest, enjoyment, happiness, relaxation	Perceived stress (high vs. low), neuroticism	

Study	Sample	Sampling	Variables	Individual differences	Notes
VAN ECK 1996; VAN ECK, NICOLSON & BERKHOF 1998	88 white-collar employees	5 × 10	Activity, location, mood, physical symptoms, appraisal of activity (effort, difficulty, enjoyment, challenge, worrying, stressful events, salivary cortisol)	Locus of control, life satisfaction, well-being	Compared work vs. leisure activities
HAWORTH, JARMAN & LEE 1997	16 clerical workers	7 × 8	Activity, motivation, enjoyment, interest, control	Sense of coherence (high vs. low)	
SHIU 1998	20 public health nurses	7 × 6	Activity, mood states, task-related goal progress, control, role-juggling	Extraversion, introversion	Sampling repeated during first 6 months of new job
BRANDSTÄTTER & GAUBATZ 1997	30 new office employees	10 × 6 (× 4)	Activity, location, social context, mood, freedom of choice of activity		
TOTTERDELL & FOLKARD 1992	8 security guards	28 × 8	Mood, cognitive test performance		Hand-held computer
	17 air traffic controllers	20 × 3	Mood, cognitive test performance		
	23 nuclear-power-plant workers	8 × 8	Mood, cognitive test performance		

TABLE 5.1. (CONTINUED)

| STUDY | SAMPLE CHARACTERISTICS | ESM ($D \times B$)[a] | MEASURES USED IN THE ANALYSIS | | |
			BEEP LEVEL	SUBJECT LEVEL	NOTES
SMITH, TOTTERDELL & FOLKARD 1995	22 nuclear-power-plant workers	4×4 + 4×5	Alertness, NASA workload items, cognitive performance	Type of work (engineers & reactor operators vs. craftsmen & maintenance operators)	Examined effects of time-on-shift; type of shift (day, evening, night)
TOTTERDELL, SPELTEN, BARTON, ET AL. 1995	61 nurses	28×8	Mood (alert, cheerful, calm), NASA workload, cognitive performance	Type of shiftwork (rotating vs. permanent night shifts), age, experience	Compared shifts (early, evening, night)
TOTTERDELL, SPELTEN, SMITH, ET AL. 1995	61 nurses	28×8	Mood (alert, cheerful, calm), NASA workload, cognitive performance		Compared work vs. rest days Compared a 14-hr night
KNAUTH ET AL. 1995	29 fire-brigade control room workers	3×8	Alertness vs. tiredness, cognitive performance, oral temperature		shift vs. a 10-hr morning shift; examined effects of time-on-shift
TEUCHMANN, TOTTERDELL & PARKER 1999	7 accountants	28×3	Mood, emotional exhaustion, time pressure, perceived control		Compared high-demand vs. normal work periods

[a] Column (d x b) refers to days (d) and beeps per day (b) during ESM sampling period.

SAMPLING FRAMES

ESM studies in the workplace have ranged in length from 3 to 28 days (see table 5.1). In a few longitudinal studies, discrete ESM sampling periods have been repeated within a longer time frame to investigate, for example, the effects of changing shift schedules (Williamson, Gower, and Clarke 1994) or adjustment to a new job over time (Brandstätter and Gaubatz 1997). In the majority of studies, sampling has taken place on consecutive days, including weekends as well as workdays (and extending beyond work hours into leisure time). This design is not mandatory, but it is difficult to draw conclusions about the influences of the work environment on mood, behavior, and other aspects of daily experience if no comparable data have been collected in other contexts. Moreover, there is abundant evidence that work experiences "spill over" into leisure and family life, and vice versa (Bolger et al. 1989; Williams et al. 1991).

Time-sampling intervals were typically between 90 minutes and 2 hours, from 8 a.m. to 10 p.m., which means that subjects received signals between 7 and 10 times each day. The drawbacks of either fixed-interval or completely random "beep" schedules have been discussed elsewhere (Delespaul 1992); the studies listed in table 5.1 all used devices that signaled subjects to complete self-reports at semi-random intervals throughout the day. The studies listed in table 5.2 also used devices to signal subjects, but in those studies, in a departure from classic ESM designs, subjects completed self-reports at fixed intervals of 2 hours.

COMPLIANCE

In general, compliance with ESM in workplace studies has been high. The number of valid self-reports obtained, expressed as a percentage of total beeps, averaged above 80% (range 70% to 88%) in the 5- to 10-day studies listed in table 5.1. As one would expect, compliance appears to have been lower in the longer studies listed in table 5.2, ranging from 50% to 72%. There is also evidence that compliance rates may decline over time. For example, security workers completed fewer responses in the second half compared to the first half of a 28-day sampling period (Totterdell and Folkard 1992). Compliance rates have also been found to vary as a function of occupational level. Csikszentmihalyi and Larson (1987) reported that blue-collar workers responded to an average of 73% of all signals, as compared to 85% for clerical workers and 92% for managers. Surprisingly, compliance rates are higher during work hours than in leisure hours (Totterdell and Folkard

TABLE 5.2.
ESM STUDIES OF CHRONIC ILLNESS

STUDY	SAMPLE CHARACTERISTICS	ESM $(D \times B)$[a]
DEPRESSION		
BARGE-SCHAAPVELD ET AL. 1995	21 primary-care patients, before vs. after 6 weeks of treatment	$6 \times 10 \ (\times 2)$
BARGE-SCHAAPVELD ET AL. 1999	63 primary-care patients; 22 normal controls	6×10
KRAAN ET AL. 1992	CMHC patients (16 current, 6 remitted); 4 normal controls (pilot)	6×10
MERRICK 1992	Adolescent patients (7 current, 7 recovered); 14 normal controls	7×8
ANXIETY DISORDERS		
DIJKMAN-CAES ET AL. 1993	65 CMHC and clinic patients with panic disorder; 20 normal controls	6×10
EATING DISORDERS		
JOHNSON & LARSON 1982; LARSON & ASMUSSEN 1992	15 bulimia patients; 24 normal controls	7×7
STEIGER ET AL. 1999	Bulimia patients (55 current, 18 former); 31 psychiatric patient controls	6 to 22[b]
PERSONALITY DISORDERS		
FARCHAUS-STEIN 1996	15 borderline patients; 4 anorexia nervosa controls; 10 normal controls	10×5
CHRONIC STRESS		
VAN ECK 1996; VAN ECK ET AL. 1996, 1998	42 employees with high perceived stress; 46 low-stress controls	5×10
FATIGUE SYNDROMES		
STONE ET AL. 1994	8 patients with chronic fatigue; 21 normal controls	$26 \times 5; 15 \times 6$
VAN DIEST & APPELS 1991	20 men with vital exhaustion; 10 normal controls	21×6
CHRONIC PAIN		
LOUSBERG ET AL. 1997; VENDRIG AND LOUSBERG 1997	57 chronic pain patients	6×8

		(d × b)
FIBROMYALGIA		
AFFLECK ET AL. 1996, 1998	50 patients	30 × 3
RHEUMATOID ARTHRITIS		
CRUISE ET AL. 1996; STONE ET AL. 1997	35 patients	7 × 7
MIGRAINE HEADACHE		
HONKOOP ET AL. 1999	56 patients	70 × 6
SORBI, HONKOOP & GODAERT 1996	4 patients (pilot study)	70 × 6
ASTHMA		
SMYTH ET AL. 1999	20 adult asthmatics	10 × 5
DIABETES		
SCHANDRY & LEOPOLD 1996	68 IDDM patients	28 × 2
ALCOHOL ABUSE; DRUG ABUSE; SMOKING		
CARNEY ET AL. 1998	48 moderate drinkers	30[c]
COLLINS ET AL. 1998	Heavy drinkers in treatment vs. wait-list	56 × 6
LARSON, CSIKSZENTMIHALYI & FREEMAN 1992	19 adolescent users of alcohol or marijuana	7 × 8
KAPLAN 1992	20 heroin addicts	6 × 10
LITT, COONEY & MORSE 1998	27 alcoholics	21 × 8
SHIFFMAN ET AL. 1994	57 cigarette smokers/alcohol users	7 × 5

[a] Column (d x b) refers to days (d) and beeps per day (b) during ESM sampling period.

[b] Reports were event-contingent (social interactions).

[c] Reports were event-contingent (drink consumption).

1992; van Eck, Nicolson, and Berkhof 1998; Williams et al. 1991). This may be due to the fact that sampling in the workplace is experienced as less annoying and less disruptive than sampling during leisure time. In addition, during the weekends subjects are more likely to be asleep in the morning and thus have the beeper turned off (van Eck, Nicolson, and Berkhof 1998).

Van Eck (1996) found little evidence for selective bias in missing responses when subjects were awake; however, a small decline in compliance occurred around 5:00 p.m. while subjects commuted by car or bicycle from work to home. Subjects with high perceived stress had rates of compliance similar to the rates of those with low perceived stress; in other words, stress does not necessarily reduce compliance. "High-stress" subjects did rate the beeps as slightly more disturbing than "low-stress" subjects did, but both groups reported very low method-induced annoyance on average.

METHOD REACTIVITY

In general, mean responses on ESM measures have not been found to change significantly over sampling periods of a week. However, since the within-individual variance in responses tends to decrease from the first to the second half of the week (Csikszentmihalyi and Larson 1987) (with the greatest decrease following the first day of sampling) (Delespaul 1995), it is often useful to add an extra run-in day (when data are collected but not used in the analysis) to ESM sampling procedures.

CHOICE OF MEASURES

Table 5.1 summarizes ESM measures that have been used in workplace studies, differentiating between the repeated measures at the "beep level" and those at the "subject level": cross-sectional measures that are hypothesized to moderate the processes under investigation at the beep level. Many studies also include repeated measures at an intermediate level, such as assessments of sleep quality upon awakening (see the last column, "Notes"). These variables allow within-individual contrasts between periods of time (e.g., day of the week, type of shift, pre- and posttreatment) that are relevant to the hypothesis being tested.

Most ESM workplace studies have included some subset of the following beep-level measures: context (current activity, location, and social setting), mood states, cognitive efficiency (concentration and alertness), and appraisal of the current activity in terms of intrinsic motivation, enjoyment, challenge, and skills. Other measures with clear relevance to work experiences include perceived goal progress, role-juggling, and stressful events, including negative interactions with colleagues. Totterdell, Spelten, Smith, and colleagues (1995) have adapted the NASA Workload Scale for repeated assessments; the seven items in the scale are mental demand, physical demand, time pressure, frustration, effort, effectiveness, and work satisfaction. These researchers have also developed handheld computer–administered cognitive-performance tests designed to assess aspects of reaction time and short-term memory processes (for a description of the development of these performance measures, see Totterdell and Folkard 1992). Finally, we note that ESM studies of physiological measures such as blood pressure (Shapiro, Jamner, and Goldstein 1993) and salivary cortisol (van Eck et al. 1996) also have shed light on potential health effects of workplace stress.

SELECTED FINDINGS

Time use. One of the most striking findings about time use is that employees in the workplace are actually working only 65% of the time. The remaining time is fairly equally divided between eating, socializing with colleagues, and talking on the phone with family and friends (Kubey and Csikszentmihalyi 1990). Clerical workers spend even less time working on the job than blue-collar workers or managers (Csikszentmihalyi and LeFevre 1989). (With many workers now having access to e-mail, the Internet, and computer games, new forms of not working have arisen in recent years.) A related finding concerns the percentage of time spent thinking about the task at hand. Studies indicate that workers focus their attention on the current activity only about 50% to 60% of the time and spend the rest of the time daydreaming (Donner 1992). This information underscores the usefulness of ESM in studies of productivity, as retrospective estimates of time use are generally inaccurate and are likely to be further biased by social desirability (or wishful thinking).

The subjective experience of work. Employee well-being has been linked to job performance and other measures of productivity (Warr 1999). Therefore, it seems reasonable to assume that ESM measures of well-being, such as high positive affect, low negative affect, and enjoyment of current activity (Barge-Schaapveld et al. 1999; deVries, Delespaul, and Nicolson 1999) will show a close connection to current work performance. ESM studies have consistently shown that working is associated with worse-than-average mood states and with relatively low enjoyment, and that individuals would generally prefer to be doing something else (Barge-Schaapveld et al. 1997; Brandstätter and Gaubatz 1997; Csikszentmihalyi and LeFevre 1989; Haworth, Jarman, and

Lee 1997; van Eck 1996). This is particularly true when work experiences are compared to leisure. However, work is associated with above-average levels of concentration and unselfconsciousness and is more likely than other activities to be intellectually challenging (Csikszentmihalyi 1990). In fact, ESM studies have shown that the vast majority of experiences involving "flow" (i.e., optimal experiences) occur in the context of work rather than leisure, and this holds true for assembly-line workers as well as managers (Csikszentmihalyi and LeFevre 1989).

The necessity of switching back and forth between different tasks, either within or across work and family roles, can interfere with productivity and lower general well-being. Aspects of this hypothesis have been investigated in two ESM studies of working mothers, where women reported task-juggling between work and family roles on 18.5% of all reports, and juggling within a role on 34.6% of reports. As expected, when women juggled between roles, positive affect and task enjoyment were lower, and negative affect was higher (Williams et al. 1991). In a study of nurses, role-juggling in the last 30 minutes was reported on 48% of all reports (Shiu 1998). Role-juggling has not been studied with ESM in working men, but experiences at work do typically spill over into family life. Larson and Richards (1994), sampling family members simultaneously, found that husbands' emotions were often transmitted to their wives after men arrived home at the end of a workday.

Effects of work organization. ESM is particularly well suited for investigating the effects of shift work on employee well-being and performance. A reduction in productivity and an increase in performance errors may be more likely during certain kinds of shifts, shift systems, or overtime within a shift. As demonstrated by Totterdell, Spelten, Barton, and colleagues (1995) in the United Kingdom, characteristics of the shift system (e.g., rotating versus permanent night shifts), type of shift (e.g., night, day, or evening), and number of hours into a particular shift all had measurable effects on self-rated mood, alertness, and workload, as well as on computer-assessed cognitive-performance measures. Furthermore, more than one rest day was needed for full recovery from consecutive work shifts for nurses (Totterdell, Spelten, Smith, et al. 1995). In nuclear-power-plant workers, alertness tended to drop off near the end of the day and during evening shifts, but cognitive-test performance was worst during the night shift (Smith, Totterdell, and Folkard 1995). A study of a fire-brigade control room showed that 14-hour night shifts posed unacceptable risks, because of a sizable decrease in alertness and reaction time (Knauth et al. 1995). This kind of approach could easily be extended to examine the effects of interventions designed to improve employee well-being or productivity such as regular work breaks.

ESM Studies of Chronic Illness

Soon after ESM was developed, researchers began to apply it in studies of chronic psychiatric disorders (deVries 1992b; deVries 1987). In the past decade, ESM applications have expanded to include a wide range of psychosomatic disorders, as illustrated in table 5.2. Many of these chronic conditions are known to affect a substantial percentage of working individuals.[2] ESM is particularly well suited to behavioral medicine and psychiatric research, since most illness symptoms vary in response to external as well as internal stimuli. ESM allows us to move out of the clinic and the laboratory to document the course of illnesses and their effects on daily experience at the times and places they occur (Affleck et al. 1999; deVries 1992a; Stone and Shiffman 1994).

PARTICIPANTS

Participants in the studies listed in table 5.2 were recruited in treatment settings (e.g., through general practice or specialty clinics) or, in the case of individuals with subclinical symptoms or undiagnosed syndromes, via screening or advertising in the community. "Snowball sampling" has been used to identify hidden populations such as heroin addicts (Kaplan 1992). Although findings suggest that volunteers for ESM studies in community samples may be less anxious and generally better adjusted than individuals who refuse to participate (Waite, Claffey, and Hillbrand 1998), little is known about biases that may operate in recruiting clinical samples. In our own experience, willingness to take part in a study depends in large part on the ability of the researcher to create an alliance with the patient, emphasizing the potential benefits of the study for both understanding the general nature of the disorder and obtaining insights into the patient's particular symptoms.

COMPLIANCE

DeVries (1992c) has summarized the most important elements for successful ESM sampling of psychiatric outpatients. Creating a research alliance not only with the patient but also with family members and the therapist is of paramount importance. Without the support of their social network, depressed patients, for example, are harder to recruit and more likely to drop out of ESM studies (Wilson et al. 1992). A thorough briefing session, in which

---

2. We have excluded from the current review studies of disorders like schizophrenia, dissociative identity disorder, and geriatric depression, which are unlikely to affect a substantial proportion of the working population.

patients are taught how to fill out ESM forms, is also essential. The same principles apply to psychosomatic illness. Although cognitive and motivational problems may be less prevalent in this group than in psychiatric patients, ESM researchers still need to be careful to avoid placing an extra burden on anyone suffering from a health problem.

The figures on compliance for the ESM studies reviewed here are somewhat surprising because the percentage of signals patients responded to did not differ significantly from the percentage responded to by healthy controls (Dijkman-Caes 1993). However, it appears that psychiatric outpatients (Dijkman-Caes 1993) and individuals with high perceived stress (van Eck 1996) experienced participation in an ESM study as more annoying or disruptive of daily activities than did controls.

Initial pilot studies on depression suggest that this disorder poses a particularly serious methodological challenge, because patients were difficult to recruit and had high dropout rates. Furthermore, those who completed a week of sampling had relatively low compliance rates. Patients who were elderly or had a low educational background, additional somatic disorders, or severe cognitive symptoms were the least likely to comply with the sampling protocol (Kraan et al. 1992; Wilson et al. 1992). Although such obstacles undeniably influence the nature of the sample, later studies in both primary- and secondary-care settings have had better success in recruiting depressed subjects, limiting the number of dropouts, and obtaining compliance (Barge-Schaapveld et al. 1999; Barge-Schaapveld et al. 1995; Peeters et al. 2003).

In passing, we note that depressed patients' compliance did not change following six weeks of pharmacological treatment. However, treatment responders showed a significant decrease in the average length of time it took to respond to a beep by completing an ESM form (3.6 minutes pretreatment versus 2.9 minutes posttreatment). In contrast, nonresponders to treatment showed no change in their average response time (4.4 pretreatment versus 4.1 minutes posttreatment) (Barge-Schaapveld et al. 1995). This suggests that the beep-to-response interval might serve as an index of cognitive impairment in depression.

Other "difficult" groups that have been investigated with ESM are substance abusers and alcoholics. Specific issues with regard to recruitment, compliance, failure to adhere to the protocol, and influences of social desirability on the accuracy of self-reports have been discussed by Kaplan (1992) and Litt, Cooney, and Morse (1998); both studies also suggest some solutions to these methodological problems. Since ESM has been effectively used with these "difficult" groups as well as with patients suffering from schizophrenia (deVries and Delespaul 1989) and geriatric depression (Voelkl and Mathieu

1993), researchers can be confident that few problems with compliance are likely to occur in studies of chronically ill individuals who are able to work.

METHOD REACTIVITY

Changes over time in mean levels or in variability in ESM measures could indicate that the method itself was influencing behavior, mood, or symptom perception. To rule out this possibility, temporal patterns in results have been investigated. Fortunately, it appears that mood and symptom levels do not systematically change over the course of week-long studies (Cruise et al. 1996; Dijkman-Caes 1993). Moreover, analysis of linear trends in data collected from moderate drinkers over 30 days of continuous self-monitoring showed no change in patterns of reported alcohol consumption over time, again indicating that reactivity effects are small (Carney et al. 1998). However, certain individuals may be more reactive to ESM procedures than others. Likewise, anecdotal evidence suggests that ESM may have influences on symptom perception and on illness and coping behaviors that may not appear as linear trends in the overall sample (Affleck et al. 1999). This is an important question for future research.

Considering the widespread use of self-monitoring techniques in behavior therapy (Nelson 1977), the failure to document clear effects of ESM on symptoms or behavior may seem surprising. However, in contrast to therapeutic self-monitoring, ESM lacks a feedback loop (Kazdin 1974). Any feedback concerning a patient's ESM reports occurs after the period of data collection. In case studies, this feedback has indeed been successfully used as part of the therapy (Delle Fave and Massimini 1992; Toth-Fejel, Toth-Fejel, and Hedricks 1998).

SAMPLING FRAMES

The majority of studies reviewed in table 5.2 lasted from 5 to 10 days and consisted of 5 to 10 beeps per day. However, a number of studies involved considerably longer periods, ranging from 21 to 70 consecutive days. The choice was typically based on known features of the illness process, for example, the probable frequency and duration of migraine attacks (Honkoop et al. 1999). Surprisingly, in long studies, compliance does not necessarily decrease over time. For example, in a pilot study lasting 70 days with 6 signals per day, four migraine patients maintained an overall response rate of 93% (Sorbi, Honkoop, and Godaert 1996). Likewise, in a 26-day study, chronic fatigue patients maintained a compliance rate of 88% (Stone et al. 1994).

CHOICE OF MEASURES

In addition to the "standard" measures (activity, location, social context, mood, evaluation of current activity, and concentration), most ESM studies of chronic illness include illness-specific measures of symptoms. These can be primarily somatic (e.g., pain, shortness of breath, hunger, fatigue) or primarily psychological (e.g., panic, craving, agitation, slowness of thought). Symptom lists are usually based on diagnostic criteria for the disorder, sometimes supplemented with items developed through focus groups (Kraan et al. 1992). Researchers have investigated the construct validity of the ESM scales by comparing results with those obtained with accepted cross-sectional instruments (Barge-Schaapveld et al. 1995; Honkoop et al. 1999; Lousberg et al. 1997). In addition to symptoms of the disorder, ESM has been used to assess known side effects of pharmacological treatment (Barge-Schaapveld and Nicolson 2002).

Recent studies have also demonstrated the feasibility of adding objective symptom measures to ESM protocols such as salivary cortisol in chronic stress (van Eck et al. 1996), blood glucose levels in diabetes (Schandry and Leopold 1996), and peak expiratory flow rate in asthma (Smyth et al. 1999). Researchers may also be interested in how environmental triggers may exacerbate symptoms, for example, how pollen counts are associated with symptoms of hay fever (Kessler et al. 2001), or how weather conditions affect pain and fatigue in arthritis (Gorin et al. 1999). However, these studies can be difficult to undertake because the effects of environmental triggers are likely to be delayed.

SELECTED FINDINGS

Time use. Not surprisingly, illness can influence how, where, and with whom people spend their time. ESM studies of psychiatric disorders suggest that time spent in work and social activities as well as the balance between active and passive leisure pursuits may be particularly sensitive indicators of clinical state. This is particularly true in depression. Merrick (1992) reported that depressed adolescents spend significantly less time in productive activities such as schoolwork or a job than either recovered or control subjects. Furthermore, although the three groups did not differ in total leisure time, depressed adolescents spent dramatically more time engaged in passive leisure activities (watching TV, reading, thinking) and less time socializing than adolescents in the other two groups did. Depressed primary-care patients were less likely to be working and more likely to be doing nothing than healthy controls were (Barge-Schaapveld et al. 1999).

In a secondary analysis of ESM data, we found an inverse relationship between average time spent in productive activities and average time spent doing nothing for different diagnostic groups (those who had pain, anxiety disorders, depression, schizophrenia, good health). Patients with schizophrenia, for example, reported working 4.9% of the time and doing nothing 25% of the time, whereas these figures were 22.1% and 6.1%, respectively, for healthy control subjects. Across groups, time spent doing nothing was associated with low positive affect and high negative affect, whereas work and household chores (although not highly preferred activities) were associated with average happiness and, especially in the psychiatric disorders, with relatively low negative mood (Barge-Schaapveld et al. 1997).

Longitudinal studies have shown how treatment can help normalize time-use patterns. Barge-Schaapveld and colleagues (1995), for example, found that responders to six weeks of antidepressant treatment showed greater increases in time spent doing chores and greater decreases in passive leisure time than did nonresponders. In a case study of a woman with agoraphobia, time-use patterns derived from nine ESM sampling periods over the course of a year of therapy showed a gradual decrease in TV watching paralleled by an increase in active leisure and social activities (Delle Fave and Massimini 1992).

Effects of illness on subjective experience in daily life. Studies of health-related quality of life have focused attention on the profound impact that illness can have on the performance of daily activities and on subjective evaluations of these activities in terms of motivation, enjoyment, and ability (Guyatt, Feeny, and Patrick 1993; Hays et al. 1995). To date, ESM studies of chronic illness have focused more on contextual variables that influence symptom expression than on the effect of illness, or symptom fluctuations on daily functioning. For example, anxiety patients are less likely to experience panic at work than when they are less actively engaged (Dijkman-Caes et al. 1993). Similarly, schizophrenic patients are less likely to experience hallucinations when working (Delespaul 1995). Although at least some of the participants in the ESM studies listed in table 5.2 were employed, published reports provide no information about the impact of illness on work experiences or performance. A study of chronic stress in white-collar workers provides some insights that may be relevant to depression as well as to stress.

Van Eck (1996) investigated how male white-collar employees with high levels of perceived stress differed from a low-stress control group in daily experience (including time use, mood, psychosomatic symptoms, and stressful events) and neuroendocrine profiles. The high-stress (HS) group, although not in treatment for any psychological complaint, displayed elevated levels of depressive, anxious, and psychosomatic symptomatology. They reported lower levels of enjoyment and perceived skill, and greater effort required to perform routine daily activities than low-stress (LS) controls. In both groups, work was rated as more challenging and requiring greater effort than other activities, but this was especially true for the HS group, for whom work was also the least enjoyable daily activity. The HS group also reported significantly more frequent stressful work events; in particular, HS subjects experienced nearly twice as many negative interactions with colleagues. Work events were also rated as more stressful by HS than by LS subjects. It is important to mention that this study focused on stress both at work and at home; HS subjects also reported more frequent and stressful events at home, especially with their partners and children, than LS subjects did.

Future studies of chronic illness in the workplace should consider responses to stressful daily events, because they are likely to have negative effects on performance. Daily events have been shown to trigger or exacerbate illness symptoms in a number of ESM studies. In a study of rheumatoid arthritis patients, daily stressors were associated with increased pain (Stone et al. 1997). ESM reports from migraine patients indicated that daily hassles were more frequent and more stressful in the two days preceding a migraine attack than in matched control periods (Sorbi, Honkoop, and Godaert 1996). Finally, higher levels of chronic stress were associated with greater increases in negative mood and decreases in positive mood in response to daily stressors in working men (van Eck, Nicolson, and Berkhof 1998).

Within-subject variability. ESM studies have clearly confirmed one of the initial tenets underlying the development of the method: that chronic illnesses are not constantly "present" in the lives of afflicted individuals. Moments when symptoms are high in intensity alternate, often within the same day, with milder or even symptom-free periods. This pattern has been shown, for example, to apply to arthritic pain (Stone et al. 1997), drug craving (Kaplan 1992), airway constriction (Smyth et al. 1999), and hypoglycemic symptoms (Schandry and Leopold 1996), to name just a few conditions. Furthermore, ESM studies that have examined variances as well as mean levels provide evidence for higher intra-individual variability in mood and well-being in certain disorders, compared to healthy controls. Increased variability could reflect underlying diurnal patterns in disease expression (Stone et al. 1994, 1997) but may also be a sign of general liability and poor regulation of emotional states (Barge-Schaapveld et al. 1999; Farchaus-Stein 1996; Johnson and Larson 1982).

CONCLUDING REMARKS

Researchers, policy analysts, and others concerned with the health and performance of workers need to use a range of techniques to study the productivity of workers and the effects of illness on work performance. Information collected through ESM provides an excellent complement to the other types of data-collection techniques described in the other chapters in part 1 of this book.

As reviewed in this chapter, ESM has already been successfully employed to study a variety of physical and mental health conditions as well as the work performance of study participants. Some unique features of ESM (e.g., the ability to make repeated assessments over time) make it especially useful (or perhaps even the method of choice) for certain investigations, such as studies of rapidly changing phenomena. The immediacy with which respondents report on experienced phenomena also enables researchers to avoid the problem of recall bias, which poses a substantial threat to the validity of many self-report surveys. In the future, opportunities may exist to reanalyze previously collected ESM data to identify the effects of chronic disease on work performance. Additional future applications of ESM involving de novo ESM data collection among workers are also likely. Ongoing methodological and technical refinements of ESM should continue to enhance the utility of ESM data collection in such future applications.

REFERENCES

Affleck, G., H. Tennen, S. Urrows, P. Higgins, M. Abeles, C. Hall, P. Karoly, and C. Newton. 1998. Fibromyalgia and women's pursuit of personal goals: A daily process analysis. *Health Psychology* 17, no. 1: 40–47.

Affleck, G., S. Urrows, H. Tennen, P. Higgins, and M. Abeles. 1996. Sequential daily relations of sleep, pain intensity, and attention to pain among women with fibromyalgia. *Pain* 68:363–68.

Affleck, G., A. Zautra, H. Tennen, and S. Armeli. 1999. Multilevel daily process designs for consulting and clinical psychology: A preface for the perplexed. *Journal of Consulting and Clinical Psychology* 67:746–54.

Alliger, G. M., and K. J. Williams. 1993. Using signal-contingent experience sampling methodology to study work in the field: A discussion and illustration examining task perceptions and mood. *Personnel Psychology* 46:525–49.

Barge-Schaapveld, D. Q., and N. A. Nicolson. 2002. Effects of antidepressant treatment on the quality of daily life: An experience sampling study. *Journal of Clinical Psychiatry* 63:477–85.

Barge-Schaapveld, D. Q., N. A. Nicolson, J. Berkhof, and M. W. deVries. 1999. Quality of life in depression: Daily life determinants and variability. *Psychiatry Research* 88:173–89.

Barge-Schaapveld, D. Q. C. M., N. A. Nicolson, P. A. E. G. Delespaul, and M. W. deVries. 1997. Assessing daily quality of life with the Experience Sampling Method. In *Quality of life in mental disorders,* ed. H. Katsching, H. Freeman, and N. Sartorius. Chichester, NY: John Wiley.

Barge-Schaapveld, D. Q., N. A. Nicolson, R. G. van der Hoop, and M. W. deVries. 1995. Changes in daily life experience associated with clinical improvement in depression. *Journal of Affective Disorders* 34:139–54.

Bolger, N., A. De Longis, R. C. Kessler, and E. Wethington. 1989. The contagion of stress across multiple roles. *Journal of Marriage and the Family* 51:175–83.

Bradburn, N. M., L. J. Rips, and S. K. Shevell. 1987. Answering autobiographical questions: The impact of memory and inference on surveys. *Science* 236:157–61.

Brandstätter, H., and S. Gaubatz. 1997. Befindenstagebuch am neuen Arbeitsplatz in differentialpsychologischer Sicht (Time sampling daily experiences of newcomers to a workplace: An individual difference perspective). *Zeitschrift für Arbeits- und Organisationspsychologie* 41:18–29.

Brown, G. W., and T. Harris. 1978. *Social origins of depression: A study of psychiatric disorder in women.* New York: John Wiley.

Carney, M. A., H. Tennen, G. Affleck, F. K. Del Boca, and H. R. Kranzler. 1998. Levels and patterns of alcohol consumption using timeline follow-back, daily diaries, and real-time "electronic interviews." *Journal of Studies on Alcohol* 59:447–54.

Cochran, W. G. 1963. *Sampling techniques.* New York: John Wiley.

Collins, R. L., E. T. Morsheimer, S. Shiffman, J. A. Paty, M. Gnys, and G. D. Papandonatos. 1998. Ecological momentary assessment in a behavioral drinking moderation training program. *Experimental and Clinical Psychopharmacology* 6, no. 3: 306–15.

Cruise, C. E., J. Broderick, L. Porter, A. Kaell, and A. A. Stone. 1996. Reactive effects of diary self-assessment in chronic pain patients. *Pain* 67:253–58.

Csikszentmihalyi, M. 1990. *Flow: The psychology of optimal experience.* New York: HarperCollins.

Csikszentmihalyi, M., and T. J. Figurski. 1982. Self-awareness and aversive experience in everyday life. *Journal of Personality* 50:15–28.

Csikszentmihalyi, M., and R. Larson. 1987. Validity and reliability of the Experience-Sampling Method. *Journal of Nervous and Mental Disease* 175:526–36.

———. 1992. Validity and reliability of the Experience Sampling Method. In deVries 1992b.

Csikszentmihalyi, M., R. Larson, and S. Prescott. 1977. The ecology of adolescent activity and experience. *Journal of Youth and Adolescence* 6:281–94.

Csikszentmihalyi, M., and J. LeFevre. 1989. Optimal experience in work and leisure. *Journal of Personality and Social Psychology* 56:815–22.

Delespaul, P. A. E. G. 1992. Technical note: Devices and time-sampling procedures. In deVries 1992b.

————. 1995. Assessing schizophrenia in daily life: The Experience Sampling Method. Ph.D. diss., University of Limburg.

Delle Fave, A., and A. Massimini. 1992. The ESM and the measurement of clinical change: A case of anxiety disorder. In deVries 1992b.

DeVries, M. W. 1987. Investigating mental disorders in their natural settings. *Journal of Nervous and Mental Disease* 175:509–13.

————. 1992a. The experience of psychopathology in natural settings: Introduction and illustration of variables. In deVries 1992b.

————, ed. 1992b. *The experience of psychopathology: Investigating mental disorders in their natural settings.* Cambridge: Cambridge University Press.

————. 1992c. Practical issues in psychiatric applications of ESM. In deVries 1992b.

DeVries, M. W., and P. A. E. G. Delespaul. 1989. Time, context, and subjective experience in schizophrenia. *Schizophrenia Bulletin* 15:233–44.

DeVries, M. W., P. A. E. G. Delespaul, and N. A. Nicolson. 1999. Experience Sampling Method (ESM). In *Compendium of quality of life instruments,* ed. S. Salek. Chichester, Eng.: John Wiley.

Dijkman-Caes, C. I. M. 1993. Panic disorder and agoraphobia in daily life. Ph.D. diss., Maastricht University.

Dijkman-Caes, C.I.M., M. W. deVries, H. F. Kraan, and A. Volovics. 1993. Agoraphobic behavior in daily life: Effects of social roles and demographic characteristics. *Psychological Reports* 72:1283–93.

Donner, E. 1992. Expanding the experimental parameters of cognitive therapy. In deVries 1992b.

Eisenhower, D., N. A. Mathiowetz, and D. Morganstein. 1991. Recall error: Sources and bias reduction techniques. In *Measurement errors in surveys,* ed. P. P Biemer, R. M. Groves, L. E. Lyberg, N. A. Mathiowetz, and S. Sudman. New York: John Wiley.

Farchaus-Stein, K. 1996. Affect instability in adults with a borderline personality disorder. *Archives of Psychiatry Nursing* 10:32–40.

Gorin, A. A., J. M. Smyth, J. N. Weisberg, G. Affleck, H. Tennen, S. Urrows, and A. A. Stone. 1999. Rheumatoid arthritis patients show weather sensitivity in daily life, but the relationship is not clinically significant. *Pain* 81:173–77.

Guyatt, G. H., D. H. Feeny, and D. L. Patrick. 1993. Measuring health-related quality of life. *Annals of Internal Medicine* 118:622–29.

Haworth, J., and S. Evans. 1995. Challenge, skill, and positive subjective states in the daily life of a sample of YTS students. *Journal of Occupational and Organizational Psychology* 68:109–21.

Haworth, J. T., M. Jarman, and S. Lee. 1997. Positive psychological states in the daily life of a sample of working women. *Journal of Applied Social Psychology* 27:345–70.

Hays, R. D., K. B. Wells, C. D. Sherbourne, W. Rogers, and K. Spritzer. 1995. Functioning and well-being outcomes of patients with depression compared with chronic general medical illnesses. *Archives of General Psychiatry* 52:11–19.

Honkoop, P. C., M. J. Sorbi, G. L. Godaert, and E. L. Spierings. 1999. High-density assessment of the IHS classification criteria for migraine without aura: A prospective study. *Cephalalgia* 19:201–6.

Hormuth, S. E. 1986. The sampling of experiences in situ. *Journal of Personality* 54:262–93.

Johnson, C., and R. Larson. 1982. Bulimia: An analysis of moods and behavior. *Psychosomatic Medicine* 44:341–51.

Kaplan, C. D. 1992. Drug craving and drug use in the daily life of heroin addicts. In deVries 1992b.

Kazdin, A. E. 1974. Reactive self-monitoring: The effects of response desirability, goal setting, and feedback. *Journal of Consulting and Clinical Psychology* 42:704–16.

Kessler, R. C., D. M. Almeida, P. Berglund, and P. Stang. 2001. Pollen and mold exposure impairs the work performance of employees with allergic rhinitis. *Annals of Allergy, Asthma, and Immunology* 87:289–95.

Knauth, P., J. Keller, G. Schindele, and P. Totterdell. 1995. A 14-H night-shift in the control room of a fire brigade. *Work and Stress* 9:176–86.

Kraan, H., H. Meertens, M. Hilwig, L. Volovics, C. I. M. Dijkman-Caes, and P. Portegijs. 1992. Selecting measures, diagnostic validity and scaling in the study of depression. In deVries 1992b.

Kubey, R., and M. Csikszentmihalyi. 1990. *Television and the quality of life: How viewing shapes everyday experience.* Hillsdale, NJ: Lawrence Erlbaum Associates.

Larson, R. and L. Asmussen. 1992. Bulimia in daily life: A context-bound syndrome. In DeVries 1992b, 167–79.

Larson, R., M. Csikszentmihalyi, and M. Freeman. 1992. Alcohol and marijuana use in adolescents' daily lives. In deVries 1992b, 180–92.

Larson, R., and P. A. E. G. Delespaul. 1992. Analyzing experience sampling data: A guide book for the perplexed. In deVries 1992b.

Larson, R., and M. Richards. 1994. *Divergent realities: The emotional lives of mothers, fathers, and adolescents.* New York: Basic Books.

Litt, M. D., N. L. Cooney, and P. Morse. 1998. Ecological Momentary Assessment (EMA) with treated alcoholics: Methodological problems and potential solutions. *Health Psychology* 17:48–52.

Little, R. J. A., and D. B. Rubin. 1987. *Statistical analysis with missing data.* New York: John Wiley.

Lousberg, R., A. J. Schmidt, N. H. Groenman, L. Vendrig, and C. I. Dijkman-Caes. 1997. Validating the MPI-DLV using experience sampling data. *Journal of Behavioral Medicine* 20:195–206.

Massimini, F., and M. Carli. 1988. The systematic assessment of flow in daily experience. In *Optimal experience: Psychological studies of flow in consciousness,* ed. M. Csikszentmihalyi and I. S. Csikszentmihalyi. Cambridge: Cambridge University Press.

Merrick, W. A. 1992. Dysphoric moods in depressed and non-depressed adolescents. In deVries 1992b, 148–56.

Moneta, G. B., and M. Csikszentmihalyi. 1996. The effect of perceived challenges and skills on the quality of subjective experience. *Journal of Personality* 64:275–310.

Morgado, A., N. Raoux, M. Smith, J. F. Allilaire, and D. Widlocher. 1989. Subjective bias in reports of poor work adjustment in depressed patients. *Acta Psychiatrica Scandinavica* 80:541–47.

Nelson, R. O. 1977. Assessment and therapeutic functions of self-monitoring. In *Progress in behavior modification,* ed. M. Hersen, R. M. Eisler, and P. M. Miller. New York: Academic Press.

Peeters, F., N. A. Nicolson, J. Berkhof, P. Delespaul, and M. deVries. 2003. Effects of daily events on mood states in major depressive disorder. *Journal of Abnormal Psychology* 112:203–11.

Reis, H. T., and S. L. Gable. 2000. Event-sampling and other methods for studying everyday experience. In *Handbook of research methods in social and personality psychology,* ed. H. T. Reis and C. M. Judd. Cambridge: Cambridge University Press.

Robinson, J. 1977. *How Americans use time: A social-psychological analysis of everyday behavior.* New York: Praeger.

Ross, M. 1989. Relation of implicit theories to the construction of personal histories. *Psychological Review* 96:341–57.

Rubin, D. B. 1987. *Multiple imputation for nonresponse in surveys.* New York: John Wiley.

Savon-Williams, R. C., and D. H. Demo. 1983. Situational and transitional determinants of adolescents' self-feelings. *Journal of Personality and Social Psychology* 44:824–33.

Schandry, R., and C. Leopold. 1996. Ambulatory assessment of self-monitored subjective and objective symptoms of diabetic patients. In *Ambulatory assessment: Computer-assisted psychological and psychophysiological methods in monitoring and field studies,* ed. J. Fahrenberg and J. Myrtek. Seattle: Hogrefe and Huber.

Schiefele, U., and M. Csikszentmihalyi. 1995. Motivation and ability as factors in mathematics experience and achievement. *Journal for Research in Mathematics Education* 26:163–81.

Schwartz, J. E., and A. A. Stone. 1998. Strategies for analyzing Ecological Momentary Assessment data. *Health Psychology* 17:6–16.

Shapiro, D., L. D. Jamner, and I. B. Goldstein. 1993. Ambulatory stress psychophysiology: The study of "compensatory and defensive counterforces" and conflict in a natural setting. *Psychosomatic Medicine* 55:309–23.

Shiffman, S. 2000. Real-time self-report of momentary states in the natural environment: Computerized Ecological Momentary Assessment. In *The science of self-report: Implications for research and practice,* ed. A. A. Stone, J. S. Turkkan, C. A. Bachrach, J. B. Jobe, H. S. Kurtzman, and V. S. Cain. Mahwah, NJ: Lawrence Erlbaum Associates.

Shiffman, S., L. A. Fischer, J. A. Paty, M. Gnys, M. Hickcox, and J. D. Kassel. 1994. Drinking and smoking: A field study of their association. *Annals of Behavioral Medicine* 16, no. 3: 203–9.

Shiffman, S., and A. A. Stone. 1998. Ecological Momentary Assessment: A new tool for behavioral medicine research. In *Technology and methods in behavioral medicine,* ed. D. S. Krantz and A. Baum. Mahwah, NJ: Lawrence Erlbaum Associates.

Shiu, A. T. 1998. The significance of sense of coherence for the perceptions of task characteristics and stress during interruptions amongst a sample of public health nurses in Hong Kong: Implications for nursing management. *Public Health Nursing* 15:273–80.

Smith, L., P. Totterdell, and S. Folkard. 1995. Shiftwork effects in nuclear power workers: A field study using portable computers. *Work and Stress* 9:235–44.

Smyth, J. M., M. H. Soefer, A. Hurewitz, A. Kliment, and A. A. Stone. 1999. Daily psychosocial factors predict levels and diurnal cycles of asthma symptomatology and peak flow. *Journal of Behavioral Medicine* 22:179–93.

Sorbi, M. J., P. C. Honkoop, and G. L. R. Godaert. 1996. A signal-contingent computer diary for the assessment of psychological precedents of the migraine attack. In *Ambulatory assessment: Computer-assisted psychological and psychophysiological methods in monitoring and field studies,* ed. J. Fahrenberg and J. Myrtek. Seattle: Hogrefe and Huber.

Steiger, H., L. Gauvin, S. Jabalpurwala, J. R. Seguin, and S. Stotland. 1999. Hypersensitivity to social interactions in bulimic syndromes: Relationship to binge eating. *Journal of Consultative and Clinical Psychology* 67, no. 5: 765–75.

Stone, A. A., J. E. Broderick, L. S. Porter, and A. T. Kaell. 1997. The experience of rheumatoid arthritis pain and fatigue: Examining momentary reports and correlates over one week. *Arthritis Care and Research* 10:185–93.

Stone, A. A., Broderick, J. E., L. S. Porter, L. Krupp, M. Gnys, J. A. Paty, and S. Shiffman. 1994. Fatigue and mood in chronic fatigue syndrome patients: Results of a momentary assessment protocol examining fatigue and mood levels and diurnal patterns. *Annals of Behavioral Medicine* 16:221–34.

Stone, A. A., R. C. Kessler, and J. A. Haythornthwaite. 1991. Measuring daily events and experiences: Decisions for the researcher. *Journal of Personality* 59:575–607.

Stone, A. A., and J. M. Neale. 1982. Development of a methodology for assessing daily experiences. In *Advances in environmental psychology: Environment and health,* ed. A. Baum and J. E. Singer, 49–83. Hillsdale, NJ.: Lawrence Erlbaum Associates.

Stone, A. A., and S. Shiffman. 1994. Ecological Momentary Assessment (EMA) in behavioral medicine. *Annals of Behavioral Medicine* 16:199–202.

Stone, A. A., Shiffman, S. S., and M. W. deVries. 1999. Ecological Momentary Assessment. In *Well-being: The foundations of hedonic psychology,* ed. D. Kahneman, E. Diener, and N. Schwarz. New York: Russell Sage Foundation.

Szalai, A., P. Converse, P. Feldheim, et al. 1972. *The use of time.* The Hague, Neth.: Mouton.

Teuchmann, K., P. Totterdell, and S. K. Parker. 1999. Rushed, unhappy, and drained: An experience sampling study of relations between time pressure, perceived control, mood, and emotional exhaustion in a group of accountants. *Journal of Occupational Health Psychology* 4, no. 1: 37–54.

Toth-Fejel, G. E., G. F. Toth-Fejel, and C. A. Hedricks. 1998. Occupation-centered practice in hand rehabilitation using the Experience Sampling Method. *American Journal of Occupational Therapy* 52:381–85.

Totterdell, P., and S. Folkard. 1992. In situ repeated measures of affect and cognitive performance facilitated by the use of a hand-held computer. *Behavior Research Methods, Instruments, and Computers* 24:545–53.

Totterdell, P., E. Spelten, J. Barton, L. Smith, and S. Folkard. 1995. On-shift and daily variations in self-report and performance measures in rotating-shift and permanent night nurses. *Work and Stress* 9:187–97.

Totterdell, P., E. Spelten, L. Smith, J. Barton, and S. Folkard. 1995. Recovery from work shifts: How long does it take? *Journal of Applied Psychology.* 80:43–57.

Van Diest, R., and A. Appels. 1991. Vital exhaustion and depression: A conceptual study. *Journal of Psychosomatic Research* 35, no. 4–5: 535–44.

Van Eck, M. 1996. Stress, mood, and cortisol dynamics in daily life. Ph.D. diss., University of Maastricht.

Van Eck, M., H. Berkhof, N. Nicolson, and J. Sulon. 1996. The effects of perceived stress, traits, mood states, and stressful daily events on salivary cortisol. *Psychosomatic Medicine* 58:447–58.

Van Eck, M., N. A. Nicolson, and J. Berkhof. 1998. Effects of stressful daily events on mood states: Relationship to global perceived stress. *Journal of Personality and Social Psychology* 75:1572–85.

Vendrig, A. A., and R. Lousberg. 1997. Within-person relationships among pain intensity, mood, and physical activity in chronic pain: A naturalistic approach. *Pain* 73, no. 1: 71–76.

Voelkl, J. E., and M. A. Mathieu. 1993. Differences between depressed and non-depressed residents of nursing homes on measures of daily activity involvement and affect. *Therapeutic Recreation Journal* 27:144–55.

Waite, B. M., R. Claffey, and M. Hillbrand. 1998. Differences between volunteers and non-volunteers in a high-demand self-recording study. *Psychological Reports* 83:199–210.

Warr, P. 1999. Well-being and the workplace. In *Well-being: The foundations of hedonic psychology,* ed. D. Kahneman, E. Diener, and S. Schwarz. New York: Russell Sage Foundation.

Williams, K. J., J. Suls, G. M. Alliger, S. M. Learner, and C. K. Wan. 1991. Multiple role juggling and daily mood states in working mothers: An experience sampling study. *Journal of Applied Psychology* 76:664–74.

Williamson, A. M., C. G. Gower, and B. C. Clarke. 1994. Changing the hours of shift-work: A comparison of 8- and 12-hour shift rosters in a group of computer operators. *Ergonomics* 37:287–98.

Wilson, K. C. M., R. Hopkins, M. W. deVries, and J. R. M. Copeland. 1992. Research alliance and the limit of compliance: Experience sampling with the depressed elderly. In deVries 1992b.

CHAPTER 6

Estimating the Dollar Costs of Productivity Losses Due to Illness: An Application of O*NET

LANCE ANDERSON, SCOTT H. OPPLER,
AND ANDREW ROSE

INTRODUCTION

Even though a better understanding of the productivity costs of illness could lead corporations to make sounder health care decisions and governments to develop more effective health care policies, productivity research continues to be of limited use to stakeholders. Unfortunately, studies have tended to focus on the impact of a particular illness on a specific measure of productivity (e.g., absenteeism) and thus lack generalizability. For example, given only the finding that certain types of arthritis affect the productivity of word processors, it would be difficult to estimate the impact of arthritis on the productivity of truck drivers.

The research on work performance has not traditionally been linked with medical findings to address the costs of illness. However, the advent of the 'Occupational Information Network of the Department of Labor (DOL) called O*NET (Peterson et al. 1999; U.S. Department of Labor 2005) should make it much easier for researchers to estimate the impact of illnesses and their treatments on productivity. Containing information on the roughly 250 characteristics of all the occupations in the U.S. economy, O*NET has led to the construction of a model that links illness to productivity across all occupations. We begin this chapter by describing this new model. We then discuss the research tools (such as O*NET and the O*NET Content Model) needed to conduct research according to the model. Finally, we outline a sample research plan using the model and these research tools.

THE MODEL

Figure 6.1 shows a model for studying the relationship between illness and productivity. According to this model, the effects of a particular illness on productivity are mediated by its direct effects on the use of abilities, skills, and work styles that, in turn, have a direct influence on productivity. This model is based on the premise that individuals who are ill cannot perform their jobs as well as they can when they are not ill because they cannot use their abilities, skills, and work styles to the fullest extent.

The constructs depicted in the model include

- *Illness:* the degree of illness, including common and temporary illnesses (e.g., influenza) and more serious and permanent disabilities (e.g., multiple sclerosis).
- *Productivity:* the effectiveness and value of work behavior and its outcomes for an occupation or occupations. This definition is adapted from the Society for Industrial and Organizational Psychology (1987) definition of *performance*. Productivity can be measured through various means, including work samples, simulations, knowledge tests, self-report, and supervisor ratings of job performance.
- *Abilities:* relatively enduring attributes of an individual's capability for performing a particular range of different tasks (Fleishman, Costanza, and Marshall-Mies 1999). This is not to say that abilities are impervious to outside influences, only that in the absence of such influences they are generally considered to be stable constructs of individual differences. Examples of abilities are reaction time, selective attention, and static strength.
- *Skills:* capabilities to implement procedures for working with or applying knowledge within a central performance domain (Mumford, Peterson, and Childs 1999). Example skills include critical thinking and negotiation.
- *Work Styles:* personality characteristics that are either relevant to job performance or may facilitate development of relevant knowledge and skills (Borman, Kubisiak, and Schneider 1999). Examples of work-style constructs include initiative, cooperation, self-control, dependability, and innovation.

The arrow pointing from illness to the block representing abilities, skills, and work styles represents the hypothesized causal relationship between the dichotomous variable "whether the person has a particular illness" and the abilities, skills, and work styles of an individual. According to this hypothesis, which assumes that illness affects an individual's use of various abilities, skills, or work styles, individuals with an illness will demonstrate less use of these abilities, skills, and work styles (all else being equal).

The model also shows an arrow pointing from the block of abilities,

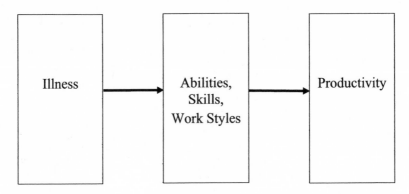

Figure 6.1. Model for examining the influence of illness on productivity as mediated by abilities, skills, and work styles

skills, and work styles to occupational productivity. This arrow represents the hypothesis that an individual's productivity in a particular occupation is affected by his or her use of various abilities, skills, and work styles.

The model posits that if an illness has a demonstrable effect on the use of one or more abilities, skills, or work styles that are, in turn, related to productivity in a given occupation, the productivity of individuals experiencing the illness will be affected. To the extent that the abilities, skills, or work styles affected by the illness are not associated with productivity in a particular occupation, it may not be reasonable to draw such a conclusion.

This model enables researchers to provide generalizable results because abilities, skills, and work styles that are important for one occupation are also likely to be important for other occupations. In a simpler model, in which there was only one arrow pointing directly from the illness to productivity, research could examine only the performance of persons in one particular occupation with and without one particular illness and thus would lack generalizability. With the alternative model proposed here, the effects of a particular illness on productivity in virtually any occupation could potentially be estimated, as long as researchers determine

- the impact of the illness on the use of a limited set of abilities, skills, or work styles and
- the relevance of those abilities, skills, or work styles to the given occupation.

Once the relationship between an illness and the use of various abilities, skills, and work styles is established, it can be applied to each occupation where those abilities, skills, and work styles are used.

Establishing the impact of illness on the use of abilities, skills, or work styles should be relatively straightforward. For some illnesses, extensive research has documented the abilities affected and the degree to which they are affected (e.g., Kay et al. 1997). For illnesses for which there is little research of this type, the relationship between the illness and the use of abilities, skills, or work styles could be established through clinical testing. For example, individuals affected and unaffected by the illness could be administered tests designed to reflect the use of certain abilities, skills, or work styles.

To some readers, establishing the impact of abilities, skills, and work styles on occupational performance may appear difficult. However, a great deal of research has already been done on this subject. For example, as Schmidt and Hunter (1998) and many others have pointed out, cognitive ability is important to the performance of all jobs, not just to those requiring a great deal of problem-solving, analysis, or decision-making. Furthermore, a database describing all occupations and the abilities, skills, and work styles associated with them has recently been developed by the DOL (Peterson et al. 1999; U.S. Department of Labor 2000). This database has thus made possible research using our new model.

TOOLS FOR CONDUCTING THE RESEARCH

Three tools are needed to conduct research according to our model:

- The Department of Labor's Occupational Information System (O*NET),
- Meta-analysis and validity generalization, and
- Utility analysis

We describe each tool below, highlighting how it can help to estimate the impact of illness on productivity.

O*NET

O*NET is an occupational information system developed by the DOL (Peterson et al. 1999; U.S. Department of Labor 2000) to replace the Dictionary of Occupational Titles (DOT), DOL's previous system for describing occupations. O*NET provides a system for collecting and reporting information on roughly 250 descriptors for all occupations in the U.S. economy. O*NET represents all of the positions in the economy with 1,122 occupations, where positions involving similar functions are clustered into the same occupation. The actual number of occupations in the database will change as U.S. jobs change over time. O*NET data is organized into a database, and the information is reported via software that can be downloaded from the Internet free of charge (U.S. Department of Labor 2000). O*NET is intended to have many different types of users, including career counselors, job seekers, policymakers, and researchers.

Since 1995, when research on the O*NET prototype began in earnest, the Social Security Administration (SSA) has been examining whether O*NET can be used effectively to assist in determining whether claimants for disability insurance are unable to work because of their disability. The conceptual framework for this chapter is based on the SSA's efforts to examine O*NET's usefulness in determining disability.

THE O*NET CONTENT MODEL

O*NET is built around a content model (see fig. 6.2) that organizes the descriptors or variables used to describe all occupations. The content model is based on three premises:

1. The characteristics of all occupations can be quantified via these descriptors,
2. All occupations can be viewed through multiple perspectives or windows, and
3. Occupational characteristics can be described and used at multiple levels of specificity.

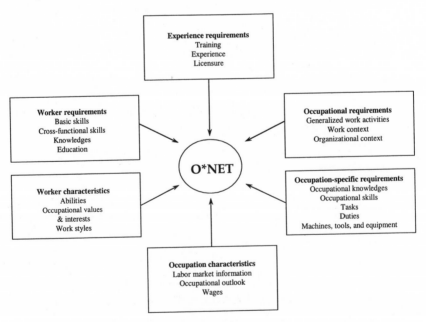

Figure 6.2. The O*NET content model

The O*NET content model places each of the descriptors into one of 19 domains that are, in turn, grouped into six broad areas. The domains each represent an individually complete and separate taxonomy for envisioning the world of work. The O*NET domains most relevant to linking illness to job performance include *abilities, skills, work styles, generalized work activities,* and *work context*

There are 52 descriptors in the *abilities* domain (see list, below). The ability descriptors and the descriptor measures for the abilities domain were drawn from Fleishman's ability requirements taxonomy and the Fleishman Job Analysis Survey, both of which are based on 40 years of research (Fleishman and Mumford 1988). The constructs in this domain include basic cognitive, psychomotor, physical, and sensory abilities, virtually all of which have been demonstrated to be relevant to many jobs. Titles for the descriptors in the *abilities* domain are provided in the list.

There are 46 descriptors in the *skills* domain (Mumford, Peterson, and Childs 1999). The skills domain in O*NET is an expansion of the research performed by the DOL Secretary's Commission on Achieving Necessary Skills (SCANS 1992). The skill descriptors are organized into categories including "basic skills," "problem solving skills," "social skills," "technological skills," "systems skills," and "resource management skills." Like abilities, skills may mediate the relationship between illness and job performance. However, skills by their nature are highly amenable to education, experience, and practice, so the influence of illness on skills may be more oblique and thus more difficult to demonstrate.

There are 17 descriptors in the *work styles* domain (Borman, Kubisiak, and Schneider 1999). The work-style descriptors are based on various efforts to identify occupationally relevant personality characteristics (Goldberg 1993; Guion 1992; Hogan and Hogan 1992; Hough 1992; Saville and Holdsworth 1990; Tupes and Christal 1992). All of the work styles are likely to be relevant to virtually any occupation.

The *generalized work activities* (GWAs) domain contains 42 descriptors, each of which pertains to an aggregation of similar job activities or behaviors that underlies the accomplishment of major work functions (Jeanneret et al. 1999). The GWA descriptors are based on reviews and analyses of previous task-analysis inventories, and some of them have been used previously on the Position Analysis Questionnaire (PAQ) (McCormick, Jeanneret, and Mecham 1972), a widely used tool for development of compensation and selection systems. They fit into four categories, including information input (e.g., "monitoring processes, materials, or surroundings"), mental processes (e.g., "processing information"), work output (e.g., "handling and moving objects"), and interacting with others (e.g., "resolving conflicts and negotiating with others").

Cognitive Abilities
  Verbal Abilities
    1. Oral comprehension
    2. Fluency of ideas
    3. Written comprehension
    4. Oral expression
    5. Written expression
  Idea generation and Reasoning
      Abilities
    6. Originality
    7. Problem sensitivity
    8. Deductive reasoning
    9. Inductive reasoning
    10. Information ordering
    11. Category flexibility
  Quantitative Abilities
    12. Mathematical reasoning
    13. Number facility
  Memory
    14. Memorization
  Perceptual Abilities
    15. Speed of closure
    16. Flexibility of closure
    17. Perceptual speed
  Spatial Abilities
    18. Spatial orientation
    19. Visualization
  Attentiveness
    20. Selective attention
    21. Time sharing
Psychomotor Abilities
  Fine Manipulative Abilities
    22. Arm-hand steadiness
    23. Manual dexterity
    24. Finger dexterity
  Control Movement Abilities
    25. Control precision

Control Movement Abilities (cont.)
    26. Multilimb coordination
    27. Response orientation
    28. Rate control
  Reaction Time and Speed Abilities
    29. Reaction time
    30. Wrist-finger speed
    31. Speed of limb movement
Physical abilities
  Physical-strength abilities
    32. Static strength
    33. Explosive strength
    34. Dynamic strength
    35. Trunk strength
  Endurance
    36. Stamina
  Flexibility, Balance, and Coordination
    37. Extent flexibility
    38. Dynamic flexibility
    39. Gross body coordination
    40. Gross body equilibrium
Sensory Abilities
  Visual Abilities
    41. Near vision
    42. Far vision
    43. Visual color disc
    44. Night vision
    45. Peripheral vision
    46. Depth perception
    47. Glare sensitivity
  Auditory abilities
    48. Hearing sensitivity
    49. Auditory attention
    50. Sound localization
    51. Speech recognition
    52. Speech clarity

Box 6.1. Descriptors in the abilities domain

The *work context* descriptors in O*NET are meant to describe conditions under which jobs are performed (Strong et al. 1999). These conditions, which are based on items found in the PAQ, pertain to the physical and sociological environment as well as to potential hazards and stressors, required body positions (e.g., sitting or standing), and type of work schedule.

The O*NET questionnaire used to gather occupational information asks respondents to make judgments about the relevance of a job descriptor for an occupation using multiple rating scales. Most of the O*NET job descriptors are rated on "level" and "importance" for each occupation. Level ratings, which reflect the complexity of the occupational demands, are made on an eight-point scale, including a scale point for "Not Relevant" and seven numeric ratings (1 = low to 7 = high). The numeric ratings are anchored at three points along the scale by concrete, commonly understood tasks. The importance scale assesses "How important is this activity to performance on this job?" (1 = Not Important to 5 = Extremely Important).

Currently, O*NET consists of two prototype databases—the incumbent database and the analyst database (Peterson et al. 1999). Data for the incumbent database have been gathered through a survey methodology, whereby representative samples of incumbents rated their occupations on hundreds of descriptors. Currently, the incumbent database contains incumbent ratings on 41 occupations. Since it will take some time to develop the full incumbent database, the DOL developed the analyst database to satisfy the immediate needs of some users. This database contains ratings made by trained job analysts on approximately 1,100 occupations.

The DOL compared the analyst and incumbent data (Peterson et al. 1999) and reached two important conclusions. First, the analyst and incumbent data are reliable. Both the incumbent and analyst ratings yielded high interrater agreement coefficients (Shrout and Fleiss 1979), with agreement coefficients generally being somewhat higher for the analysts' data. While there is some fluctuation across domains and rating scales, the median interrater agreement coefficients tend to be in the .70s and .80s for the incumbent data and in the .80s and .90s for the analyst data. Second, the analyst and incumbent data are in agreement with each other in terms of correlations, but there were some differences in mean ratings across the two databases. The correlations between analyst and incumbent ratings were .73 for level ratings of basic and cross-functional skills, .65 for knowledges, .70 for generalized work activities, .58 for work context, and .70 for level ratings of abilities. These correlations are nearly as high as the interrater agreement coefficients for the incumbent data. Even so, there are some mean differences across the ratings. For example, analysts tended to rate some of the descriptors lower than did incumbents. The differences may reflect distinct perspectives. Analysts have a cross-job perspective and take into account the importance or level of an ability or skill needed across jobs. Incumbents necessarily focus only on the job at hand. In our opinion, the substantial agreement between analyst and incumbent ratings is sufficient to warrant interim use of the analyst ratings until more incumbent ratings become available.

WAYS THAT O*NET COULD ASSIST WITH EXAMINING THE IMPACT
OF ILLNESS ON PRODUCTIVITY

O*NET can be used in many ways to improve the study of the impact of illness on productivity. The O*NET content model provides a consistent nomenclature for discussing occupational information. It also provides full taxonomies for various characteristics of work and workers. O*NET is also in agreement with the Standard Occupational Classification (U.S. Department of Commerce 2000) and thus provides an occupational taxonomy that should be useful for systematically exploring the impact of illnesses on different types of jobs, where the findings could be linked to other data including labor statistics.

O*NET's most important contribution to examining the impact of illness on productivity could be to provide data on the occupational relevance of a variety of standardized constructs that, in turn, may be associated (through extant research) with illnesses or treatments. Thus, O*NET data on each of the descriptors from the different domains described above could be applied in a research program to understand the relationship between illness or its treatment and job performance or productivity. In fact, each of these different types of descriptors could be used as a mediator variable in a model similar to that described earlier.

As noted previously, abilities are an important mediator of the illness–job performance relationship. Since illnesses (and treatments) affect the application of relevant abilities, they are bound to impact productivity in jobs where those abilities are relevant. In fact, just as an individual's capability to exhibit the appropriate work styles or to perform relevant GWAs is affected by illness (or its treatment), so, too, is job performance or productivity. Finally, since illnesses (or treatments) affect an individual's ability to tolerate a particular required work context (e.g., arthritis may prevent an individual from standing all day), they also affect job performance and productivity.

For the research plan provided here, we have chosen to focus on the abilities domain, because numerous studies have been conducted demonstrating the relationship between abilities and illnesses (Kay et al. 1997), and a large number of studies have established the relationship between abilities and job performance (Schmidt and Hunter 1998). In theory, if these two research literatures were linked, the impact of illness on productivity in any job could be estimated. Of course, a single chapter could not review a research plan including all of the potentially relevant mediator variables.

Future research should consider the merits of using skill, work-style, GWA, and work-context variables to link illness to productivity, since these variables have a demonstrable relationship to job performance. For example, GWAs and work-context variables by nature are more easily observed, and their link to job performance is therefore less tenuous than the one between abilities and performance. In the case of work styles, some research (e.g., Anderson, Brown, and Brantley 1999) suggests that many of these constructs are relevant to all work. Thus, if an illness (or treatment) affects an individual's ability to demonstrate these work styles, it also affects her or his productivity, regardless of the job. However, to use any of these constructs in a research program to link illness to productivity, they must be linked to illness, and we suspect that research in that area is less common than that linking illness to the use of abilities.

In the research plan presented here, we suggest using O*NET to obtain data on the occupational relevance of the abilities for each occupation. We also suggest using data linked to O*NET, including salary data from the Bureau of Labor Statistics databases.

Meta-Analysis and Validity Generalization

As noted above, a vast research literature examines the relationship between ability tests and performance in various jobs. Most scientifically developed, commercially available selection tests have been linked to performance in some job (Murphy, Impara, and Plake 1999). Usually this link is demonstrated through a single sample criterion-related validity study, in which the test scores of individuals are correlated with some measure of their job performance to provide an index of the validity of the test, commonly called the validity coefficient. As these studies are typically limited to one job and one organization, their results alone are of limited use to understanding the relationship between ability and performance in other jobs. In addition, often these criterion-related validity studies have inadequate sample sizes (Schmidt, Hunter, and Urry 1976) and thus give misleading results. Narrative reviews of these studies may provide erroneous findings because they do not account for various statistical artifacts such as sample-size variation, measurement error, and range restriction (Hunter, Schmidt, and Jackson 1982). To summarize these findings and allow for generalization to a wider set of organizations or jobs, the results must be cumulated in a manner that accounts for these statistical artifacts.

Meta-analysis (Hunter and Schmidt 1990) is a technique for summarizing research findings whereby study characteristics are coded and formulas are applied to account for statistical artifacts in the findings. The technique allows for estimation of the mean, variance, and confidence intervals surrounding correlation coefficients or effect sizes. While the technique can be applied to various types of research findings, a specific set of procedures can be applied when examining validity coefficients describing the relation between ability test performance and job performance. This technique is called validity generalization (Hunter, Schmidt, and Jackson 1982). The procedures generally involve

- Gathering research reports in which a test of an ability is related to job performance in one or more jobs;
- Determining, for each study, the validity coefficient(s), the sample size, and the degree of measurement error and range restriction in the predictor and the criterion;
- Coding study characteristics that may serve to moderate the relationship between job performance and test performance (e.g., the type of job involved, the industry, or the study design);
- Correcting the validity coefficient(s) for predictor and criterion measurement error and range restriction;
- Estimating the mean correlation of all of the validity coefficients weighted by study sample size;
- Estimating the variance in the validity coefficients attributable to all statistical artifacts; and
- Estimating the credibility intervals around the mean corrected validity coefficient.

The result of implementing this set of procedures would be to create a matrix of mean corrected validity coefficients bounded by credibility intervals, where each mean corrected validity coefficient would represent the relationship between an ability and the performance of a job. Production of this matrix is of course not feasible at this point, because there are not studies on every job for every ability. However, there are studies on large groups of jobs for some abilities. For example, Hunter and Hunter (1984) conducted a large meta-analysis and found that cognitive ability, psychomotor ability, and perceptual ability are all related to occupational performance in large families of jobs.

In our research plan described below, we suggest using meta-analysis and validity generalization numerous times. In particular, these techniques should be considered to examine or summarize the relationship between an illness and various abilities, or between abilities and performance in a variety of jobs.

Utility Analysis

Utility analysis is a method used by researchers to translate the effects of interventions into utility in terms of dollars (Brogden 1946). Utility analysis usually focuses on estimating the marginal utility of an intervention, or the average per person gain in utility in dollars associated with the intervention (e.g. Hunter and Schmidt 1982). Various formulas have been proposed for obtaining this estimate, but most of the formulas in use today are based on the following simple formula:

Marginal utility (or cost) of the intervention per person per year
$= (\Delta Y')(SD_y)$

Where

$\Delta Y'$ = predicted change in occupational performance associated with the intervention (expressed in terms of standard deviation units).
SD_y = the standard deviation of occupational performance in dollars for the population prior to the intervention.

The statistic $\Delta Y'$ is usually estimated using the ability test scores relevant to the intervention and a regression-based formula for combining these test scores to predict occupational performance. To estimate SD_y, Hunter and Schmidt (1982) suggest using 40% of the mean salary. In various research studies, this method has been shown to provide a conservative, yet relatively accurate, measure of the true standard deviation in performance.

In our research plan, we suggest using utility analysis to estimate the dollar costs associated with the predicted decrements in occupational performance due to illness. In doing so, we supplement the above utility analysis formula to take into account such factors as the number of persons in each occupation, the prevalence of the illness, and the number of workdays individuals are affected by the illness. If supporting research is conducted, the researcher should be able to estimate these costs for each occupation in O*NET.

RESEARCH PLAN FOR EXAMINING EFFECTS AS MEDIATED BY ABILITIES

We present our research plan for estimating the dollar impact of a particular illness on the performance of all jobs in the U.S. economy, as mediated by individuals' capacity to use abilities, in order to illustrate how to perform research using the model described earlier in the chapter. Other models and approaches could certainly be used. The steps in this plan include

- determining the abilities to examine
- estimating the effect of the illness on the use of the abilities
- obtaining estimates of the intercorrelation of the abilities measures
- obtaining estimates of validity coefficients
- adjusting correlation estimates for measurement error
- developing and applying equations to predict performance decrements for each occupation
- applying utility analysis
- calculating upper and lower bound estimates

The plan is presented below in a "barebones" outline to quickly give the reader a brief overview of how we envision conducting the research. This outline leaves room for the skilled researcher to add features such as the use of multiple and different measures of the same construct, reliability checks, and identification of potential moderators of various relationships. Our research plan outline assumes that when possible, researchers will employ basic research-design principles (e.g., random sampling, random assignment, and use of reliable measures).

Determine the Abilities to Examine

To determine which abilities to examine, we recommend reviewing the literature on the illness. For many illnesses, thousands of studies have been conducted that show the impact of the illness on abilities. While this impact may not be consistent across all individuals, some generalizations may be possible. In many cases, the definition of the illness or disorder will list the abilities that are affected. To ensure that important abilities are not missed, we recommend reviewing Fleishman's taxonomy of abilities as provided in O*NET (Fleishman, Costanza, and Marshall-Mies 1999). This taxonomy is arranged hierarchically, with varying levels of specificity at each level of the hierarchy. Therefore, broad abilities (e.g., cognitive ability) or specific abilities (e.g., selective attention) could be reviewed using it. Experts on the illness could review the taxonomy and identify those abilities that would likely be affected by the illness. Researchers should carefully consider those abilities that have already been linked to performance in a variety of jobs, because if these abilities are affected, the illness is likely to have a meaningful impact on productivity across the economy.

Estimate the Effect of the Illness on the Use of the Abilities

After the abilities are identified, the effect of the illness on those abilities must be quantified. In particular, the ability use of persons with the illness must be compared with the ability use of persons without the illness. This difference in the use of each ability can then be converted to an effect size. The effect size could be calculated based on findings from extant research or original research.

As discussed earlier, it is likely that studies examining the relationship between the illness and ability use already exist. If there are multiple studies, meta-analytic techniques (Hunter and Schmidt 1990) can be applied to cumulate the findings and adjust them for statistical artifacts. Such meta-analyses may already have been conducted for some illnesses.

For some illnesses, the impact on abilities may be difficult to establish through previous research. In these cases, original research may have to be performed, where persons with and without the illness are administered tests measuring abilities of interest. Such original research will require careful research design that addresses the issues associated with studying the particular illness. A description of such a research design is beyond the scope of this chapter. At a minimum, however, researchers should take care to select measures that are reliable and valid indicators of the abilities. Fleishman and Reilly (1992) provide examples of measures of each ability in the taxonomy.

Regardless of whether extant or original research is used to establish the link between the illness and ability use, the effect size (d) (Cohen 1992) can be calculated to express the effect in terms of standard deviation units. To calculate d, the researcher would subtract the mean test score for persons without the illness (asymptomatic condition) from the mean test score for persons with the illness (symptomatic condition) and divide the difference by the standard deviation for the asymptomatic condition. This effect size can then be used in calculations explained below.

Obtain Estimates of the Intercorrelation of the Abilities Measures

The ability measures will likely correlate with one another. This intercorrelation must be considered when attempting to gauge the overall impact of an illness on occupational performance. Failure to do so would lead to an overemphasis on correlated measures. The methods for considering these intercorrelations involve use of multiple regression techniques that we discuss below. Before that, however, it is important to obtain these intercorrelations. Perhaps the best way to do it is to administer the ability test measures to a representative and reasonably large sample of individuals without the illness and use the resulting data to calculate the correlations among the measures.

Obtain Estimates of Validity Coefficients

The notion here is to characterize, in the form of correlation, the relationship between individuals' capacity to use each ability and their performance in each occupation in the economy. There are numerous ways that these correlations or validity coefficients could be estimated. Here is a series of steps describing one approach.

- For each ability of interest, review the literature to identify previously conducted meta-analyses where the correlation between measures of the ability and job performance in one or more jobs or types of jobs is estimated.
- If no meta-analyses exist, or if the existing ones are incomplete, conduct a literature review and meta-analysis of existing empirical criterion validation studies where measures of the ability were correlated with measures of job performance. Cumulate the findings and correct them for sampling error, range restriction, and measurement error.
- As part of each meta-analysis, examine whether occupation type affects the size of the corrected validity coefficients. When possible and necessary, establish different corrected validity coefficients for each occupation or cluster of occupations. This may not be necessary in many cases because the magnitude of the validity coefficient may not vary appreciably across occupations. At a minimum, however, this step should allow the researcher to establish a range of validity coefficients if there are well-documented empirical validation studies.
- Match each O*NET occupation, or cluster of O*NET occupations, to the results of the meta-analyses. This could be done by examining the mean ratings provided by O*NET for each worker characteristic.
- For O*NET occupations that cannot be matched to meta-analytic findings, obtain estimates of the validity coefficients from experts (Hirsh, Schmidt, and Hunter 1986). Provide experts with (1) a description of the ability, (2) a description of instruments measuring that ability in individuals, and (3) information from O*NET on each occupation including mean ratings specific to each relevant ability. Have the experts estimate the validity coefficient for each ability and occupation pairing. To save time and money in obtaining these estimates, you could ask the experts to provide these estimates for approximately 300 representative occupations rather than all 1,122 O*NET occupations. . The policies used by the experts could be captured analytically, and then these policies could be applied to the remainder of the occupations. The method for doing this is explained briefly in a later step.

The output of these steps would be a series of estimated mean validity coefficients describing the relationship between ability measures and job performance for a sample of occupations in O*NET.

Adjust Correlation Estimates for Measurement Error

In previous steps in the research plan, we discussed obtaining various correlation coefficients. Using the techniques described above, virtually all of these correlation coefficients would be estimated among variables that are measured imperfectly and would thus be underestimates of the true relationship between the variables. Use of these biased correlations in later calculations would bias the results.

To obtain a more accurate estimate of the true correlations, we suggest correcting the estimates for "attenuation" (Spearman 1904). Spearman's formula for correction for measurement error should be applied using the reliability statistics available for each of the measures to estimate the amount of the measurement error. When reliability statistics are not available, we suggest using conservative estimates of the amount of error with which the variables were measured. These analyses will provide a revised estimate for each correlation, assuming that the variables are measured perfectly.

Develop and Apply Equations to Predict Performance Decrements for Each Occupation

The purpose of this step is to conduct data analyses in order to obtain estimates of occupational performance decrements. In particular, this step includes procedures to

- Develop predicted correlation estimates for remaining O*NET occupations,
- Develop equations for predicting performance in each of the 1,122 O*NET occupations given the ability test scores, and
- Insert the appropriate values in these equations to obtain a predicted performance score for each effect associated with the burden of illness.

Details of these data analyses are provided below.

DEVELOP PREDICTED CORRELATION ESTIMATES FOR REMAINING O*NET OCCUPATIONS

Given the corrected correlation estimates for the representative sample of 300 occupations, we suggest developing predicted estimates for the correlation between each of the clinical trials tests and occupational performance for the remaining 822 occupations not included in the expert judgment task. To do this, we suggest using a policy-capturing, or lens-model, approach (Brunswik 1952, 1956, 1955). Through the policy-capturing approach, the policy of each expert for estimating the correlation coefficient for a given test can be "captured" by conducting a multiple regression and developing a multiple-regression equation. The criterion or dependent variable for each of these regressions would then be the corrected estimated correlation between the test and occupational performance. The independent variables (also called predictors or "cues") would be the ability ratings provided for each of the 300 occupations in the O*NET database. This procedure would require computing $k \times j$ regressions—one for each of the k ability measures for each of the j experts.

Then, for each of the experts, we suggest developing predicted correlations for each test for each of the other 822 occupations, by taking the regression equation for each test and inserting the relevant ability ratings from the O*NET database for that occupation. Next, take the mean of the predicted correlations across all of the experts for each test for each of the 822 occupations. Completion of this procedure will provide estimates or predicted estimates of the validity coefficients for each of the ability measures relative to each occupation in O*NET.

DEVELOP EQUATIONS FOR PREDICTING PERFORMANCE DECREMENTS FOR EACH OCCUPATION

Given the corrected correlations calculated earlier, we suggest developing for each of the 1,122 occupations an equation for optimally combining the clinical-trial test scores to predict occupational performance. By inserting the effect sizes calculated earlier, one can use these equations to estimate performance decrements associated with the burdens of illness. These equations can be developed by computing a multiple-regression equation for each occupation, where the criterion or dependent variable in each multiple regression is occupational performance and the independent variables or predictors are the ability measures.

There are many advantages to using these multivariate regression equations to relate the ability test scores to occupational performance. The multiple correlations associated with the regression should provide an indication of the overall impact of the abilities on occupational performance after accounting for any shared effects or covariation among the ability tests. Therefore, with knowledge of the impact of the illness on these abilities, one can better gauge the impact of the illness on occupational performance. The regression equations also provide the optimum combination of ability test scores needed to predict performance in each occupation. Finally, development of separate equations for each occupation should allow for interactions in the relevance of the abilities for different occupations.

To derive standardized regression weights needed for each equation that will be used to predict performance in each occupation, compute a multiple regression using a correlation matrix assembled from the following corrected correlations calculated in a previous step:

- The $k \times k$ matrix of ability test performance correlations, where k is the total number of ability measures; and
- The $k \times 1$ matrix of correlations between the k ability tests and performance in the occupation.

Following this procedure, there will be a different correlation matrix for each of the 1,122 O*NET occupations and hence a different regression equation for predicting performance decrements for each of the occupations.

ESTIMATE THE IMPACT OF THE BURDENS OF DISEASE OR
TREATMENT ON PERFORMANCE OF EACH OCCUPATION

The intention of this activity is to estimate the impact of the burden of illness for each occupation in terms of a standardized predicted job-performance score. This should be done by inserting the appropriate d statistics (calculated earlier) into the equations for each occupation. For example, to estimate the burden of the illness on the performance of registered nurses, one would use an equation developed specifically for that occupation. This equation can be represented as

$$\Delta Y_{(Registered\ Nurse,\ illness)}' = B_{(Registered\ Nurse,1)} d_{(illness,1)} + B_{(Registered\ Nurse,2)} d_{(illness,2)} \\ + \ldots B_{(Registered\ Nurse,11)} d_{(illness,11)}$$

Where

$\Delta Y_{(Registered\ Nurse,\ illness)}'$ = predicted decrement in occupational performance due to the illness for the occupation Registered Nurse.

$B_{(Registered\ Nurse,1)}$ = standardized regression weight associated with ability test number 1 for the occupation Registered Nurse. Each equation will have a standardized regression weight for each of the k ability tests.

$d_{(illness,1)}$ = effect size for illness on ability test number 1. These effect sizes will have been calculated in an earlier step. Each equation should have places to insert effect sizes for each of the k ability tests.

Apply Utility Analysis

In this step, the researcher should take the predicted decrements in occupational performance as estimated above, and apply utility analysis to estimate the dollar impact of those decrements. For each occupation or set of occupations, an adaptation of the utility analysis formula discussed earlier could be used. The formula can be represented as

$$Cost_{illness} = (\Delta Y_{illness})(SD_y)(N)(Prevalence)(Workdays\ Affected/250)$$

Where

> $Cost_{illness}$ = Economy-wide annual dollar costs of productivity losses due to illness for the occupation(s) of concern;
> $\Delta Y_{illness}$ = Occupational performance decrement due to illness (listed in standard deviation units);
> SD_y = Standard deviation of performance in dollars for the occupation(s) of concern, estimated as 40% of the mean salary for the occupation (Schmidt, Hunter, and Pearlman, 1982);
> N = Number of workers in the occupation(s);
> *Prevalence* = Percentage of workers affected by the illness;
> *Workdays affected* = For each worker affected, the average number of days affected by the illness in a given year.

Using this formula, the annual cost of the burden of the illness can be calculated for each occupation. By summing the results across occupations, the impact on the entire economy can be estimated.

Calculate Upper and Lower Bound Estimates

The estimation technique described above will not provide error-free estimates. One potential source of error is the experts' estimation of various validity coefficients. For instance, some experts may provide underestimates of the true values, while others may provide overestimates. To obtain an indication of the potential error in the estimates, we suggest developing upper and lower bound estimates of the dollar costs associated with productivity losses. To do this, calculate a credibility interval around each of the mean estimated correlations using procedures described in Hunter and Schmidt 1990. These credibility intervals will provide an upper and lower bound estimate of the correlations. The research should carry these upper and lower bound correlation estimates through all of the calculations to eventually provide upper and lower bound estimates of the dollar costs of productivity losses due to illness or its treatments. These upper and lower bound estimates should be of help to decision-makers, policymakers, and consumers who may eventually be reviewing the findings of this study.

CONCLUSION

Productivity research has often been of limited use to stakeholders because it typically lacks generalizability. In this chapter we describe a model to estimate the productivity implications of an illness for each and every occupation in the economy, a model that involves the use of various research tools including clinical trials, meta-analysis, expert judgment, utility analysis, and the DOL's O*NET.

The model suggests that the effects of an illness on productivity are mediated by the effects on the use of one or more abilities, skills, and work styles. This model is based on the premise that an individual burdened by an illness cannot perform his or her job up to par because abilities, skills, or work styles have been impaired.

The model requires that researchers determine

- The relationship between the burden of the illness and the use of a limited set of abilities, skills, and work styles and
- The relevance of those abilities, skills, and work styles to each occupation.

The first set of relationships should be available through extant research on the impact of different illnesses. To establish the second set of relationships, we suggest taking a series of research steps that involve obtaining expert judgments on the correlation between performance in each occupation and in each of various ability, skill, or work-style measures, and then using these correlations to form separate regression equations for predicting performance in each of the occupations in the economy. These numbers can then be converted to dollar costs by applying classical utility analysis. Armed with accurate data about productivity costs, both businesses and governments can make more informed decisions about health care practices and policies.

REFERENCES

Anderson, L. A., J. L. Brown, and L. B. Brantley. 1999. *Identification of general requirements of work*. Washington, DC: American Institutes for Research.

Borman, W. C., U. C. Kubisiak, and R. J. Schneider. 1999. Work styles. In Peterson et al. 1999, 213–26.

Brogden, H. E. 1946. On the interpretation of the correlation coefficient as a measure of predictive efficiency. *Journal of Educational Psychology* 37:65–76.

Brunswik, E. 1952. *The conceptual framework of psychology.*. Chicago: University of Chicago Press.

———. 1955. Representative design and probabilistic theory in a functional psychology. *Psychological Review* 62:193–217.

———. 1956. *Perception and the representative design of experiments*. Berkeley: University of California Press.

Cohen, J. 1992. *Statistical power analysis for the behavioral sciences*. Rev. ed. New York: Academic Press.

Fleishman, E. A., D. Costanza, and J. Marshall-Mies. 1999. Abilities. In Peterson et al. 1999, 175–96.

Fleishman, E. A., and M. D. Mumford. 1988. Ability requirement scales. In *Job analysis handbook for business, industry, and government*, ed. S. Gael, 2:917–35. New York: John Wiley.

Fleishman, E. A., and M. E. Reilly. 1992. *Handbook of human abilities: Definitions, measurements, and job task requirements*. Palo Alto, CA: Consulting Psychologists Press.

Goldberg, L. R. 1993. The structure of phenotypic personality traits. *American Psychologist* 48:26–34.

Guion, R. M. 1992. Matching position requirements and personality: Industrial and organizational psychology. Symposium conducted at the 7th annual meeting of the Society for Industrial and Organizational Psychology, Montreal, Canada.

Hirsh, H. R., F. L. Schmidt, and J. E. Hunter. 1986. Estimation of employment test validities by less experienced judges. *Personnel Psychology* 39:337–44.

Hogan, R., and J. Hogan. 1992. *Manual for the Hogan Personality Inventory*. Tulsa, OK: Hogan Assessment Systems.

Hough, L. M. 1992. The "big five" personality variables—construct confusion: Description versus prediction. *Human Performance* 5:139–55.

Hunter, J. E., and R. F. Hunter. 1984. Validity and utility of alternative predictors of job performance. *Psychological Bulletin* 96:72–98.

Hunter, J. E., and F. L. Schmidt. 1982. Quantifying the effects of psychological interventions on employee job performance and work force productivity. *American Psychologist* 38:473–78.

———. 1990. *Meta-analysis: Correcting error and bias in research findings*. Beverly Hills, CA: Sage Publications.

Hunter, J. E., F. L. Schmidt, and G. B. Jackson. 1982. *Meta-analysis: Cumulating research findings across studies*. Beverly Hills, CA: Sage Publications.

Jeanneret, P. R., W. C. Borman, U. C. Kubisiak, and M. A. Hanson. 1999. Generalized work activities. In Peterson et al. 1999, 105–26.

Kay, G. G., B. Berman, S. H. Mockoviak, C. E. Morris, D. Reeves, V. Starbuck, E. Sukenik, and A. G. Harris. 1997. Initial and steady-state effects of diphenhydramine and loratadine on sedation, cognition, mood, and psychomotor performance. *Archives of Internal Medicine* 157:2350–56.

McCormick, E. J., P. R. Jeanneret, and R. C. Mecham. 1972. A study of job characteristics and job dimensions as based on the Position Analysis Questionnaire. *Journal of Applied Psychology Monograph* 56:346–68.

Mumford, M. D., N. G. Peterson, and R. A. Childs. 1999. Basic and cross-functional skills. In Peterson et al. 1999.

Murphy, L., J. Impara, and B. Plake. 1999. *Test in print V: An index to tests, test reviews, and the literature on specific tests.* Lincoln, NE: Buros Institute.

Peterson, N. G., M. D. Mumford, W. C. Borman, P. R. Jeanneret, and E. A. Fleishman, eds. 1999. *O*Net: An occupational information network.* Washington, DC: American Psychological Association.

Saville, P., and R. Holdsworth. 1990. *Occupational personality questionnaire manual.* Surrey, U.K.: Saville and Holdsworth.

SCANS. 1992. *Learning a living: A blueprint for high performance.* Washington, DC: U.S. Department of Labor.

Schmidt, F. L., and J. E. Hunter. 1998. The validity and utility of selection methods in personnel psychology: Practical and theoretical implications of 85 years of research findings. *Psychological Bulletin* 124:262–74.

Schmidt, F. L., J. E. Hunter, and K. Pearlman. 1982. Assessing the economic impact of personnel programs on workforce productivity. *Personnel Psychology* 35:333–47.

Schmidt, F. L., J. E. Hunter, and V. W. Urry. 1976. Statistical power in criterion-related validation studies. *Journal of Applied Psychology* 61:473–85.

Shrout, P. E., and J. L. Fleiss. 1979. Intraclass correlations: Uses in assessing rater reliability. *Psychological Bulletin* 86:420–28.

Society for Industrial and Organizational Psychology. 1987. *Principles for the validation and use of personnel selection procedures.* 3rd ed. College Park, MD: Society for Industrial and Organizational Psychology.

Spearman, C. 1904. General intelligence objectively determined and measured. *American Journal of Psychology* 15:201–93.

Strong, M. H., P. R. Jeanneret, M. McPhail, B. R. Blakely, and E. L. D'Egidio. 1999. Work context: Taxonomy and measurement of the work environment. In Peterson et al. 1999.

Tupes, E. C., and R. E. Christal. 1992. Recurrent personality factors based on trait ratings. *Journal of Personality* 60:225–51.

U.S. Department of Commerce. 2000. *Standard Occupational Classification system.* http://www.bls.gov/soc/home.htm.

U.S. Department of Labor. 2005. O*NET OnLine. http://online.onetcenter.org.

CHAPTER 7

Labor-Market Consequences of Health Impairments

THOMAS DELEIRE AND WILLARD G. MANNING

INTRODUCTION

As a growing body of research now shows, health impairments increase absenteeism, lower labor-force participation, and reduce on-the-job productivity, causing economic losses for workers, companies, and society at large. Given the prevalence of both chronic and acute illnesses among workers, policymakers have shown considerable interest in theoretical models that provide a framework for estimating the social cost of health impairments from injuries or illnesses. This calculus is, in turn, a necessary step in conducting cost-effectiveness analyses of potential health interventions from a societal perspective. In this chapter we present a set of microeconomic models that take into consideration the impact of illness on labor-market behavior. Our approach suggests that several common measures of labor-market impact lead to a biased assessment of the costs of illness and health impairment. In fact, if the illness is prevalent or the impact of health on productivity is large, then the effects on labor-market equilibriums are likely to be substantial. In other words, it appears that at present, policy analysts may be underestimating the social costs of illness.

We begin by defining productivity and health and move on to a presentation of several economic models of the indirect (labor-market) costs of worker injuries, progressing from a simple model to more complex scenarios. We then provide a brief overview of both the empirical economics literature on the labor-market effects of health impairments and the cost-of-illness (COI) literature. Although the COI studies include estimates of the labor-market consequences of health impairments, they fail to factor in all the relevant labor-market behavior. What may be true at the level of the individual firm may not be true in the aggregate. In our conclusion we summarize the implications of our key findings for health care policy.

ECONOMIC APPROACHES TO IDENTIFYING THE LABOR-MARKET EFFECTS OF HEALTH IMPAIRMENTS

In this section we employ several economic models to examine the effect of health impairments on labor-market outcomes. First, we define what we mean by productivity and health impairments. Second, we present a simple model of a firm's labor demand, from which we can derive the majority of our results relating the effects of a health impairment on wages and employment. Third, we incorporate health-related effects on the labor supply of workers into our model.[1] In each of these models, we show how the labor-market effects are related to the productivity effects and determine the employer and social costs of health impairments or illnesses and, by extension, of treatment as well.

Defining Productivity and Health

There are a number of definitions of productivity or changes in productivity in health-service research and in the applied-economics literatures. The measures in the health service literature include changes in labor-force status, especially job loss or return to work, hours or weeks worked, and (less often) physical productivity when working and time on-task. In contrast, the economics literature tends to equate productivity with output per worker while the worker is on the job, typically output per hour worked. Because of the lack of agreement, we consider both types of measures.

Rather than addressing each type of productivity separately, we examine the overall effect of health impairments on labor-market behavior. Thus, we consider *productivity* quite broadly as anything affecting labor-market behavior by firms and workers, although we use it in the specific sense of productivity on the job. In order to do the calculations needed for cost-benefit, cost-effectiveness, and cost-of-illness analyses, it is essential to look at production and employee, employer, and market-level behavior.

In the following sections, we consider two ways in which a health im-

---

1. In this paper we do not allow either firms or workers to adjust to the risk of illnesses. Thus, we do not deal with the implications of formal and informal employer-provided sick leave and disability insurance, compensating wage differentials, or moral hazard.

pairment affects productivity. In the first scenario, the health impairment reduces the worker's marginal product while he or she is on the job, and the
firm can distinguish health-impaired workers from healthy workers. In the
second scenario, the health impairment increases the absenteeism rate or reduces labor-force participation but does not reduce on-the-job productivity
per se. In this case, the firm cannot distinguish between healthy and health-
impaired workers. While the distinction between marginal product on the
job and absenteeism has little impact on the models we discuss below, it does
have consequences both for policy choices and for the practical issue of data
collection and analysis.[2]

A Simple Model of Productivity and Labor Demand

Our starting point is the standard neoclassical model of the labor-leisure
choice by consumers/workers and the production and input choices by a perfectly competitive, profit-maximizing firm.[3] In this model, an individual firm
will hire or buy inputs up to the point where the value of the incremental production of the last unit of that input (output price times the marginal product of that unit) just equals the input's price. Thus, for a worker, the output
price times the incremental (or marginal product) of another unit of labor
just equals her or his wage. To cite an example, if a firm hires workers at $10
an hour, the first few workers hired will have a higher marginal product of
labor, one that is likely to amount to more than the $10-per-hour wage. As the
firm continues to hire workers, the new hirees will add less and less to total
productivity. Thus, implicit in this analysis is the assumption that the marginal product of labor is positive but declining. In other words, the more
workers added to the firm's labor force, the lower the marginal product of

2. The following two scenarios are equivalent in terms of their economic effect on levels of employment. First, employees are covered at a wage rate w^{**}, $100x\%$ are too sick to
work on any given date, and the firm will hire workers as long as their marginal revenue
product—$p(1 - x)MPL$—equals the wage rate w^{**}. Second, there is no sick leave, the market wage rate is $w^{**}/(1 - x)$, and firms hire until the marginal product of an additional
worker equals the wage paid to workers while on the job.

3. We can relax the assumption that firms are perfectly competitive in output markets
and price-takers in input markets without changing the qualitative pattern described below.
Relaxing such assumptions may have important quantitative impacts for some applications.

We use a one-period model for ease of exposition. For many health impairments from
injury or illness, the consequences for labor-market behavior can span several periods.
Some health interventions also have costs and benefits that span several periods. In such
cases, the analysis should be extended to include these intermediate-to-longer-term effects.

labor of each new worker. A profit-making firm will not hire labor that cannot produce enough to pay its wage cost. For firms to earn a profit or break even after paying for all of the inputs, any increases in input costs will reduce the number of firms in the market. Higher input costs increase the average cost of doing business. Unless the price in the output market rises, some firms will have average costs above prices, earn negative profits, and go out of business. Thus, the number of firms in the market is also a declining function of the prevailing wage rate and other input unit costs for the factors of production (for example, capital).

By definition, the firm's demand curve for labor is the marginal product of labor multiplied by price as a function of the wage rate. The overall demand for labor in the labor market is simply the sum of the quantities of labor demanded by all of the firms (which are operating in the market at those input and output prices) as a function of the market wage rate. These assumptions imply that the overall (or labor-market-level) demand curve for labor is downward sloping in the wage rate, and that all firms will continue to employ workers so long as the competitive wage is less than or equal to price (of the product of the firm) times the marginal product of the last worker hired.[4]

To keep matters simple, we will ignore the role of sales, excise, and profit taxes on firms, of income and wage taxes, and of the differential tax treatment of fringe benefits. This analysis assumes that a typical worker who experiences the onset of a health impairment or illness will become less productive while he is working at his current occupation; that is, while he is physically on the job. We also assume that the health-related productivity loss can be measured for a typical worker and that this loss is $100x\%$ of what would have been produced without the decrease in health status where $0 < x < 1$ where x refers to the proportional reduction in productivity due to a health impairment. When ill, the worker produces only $(1 - x)$ 100% of what she or he would have produced in good health. For example, say an executive secretary has a sinus infection that reduces her on-the-job productivity by $x = 0.2$. On a normal eight-hour day, she completes 40 letters; on health-impaired days, she produces only 32 letters $[(1 - .2) \times 40]$. For simplicity, we will also assume that the onset of the health impairment does not affect the worker in terms of utility (i.e., overall well-being) or any factor that would influence his or her labor supply; we will relax this assumption in the section entitled "Models for Health Impairments and Labor Supply."

---

4. The area under the demand curve gives the value of the total productivity of labor up to a specific level of labor because it is the marginal product of labor multiplied by price, holding all other factors constant.

EFFECT ON WAGES AND EMPLOYMENT

A decline in worker productivity will cause the firm's and the market's labor-demand curve to shift left in figure 7.1. Thus, at any given market wage rate, the firm will demand fewer hours of work. Consider the case where the firm can distinguish health-impaired workers from nonimpaired workers and where a health impairment affects marginal product on the job. The health impairment reduces the marginal product of labor from MP_L to $(1 - x) MP_L$, where MP_L is a shorthand for the marginal product of labor, holding all other factors of production constant. That is, at a given wage, w, firms will be less willing to employ workers who are impaired than they would had the workers not been impaired at all. The effect of a decline in productivity on labor demand at the market level is displayed in figure 7.1. L_1^D represents the firm's demand for nonimpaired workers and L_2^D represents the firm's demand for impaired workers.

Because labor supply is upward sloping, both wages and employment

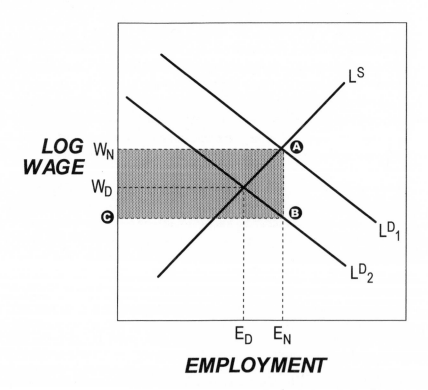

Figure 7.1. The effect of health impairments on labor demand

will fall. Wages fall in response to the decline in labor demand because health-impaired workers produce less at work. Further, some firms may no longer be able to break even or earn profits if they have to pay for L hours of labor but receive only $(1 - x)$ L hours of effort. In addition, some workers will voluntarily leave the firm and will seek employment elsewhere (or will leave the labor force entirely) in response to falling wages. Thus, under the new equilibrium, the firms will employ E_D workers with a health impairment or disability, compared to E_N—the employment level had these workers remained healthy. Health-impaired workers will receive a wage w_D, compared to w_N, the wage these workers would have received had they remained healthy.

In figure 7.1, the decline in productivity associated with illness and health impairment is measured as the vertical difference between the demand curves for disabled workers and for nondisabled workers, in this case: $p (1 - x) MP_L$.[5] On the graph, this distance is measured by the distance AB, which we have assumed to equal a 100x% loss in productivity. The distance AB, therefore, is the productivity loss for a typical worker due to the onset of the health impairment. Because the vertical axis is measured in log dollars, and the effect of this health impairment is a proportional shift downward in productivity, the shift in the demand curve is parallel to the original, perfectly healthy demand curve for labor because of the uniform 100x% shift in productivity.

This simple labor-demand model yields four results. First, the wage decline resulting from the onset of the health impairment is less than the loss in productivity for any single worker, 100x%, whenever the labor supply is upward sloping. Wages of health-impaired workers decline by an amount that is less than the individual decline in productivity because some workers voluntarily leave the labor force (or firm) in response to the decline in wages that follows the onset of the health impairment. Therefore, the log wage difference between healthy workers and workers with some health impairment $(w_N - w_D)$ will be less than the productivity effect of the health impairment for a typical worker, $AB = p(1 - x)MP_L$. Second, the percentage decline in wages will equal the percentage decline in productivity only in the case when labor supply is perfectly inelastic (and, therefore, the labor-supply curve is vertical). An inelastic labor-supply curve is one in which the quantity of workers is not very responsive to the wage rate. The wage elasticity of supply is the

5. We ignore the possibility of entry and exit of firms from the industry. As the extent of the impairment x increases, some firms will exit. This will shift the demand curve further to the left than is shown in figures 7.1 and 7.2.

A

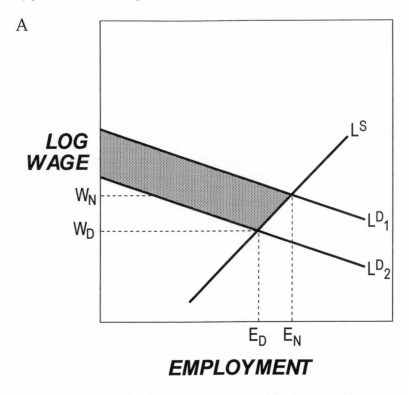

Figure 7.2a. The social loss from health impairment based on labor-demand model

percentage change in labor supplied divided by the percentage change in the wage. For example, if the wage rate increases by 10% and the hours supplied increase by less than 10%, then the supply is inelastic with respect to wages. If the hours supplied increase by more than 10%, then the supply is elastic. Third, there will be no decline in wages if the supply of labor is perfectly elastic, meaning that the labor-supply curve is horizontal or that the quantity of workers is extremely responsive to the wage rate. In that case, the effects of the health loss are limited to reductions in the amount of labor demanded by the firms and a reduction in the profitability of the firms. Finally, workers will absorb all of the decrease in productivity as a reduction of 100x% in wage rates if the supply of labor is perfectly inelastic (the supply curve is vertical) and fixed.

The social costs associated with a decline in productivity resulting from the onset of a health impairment are depicted in figures 7.2a and 7.2b. The social loss in figure 7.2a is given by the cross-hatched area corresponding to the area between the two demand curves that is northwest of the supply

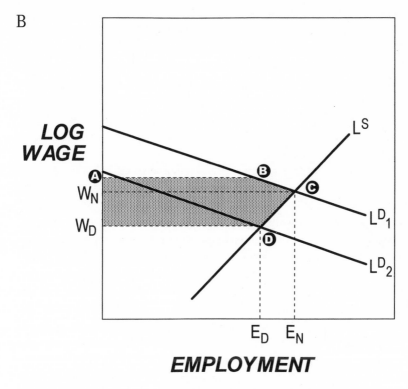

B

Figure 7.2b. A convenient approximation of the social loss from health impairment based on labor-demand model

curve. If the demand and supply curves are linear and if the shift in costs is additive, then the cross-hatched area in figure 7.2b is the same as the cross-hatched area in figure 7.2a. Otherwise, the area in figure 7.2b is an approximation to the true social loss in figure 7.2a. As a practical proposition, it is much easier to use the approximation in figure 7.2b, which relies on readily observable information. To carry out the approximation in figure 7.2b, one needs to know only the two levels of employment and the two wage levels, or to have estimates for each. In contrast, to figure out the exact amount in figure 7.2a, one needs to know the whole demand curve (before and after the shift).

The nature of the shift in productivity can have a major effect on the quality of the approximation. If the shift is truly a proportional one, such as the one considered in figure 7.2a, then the shift in the demand curve as a function of log wage is additive. However, if we plot labor versus the actual wage, then the demand curves will be further apart on the left than they are on the right, because a constant proportion of a larger number is bigger than the constant proportion of a small number. In that case, the usual welfare approximation (the cross-hatched area in figure 7.2b) provides an underestimate of the welfare impact of a change in health impairment or illness. In contrast, if the effect of health impairment is additive—an additive constant, not a proportional reduction in the marginal product of an affected worker—then the usual welfare approximation (the cross-hatched area in figure 7.2b) may provide a reasonable approximation of the welfare impact of a change in health impairment or illness.

Hidden in this discussion is an additional set of second-order effects of an increase in illness or health impairment. As the productivity of the affected workers falls, firms will substitute other inputs, such as other sources of labor, along with capital, for the impaired workers. Thus, there will be spillover effects into other input markets. As the productivity of labor falls, both the marginal and the average cost of producing a given level of output will increase. As the average cost of doing business rises, some firms will find that their average cost exceeds the price of that output in the market. If this shortfall occurs for any length of time, some of these firms will go out of business. Among those remaining in the market, the higher the marginal cost of producing the firm's output, the less each firm will produce at a given price in the output market. The combined result will be a reduced supply of the product in output markets (the supply curve will shift to the northwest in the output market) and a consequent increase in the price in that output market. The magnitude of these second-order effects will depend on the prevalence of the illness or the injury rate, the degree of substitution of the affected type of labor for other inputs, and the cost share of the affected input. The higher the prevalence rate for the disease, the lower the elasticity of substitution; and the higher the cost share, the greater the impact on related input and output markets. We suspect that these general equilibrium effects will be negligible in many cases, but not necessarily in all.

THE SOCIAL LOSS OF HEALTH IMPAIRMENTS

The social loss of health impairments can be divided into two parts, the loss in producer surplus to the firm resulting from employing fewer workers (some of whom are, in turn, less productive) and the loss to workers resulting from lower wages and fewer jobs. Since losses to third parties including the loss of revenue from income taxes and corporate taxes and the increase in government expenditures going to disability and unemployment benefits represent transfers from one group to another, they do not affect the calculation of lost social welfare.[6] Third-party transfers do, however, affect the relative losses to the firm and to the worker and therefore affect the incentives to avoid injuries and disabling health impairments.

The social loss can be measured in figure 7.2b by the area w_D-A-B-C-D. The social loss stems from two effects—fewer health-impaired individuals are employed, and those who remain employed are less productive. The social loss is borne both by the firm and by workers. The region w_N-A-B-C is the loss to the firm while the region w_D-w_N-C-D is the loss to workers. If labor supplied to the market is perfectly inelastic (i.e., if there is a vertical supply curve), the entire social loss is borne by workers. The literature indicates that the supply of labor is inelastic for both men and women, but not perfectly inelastic.

The social loss implied by the labor-demand model differs from that suggested elsewhere in the literature. For example, chapter 6 in this volume suggests that the social loss resulting from health impairments can be measured by the change in performance (measured in standard deviation units) multiplied by the standard deviation of earnings. This measure of the social loss is depicted graphically in figure 7.1 by the region w_N-A-B-C. Thus, the productivity loss estimate of the social cost of health impairments is larger than the estimate of the social loss from the labor-demand model. If the demand and supply curves are linear, and the shift in demand is parallel to the healthy demand curve, then the loss formula xwE_N overstates the social loss based on the labor demand model by $xw(E_N - E_D)/2$. The two estimates will be equal only when labor supply is perfectly inelastic, and $E_N = E_D$.

The labor demand model implies that for two reasons empirical estimates of the wage loss associated with illness and health impairments (or the gains from treatment of health impairment) will not generally correspond to the estimates of the productivity loss such as those in the literature. First, wages will not fall to the full extent of the productivity loss for a typical worker as long as supply curves slope upward. Some workers will voluntarily leave the labor force, increasing the productivity of the remaining workers, and some firms will exit. Second, the social value of the time of workers who voluntarily leave is not zero. These workers will either find employment in another industry or occupation, engage in home production, or consume leisure.

The extent to which firms and workers have incentives to prevent injuries or to take actions to improve health is determined by the respective

6. The transfer payments should be included if the analysis or policy concerns are those of the agency providing the transfers. One of the early studies by Javitt and his colleagues found that the savings in transfer payments offset the costs of additional screening and treatment for diabetic retinopathy. The perspective for that analysis was the federal government.

magnitudes of the costs of impairments to each group. The magnitudes of the costs from health impairments borne by the firm and by workers are determined, in part, by the elasticity of labor supply. If the labor supply is perfectly inelastic, the entire cost of the decline in productivity associated with a health impairment is borne by workers in the form of lower wages; because the firm bears no cost, it has no incentive to reduce injuries or to improve the health of its workers. At the opposite extreme, if labor supply is perfectly elastic, then the entire cost of the productivity loss associated with a health impairment will be borne by the firm. Impaired workers will shift their employment to a different sector if wages fall.

Models for Health Impairments and Labor Supply

The labor-demand analysis presented in the section entitled "A Simple Model of Productivity and Labor Demand" explicitly assumes that labor supply is not affected by the advent or threat of health impairments. However, to the extent that health-impaired individuals are less willing to supply their labor services to the market, the onset of a health impairment will lead to even larger employment losses than suggested by the labor-demand model. The effect of health on labor supplied by a worker is of an ambiguous sign; in other words, theory does not allow us to determine whether it is positive or negative on a priori grounds. (See Deaton and Muellbauer 1980, chap. 11, for a description of the basic labor-leisure model.) On the one hand, an increase in health may increase the utility from consuming leisure, thus reducing the willingness of consumers to work as much. On the other, better health may increase the utility from consuming other goods and services that must be purchased with income earned by selling leisure time in the labor market. Alternatively, improved health may increase the utility from leisure enough to compensate for the increased utility of other goods and services. As health improves, a worker will spend less time going to see physicians, thus increasing the time available for both labor and leisure; see Currie and Madrian 1999 for a review of the empirical literature. Which of these two forces is larger will determine the overall direction of the effect of an improvement in health status on leisure consumed and labor time sold. If patients can improve their health status by seeking medical care, and if seeking care takes time from other activities (leisure or work), then the effect of improved health is still ambiguous.

In contrast to the theory, the empirical evidence supports the assumption that better health increases labor supplied. Health can affect labor supply for many reasons, including the facts that health-impaired individuals may have greater nonwork time needs for going to a physician and for personal maintenance, and that health-impaired individuals are more likely to be eligible for cash and noncash disability benefits that place work restrictions on program participants.

The reader should note that nothing in the preceding section would change if we considered that health impairments and illness increased absenteeism instead of simply reducing on-the-job productivity. So far, in our description of market responses to impaired health, we have focused on a model in which the employer hires more labor than she actually uses, with the difference being impaired health or work-loss days. This is implicitly a model with fully covered sick leave. Now, we would like to turn to a model where the employee nominally bears directly all of the risk of health impairment or work loss. This model reflects the situation in the United States, where a substantial fraction of the workforce does not have sick leave as a formal benefit. According to the Department of Labor, in 1997, 95% of full-time employees in medium to large firms had paid vacation benefits, but only 56% had paid sick leave (Bureau of Labor Statistics 1999).

Let's consider a stylized situation in which employers go to a hiring hall or labor exchange to hire workers as needed. Workers may have differing skills, but none of these differences constitute firm-specific human capital. If a potential worker is too ill to work on a specific day, then he or she does not go to the labor exchange. Under this model (depicted in figure 7.3), a 100x% reduction in health status leads to a corresponding downward shift in the supply of labor. If there was a supply curve L_0 at a given wage w when all potential workers were healthy, there will be $L_1 = (1 - x)L_0$ when some 100x% are too ill to offer work. In this case, the market will observe a leftward shift in the labor supply when health impairments and illness increase absenteeism or withdrawals from the labor force. This will lead to a reduction in labor used from L_0 to L_1, and a rise in the wage rate paid by the firm from w_0 to w_1.

In this case, impaired workers have fewer hours and higher wage rates than indicated earlier, but their earnings (equal to wages times hours) have actually fallen since they, in contrast to employers, are bearing the full cost of the reduction in time available for work. Part of the difference is in the wages for hours actually worked (these wages are now higher) versus the wage for all hours (worked plus out sick, which are lower). This distinction between wages for the types of hours is an important one and is often a potential source of confusion.

If we consider the case where illness and health impairments do not reduce productivity but do reduce labor supply, labor supply could fall either because working while ill or impaired causes pain, or because the worker now has less time available to split between work and leisure. This result is displayed in figure 7.3. The social losses for this decline in labor supply are displayed by the cross-hatched area in figure 7.3. The social losses depicted

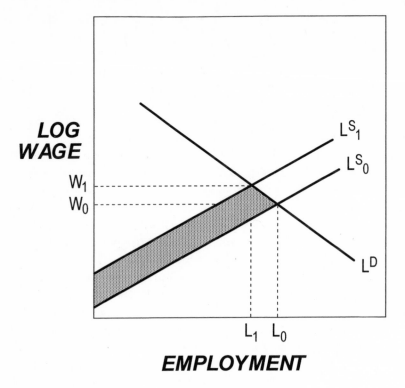

Figure 7.3. Labor-supply effects
Note: $w_1 - w_* = pMP_L$

there suggest that there will be even larger economic losses than those measured by the productivity chapters in this volume because of the shifts in the
market's equilibrium wage structure and the effects on employers.

A Model with Both Demand and Labor Shifts

If the illness or impairment is prevalent in its extent and serious in its impact
on workers' output or firm behavior, then there will be a series of shifts in the
equilibrium levels of employment and wages that extend beyond a simple
shift in absenteeism and labor-force participation, or increased productivity
while on the job. As we have shown, a reduction in the physical productivity
of workers on the job due to either illness or impairment will lead to

1. Reductions in the demand by firms for the affected types of labor,
2. An increase in the use of substitute types of labor and capital, and

3. A drop in the wage rate for the types of labor affected by the illness or impairment, with the change being *less* than that indicated by the productivity shift alone.

The usual approximations to the welfare loss are likely to be too conservative, that is, too small, unless all shifts in productivity are the same across all levels of employment, or unless only a few individuals are affected.

In addition to shifts in the demand for labor by firms, an increase in illness or health impairment will also shift the supply of labor by workers or potential workers. The resulting increases in time taken to seek health care, absenteeism for sickness, and exits from the labor force will lead to a leftward shift in the supply of labor. The result will be higher wages than would have existed if the effect of illness or health impairment affected only physical productivity of workers on the job. It is even conceivable that the reduction in labor supply will push wages beyond the pre-illness or pre-impairment level if the labor-supply shifts are larger than the labor-demand shifts—if shifts in labor-force participation and absenteeism are larger than the shifts in the physical productivity of a worker while on the job. In any case, there will be less labor employed than would have been the case in the absence of the illness or impairment.

If we combine the shifts in both the demand for labor (due to productivity shifts) and the supply of labor (due to absenteeism and labor-force participation) into an overall assessment of labor-market impact, we have the situation displayed in figure 7.4. The economic impact of the joint shifts would include the cross-hatched areas in figure 7.4. This area is likely to be much larger than that associated with simple shifts in physical productivity of workers on the job alone in figure 7.2a. The usual approximation would apply only if labor supply were inelastic and insensitive to the level of illness and/or impairment. A similar argument can be made that just looking at labor-force participation, hours worked, or absenteeism will cause the usual approximation to be an underestimate of impact unless the demand for labor was perfectly price-elastic and insensitive to the level of illness or impairment.

The loss portrayed in figure 7.4 is itself incomplete in the sense that it does not reflect the entire impact of shifts in the labor market for three reasons. First, it fails to fully capture the adverse economic effect of increases in risk-bearing by workers due to the increased risk in wages and incomes if moral hazard is present or the insurance market's imperfections lead to incomplete coverage. Second, changes in input prices will have spillover effects on output markets. Third, changes in the wage and productivity of one type of labor due to illness or impairment will lead to shifts in the demand for identifiably healthier and more productive workers as well as reassessments of the labor-capital mix employed by firms.

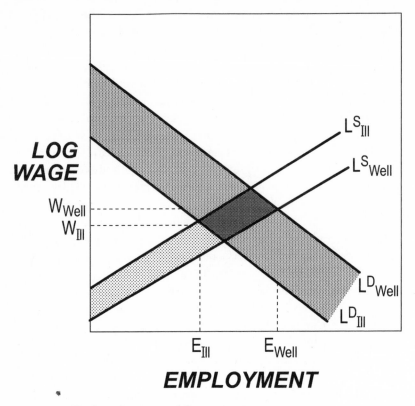

Figure 7.4. Welfare losses from increased illness or impairment

The Special Case of a Single Firm Affected

The preceding discussion is concerned largely with the effects of changes in illness and health impairment that are industry-wide. By extension, the measures are ones that would be useful if one were assessing the cost-effectiveness of an intervention that would be applied across the population. In some situations, an analyst assessing the impact of an illness, an impairment, or an intervention to treat illness and impairment may have a much narrower focus. For example, one may be interested in studying what happens when a single firm is affected or has a health intervention. If the firm in question is a perfectly competitive firm in both the output and input (labor) markets, then there will be no impact on output supply or output prices, and a negligible impact on labor supply, demand, and wages.

At the firm level (see fig. 7.5), the supply of labor is perfectly elastic in the absence of firm-specific human capital (that is, knowledge specific to the firm that an impaired worker, in contrast to a new temporary worker, has access to). Thus, on the one hand, a health-related shift in productivity for the firm's workers while on the job will lead to a reduction in the firm's demand for labor, a fall in the hours worked, and a fall in the firm's profitability, but no change in the wage rate. On the other hand, if the health-related shift is a change in absenteeism rather than a change in on-the-job productivity, then there are no changes in the firm's behavior unless there is a loss in firm-specific human capital or unless there are transaction costs of hiring temporary workers. Because the firm is small relative to the size of the labor market, there will be no change in the wage rate faced by that firm. The major difference between the productivity and absenteeism cases concerns who bears the effects of the health impairment: the firm, the workers, or some combination. Changes in productivity while on the job caused by increased health impairments and illness will reduce the firm's profits by the area between the firm's demand for labor before and after the change in impairment in figure 7.5; because the price in the output market is not affected by the

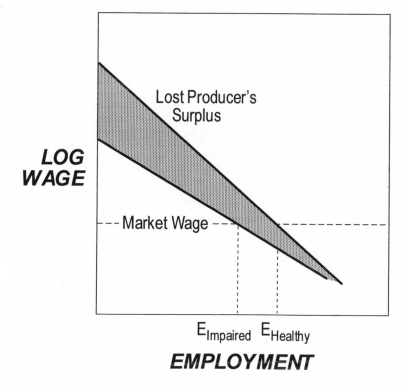

Figure 7.5. Effect of health impairments on firm's labor demand

decisions of a single firm, the price does not change. All of the shift is a shift in the marginal product of labor. The shift in wages paid will be $w(E_N - E_D)$ If, in addition, there is a change in absenteeism, then there may be an adverse effect on the firm's profits and the wages of workers that depends on the extent of sick leave and how much workers work together in teams. For more discussion on this last point, see chapter 9 in this volume.

Frictional Costs of Illness and Health Impairment

The discussion so far has ignored the frictional costs of illness to employers. If workers have specialized knowledge, there may be an additional social cost due to illness. Consider a modification of the hiring-hall or labor-exchange model mentioned above, so that there is no formal sick leave or disability. When a specific employee is ill or out on disability leave, the firm will go to the labor exchange or a temporary help agency to find a temporary replacement. The temp worker may be equally skilled but may not have all of the job-specific knowledge of the employee that she or he is replacing. As a result, there is a drop in productivity associated with the use of the temp employee. This is an example of the frictional cost of illness described by Brouwer, Koopmanschap, and Rutten (1997) and Koopmanschap and colleagues (1995). The first-order effects of this difference in productivity will be captured in the differences in wages, but there will also be second-order effects. As illness and impairment increase, the demand for temp employees will expand and their wages will rise, all other things remaining equal, while wages for regular workers will fall.

The recent work by Murray, Nicholson, Pauly, and Berger (chapter 9 in this volume) on absenteeism and the impact on employers and employees is related to the frictional-cost approach. These authors consider the disruptions that occur when a worker is absent. They deal specifically with the case where work is done in teams and the operation of the team may be compromised by the absence of a member. Thus they consider cases where the loss in productivity is greater than that described in our initial model for health-related shifts in labor demand because of shifting productivity.

REVIEW OF EMPIRICAL ECONOMICS
LITERATURE ON THE LABOR-MARKET EFFECTS
OF HEALTH IMPAIRMENTS

In our review of literature, we do not include the empirical economics literature that has sought, among other things, to measure the extent of wage losses stemming from the onset of disabilities and illness. This literature has also tried to measure the impact of insurance mechanisms, such as worker's compensation and health insurance, on wages and compensating wage differentials. A substantial part of the labor literature in this area has been concerned with trying to assess the causal effect of health on labor-market outcomes, as distinct from the impact of income and other labor-market behaviors on health, and with addressing methodological issues that could bias the estimates. There are several excellent reviews available in the literature, including Currie and Madrian 1999 for the labor impacts of health, Gruber 2000 for health insurance, and Moore and Viscusi 1990 for compensating wage differentials.

There is a related literature on the COI that estimates some of the labor-market consequences of illness and health impairment. That literature includes in its estimates the health-sector costs of treating the illness and the "indirect" costs in terms of labor-market consequences (other than time-in-treatment). Although originally based on market transactions and human-capital theory, the COI studies now include estimates of the cost of nonmarket transactions, such as informal care-giving. Typically these studies use observed differences in labor-market participation, hours, wages, and earnings to estimate how labor contributions would change if the illness, impairment, or injury were eliminated. In this sense, they are very similar to some of the labor-market studies reviewed by Currie and Madrian (1999).

If such labor and COI studies stopped at estimating the impact on an individual of illness or impairment, then we would have relatively few questions about the estimates. Unfortunately, these individual assessments of the cost of illness are summed over the population to provide a total or societal estimate of cost. What is true at the individual level may not be true in the aggregate. The following example also points to how other methods tend to underestimate economic losses: if we observed two samples of observationally equivalent women, who differed only in that one set was clinically depressed and the other was not, then the difference in labor behavior and earnings would provide us an approximation of what would happen if one of the depressed women was not depressed. To the extent that depression affects productivity while on the job, the firm's and the industry's demand for women workers will increase (shift outward) when depression is eliminated, because their marginal product of labor increases. To the extent that depression increases absenteeism and withdrawal from the labor force, eliminating depression would shift the supply of labor outward (to the right). The net effect will depend on the relative magnitude of these effects. But it seems unlikely that women's wages and firms' decisions about labor and capital would not be affected by the change in depression. Based on current estimates of the prevalence of depression among women, these shifts could be noticeable (Ettner, Frank, and Kessler 1997).

To the extent that a disease or impairment is prevalent, and that its effect on either the firm's demand for labor or the supply of labor is large, aggregating individual estimates of the cost of illness will provide a systematically biased and incomplete assessment of what would happen if the disease were eliminated, as a comparison of figure 7.4 with the earlier figures indicates.

CONCLUSION

The impact of illness and health impairments on labor markets and social welfare is complex. Assessments that look only at shifts in productivity, changes in labor-force participation, or absenteeism rates do not provide an accurate picture. The economic models presented here suggest that there is not a simple one-to-one correspondence between measured productivity losses per worker and the social losses to firms and to workers that we would expect to observe in the marketplace. Much of the work to date has looked at shifts in either the firm's or the worker's behavior, without considering the effects of these shifts on either the equilibrium at the labor-market level or on general equilibrium. Considering the broader impact of illness and impairment leads to somewhat different conclusions about the economic consequences of illness and impairment. In particular, as noted above, for prevalent diseases such as depression, the social costs are probably much greater than commonly assumed. To the extent that public policy is influenced by either cost-effectiveness analyses or cost-of-illness studies, the true social costs of treatments or diseases with substantial impacts on labor-market effects could be substantially understated because the literature has typically ignored labor-market consequences. In cases where there are major shifts in productivity while on the job (shifts in the marginal product of labor), the usual methods will understate the economic consequences because they largely omit the impact of illness on the profits of firms. By the same logic, use of similar methods applied to the costs of treating diseases will probably understate the benefits (or cost reductions or productivity improvements) associated with new interventions if they shift productivity on the job or lead to changes in market equilibriums if widely adopted.

ACKNOWLEDGMENTS

We received helpful comments from Alan Garber, Werner Brouwer, Stephen Almond, and workshop participants at the University of Chicago and the 2001 International Health Economics Association Meetings.

REFERENCES

Brouwer, W. B., M. A. Koopmanschap, and F. F. Rutten. 1997. Productivity costs measurement through quality of life? A response to the recommendation of the Washington panel. *Health Economics* 6:253–59.

Bureau of Labor Statistics, U.S. Department of Labor. 1999. *Employee benefits in medium and large private establishments, 1997.* 1999. Available from http://statsbls.ebshome.htm (January 24, 2003).

Currie, J., and B. Madrian. 1999. Health, health insurance, and the labor market. In *Handbook of labor economics,* ed. O. Ashenfelter and D. Card. New York: Elsevier Science.

Deaton, A., and J. Muellbauer. 1980. *Economics and consumer behavior.* Cambridge: Cambridge University Press.

Ettner, S. L., R. Frank, and R. C. Kessler. 1997. The impact of psychiatric disorder on labor market outcomes. *Industrial and Labor Relations Review* 51:64–81.

Gruber, J. 2000. Health insurance and the labor market. In *Handbook of health economics,* ed. A. J. Culyer and J. P. Newhouse. New York: Elsevier Science.

Koopmanschap, M. A., F. F. Rutten, B. M. van Ineveld, and L. van Roijen. 1995. The friction cost method for measuring indirect costs of disease. *Journal of Health Economics* 14:171–89.

Moore, M. J., and W. K. Viscusi. 1990. *Compensating mechanisms for job risks: Wages, workers' compensation, and product liability.* Princeton, NJ: Princeton University Press.

PART TWO

Stakeholder Perspectives

CHAPTER 8

Overcoming Barriers to Managing Health and Productivity in the Workplace

DENNIS P. SCANLON

When it comes to the bottom line, I would say that HR (Human Resources) has been a bit out to lunch. . . . But their understanding of the bottom line has improved over the past few years, and I do believe that most HR executives are striving to better understand how their decisions and actions can truly affect the bottom line.
—Robert McDonald, 2000

The cost of health care is increasing at such an alarming rate that controlling it has become the No. 1 priority, up from No. 2 among HR professionals, according to a recent Mercer survey, with 84% of employee benefit specialists citing health care costs as their No. 1 priority.
—E. M. Parmenter, 2003

INTRODUCTION

The challenge and the opportunity for Human Resource (HR) departments generally, and health-benefit managers within HR departments specifically, are widely acknowledged. The recent economic recession coupled with annual double-digit increases in health care costs year after year has moved health care benefits to the front of the agenda at many companies. According to a U.S. Chamber of Commerce survey, employee benefits cost an average of 37.5% of payroll in 2000, or an average of $16,167 per employee annually. The cost of health insurance has historically been one of the largest of these cost items, averaging 10.5% of payroll (Parmenter 2003). Benefit administrators, HR directors, and CEOs are all clamoring for reasonable solutions to address what appears to be an impending train wreck (Pugh 2003).

To illustrate the burden for specific companies, General Electric's health-benefit spending hit $1.4 billion in 2002, up 45% since 1999, an increase of $2,350 per employee (Hansen 2003). Similarly, a Wall Street analyst described General Motors Corporation, which has the largest retiree population of all private U.S. employers, as an "HMO with wheels" (Hakim 2003)—in other words a health care company that produces cars to pay for its employee and retiree health and pension benefits. The picture worsens when the costs of other work health-related programs (e.g., worker's compensation and disability) are included. In short, the cost of providing health-related benefits is affecting the bottom line at many firms, eating away at corporate profitability and affecting global competitiveness.

To address these issues, companies have been pursuing a variety of options, ranging from increasing employee contributions for health insurance to contracting with various forms of managed-care organizations, to exploring Health Savings Accounts (HSAs) and defined-contribution plans (Lipson and De Sa 1996; Parmenter 2003). While cost-saving approaches may improve the bottom line in the short term, it is uncertain how these approaches will affect employee health in the longer term. For example, Rosenheck and colleagues (1999) found that savings from lower mental health care utilization by employees at one company due to increased copayments were offset by increased use of other health care services and lost workdays. Some experts believe that a more radical approach is needed, such as a single-payer government-run system that removes employers from the equation altogether (Woolhandler, Campbell, and Himmelstein 2003).

Less radical but unorthodox nonetheless are programs that both recognize the link between positive health and employment productivity and attempt to manage health in employed settings. The term used to describe these programs is *health and productivity management* (HPM), defined by the Institute for Health and Productivity Management as "the integrated management of data and services related to all aspects of employee health that affect work performance." HPM "includes measuring the impact of targeted interventions on both health and productivity" (Institute for Health and Productivity Management 1998–2004). While the link between good health and productivity may seem intuitive, few employers have paid more than lip service to this connection. Findings from a recent report by the Midwest Business Group on Health and the Juran Institute shed light on the opportunity for employers engaged in HPM. The report estimated that about $1,500 per employee covered by employment-based health insurance can be attributed to waste due to overuse and underuse of appropriate medical services as well as to medical errors. In addition, the report estimated that employers lose another $400–$750 per employee annually in lost productivity associated with these problems (Midwest Business Group, Juran Institute, and Severyn Group 2002).

A paradox is evident: why are few companies aggressively engaged in HPM when sophisticated techniques for measuring the relationship between work and productivity exist (see part 1 of this volume), effective health interventions are available for early detection and treatment of many acute and chronic conditions, and economists recognize that better employee health makes sense for the corporate bottom line (as discussed throughout part 2)?

In this chapter I identify barriers that prevent health and productivity from being more formally managed by firms, discuss options for removing the barriers, and offer specific examples of firms that have been successful in implementing HPM.

BARRIERS TO HEALTH AND PRODUCTIVITY MANAGEMENT WITHIN FIRMS

Benefit Staffing Constraints

The benefit staff is housed under Human Resources in most firms; a recent survey indicates that 79% of employee benefit departments report directly to HR (Huth 2001). More important, the number of staff dedicated to employee benefits in firms is small, ranging from an average of 2.5 full-time-equivalent (FTE) employees at firms with less than 1,000 employees to 10 FTEs for firms with more than 5,000 employees. Add the fact that the average employee benefit department staff had almost 5 fewer employees in 2000 than in 1991 (Huth 2001), and it is easy to see why staff-resource constraints may be a significant barrier to addressing health and productivity issues.

In addition, those working in employee benefits often have multiple responsibilities besides administering employer-sponsored health care, such as contracting and managing life and disability insurance as well as worker's compensation plans. Hence, benefit employees are not necessarily trained in health-benefit administration. Knowledge limitations regarding the delivery, organization, and financing of health care may present significant barriers for employee benefit personnel when it comes to developing effective solutions for addressing the corporate health care crisis. Indeed, corporate health-benefit management is not one of the traditional career choices for students graduating from programs in health administration.

Silo Model of Benefits Management versus Population Health Approach

Given how employment-based health and benefit programs are structured at most firms, it is not surprising that HPM programs have received little attention. As figure 8.1 illustrates, the many employer-sponsored health programs have typically been managed in silos. Each program is unrelated to the others, and the major role of benefit staff is to select and contract with vendors. For many programs, such as health benefits, disability, and even worker's compensation, firms have viewed the vendors as *insurance* providers rather than as population health managers. Worker's compensation, for example, is insurance to protect both the employer and the employee against the financial costs associated with injury in the workplace. Health insurance protects employees against the potentially significant costs of medical care for themselves and their family members.

Population health management refers to the comprehensive identification and management of the entire health needs of a population, including preventive care, care for acute and chronic conditions, and health care needs related to employment. Figure 8.2 illustrates what a population health-management approach would look like, with the link between the various health-related programs and the core representing the impact of each program individually and collectively on productivity and profits.

Thus, in a population health-management approach, Employee Assistance Programs (EAPs) would be linked with worker's-compensation and general health-benefit programs. After all, the services provided by EAPs can have significant ripple effects throughout the company. Take, for example, the early detection of substance abuse, which might result in fewer on-the-job injuries and fewer worker's compensation claims. Reductions in overall health care utilization might also occur, as substance abuse is typically associated with other illnesses. Finally, productivity would probably be improved because of a lower incidence of absenteeism and presenteeism.

To date, rather than taking an integrated approach to benefit management, most companies have focused on selecting vendors that provide insurance protection and administrative services at the most favorable rates. Integrated HPM programs are often not even available under traditional modes of vendor contracting. With benefit managers facing evaluations based on their success in reducing cost rather than generating savings, they have little incentive to take a holistic view.

Moving from risk bearer / claims processor to health manager changes the employer-vendor relationship because it requires active coordination and planning for the care of the designated population (e.g., disabled, injured,

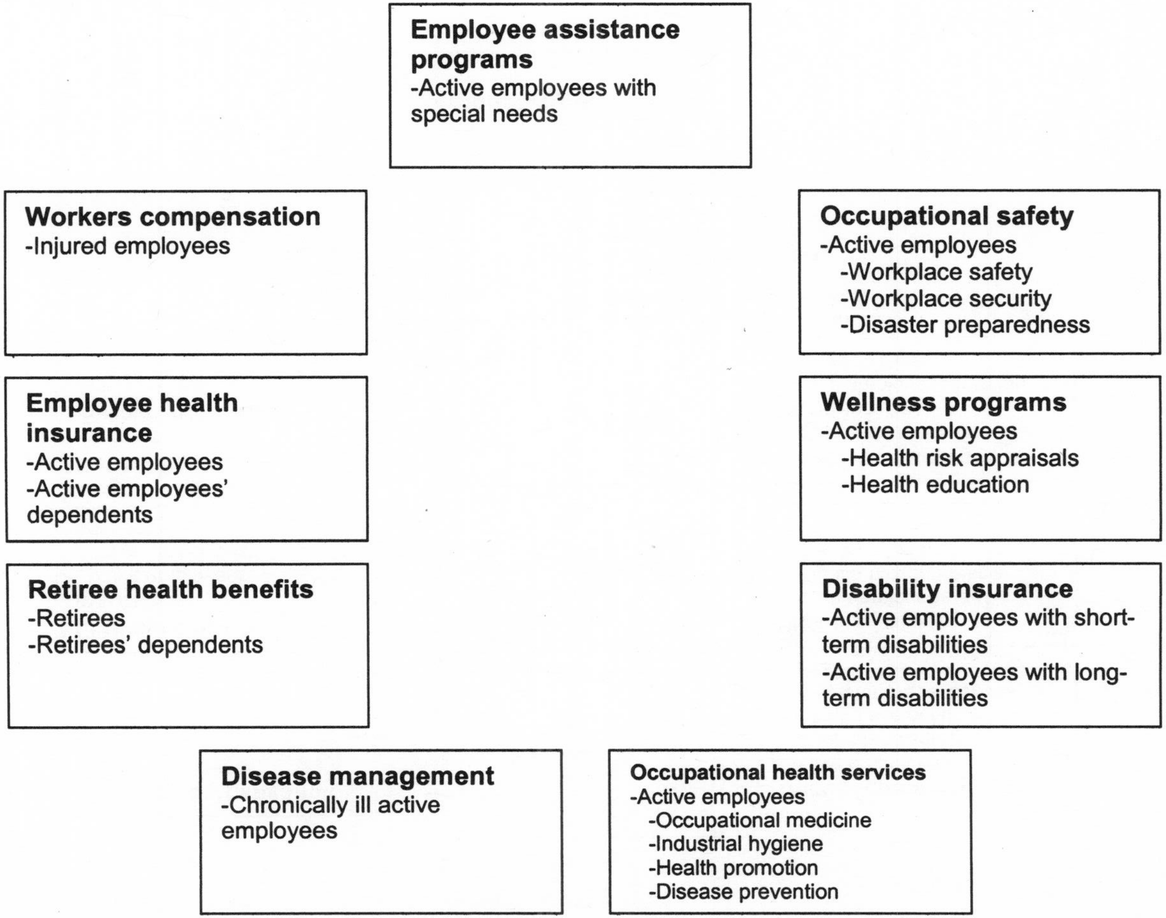

Employee assistance programs
-Active employees with special needs

Occupational safety
-Active employees
-Workplace safety
-Workplace security
-Disaster preparedness

Wellness programs
-Active employees
-Health risk appraisals
-Health education

Disability insurance
-Active employees with short-term disabilities
-Active employees with long-term disabilities

Occupational health services
-Active employees
-Occupational medicine
-Industrial hygiene
-Health promotion
-Disease prevention

Workers compensation
-Injured employees

Employee health insurance
-Active employees
-Active employees' dependents

Retiree health benefits
-Retirees
-Retirees' dependents

Disease management
-Chronically ill active employees

Figure 8.1. Employment-based health benefits / management programs

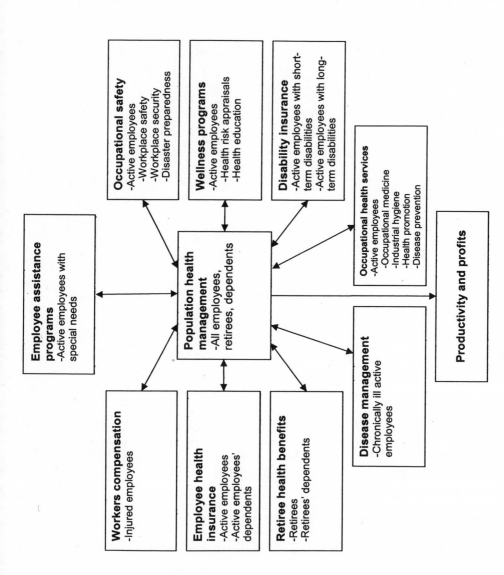

Figure 8.2. Population-health management program

sick, etc.). Active coordination requires the vendor to monitor the types of treatments provided by physicians and to hold providers accountable for employee health and productivity. As Wagner's chronic care model (CCM) suggests, effective care requires engagement on the part of both health care practitioners and patients (Wagner et al. 2001).

Unfortunately, engaging individual physicians is challenging for several reasons. First, providers often view care-management programs as a threat to their autonomy. Second, in most managed-care arrangements, providers are not employed by the managed-care organization (MCO) and only a portion of their overall patient business may be attributed to the MCO, making accountability difficult. In fact, physicians often contract with multiple managed-care organizations in the same market (Chernew et al. 2004). Third, most programs have not yet developed effective incentives for encouraging provider compliance, and measuring provider compliance is not always possible given current information systems. As if these issues were not enough, many clinical-care guidelines do not take into account the effect of illness on job productivity, and many programs are just beginning to link the effects of treatment-management programs to productivity outcomes.

Engaging consumers is also a challenge. Concerns about access to care (i.e., restricted provider choice and utilization management), poor quality, and cost-cutting have resulted in a swift movement away from plans with formal care-management activities and toward plans that provide access to broad networks of providers (e.g., preferred-provider organizations [PPOs]), with little or no population health-management functions (Peterson 1999; Scanlon et al. 2001). Hence, employers interested in HPM programs are faced with consumers and providers who are reluctant to embrace structured care-management programs.

Cost-Minimization versus Value-Based Health Care Purchasing

The traditional approach to benefit management has focused narrowly on expenditures rather than on the value received for those expenditures. In his book *Costing Human Resources*, Wayne Cascio argues that management based on sound economic valuation has historically been lacking across all functions of human resource management, preventing it from competing with other departments for investment resources: "The need to evaluate Human Resources Management activities in *economic* terms, however is becoming increasingly apparent. In the current climate of rising costs for labor, energy, and raw materials, operating executives justifiably demand estimates of the expected costs and benefits of HR programs. Developing such measures requires an interdisciplinary approach that incorporates information from accounting, finance, economics, and behavioral science" (Cascio 2000, 1). As Cascio suggests, benefit managers need to understand the type of information chief financial officers and other corporate decision-makers require. Specifically, they must begin to assess the value received for current health-benefit expenditures, and they should compare that value to what could be obtained from alternative approaches. To establish the value of benefit programs, it is not enough to hypothesize a correlation between a proposed health-management program and an increase in productivity. Instead, these benefits must be converted into dollars in order to demonstrate their value.

In finance vernacular, the return from potential investments is known as the internal rate of return (IRR). The IRR is derived from *net present value analysis* (NPV) and estimates the amount of financial benefit generated from a dollar invested in a proposed program. The computation of the IRR allows financial officers to compare the value of different investment opportunities (i.e., the opportunity cost of investments), or even decrements in value resulting from reducing investments in certain projects. For investments in equipment such as a new machine for an assembly line, companies usually have sound information regarding the increased productivity (e.g., extra widgets produced per day) likely to result from the new machine relative to the current machine. Firms also have information such as the expected life of the machine and costs of maintenance. All of this can be used to compute the expected lifetime value of the machine relative to the overall investment.

However, computation of an IRR for health-benefit programs is much more complex. Consider, for example, an IRR for an investment in a HPM program, such as an employee assistance program (EAP). While the direct costs of such a program may be known with certainty (e.g., the cost to contract with an EAP vendor), the indirect costs and benefits of the program are much less certain. Indirect costs include items such as the cost of medical care (e.g., outpatient visits, diagnostic tests, and medications) that results from identifying employees with conditions in need of treatment. The benefits would include the dollar value of medical care (e.g., lengthy hospitalizations) avoided by identifying problems at an earlier stage, lower rates of work absenteeism, and increased work productivity.

Unlike the assembly line machine, the indirect costs and benefits of such programs are typically less well known and require broad assumptions, making the IRR computation uncertain. HPM programs for which an IRR calculation is possible have not been studied extensively. Unfortunately, the research on the costs and benefits of treatment programs is scant for many types of care.

Some large firms are beginning to use value-based purchasing (VBP) techniques to understand the benefit received for health care expenditures (Scanlon, Chernew, and Doty 2002). For example, the Health Plan Employer Data and Information Set (HEDIS) data was developed by large employers to monitor the value received for HMO premiums, with HEDIS measuring key process indicators across entire health-plan populations (e.g., compliance with recommended immunizations or cancer screenings), as well as member satisfaction with health-plan service (e.g., the Consumer Assessment of Health Plans Survey measures). More sophisticated evaluation has emerged for specific programs, such as disease-management programs for health-plan members with specific chronic illnesses (e.g., diabetes, asthma), but the value of these programs is not well established (Selby et al. 2003), particularly in the short run.

The eValue8 group is a purchasing coalition that attempts to obtain details about the care that health plans provide to members. The eValue8 purchasers have developed a detailed request for information (RFI) that asks plans about compliance with guidelines for treatment of chronic illness, management of pharmacy utilization, and implementation of practices that promote patient safety. While the eValue8 effort is promising, the project faces some serious obstacles. Unfortunately, many health plans are unable to provide answers to the questions that are asked because of a lack of easily accessible electronic information about the treatment provided by individual physicians. For example, in eValue8's 2003 survey, the purchasers asked plans to report aggregate cost and benefit information for their diabetes disease-management programs in order to estimate the return on investment of these initiatives. However, few plans were able to report this information. In addition, the RFI focuses on the care that HMOs and PPOs provide to insured populations; it has not yet attempted to integrate other workplace health programs.

Yet, despite enormous growth in recent years, value measurement of health programs is still in its infancy. Its growth has been hampered by the short-term focus on costs, by the recent movement away from managed-care contracts, and by the inactivity of all but the largest employers (Gabel, Hunt, and Hurst 1998). Furthermore, measurements continue to focus more on clinical indicators than on productivity indicators.

Inadequate Supply of Organized HPM Vendors

While a growing number of studies cite evidence about the value of unique care-management approaches such as, for example, coordinated worker's compensation management and behavioral health case management, few vendors offer these programs. Knowledgeable employers may be hard pressed to find integrated HPM programs in their own communities. Employers could theoretically establish their own programs by contracting directly with health care providers, but such activity is beyond the scope of most benefit departments, even in the very largest companies.

As a rule, market availability is determined in part by employer and purchaser demand as well as the interest of providers in developing these "managed arrangements." Unfortunately, providers are unlikely to offer integrated health-management programs until financial incentives change to reward their development.

Health Payments Are Not Linked to Outcomes

Vendors for the various programs portrayed in figure 8.1 have rarely been paid based on performance measures that capture either the health or the productivity of their populations. Instead, vendors have been paid for assuming claims risk and providing administrative services. In fact, in its recent report entitled *Crossing the Quality Chasm: A New Health System for the 21st Century,* the Institute of Medicine (U.S.) Committee on Quality of Health Care in America (2001) cited the need for innovative payment systems that reward health care providers for delivering effective care as opposed to paying for services regardless of effectiveness, or even whether the service is needed. Payment systems based on outcomes for entire employed populations might even encourage providers to develop integrated programs that cover many of the functions in figure 8.2, rather than individually supplying these programs in silos. As a first step, providers must be educated on the needs and objectives of health care payers and must learn techniques for managing the comprehensive needs of patients across the continuum, including measuring the impact of care on employment outcomes.

Health Insurance Portability and Accountability Act (HIPAA)

Another barrier for the development of integrated HPM programs is the 1996 Health Insurance Portability and Accountability Act (HIPAA). Contrary to the name of the legislation, its most far-reaching aspects contain regulations regarding the collection, sharing, transfer, and use of health-related information. HIPAA has specific implications for employer-sponsored health and benefit programs, both in terms of how employers can access information regarding employee health and how contracted vendors can use such information (Stanton, Scheidt, and Bassier 2003). Hence, HIPAA has made many employers and vendors vigilant about protecting the health information of employees, retirees, and beneficiaries, perhaps to the detriment of integrated HPM programs, which require linking employees' records in a population health-management database (as in figure 8.2). Although employers' wariness of HIPAA is easy to understand, it is still feasible to develop integrated population health-management programs while complying with HIPAA requirements.

Hence, while HIPAA has been viewed as a barrier to HPM integration, it is not an insurmountable one. Data accessibility is important for two reasons. First, employers cannot manage what they do not measure, and evidence about the effectiveness of HPM programs requires measurement. Second, providers need data to demonstrate the effectiveness of HPM programs. Since the majority of medical records are still kept on paper, providers and employers must work together to develop the databases that will be useful for both parties.

Multiple Geographic Locations and Off-Site Employees

Another barrier to establishing a health-management program is the challenge of coordinating benefit programs when employees and dependents are spread across multiple geographic locations. For a firm with many small retail outlets scattered across the country, or for one that has individual employees in remote locations, HPM programs may not be cost-effective. Although the retail firm could contract for integrated health-management programs in each community, the cost of selecting, monitoring, and administering these programs may be prohibitive.

Organized Labor

Even if corporate management is interested in developing an integrated HPM program, organized labor may not consent. As an illustration, consider the recent contract negotiations between the Big Three auto manufacturers (General Motors, Ford, and Chrysler) and the United Auto Workers (UAW). Facing an annual increase in health-insurance premiums of about 12%, management at the Big Three was pushing for cost sharing. However, UAW president Ron Gettelfinger recently declared, "We're not going to share costs" (Hakim 2003).

Some options for integrated HPM do not involve cost-sharing, such as one relying on restricted provider networks to manage patients with chronic illnesses, but unions are likely to reject any program that impinges on the free choice of health care provider. Organized labor may also be opposed to any efforts to measure productivity.

Although unions have historically bargained aggressively for health insurance benefits (Hansen 2003), workers are starting to realize that the cost of health care coverage is becoming unsustainable for employers. Therefore, management and labor may soon become motivated to work together to develop HPM programs that will be mutually beneficial.

SOLUTIONS FOR MINIMIZING THE BARRIERS OF HEALTH AND PRODUCTIVITY MANAGEMENT

Developing a Population Health Approach and Program Consolidation

The first step is for corporations to identify and develop linkages between existing health-related programs. A starting point for this activity is to ask, for each program in figure 8.1, variations on the five questions posed by Kessler and Stang in chapter 14 of this volume:

- What are the most commonly occurring health problems for the relevant population of each employer-sponsored health program?
- What are the effects of these health problems for the populations covered by the program?
- What is the monetary value (loss) associated with these health problems on the company's bottom line?
- What is the availability of effective HPM interventions in reducing these health problems, and what impact would reduction of these problems have on the health program of interest, as well as related programs? How can program outcomes be measured? What is the time frame for realizing program results?
- What is the cost of these proposed interventions, and who would implement them? How could the programs be implemented in an employment setting? Is implementation cost-effective?

Answers to these questions should help to identify the most promising opportunities and lead to priority-setting. While it will be challenging for many firms to answer these questions given the barriers identified above, the measurement strategies reviewed in this book highlight useful approaches to obtaining the necessary information.

Developing the Supply of Integrated HPM Programs

Employers need to send stronger signals to health insurers and health care providers about the demand for integrated HPM so that providers will have an incentive to develop these products. To date, employer actions have been sending the opposite signal, as firms have been shifting away from managed insurance products toward discounted fee-based arrangements. In addition, while employers have begun to request performance measures from health plans, few employers have requested information about productivity indicators such as absenteeism.

Providers should also realize the potential market niche of comprehensive integrated health-management programs that demonstrate value. Achieving this next level of sophistication will require investments in information technology to monitor and manage employees and patients across the continuum of care. It will also require strong coordination and commitment to protocols and guidelines across providers. The development of smaller, exclusive provider networks capable of managing care and demonstrating value may well be necessary. To date, both employers and consumers have been wary of restricted networks and provider access. However, if employers send the right signals, providers will see a competitive advantage to developing new population health-management approaches.

Developing an Information Infrastructure

As mentioned above, both the demand for and the supply of integrated HPM programs is limited by a significant information gap in the marketplace. Traditionally, benefit program administrators used a silo approach, and vendors have provided insurance rather than population health management. However, the information problem in health care goes well beyond employment-based benefit settings, resulting in significant limitations and underachievement of the entire U.S. health care system. The Committee on Quality of Health Care recently made the following recommendation: "Congress, the executive branch, leaders of health care organizations, public and private purchasers, and health informatics associations and vendors should make a renewed national commitment to building an information infrastructure to support health care delivery, consumer health, quality measurement and improvement, public accountability, clinical and health services research, and clinical education. This commitment should lead to the elimination of most handwritten clinical data by the end of the decade" (Institute of Medicine [U.S.] Committee on Quality of Health Care in America 2001, 17).

As this report argues, both private-sector purchasers (i.e., employers) and health care providers have a role to play in the development of information systems. For purposes of developing HPM programs, investments need to be made at both the purchaser and the provider levels. For health care providers, the benefits of automating patient and clinical information offer enormous promise from reduction in drug errors to instant access to a patient's medical record by all authorized providers, to clinical decision support including up-to-date information on the latest medical treatments and scientific evidence. To be useful for managing the health of employed populations and breaking down the silo approach to health-benefit management, provider-level systems must interact with the information systems of employers, or at least be able to link de-identified aggregate-level clinical information with productivity information.

For employers, the starting point is to develop *data warehouses* by merging information from their multiple health-related programs into a database in order to understand the linkages between these programs and the potential for integration and improvement. The ability to answer the questions outlined above will depend on the degree to which such information can be merged. Employers should also think about collecting and managing information on employment outcomes and productivity, as the chapters in the first part of this volume discuss.

The development of state-of-the-art information systems and the linkage of data across purchaser and provider functions will provide opportunities for developing integrated HPM programs that are cost-effective. In a utopian world, providers would be able to monitor the link between health conditions and job performance, resulting in a better understanding of the health care needs and treatment options of employees. Providers could also manage the simultaneous needs of patients and employers in one program, breaking down the silos that currently exist in health-benefit management. Finally, innovative approaches to providing patient care such as electronic visits and telemedicine can be developed.

In short, creation of an information infrastructure is probably the most important ingredient for developing integrated HPM programs in employment settings. The two biggest barriers to developing such information systems are the investments required by health care providers and the cultural barriers of medicine, which has been slow to adopt information technology. Purchasers should take note of these barriers, particularly the financial investment required of providers to implement an information infrastructure. But the wide use of information systems will pay off in terms of better quality and efficiency.

Paying for Performance: Linking Health Payment Systems to Outcomes

As the discussion about information technology suggests, employers and other health care purchasers should develop financial incentives that reward investments and activities that meet purchaser goals. While this seems obvious, health care payment systems have not been developed in this fashion because of both the narrow focus on insurance rather than population health management and the lack of sound outcome or process measurements on which to base provider payments.

Another barrier to the development of innovative payment systems by employers is that very large employers represent only a fraction of any health care provider's business. Hence, pay-for-performance systems will produce a meaningful economic incentive only when multiple employers pool performance information. Forward-thinking measurements and payment programs could be developed to encourage linkages between the various health programs managed by employers (general health insurance benefits, worker's compensation, EAP, etc.). The Institute of Medicine's Committee on Quality of Care also addressed the payment issue:

> Although some purchasers are pursuing payment approaches that include rewards for quality, all existing methods could be modified to create stronger incentives for quality improvement. Purchasers should identify ways to (1) recognize quality, (2) reward quality, and (3) support quality improvement. For example, quality could be recognized by developing better quality measures and making their results more broadly available to covered populations, whether through new forms of information or improvements in the ways existing information is shared. Quality could be rewarded by using direct payment mechanisms or by redirecting volume to health plans and providers recognized for providing high-quality care by offering stronger incentives for people to seek out better quality care (e.g., adjustments to out-of-pocket costs). Quality improvement could be supported by exploring the potential for shared-risk arrangements that could encourage making significant changes in care processes to improve quality. Although more fundamental change may be required in the long run, immediate improvements can and should be pursued. (Institute of Medicine [U.S.] Committee on Quality of Health Care in America 2001, 182)

Although payments have historically been fee-for-service based, some employers have begun experimenting with performance-based payment systems. For example, General Electric, Verizon, and a handful of other purchasers have developed *Bridges to Excellence,* a pilot program that rewards individual physicians and practices for complying with recommended guidelines for treating patients with chronic illnesses such as diabetes (Prince 2003). General Motors, which has been evaluating health plans using HEDIS and CAHPS data and the eValue8 RFI data, reduces the monthly out-of-pocket costs to salaried employees who choose the better-rated plans. The Leapfrog Group has established an "incentives and rewards" program in which six pilots are being led by individual employers or purchasing coalitions to develop and implement incentives for hospitals to adopt Leapfrog's hospital-based patient safety leaps (Leapfrog Group 2003). Finally, all of these efforts are being aided by the recent announcement by Centers for Medicare and Medicaid Services of its pay-for-performance program (Pear and Walsh 2003).

However, these innovative employer-based payment programs focus on general health insurance benefit programs rather than on other work-health programs. In addition, the value/benefit measures have not been linked to job outcomes or productivity. Future efforts should consider these linkages, as well as other innovative payment approaches such as multiyear contracts, bundled or blended payments, and risk-adjusted payments.

Incentivizing the Healthy Behavior of Employees

Skyrocketing health care costs are affecting not only corporate competitiveness but also employee job security and wages. Thus, like employers and providers, employees and those who represent employees (e.g., organized labor) have a direct interest in discussions about HPM programs.

At a macro level, employees need to be better educated about the cost of health care and employment-related health-benefit programs as well as the rate at which these expenditures have been growing. Employees should understand the link between health and job productivity as well as the impact of absenteeism and presenteeism on the bottom line. Finally, employees should be educated about population health-management approaches to care delivery. While much of the consumer criticism generated in the managed-care backlash debate was valid, consumers should not overlook the advantages that can be achieved by appropriately run managed-care programs.

At the micro level, employers should explore approaches that provide incentives for employees to engage in healthy behaviors. For example, some companies have reduced out-of-pocket contributions for health-insurance premiums for employees who complete an annual health–risk appraisal questionnaire. Other companies provide incentives for smoking cessation or wellness, or for using generic rather than brand-name drugs. The development of an integrated HPM will be unsuccessful without the support of individual employees and organized labor.

EXAMPLE

One example of an integrated HPM is the Minnesota Health Partnership and Coordinated Health Care and Disability Prevention Program. The Minnesota Health Partnership (MHP) is a coalition of private and public-sector employers, health care provider groups, and health plans that received funding from the Robert Wood Johnson Foundation to develop, test, and evaluate a pilot program. The program integrates treatment for both work-related and non-occupational disability and provides education for general physicians (those not trained in occupational medicine or worker's compensation management) about disability prevention and disability management in employed populations (McGrail et al. 2002).

The project, which originated with a group of Minneapolis employers (the Buyer's Health Care Action Group [BHCAG]), is based on two observations: that roughly two-thirds of lost income due to disability-related absence in the United States stems from nonworkplace injury or illness, and that community physicians are typically both unaware of this link and unfamiliar with effective techniques for managing these patients' return to the workplace.

Many employers have developed worker's compensation programs to address treatment for work-related injuries, but these programs rarely address the needs of patients with work absence due to nonoccupational conditions (McGrail et al. 2002). The objectives of the MHP program were to "decrease morbidity associated with inactivity and worklessness, decrease long-term medical and indemnity costs, and improve patient satisfaction with their health care" (McGrail et al. 2002, 44). After extensive study, the Minnesota employers identified several problems with the traditional system:

> For instance employers frequently found minimal communication between workers' compensation risk management and general health and disability benefits personnel, which led to an internal lack of accountability for total employee health and productivity. Job accommodations for non-work related conditions often were not pursued as aggressively as for work-related injuries, and disability benefits sometimes were used to solve personnel problems. At the same time, employees directed to specific occupational health providers for workers' compensation conditions often voiced concern over lack of provider choice in comparison to the options available to coworkers with nonoccupational health problems.
>
> Employers also perceived that, in general, primary care providers in the general health care system did not address disability prevention,

or emphasize appropriate activity to their patients as a component of their health message. Other than in occupational health, employers reported that physicians and other health care providers seemed to believe that an effort to encourage early return for their patients, even in a modified work status, was contrary to their role as patient advocates. A lack of trust in the employer's ability to maintain a safe work environment, as well as a lack of understanding of the actual work place, appeared to be contributing factors. Meetings with physicians revealed that, as a group, they felt poorly trained to determine what is appropriate activity for patients, and were most comfortable with a "don't ask, don't need to advise" approach. (McGrail et al. 2002, 45)

The employers' review led to the development of a pilot program that involved relying on existing organized multispecialty physician groups, known as "care systems" in Minneapolis, to manage the care of all disabled patients, regardless of whether the disability occurred in the workplace. In addition, traditional occupational disability accommodations usually reserved for workplace injuries were extended to employees with nonoccupational injuries and illnesses. To bridge this gap, BHCAG and its contracted care systems provided extensive education for its physicians and health care providers about disability management and return-to-work activity. In addition, human resource departments of the participating employers were educated regarding workplace accommodations under this new medical-care-management arrangement. While the results of the program have yet to be published, the MHP continues to assess both the costs and benefits associated with this novel integrated disability health-management program.

CONCLUSION

Despite the vast research cited throughout this book linking health and productivity, few employers are actively engaged in integrated health productivity management programs. This chapter has outlined barriers to using HPM in employment settings and has proposed some strategies for making HPM a more frequently pursued objective. Both employers and providers need to consider the following questions: *Is there a better way to produce health in employed populations? Is there a market for producing health and productivity?* Current evidence suggests that the market for HPM may be growing, but only time will tell if HPM becomes more than a short-lived buzzword.

The staggering recent increases in health care costs suggest that the window of opportunity for HPM is now, because employers can ill afford to continue to spend more and more money on health-related benefits without receiving more value for these expenditures. At present, employers are keenly interested in alternative arrangements that are likely to be more effective and efficient. The chapters in the first part of this volume outline a variety of methods for empirically addressing the relationship between health and productivity. Employers and the research community should realize that these tools are key to providing the necessary information for employers to become more effective value-based health purchasers. In addition, these tools will provide information that providers need in order to develop effective programs for managing the health of employed populations.

The literature generated by these research tools may eventually lead to broad-based changes in how the health of employed populations is managed and monitored. If that much can be accomplished, then the field will have made great leaps, and both employers and employees will have benefited.

REFERENCES

Cascio, W. F. 2000. *Costing human resources: The financial impact of behavior in organizations.* 4th ed. Cincinnati: South-Western College Publishing.

Chernew, M., W. Wodchis, D. P. Scanlon, and C. McLaughlin. 2004. Overlap in HMO physician networks. *Health Affairs* 23, no. 2: 91–101.

Gabel, J. R., K. A. Hunt, and K. M. Hurst. 1998. When employers choose health plans: Do NCQA accreditation and HEDIS data count? Commonwealth Fund, New York.

Hakim, D. 2003. Their health costs soaring, automakers are to begin labor talks. *New York Times,* July 15, final ed., C1.

Hansen, F. 2003. Cost-sharing will dominate talks. *Workforce* 82:16.

Huth, S. A. 2001. Technology is now prime information tool for benefits managers, survey reports. *Employee Benefit Plan Review* 56:14–20.

Institute for Health and Productivity Management. 1998–2004. *What is health and productivity management, anyway?* http://www.ihpm.org.

Institute of Medicine (U.S.) Committee on Quality of Health Care in America. 2001. *Crossing the quality chasm: A new health system for the 21st century.* Washington, DC: National Academy Press.

Leapfrog Group. 2003. Basic incentives and rewards toolkit for frogs. White paper, vol. 2003, Leapfrog Group, Washington, DC.

Lipson, D. J., and J. M. De Sa. 1996. Impact of purchasing strategies on local health care systems. *Health Affairs* 15:62–76.

McGrail, M. P., Jr., M. Calasanz, J. Christianson, C. Cortez, B. Dowd, R. Gorman, W. H. Lohman, D. Parker, D. M. Radosevich, and G. Westman. 2002. The Minnesota Health Partnership and Coordinated Health Care and Disability Prevention: The implementation of an integrated benefits and medical model. *Journal of Occupational Rehabilitation* 12:43–54.

Midwest Business Group on Health, Juran Institute Inc., and The Severyn Group Inc. 2002. *Reducing the costs of poor-quality health care through responsible purchasing leadership.* Midwest Business Group on Health, http://www.mbgh.org/pdf/Cost%20of%20Poor%20Quality%20Report.pdf.

Parmenter, E. M. 2003. Controlling health care costs: Components of a new paradigm. *Journal of Financial Services Professionals* 57:59.

Pear, R., and M. W. Walsh. 2003. Medicare to pay bonuses for best of hospital care. *New York Times*, July 11, final ed., 10.

Peterson, M. A. 1999. Introduction: Politics, misperception, or apropos? *Journal of Health Politics, Policy, and Law* 24:873–86.

Prince, M. 2003. Pay-for-performance plans seek to cut costs: Bonuses paid for quality health care. *Business Insurance*, April 28, 4.

Pugh, T. 2003. Health-plan premiums spike 14 pct. in one year. *Philadelphia Inquirer*, September 10, CO1.

Rosenheck, R. A., B. Druss, M. Stolar, D. Leslie, and W. Sledge. 1999. Effect of declining mental health service use on employees of a large corporation. *Health Affairs* 18:193–203.

Scanlon, D. P., M. Chernew, and H. Doty. 2002. *Evaluating the impact of value-based purchasing initiatives: A guide for purchasers.* Agency for Healthcare Research and Quality (AHRQ) publication no. 02-0029. Rockville, MD: AHRQ.

Scanlon, D. P., M. Chernew, H. E. Doty, and D. G. Smith. 2001. Options for assessing PPO quality: Accreditation and profiling as accountability strategies. *Medical Care Research and Review* 58:70–101.

Selby, J. V., D. P. Scanlon, J. Elston-Lafata, V. Villagra, J. Beich, and P. R. Salber. 2003. Determining the value of disease management programs. *Joint Commission Journal on Quality and Safety* 29, no. 19: 491–99.

Stanton, T., K. Scheidt, and S. A. Bassier. 2003. What every employer needs to know about the HIPAA privacy rules. *Employee Benefit Plan Review* 57:21–26.

Wagner, E. H., B. T. Austin, C. Davis, M. Hindmarsh, J. Schaefer, and A. Bonomi. 2001. Improving chronic illness care: Translating evidence into action. *Health Affairs* 20:64–78.

Woolhandler, S., T. Campbell, and D. U. Himmelstein. 2003. Costs of health care administration in the United States and Canada. *New England Journal of Medicine* 349:768–75.

CHAPTER 9

Investing in Health to Boost Employee Productivity: The Employer's Perspective

JAMES F. MURRAY, SEAN NICHOLSON, MARK PAULY, AND MARC L. BERGER

INTRODUCTION

As argued throughout this book, corporate America would benefit from shifting to an investment approach toward all health-related expenditures, including health-promotion services and health care coverage for employees. As with any other investment, an employer should estimate both the projected returns from an investment in health coverage/programs and the related costs. While this cost-benefit calculus has been applied to health issues from a societal perspective (Berger et al. 2001; Gold et al. 1996), its practical application in the design and administration of employee health benefits and programs has yet to occur. A major reason why the business community has been hesitant to embrace this approach has been the difficulty of quantifying the impact of health benefits and improvement programs on workforce productivity.

To maximize output, companies need to maximize workforce productivity at a given level of labor and costs (including health-related costs). Thus, employers need to make decisions from a systemwide perspective, taking into account the labor market as well as employees' preferences. In fact, by simply shifting benefit costs to workers or by minimizing costs, a company may actually cause harm to its productive capacity. For example, inadequate health benefits might lead workers to make demands for higher cash wages and cause drops in morale along with increases in absenteeism, presenteeism, on-the-job accidents, and employee turnover. Employers make many investment choices in their strategy to attract and retain employees (e.g., signing bonuses, moving expenses, compensation incentives). This chapter focuses on the employer investment in employee health.

The principal challenge for employers is to improve the design and management of health expenditures in a way that maximizes the return on their investment. Because health is a quantifiable measure and outcomes such as productivity and health status can be measured by a variety of available instruments, it is helpful to conceptualize health as a commodity. In other words, employee health, like any other resource, has a monetary valuation. A comprehensive approach to health investments should therefore include the impact of health-related variables on costs and revenues. How much of workforce productivity is health-related? What impact do changes in workforce health status have on productivity? What impact do changes in the effectiveness of health care interventions (as reflected by quality, for example) have on productivity, and at what cost?

CURRENT APPROACHES TO QUANTIFYING THE RETURN ON EMPLOYEE HEALTH-RELATED INVESTMENTS

Determining the value of health-related investments in employees must be multifaceted, addressing all aspects of how health affects or is affected by the work environment. These investments must be put into the context of other

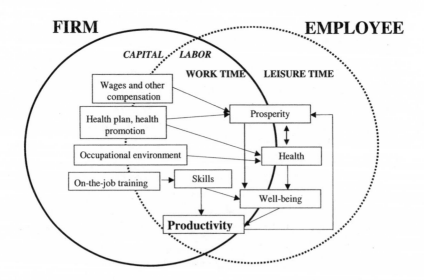

Figure 9.1. Interrelationships of work environment and productivity cost components

TABLE 9.1.

INDIRECT COST OF ILLNESS FROM THE

INDIVIDUAL, SOCIETAL, AND EMPLOYER PERSPECTIVES

	INDIVIDUAL PERSPECTIVE	SOCIETAL PERSPECTIVE	EMPLOYER PERSPECTIVE
DEFINITION	Value of a human life in terms of a person's income and value of leisure time	Value of a human life in terms of a person's potential income generation	Cost of the disease to the employer from illness and/or death
CALCULATION			
MORTALITY	The Ultimate Loss Effect on family	Present value of forgone future income	Cost of replacing workers (hiring and training)
MORBIDITY	Loss of income (e.g., unpaid sick-leave days, decrement in income when on disability) and loss of leisure time	Lost income from missed work	Work loss, idle assets, and nonwage costs (e.g., benefits and fixed payroll costs)

employee benefits such as compensation, nonhealth benefits, training, and career development. All investments in employees affect employee well-being and the wage levels required to compete in the labor market and contribute to the productivity of the workforce (fig. 9.1). The impacts of these investments, we will argue, are uniquely related to the nature of the work the employees are performing and the characteristics of the employer. Therefore, the employer perspective on the value of health is not the same as the societal or individual perspective.

Three Perspectives: Individual Worker, Societal, and Employer

Health investments have typically been quantified through the relatively narrow prism of mortality (i.e., life-years saved), morbidity, and associated indirect costs such as absenteeism and presenteeism. However, the precise evaluation of these indirect costs depends on whether one is taking the perspective of the individual, the employer, or society (See table 9.1).

From an individual worker's perspective, indirect costs include factors such as an impaired ability to earn income or to engage in leisure activities due to morbidity (or the loss of life) as well as the lost economic contributions for dependents due to premature death. These dimensions are usually measured in terms of lost income plus the value of lost leisure time.

From the societal view, the measurement of indirect costs is based on the premise that the value of an individual's work to society is equal to a person's potential income (Gold et al. 1996). (That the individual often consumes most of what he or she produces is considered irrelevant.) This measure of value can be further refined along the two dimensions of morbidity and mortality. The impact of avoidable mortality is measured in terms of the present value of forgone future income. The impact of morbidity is measured in terms of lost income from missed work.

From an employer's perspective, the valuation of morbidity and mortality include only the costs that affect the employer, not society as a whole. An employer's valuation of work loss may include, but need not be restricted to, the following:

1. Higher wage costs;
2. Lost production;
3. Idle assets;
4. Employee turnover; and
5. Other nonwage costs incurred by the employer (e.g., benefits, indirect business taxes, nontax liabilities).

The cost of mortality to the employer generally excludes the present value of future earnings forgone due to premature death. The wage offset (if any) in firms with less effective benefit plans and consequent higher mortality may be greater or less than the present value of lost future income (depending on worker information and the value the employer places on longevity). The firm's cost of morbidity also includes the cost of idle assets and nonwage factors as well as other expenditures the employer makes to mitigate the effect of absences (such as additional staffing, overtime pay, hiring of more costly or less productive temporary workers, and additional inventory).

These differences in perspective have a profound impact on the valuation of morbidity and mortality to indirect costs. In the societal perspective, the estimate of indirect costs stems largely from premature mortality and the present value of lost future income. For example, using the societal perspective, the American Heart Association estimated that indirect costs for coronary heart disease (CHD) were $46.7 billion in 1999. Of this amount, $6.9 billion (19%) was due to morbidity. The remaining $39.8 billion (81%) was due to mortality (American Heart Association 1999). Using the employer perspective and assuming no wage offset, we, along with others, have reported that the indirect cost to employers was a total of $4,298 per employee with CHD per year (Guico-Pabia et al. 2001). The overwhelming component of indirect cost was related to morbidity (95.2%) rather than mortality (4.8%).

The most frequently used method of estimating indirect costs is the lost-wages method (sometimes called the "human capital" method, even though discounted future lost wages are sometimes not fully taken into account in the measure, and the value of lost leisure is usually not included). The method is straightforward. According to the neoclassical economic model, wage rates are equal to the value of marginal revenue generated by an additional worker under full employment. Thus, indirect costs are quantified in terms of forgone earnings (Osterhaus, Gutterman, and Plachetka 1992). Lost production is measured using gross compensation at the individual level, and the absenteeism loss to a firm providing sickness benefits (in the form of continuation of wage payments) is calculated by multiplying the estimated number of workdays missed by the estimated average daily earnings. Of course, if there are no sickness benefits and the worker does not receive the daily wage for a missed workday, the cost still equals the lost wage, but now the worker incurs the cost in the short run. Presenteeism, which is defined as the percentage of productivity reduction on days worked with symptoms, is typically measured by employee self-report (Legg et al. 1997; Osterhaus, Gutterman, and Plachetka 1992).

While the lost-wages approach is founded in economic theory, estimation of indirect costs using this method from a societal perspective usually makes some simplifying assumptions. It considers only monetary compensation and ignores other dimensions that have intrinsic and economic value, such as loss of leisure time and the "consumption" value of any change in health status. In addition, the estimates obtained are sensitive to assumptions built into the calculation (Jacobs and Fassbender 1998). For example, some studies assume a fixed time period, while others use a variable time period, such as life expectancy. Likewise, some studies include only paid labor, others include all activities, and a few include unemployment. The method employed to value forgone paid work also varies among different studies. Most studies use the all-industry average wage to calculate the value of lost labor time; others use the minimum wage or the wage rate for a specific group. Subjectivity in these dimensions may account for the wide variation in the results.

The lost-wages method has been widely used to measure the societal costs of illness. However, this method may not provide reliable estimates of the economic consequences of disease (Koopmanschap and Rutten 1996). As Drummond pointed out (1992), a given person's work may be made up by the sick employee on his return to work after a short absence. In the short run, wage costs would then be unaffected (or possibly even reduced, if sick benefits do not fully replace wages). However, in the long run, equilibrium wages would be higher in firms that require this practice compared to those that do not.

If the unemployment rate is above the full employment level, society may not actually suffer a loss of output because the worker can be replaced with a previously unemployed person, meaning that the amount of income generated would not change. However, this calculation, in turn, assumes perfect interchangeability between workers, and assigns no value to the leisure of the unemployed.

From the employer's perspective, the unemployment rate itself does not matter, since the employer will have to pay a wage to the replacement worker even if there is high unemployment. The state of the labor market may affect the extent to which health benefits and health effects trade off against wages, since wage offsets are properties of labor markets in equilibrium, not markets with excess supply. Nevertheless, the difference in treatment of indirect costs between employer and societal perspective is perhaps greatest in times of above-normal unemployment.

The Challenges Faced by Employers in Estimating Indirect Costs

Employers attempting to estimate indirect costs face significant challenges due to the scarcity and the unproven validity of the necessary data. Several chapters in this book examine sophisticated methods for the collection and analysis of work-loss and productivity data. Three approaches are discussed:

1. Self-reported work and productivity loss (chapter 4);
2. Primary data collection using sophisticated experimental designs (chapter 5); and
3. Use of administrative data collected as part of normal work policies and procedures (chapter 2).

Currently, these methods have limited use for employers for various reasons. First, validations of self-reported work and productivity loss have focused on jobs that have quantifiable output (e.g., calls answered per hour or pieces produced per hour). Second, conversion of the work-loss time into actual effects on the company's bottom line is tenuous. As such, current measures of productivity can be used only as a qualitative measure of program benefits rather than as a generalized measure of health-related productivity. Finally, even when accurate data are available, calculation of indirect costs based on the lost-wages method is excessively simplistic, because it is based on assumptions that are unlikely to hold in general application (Pauly et al. 2002).

Assuming full employment or even above-normal employment, we contend that wages represent a lower bound for societal costs due to work loss. A more realistic model of valuing work loss would not employ the naive assumption that any single method can be applied to all firms. Specific firm and market characteristics influence whether the costs of work loss will be large or small, and how these costs will be distributed between employer and employee (Berger et al. 2001; Pauly et al. 2002). For example, a firm that depends on team performance rather than on individual performance will require a different model for valuing work loss, since a worker's absence can affect the output of the entire team. The same holds true if there is a large dependence on firm-specific human capital (e.g., knowledge workers are needed to do the job tasks) versus a small dependence on firm-specific human capital (e.g., temporary workers can easily perform the job tasks). Another important characteristic is whether the job function is labor-intensive, capital-intensive, or a combination of both. Finally, the valuation of work loss will also depend on how work loss affects the flow of output. The valuation of work loss in a firm that has large inventory (or small costs associated with variations in output) will be very different than in a firm that has small inventory (or incurs large costs associated with output shortfalls relative to the expected or desired level).

TOWARD A MORE GENERAL AND REALISTIC APPROACH FOR MEASUREMENT AND VALUATION OF WORK LOSS

Given the concerns about current methods of valuing work loss, we have proposed a new conceptual framework (Pauly et al. 2002) that we summarize informally here. We assume that a firm that offers full sickness benefits (i.e., pays wages when the employee is sick) hires workers in a labor market in competitive equilibrium, with unemployment at the normal "transitional" level. Let's also assume that workers know the wage and benefits that employers offer, and they also know the conditions of work. For example, workers know whether the firm has a policy of requiring absent workers to make up lost output with no additional compensation or whether others are expected to work harder when someone is absent. However, employers do not pay different wages to different workers based on their individual health or effort levels.

For the vast majority of firms, the consequence of any employee absence can be larger than the average output per worker. However, this outcome will not occur in jobs in which each worker works alone (or in which the worker's productivity depends only on capital). Studies of productivity effects associated with illness usually focus on jobs where the production process is essentially piecework—for example, a worker at a call-in center or an insurance claim processor (Berndt et al. 2000; Cockburn et al. 1999)—and output is easily attributable to individual workers.

In contrast, many jobs depend on teamwork, meaning that the firm's output depends to some extent on the simultaneous presence of all (or some subset of) workers. For example, jobs that involve real-time exchanges of information or materials or that depend on collective activity such as meetings or group presentations fall into this category. With such a production process, the absence of a worker who cannot be replaced with a perfect substitute typically leads to a loss of output much larger than the wage per worker. In an extreme case (e.g., an impossible-to-replace worker is absent), the team may not be able to produce any output at all.

Loss in output from an absence will be particularly large in firms that

1.   rely on team production; and/or
2.   are unable to find good substitutes at the wage rate; and/or
3.   have a time-sensitive demand for output (so the production process either cannot be postponed until the worker recovers, or can be postponed, but at a cost).

We note that not all workers need to have the same "essential" character for this phenomenon to occur. The manager of a retail store who has the responsibility to open the cash register or approve transactions may have a more costly absence than the salespersons who work individually. We have undertaken a set of case studies to determine whether jobs in firms with one or more of these characteristics can be identified and whether they are relatively common.

Case I

The packaging department at a pharmaceutical firm, whose managers we interviewed, provides an example of how the impact of an absent worker can exceed the wage when there is team production.

The department has about 150 employees who package vaccines and drugs into containers, blisters, and vials. They operate three shifts per day, five days per week to take advantage of the expensive equipment involved in the production process. The packages are produced with a series of automated workstations that cost over $1 million each. Two, three, or four employees must be situated at each workstation in order for the assembly line to function. If a single worker is absent and no qualified replacement is available, no drugs can be packaged. In this case, the cost of the absence would be the value of the team's output, not the wage of the absent worker. If the team's wages are equal to the value of their output, the cost of the absence is the sum of the team's wages and the opportunity cost of the capital equipment, a figure that greatly exceeds the wage of the single absent worker.

Since absences can be so costly in this department, managers have taken a number of steps to minimize their impact. Each day, about 5 workers are assigned to complete some manual tasks rather than to work on the auto-mated assembly line, even though these workers have been trained to operate the workstations on the assembly line. When an assembly line worker is absent, the manager replaces her or him with a manual worker and the packaging process can proceed as scheduled. The cost of an absence is therefore much less than the sum of the wages of the entire team of workers, but it is higher than the wage of the absent worker. The cost of absences should include the cost of training the manual workers to fill in for absent assembly line workers (estimated by the department manager to be 10% of the manual workers' wages) and the opportunity cost of not automating the entire department's activities. After all, the department decided not to automate the manual component of the work precisely because the availability of the manual workers minimizes the impact of an absent assembly line worker. The department therefore consciously overstaffs in one area in order to minimize total production costs, including the costs stemming from absences.

In this case study, the packaging department was able to find a replacement worker with the same productivity as the absent worker, which helped keep the cost of an absence close to the wage of the absent worker. Our second case study illustrates how the cost of work loss can greatly exceed the wage when it is difficult or impossible to find a perfect substitute.

Case II

We interviewed the office manager at a firm that employs 70 stockbrokers who are responsible for attracting investment funds from new and existing clients, offering investment advice to the clients, and servicing the accounts. The investment bank generates commissions on all client transactions. When a stockbroker is absent, the support staff on a stockbroker's team will process trades for clients who call with a specific request. However, the support staff does not have the same rapport with the client as the stockbroker and, therefore, cannot function as a perfect substitute for the absent stockbroker. The support staff can respond to the clients' requests but do not offer recommendations regarding portfolio adjustments. Likewise, the other stockbrokers in the firm cannot serve as a perfect substitute because they have an incomplete understanding of a given client's risk preferences and investment objectives. The cost of the stockbroker's absence is the difference between the commissions the stockbroker would have generated if he had been present and the commissions generated by the support staff in his absence. This cost can greatly exceed the wage because stockbrokers cannot make up the work they miss; the stock-market conditions that generated trading opportunities typically vanish by the time they return.

Our third case study highlights how the cost of an absence can exceed the wage of the absent worker when the production process cannot be postponed or when postponing the production process is itself costly.

Case III

We examined a biostatistics department at a pharmaceutical firm that is responsible for collecting and analyzing the patient-level data from clinical trials (e.g., randomized controlled trials of a new drug versus a placebo). From their analyses, they prepare reports for the Food and Drug Administration (FDA) regarding the safety and effectiveness of the drugs that are being developed. About one-half of the 250 people in the department collect data from clinical trials, verify accuracy, and enter it into the computer. The other half of the workers in the department analyze the data and prepare the FDA reports. When department members are absent, the company does not always meet its self-imposed deadline for filing a report with the FDA. As a result, there may be a delay in receiving FDA approval for selling the drug to consumers. The cost of an absence can be measured as the cost of a delay in filing the report. Experts in the pharmaceutical industry estimate that each extra day a blockbuster drug spends in development "costs" a firm approximately $1 million in the form of forgone profit (Tighe 2001). However, the actual cost of an absence never approaches this figure because managers will take steps (e.g., hire extra staff) to reduce the chance that absences will cause filing delays. In any event, delaying production carries a penalty that, all else being equal, drives the cost of an absence to an amount above the wage of the absent worker.

This new theory of the cost of work loss also emphasizes that wages may be tied to work-loss effects. Consider Drummond's example of a firm that has a policy of requiring a worker (or a team of workers) to make up output lost due to illness later at a (presumably) less convenient time, but with no specific increase in pay. In this model, such a firm will have to pay higher wages than a firm that permitted output to fall but did not burden workers with such a requirement. After the fact, the first firm may have the same productivity if work loss is high as if it is low, but it will have to pay higher wages to compensate for the greater likelihood of work at an inconvenient time or at an inconvenient pace.

Finally, the theory points out that firms may appear to suffer relatively small impacts from lost work time because they have taken costly steps to prevent or cushion such losses. In the most obvious case, a firm that expected a high absenteeism rate would hire a larger complement of workers to produce a given output than a firm that expected a low absenteeism rate. In effect, the firm chooses to have a costly stock of substitute workers who would not be needed if workers missed fewer days on average. Likewise, a firm may maintain a large inventory of finished goods, at some cost, because a "just-in-time" system fails when workers call in sick.

In the final analysis, this theory posits that the cost of absences is more than the observed short-run lost productivity. A correct measure of indirect cost must include both the cost of actual lost output and the cost of all "preventive" activities. Alternatively, a manager should not think of the cost of work loss as the answer to the question "What would happen right now if one of my workers happened to miss a workday?" Instead, he should compare his total labor cost and output when workers miss work at the current rate with what those costs and output would be if there were a permanent reduction in the rate of absenteeism. In the latter case, the ability to economize on preventive and cushioning measures will become more apparent, as will the value of increasing wages to pay workers for imposed inconvenience.

WHAT SHOULD A MANAGER DO TODAY?

The previous sections covered the theoretical underpinnings of efforts to measure the cost to the employer of work absences due to illness. As we showed, this cost is often higher than commonly assumed. In this section, we explain how managers can use this new model to make more efficient decisions about health benefits for their workers. In addition, we also address better tools that might make this process easier for managers in the future.

Estimating the ROI for Investments in Health-Related Productivity

Given the theoretical complexity of measuring workplace productivity, it is not surprising that current efforts to measure this variable tend to be imprecise. Thus, we recognize that a perfect analysis of the net benefit or return from investments in improved worker health can neither be sought nor expected. But what can be done to make the most reasonable judgment in the face of uncertainty?

Based on our model, we propose that managers should take the following initial steps:

1. Develop a benchmark monetary estimate of the cost and benefit of reducing work loss;
2. Demonstrate that it is financially significant (i.e., that the benefit is not too low and that benefit exceeds cost); and
3. Demonstrate the potential for the financial impact to be much higher (i.e., a benefit could be greater than estimated).

The initial benchmark should be the worker's wage or pay per time period. This represents the minimum value of the lost worker's output if the firm is hiring the proper number of workers. Subject to some exceptions we mention below, if a firm can suffer the loss of a day's work from a sick worker and yet not lose at least the monetary equivalent of the worker's wage, it is overstaffed. Our case studies indicate that most American firms are "lean" and limited in their staffing. Temporary drops in business can change this pattern, but the changes typically do not last long since firms tend to respond to downturns in business with disproportionately large layoffs.

Interventions whose costs per work-loss-day-avoided fall short of the wage per day can be immediately judged to pass a return on investment test—that is, they return more benefits than costs. However, some skeptical higher-level managers may question whether the wage is a proper measure since, after all, almost every department will have gone through a period of unexpectedly high absences without self-destructing. Don't we just ask other workers to pitch in and work harder or work overtime to make up for the lost worker, and don't we often train workers so they can do more than their own job in case of just this eventuality?

As we discussed at length in the previous section, such approaches lead to underestimation of the cost of illness. The workers asked to work at inconvenient times or at an inconvenient pace will eventually require higher wages (unless they were overpaid to begin with), and the extra training has a cost of its own. Even the presence of workers able to fill in by abandoning their current job may represent a de facto overstaffing, which itself has a cost. And if these measures are pursued to their efficient level, at the margin, the loss from a missed day will still be the wage per day.

As also noted above, an intervention may return more than its cost even if the intervention's cost per work-loss day avoided exceeded the daily wage. Where a firm relies on team production and has time-sensitive output requirements (and/or an inability to make perfect substitutions between workers), the cost to the firm of an absence can well exceed the worker's wage. The issue is how to determine when this is true and how to demonstrate the size of the loss. Except for those who supervise piecework employees, all managers know the essential uncertainty of measuring the precise number of workers needed to accomplish what the firm requires from their department or division. And yet managers somehow arrive at reasonable staffing levels and provide the services or outputs that keep the firm operating. Thus, managers must have some way of determining how many workers are needed to do the task at hand.

The specialized tools needed to quantify the value of lost work in these situations are not yet available, so managers will need to use less formal methods. For example, they might categorize workers in a given department or division according to the impact their absence (short-term or long-term, expected or unexpected) would have on the unit's ability to provide its required services. Relative to a benchmark job such as administrative assistant, are there jobs in which absences can cause greater loss? It would be most convincing to cite low-wage jobs that are critical to the department's ability to sustain a steady workflow. Once the point is made that damage can be greater than the wage, managers could make estimates for other jobs in terms of the relative consequences for workflow. For example, even though wellness programs may have only a limited impact on absenteeism, if these programs are directed at workers involved in team production, the payoff may be large.

From a broader perspective, even though most large organizations have some type of formal process for planning staffing needs, companies rarely distinguish between workers on the payroll and the quantity of person-hours or person-days available for work for each job type. Thus, managers need to take into account all of the following factors:

1. Total absences due to illness;
2. Partial reductions in productivity for people who come to work with an acute or chronic illness (presenteeism);
3. Vacation days and other personal days; and

4. Absences from a worker's main task due to in-service training or other such activities.

Once "effective work time" rather than days paid can be the measure of inputs, it becomes easier to quantify the value of health-related investments. While a formal measure of output is beyond the scope of most firms, approximations may be useful. As our case studies indicate, managers actually possess accurate estimates of work loss due to illness for various types of workers. The problem, therefore, stems not from the lack of knowledge but from the lack of documentation that quantifies the potential benefits. This might be surmounted through investing resources for work-loss-reduction programs at the departmental or division level and having their effects monitored directly by the responsible manager. Alternatively, companies might implement a firmwide system to track work loss, its consequences, and its change over time in response to firmwide efforts to reduce work loss.

Portfolio of Investment Choices in Health-Related Productivity

Recognizing that work loss has an impact that can be measured at the level of its minimum cost, how does a manager address it at a practical level? A manager must decide how much to invest in various programs that can potentially reduce health-related productivity losses, just as an individual investor needs to decide on the overall mix of investments in his portfolio. Likewise, the manager needs to categorize the various options according to the size of the potential investment and the expected timeframe for its maturation. Given today's measurement limitations, the manager will necessarily have to employ the human-capital method of estimating indirect costs (although, as discussed, this method often underestimates the impact).

The range of interventions includes health-promotion programs, prevention programs, redesigned benefits, selection of higher-quality health care providers, disease-management programs, and case-management programs. These interventions can be categorized according to the relative cost per employee and the planning period over which returns would be expected (see fig. 9.2).

For health-promotion programs targeted at diet and exercise, the costs are generally low and the time horizon for the benefits is long-term. For example, good evidence suggests that the costs associated with excess weight and obesity are significant (Burton, Chen, et al. 1999; Colditz 1999). The benefits of these programs tend to outweigh the associated costs (Hatziandreu et al. 1988; Nicholl, Coleman, and Brazier 1994), although the true im-

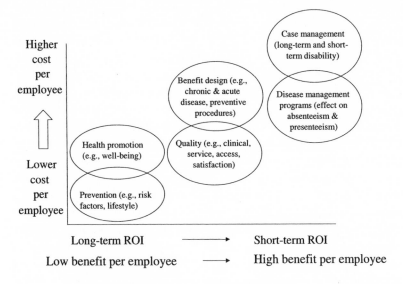

Figure 9.2. Portfolio of investments in health-related productivity

pact of exercise and weight-loss programs on work loss, productivity, and output has not been established. Nevertheless, given the strong link between BMI and health care cost (Burton, Chen, et al. 1999), it should be possible to project potential wage or quality offsets from successful programs.

Another focus of health-promotion programs has been smoking cessation. One study estimates that of the total health care costs associated with smoking, 9% are indirect costs caused by lost productivity; another study estimated the average work loss for a smoker versus a nonsmoker to be an additional two days of absence per year (Williams and Franklin 1993). However, researchers have not yet determined the impact of exercise and weight-loss programs on work loss and productivity (although Warner has modeled the potential impact using simulation analysis) (Smith and Fiore 1999).

Overall, prevention programs generally have low per-employee costs. Since the time horizon for their expected benefits is long-term, employees tend to perceive them as having relatively low value. Therefore, while they represent an important component of a portfolio in health-related productivity, they will not command the most attention from managers attempting to maximize productivity. However, other benefits may be more salient. For example, prevention programs may boost employee morale or enhance worker retention and satisfaction, thus enabling firms to keep wages down.

Like health-promotion programs, preventive services usually have also depended upon their perceived additional benefits rather than their impact on productivity. Thus, some employers have not embraced them in designing their health-benefit programs (Partnership for Prevention 1999). Preventive services are often a mix of health-promotion activities (e.g., smoking cessation, exercise, and weight loss) and clinical services such as immunizations (e.g., chickenpox, influenza) and cancer screening (e.g., mammography, cervical cancer screening). Health-promotion activities are generally not included or covered in employer's health-benefit programs; clinical services are commonly covered in HMO plans though not usually in PPO or traditional indemnity plans.

Building on the work of the U.S. Preventive Services Task Force, the Partnership for Prevention (along with its own expert panels) has established a set of priorities for employers that reflect the perceived value of a number of preventive services (Partnership for Prevention 2001), citing the clear evidence of benefit from immunizations (Hatziandreu et. al. 1994; Huse et al. 1994; White, Koplan, and Orenstein 1985). The impact and benefit of such programs extend to the employee's dependents. Yawn studied the impact of workers with children who contracted chicken pox and found that on average there were 1.68 days of work loss per case (Yawn, Yawn, and Lydick 1997). The cost of this work loss is sufficient to justify immunization as a covered benefit. Preventive services deserve a second look by employers; they are an integral part of investing in health-related productivity.

Managers place great emphasis on the design of health-insurance coverage because it constitutes the most significant portion of benefit cost. Viewed from the perspective of health-related productivity, health-insurance benefits have a shorter time horizon for the return on investment than other health programs (e.g., disease management).

Many studies have described the impact of common diseases on direct and indirect health care costs such as the following: allergies (Burton, Conti, et al. 2001), arthritis (Leigh, Seavey, and Leistikow 2001; Merkesdal et al. 2001), asthma (Ungar and Coyte 2000; Weiss and Sullivan 2001), cancer (Brown, Lipscomb, and Snyder 2001), coronary heart disease (Guico-Pabia et al. 2001; Herrin et al. 2000), depression (Birnbaum et al. 1999; Claxton, Chawla, and Kennedy 1999; Conti and Burton 1995; Greenberg et al. 1993), diabetes (Ng, Jacobs, and Johnson 2001; Songer 2001), hypertension (Kiiskinen et al. 1998), migraine (Hu et al. 1999), musculoskeletal pain (Melhorn, Wilkinson, and Riggs 2001), and rheumatoid arthritis (Birnbaum et al. 2000). Burton recently analyzed the combined effects on short-term absences, disability, and presenteeism for a set of common health care conditions (Burton, Conti, et al. 1999). However, adjusting the level or quality of health care coverage has not been shown to affect employee productivity. No studies have compared insured versus uninsured employees on worker productivity or output. In addition, measures of absenteeism attributable to specific diseases are not routinely collected. Similarly, few studies assess the impact of health-benefit design on the direct costs of disease.

However, health investments can clearly provide a positive return, because there is a window between what the health care system *could* do to decrease work loss and what it currently achieves. We discuss below a few examples of what an employer can do to make use of this window.

Many employers have taken a leadership role in requiring quality report cards such as the Health Plan Employer Data and Information Set (HEDIS) from health care providers since better-quality services both enhance patient satisfaction and improve employee health. To show the value of HEDIS and to enable employers to evaluate the return on investment in quality-based purchasing, the National Committee for Quality Assurance (NCQA) has posted on its Web site a hypothetical benefit calculator. This calculator provides an estimate of the incremental return for employers when they contract with health plans that achieve higher scores on HEDIS. (See www.ncqacalculator.com/Index.asp, the Quality Dividend Calculator.)

To use the calculator, an employer enters information about (1) employee demographics, (2) workforce management of absences, (3) replacements and their associated costs, and (4) the prevalence of eight conditions in the general population (depression, asthma, diabetes, chickenpox, heart disease, hypertension, pregnancy, and smoking). The calculator then estimates the potential total absentee days gained, total productivity days gained, and associated financial information (lowering of replacement costs, revenue impact, and reduced sick-day wages) for these eight conditions when employees receive their health care from high-quality providers as measured by HEDIS. While directly observed and validated estimates have not been established, the estimates from the Quality Dividend Calculator reflect a growing belief that improvements in health outcomes associated with high-quality health care will result in enhanced workforce productivity.

More recently, employers also have turned to case-management programs to manage disability costs. In these programs, case managers assist workers in receiving appropriate care for conditions associated with short-term disability, thereby accelerating return to work (RTW). Even though these programs carry a relatively high per-employee cost, the costs can be more than offset by decreased sickness and worker replacement costs. Merck & Company Inc. has demonstrated success in such a pilot program for its field sales employees. Health Services received same-day absence information on more than 3,000 employees nationwide and provided case management to employees disabled for more than five days. RTW was significantly improved, as reflected in an audit of 628 closed cases in comparison to United Society of Actuaries' disability duration data. According to an unpublished Merck analysis, the return on investment was estimated to exceed 100%.

Employers have also been early adopters of disease-management programs for chronic diseases prevalent in the workforce. Disease-management programs involve a systematic evidence-based approach to the treatment of illnesses across the continuum of care, including the monitoring and measurement of patient outcomes (Nebenfuhr, Jungkind, and Berger 2001). Key aspects of the programs are the proactive identification of employees with (or at risk for) particular conditions (such as asthma, migraine, depression, and diabetes) and management strategies aimed at preventing complications. Similar to case management, these programs also have relatively high per-employee costs and the potential to provide shorter-term returns through reducing absenteeism and improving productivity. To date, the documentation of the cost-effectiveness of disease-management programs has been generally informal and impressionistic (Nebenfuhr, Jungkind, and Berger 2001); results have been published in the trade literature (e.g., *Disease Management News*) rather than the peer-reviewed literature. The scope of such programs has remained small. However, in principle, an employer should be able to measure the impact of disease-management programs on absenteeism, presenteeism, and disability. Perhaps some employers might even be interested in a formal evaluation, with a control group, and accurate measures of cost and output.

Currently, a manager cannot predict or model how changes in health benefits and case-management programs will reduce the impacts of disability, absenteeism, and presenteeism on the company. Thus, it is critical that the manager monitor the impacts of these changes to have confidence in decision-making. While there is uncertainty surrounding these decisions, it is possible to make reasonable lower bound estimates based on the work that has been done in estimating indirect costs using current methods (e.g., the human capital method). Indeed, the uncertainty regarding the financial impact of changes in health benefits and case management is often smaller than that associated with other business decisions, as there is face validity to them—in other words, they make sense.

The best approach may be to start with a small, focused effort, and then expand as experience is gained. In this way a continuous quality-improvement approach can quantify results and reinforce the soundness of managerial decisions. The potential for "early wins" is significant—returning money to the corporation within a yearly budget. As we have noted, case management can provide a positive ROI in the management of sickness absences when it targets employees with time-sensitive output. Initiating programs that focus on illnesses for which productivity declines are predictable may also provide quick returns. For example, managers might start with prevention programs that decrease absenteeism caused by seasonal allergies, chickenpox, or influenza.

Clearly, medical conditions that usually result in disability or absences (e.g., low back pain, influenza) should be addressed first, as it is easier to monitor these conditions than those that usually manifest themselves in the form of presenteeism (e.g. migraine, diabetes). For this second category of conditions, an employer may want to consider implementing annual employee surveys that collect self-reported information on sickness-related absences and productivity while at work. Annual surveys can provide baseline and follow-up measures to assess the impact of programs designed to improve health-related productivity (e.g., health promotion, prevention, case management, and disease management).

CONCLUSIONS

While employers have long recognized that profitability is affected by the productivity of their workforce, health promotion and health care benefits have traditionally been viewed as a cost of doing business rather than an investment. A variety of factors are responsible for this point of view. First, since indirect costs have generally been estimated from a societal perspective rather than from the employer's perspective, they have not been considered relevant to a company's financial planning. Furthermore, even when the employer perspective has been taken, the prevalent methodology (lost wages or human capital) tends to underestimate the costs incurred. Additionally, attempts to measure lost productivity have largely been limited to those involving piecework, where one can accurately measure worker output. However, most production involves teamwork by knowledge workers for whom there are no perfect substitutes.

We have proposed a new model for categorizing production that takes into account firm-specific human capital, team production, and the time-sensitivity of output demand. This model provides a financial framework for managers to address the impact of absenteeism, presenteeism, and disability on workforce productivity.

The portfolio of possible investments in health-related productivity includes health-promotion programs, prevention programs, redesign of health benefits, selection of higher-quality health care providers, case-management programs, and disease-management programs. These interventions can be categorized according to the relative cost per employee and the planning period over which a company can expect return on its investment. Some of these programs may be readily adopted because they have a positive short-term ROI (e.g., case management for short-term disability, influenza vaccination, disease management of asthma), while others will provide returns in the longer term (e.g., coverage of preventive services, disease management of heart disease). A company can approach the size and the mix of these investments in a framework similar to that employed for other investment decisions. In this way, the "business case for quality health care" is no longer simply a catch-phrase for an employer-based health care system wanting to do the "right thing," but rather a viable management strategy for maximizing workforce productivity.

REFERENCES

American Heart Association. 1999. *1999 heart and stroke statistical update*. Dallas: American Heart Association.

Berger, M. L., J. F. Murray, J. Xu, and M. Pauly. 2001. Alternative valuations of work loss and productivity. *Journal of Occupational and Environmental Medicine* 43:18–24.

Berndt, E. R., H. L. Bailit, M. B. Keller, J. C. Verner, and S. N. Finkelstein. 2000. Health care use and at-work productivity among employees with mental disorders. *Health Affairs* 19:244–56.

Birnbaum, H. G., M. Barton, P. E. Greenberg, T. Sisitsky, R. Auerbach, L. A. Wanke, and M. C. Buatti. 2000. Direct and indirect costs of rheumatoid arthritis to an employer. *Journal of Occupational and Environmental Medicine* 42:588–96.

Birnbaum, H. G., P. E. Greenberg, M. Barton, R. C. Kessler, C. R. Rowland, and T. E. Williamson. 1999. Workplace burden of depression: Case study in social functioning using employer claims. *Drug Benefit Trends* 11:6–12.

Brown, M. L., J. Lipscomb, and C. Snyder. 2001. The burden of illness of cancer: Economic cost and quality of life. *Annual Review of Public Health* 22:91–113.

Burton, W. N., C. Y. Chen, A. B. Schultz, and D. W. Edington. 1999. The costs of body mass index levels in an employed population. *Statistical Bulletin—Metropolitan Insurance Companies* 80:8–14.

Burton, W. N., D. J. Conti, C. Y. Chen, A. B. Schultz, and D. W. Edington. 1999. The role of health risk factors and disease on worker productivity. *Journal of Occupational and Environmental Medicine* 41:863–77.

———. 2001. The impact of allergies and allergy treatment on worker productivity. *Journal of Occupational and Environmental Medicine* 43:64–71.

Claxton, A. J., A. J. Chawla, and S. Kennedy. 1999. Absenteeism among employees treated for depression. *Journal of Occupational and Environmental Medicine* 41: 605–11.

Cockburn, I. M., H. L. Bailit, E. R. Berndt, and S. N. Finkelstein. 1999. Loss of work productivity due to illness and medical treatment. *Journal of Occupational and Environmental Medicine* 41:948–53.

Colditz, G. A. 1999. Economic costs of obesity and inactivity. *Medicine and Science in Sports and Exercise* 31:S663–67.

Conti, D. J., and W. N. Burton. 1995. The cost of depression in the workplace. *Behavioral Healthcare Tomorrow* 4:25–27.

Drummond, M. 1992. Cost-of-illness studies: A major headache? *PharmacoEconomics* 2:1–4.

Gold, M. R., J. E. Siegel, L. B. Russel, and M. C. Weinstein. 1996. *Cost-effectiveness in health and medicine.* New York: Oxford University Press.

Greenberg, P. E., L. E. Stiglin, S. N. Finkelstein, and E. R. Berndt. 1993. The economic burden of depression in 1990. *Journal of Clinical Psychiatry* 54:405–18.

Guico-Pabia, C. J., J. F. Murray, S. M. Teutsch, A. I. Wertheimer, and M. L. Berger. 2001. Indirect cost of ischemic heart disease to employers. *American Journal of Managed Care* 7:27–34.

Hatziandreu, E. I., J. P. Koplan, M. C. Weinstein, C. J. Caspersen, and K. E. Warner. 1988. A cost-effectiveness analysis of exercise as a health promotion activity. *American Journal of Public Health* 78:1417–21.

Hatziandreu, E., et. al. 1994. A cost benefit analysis of the diptheria-tetanus-pertussin (DTP) vaccine. Prepared for the National Immunization Program, Centers for Disease Control and Prevention, Atlanta, GA.

Herrin, J., C. B. Cangialose, S. J. Boccuzzi, W. S. Weintraub, and D. J. Ballard. 2000. Household income losses associated with ischaemic heart disease for US employees. *PharmacoEconomics* 17:305–14.

Hu, X. H., L. E. Markson, R. B. Lipton, W. F. Stewart, and M. L. Berger. 1999. Burden of migraine in the United States: Disability and economic costs. *Archives of Internal Medicine* 159:813–18.

Huse, D. M., H. C. Meissner, M. J. Lacey, and G. Oster. 1994. Childhood vaccination against chickenpox: An analysis of benefits and costs. *Journal of Pediatrics* 124: 869–74.

Jacobs, P., and K. Fassbender. 1998. The measurement of indirect costs in the health economics evaluation literature. *International Journal of Technology Assessment in Health Care* 14:799–808.

Kiiskinen, U., E. Vartiainen, P. Puska, and A. Aromaa. 1998. Long-term cost and life-expectancy consequences of hypertension. *Journal of Hypertension* 16:1103–12.

Koopmanschap, M. A., and F. F. Rutten. 1996. The consequence of production loss or increased costs of production. *Medical Care* 34:DS59–68.

Legg, R. F., D. A. Sclar, N. L. Nemec, J. Tarnai, and J. I. Mackowiak. 1997. Cost benefit of sumatriptan to an employer. *Journal of Occupational and Environmental Medicine* 39:652–57.

Leigh, J. P., W. Seavey, and B. Leistikow. 2001. Estimating the costs of job related arthritis. *Journal of Rheumatology* 28:1647–54.

Melhorn, J. M., L. Wilkinson, and J. D. Riggs. 2001. Management of musculoskeletal pain in the workplace. *Journal of Occupational and Environmental Medicine* 43: 83–93.

Merkesdal, S., J. Ruof, O. Schoffski, K. Bernitt, H. Zeidler, and W. Mau. 2001. Indirect medical costs in early rheumatoid arthritis: Composition of and changes in indirect costs within the first three years of disease. *Arthritis and Rheumatism* 44: 528–34.

Nebenfuhr, P., K. Jungkind, and M. L. Berger. 2001. Disease management: An intermediate step toward integrated and coordinated patient care. *Disease Management* 4:173–78.

Ng, Y. C., P. Jacobs, and J. A. Johnson. 2001. Productivity losses associated with diabetes in the US. *Diabetes Care* 24:257–61.

Nicholl, J. P., P. Coleman, and J. E. Brazier. 1994. Health and healthcare costs and benefits of exercise. *PharmacoEconomics* 5:109–22.

Osterhaus, J. T., D. L. Gutterman, and J. R. Plachetka. 1992. Healthcare resource and lost labour costs of migraine headache in the US. *PharmacoEconomics* 2:67–76.

Partnership for Prevention. 1999. *Why invest in disease prevention: Results of a survey by William Mercer and Partnership for Prevention.* Washington, DC: Partnership for Prevention.

———. 2001. *Prevention priorities: Employers' guide to the highest value preventive health services.* Washington, DC: Partnership for Prevention.

Pauly, M. V., S. Nicholson, J. Xu, D. Polsky, P. M. Danzon, J. F. Murray, and M. L. Berger. 2002. A general model of the impact of absenteeism on employers and employees. *Health Economics* 11:221–31.

Smith, S. S., and M. C. Fiore. 1999. The epidemiology of tobacco use, dependence, and cessation in the United States. *Primary Care: Clinics in Office Practice* 26: 433–61.

Songer, T. J. 2001. The role of cost-effectiveness analysis and health insurance in diabetes care. *Diabetes Research and Clinical Practice* 54:S7–11.

Tighe, S. 2001. *US major pharmaceuticals: Variability among NDA review times.* New York: Merrill Lynch Capital Markets.

Ungar, W. J., and P. C. Coyte. 2000. Measuring productivity loss days in asthma patients. The Pharmacy Medication Monitoring Program and Advisory Board. *Health Economics* 9:37–46.

Weiss, K. B., and S. D. Sullivan. 2001. The health economics of asthma and rhinitis. I. Assessing the economic impact. *Journal of Allergy and Clinical Immunology* 107:3–8.

White, C. C., J. P. Koplan, and W. A. Orenstein. 1985. Benefits, risks, and costs of immunization for measles, mumps, and rubella. *American Journal of Public Health* 75:739–44.

Williams, A. F., and J. Franklin. 1993. Annual economic costs attributable to cigarette smoking in Texas. *Texas Medicine* 89:56–60.

Yawn, B. P., R. A. Yawn, and E. Lydick. 1997. Community impact of childhood varicella infections. *Journal of Pediatrics* 130:759–65.

CHAPTER 10

The Role of Health Plans in Linking Quality of Care to Labor Outcomes: Challenges and Opportunities

ARNE BECK

INTRODUCTION

In this era of rapidly escalating health care costs, health plans market their services to employers primarily on the basis of price. Although many health plans both provide large amounts of health care quality data to accrediting organizations such as the National Committee on Quality Assurance (NCQA) and the Joint Commission on Accreditation of Health Care Organizations (JCAHO) and make substantial investments in quality-assurance programs, quality has not yet emerged as a significant factor in the purchasing decisions of employers. While quality measures can gauge health-plan performance, they do not directly address what is of greater interest to employers: namely, how investing in a given health plan is likely to affect the productivity of their employees.

This chapter explores the perspective of the health plan as a stakeholder in the use of health and work productivity data. I present an overview of the health-plan perspective, highlighting some fundamental differences between the concerns of health plans and employers. Included in the discussion are differences between how health plans and employers view quality indicators (e.g., report cards) and the differences between how health plans, employers, and researchers value specific work-productivity measures. I then explore approaches to addressing these differences and present new methods of value-based purchasing and employee-benefit design that incorporate emerging work-performance assessment methods.

The discussion in this chapter is based on three assumptions. First, health plans have an opportunity to make the business case to employers that providing evidence-based care improves employees' work performance. In other words, health plans can be instrumental in creating a new mind-set in which employers see health care as an asset that can provide a positive return on investment (ROI) to their companies. Second, health plans need to work with health-service researchers to provide evidence for the impact of health care on employee productivity. Third, health plans, employers, and re-searchers need to find a common language regarding health care outcomes. Unless health plans can translate the data of researchers to employers, em-ployers are unlikely to use this valuable source of information when making health care purchasing decisions. Ultimately, health plans also need to work with employers in order to improve labor outcomes for health-plan mem-bers / employees. Effectively translating research on labor outcomes into value-based purchasing and benefit design is a first step in this direction.

HEALTH-PLAN PERSPECTIVE

Health plans are key stakeholders in the policy debate regarding health and work productivity. Employers purchase health care benefits for their employ-ees through two primary health care delivery arrangements: fee-for-service providers and managed-care organizations (MCOs). MCOs, which have dominated the health care landscape for more than a decade, in turn, actually encompass various service-delivery structures and financing mechanisms, including large, for-profit capitated networks of individual providers and not-for-profit group and staff-model HMOs.

MCOs first began to emerge on a wide-scale basis in the early 1990s, when annual increases in health care costs typically ran in the double digits. Initially, MCOs were successful in stabilizing costs, but their ability to do this has been hampered in recent years. In fact, health care inflation is now back to where it was when the managed-care revolution began. With health care costs once again rising steeply, employers are becoming increasingly con-cerned about the value of the health care services they purchase for their employees.

Differing Perspectives on Outcomes

Health plans, health-care professionals and employers all have different per-spectives on health care outcomes that are reflected in the differences in the language used by these stakeholders (see fig. 10.1). Health plans use medical as opposed to business language (e.g., signs, symptoms, and health care uti-

Traditional outcomes	**Outcomes**	Clinical outcomes
Death		Signs
Disease		Symptoms
Disability		Lab results
Discomfort		Complications
Dissatisfaction		

Perspectives

	Outcomes important to patients
	Pain
Outcomes important to payers	Anxiety
Cost	Disability
Work days lost	Disfigurement
	Death

Figure 10.1. Differences in outcomes and perspectives
Source: Adapted from diagrams presented at the conference "Implementing Outcomes Management," National Jewish Center for Immunology and Respiratory Medicine, December 6, 1991.

lization rather than terms such as the business case for health care and ROI of health care dollars). Likewise, the health care professional, who provides care according to treatment guidelines that are evidence-based and/or the product of expert consensus, focuses on treatment of the presenting problem (if acute) or optimal management of the chronic condition. Thus, outcomes related to functional status in general and work performance in particular have not been widely incorporated into the clinician's lexicon of patient outcomes, unless the discussion centers on disability for a work-related injury. By way of contrast, the employer's perspective encompasses outcomes directly related to the company's operational and financial health, namely, worker productivity, absenteeism, presenteeism, disability, and the associated costs.

At present, health plans, and in particular, MCOs, are typically guided by a public-health orientation that emphasizes preventive interventions such as immunizations and cancer screening of health-plan members. In addition to traditional public-health-oriented measures, health plans are increasingly using their information systems to facilitate population-based care as well as to create disease registries that provide aggregate clinical-outcome data (e.g., blood sugar levels of diabetic patients). These data may then be profiled, often stratified by clinic and by provider. Improved information-system capabilities have enabled health plans to enhance their care-management programs and to provide performance data that are required for NCQA accreditation.

These language differences between the research community, health plans, and employers have limited the practical value of outcome research. Health-service researchers are able to use the comprehensive, large secondary databases and data from electronic medical records collected by health plans to develop models of health care treatment outcomes and their cost-effectiveness. Unfortunately, neither health plans nor researchers have shown equal acumen in translating this evidence into actionable information for employers, such as data that either can make the business case for evidence-based health services or can be used by employers in making health care purchasing decisions. The discussion of evidence has typically not moved beyond elaborating on research designs, multivariate statistical techniques, and p values. As a result, research is just as likely to confuse as to enlighten employers interested in making evidence- or value-based purchasing decisions.

Differing Perspectives on Cost of Illness, Financing, and Benefit Design

Health plans rarely consider costs and benefits of health care services from the employer perspective primarily because they are forced to focus on their own cost structures in order to deliver medical care at a competitive price while maintaining quality and service standards. Like employers, health plans tend to view health care services from a cost and cost-control (traditional utilization management) rather than from an investment perspective.

However, for health plans, the locus of cost differs in important ways from the individual, societal, and employer perspectives. While health-plan direct costs include the costs of services delivered by health care professionals, ancillary services (e.g., home-health services), and capital equipment (e.g., imaging machines, hospitals, medical offices), indirect costs consist largely of unnecessary utilization of health services by patients. To control costs, health plans have traditionally developed utilization-management efforts that limit access to specialty care, hospital, and emergency department (ED) services. Health plans also make use of different benefit structures or copayment requirements to provide incentives for employees to reduce their utilization of high-cost services. For example, increasing the copay for ED services has been shown to reduce utilization in that care setting (Magid et al. 1997; Selby, Fireman, and Swain 1996). In response to such efforts to control the costs of care, a substantial research literature has emerged that documents the costs of various chronic conditions from the health-plan perspective (Brown, Lipscomb, and Snyder 2001; Drummond

1992; Hu et al. 1999; Merkesdal et al. 2001). However, health plans are less familiar with the emerging literature on health and productivity because they typically pay little attention to the impact of illness on employer costs incurred from work loss, disability, replacing workers (hiring and training), and nonwage costs such as employee benefits.

Another significant gap between the health-plan and employer perspective is evident in the area of financing and benefit design. At present, only a select group of large employers have the sophistication to purchase health care based on quality and value, to assess ROI, and to interpret performance metrics. In other words, most businesses lack the trained personnel who can engage in a dialogue about value-based purchasing (Young et al. 2001). Though CFOs typically understand that ROI principles can apply to employee health, these senior executives are often not directly involved in health care purchasing decisions. Moreover, most employee-benefit managers do not take an investment perspective concerning the purchase of health care. In addition, because insurers typically market health plans to employers through brokers, who are motivated by their own unique economic incentives—namely, commissions—employers rarely see information on ROI when deciding on health care purchasing options.

In addition, health plans have silos similar to those described in the discussion in chapter 9 of this book on the employer perspective. Individuals in sales and marketing departments typically are responsible for negotiating with employer groups about purchasing decisions. And, like benefit managers, salespeople often lack an understanding of how health care performance measures can be useful to employers. Likewise, although most health plans have quality-management departments that provide data on Health Plan Employer Data Information Set (HEDIS, http://www.ncqa.org/Programs/HEDIS/index.htm) measures to employers (and the larger plans typically also have health-service researchers), these specialists rarely share their expertise in performance measurement and ROI evaluation with employers.

From the health-plan perspective, the task of designing and financing a benefit package likely to provide a positive ROI can be daunting. With employers rarely willing to increase expenditures, health plans may be forced to reduce their own profit margins to pay for additional services (say, disease-management programs) that may benefit the employer in the long run. Alternatively, health plans may need to engage in cost-shifting by, for example, altering copays to encourage members to engage in specific treatments or activities (for example, wellness programs) that may increase their productivity. In any event, the basic challenge for health plans is to find ways to provide evidence-based care leading to a ROI for employers within the constraints of their cost structure.

Differing Perspectives on Health-Plan Performance Measures

To help employers make informed health care purchasing decisions based on quality as well as price, accreditation organizations such as NCQA (http://www.ncqa.org) and JCAHO (www.jcaho.org), in collaboration with their employer constituents, have developed health performance measures. The original premise behind HEDIS, the database created by NCQA, was to obtain some basic information on health care quality during a time when the only information available to employers was health care claims and associated costs. At present, health plans are required to produce several HEDIS performance measures on an annual basis. These include such indicators as childhood immunization rates, diabetic retinal exam rates, antidepressant medication continuation rates, and beta-blocker prescription rates following myocardial infarction. In addition, NCQA and other national and local accreditation and regulatory agencies require consumer-oriented measures on service quality, such as access to and satisfaction with care. Health plans invest literally tens of millions of dollars to produce the data for the multitude of quality measures now required, providing the manpower and information infrastructure to assemble the data from administrative databases or chart review and to collect survey data from samples of members. The ability of a given plan to provide HEDIS data and thus to attain NCQA accreditation makes employers more likely to include it in the array of plans offered to employees.

Unfortunately, research suggests that that the information provided in health-plan performance measures does not influence either employer purchasing decisions or consumer choice of health plans (Beyers 2003; Chernew and Scanlon 1998; Eckhart 2003; Goldfarb et al. 2003; Mainous and Talbert 1998; Mehrotra, Bodenheimer, and Dudley 2003; Mukamel and Mushlin 2001; Mukamel et al. 2000; Scanlon et al. 2002; Schultz et al. 2001; Simon and Monroe 2001; Sorokin 2000; Thompson and Harris 2001; Wedig and Tai-Seale 2002). This fact is not lost on decision-makers in health plans, who see little evidence that improved quality on HEDIS measures leads to membership growth, despite the prestige accorded to health plans that consistently score high on these measures. The attainment of high levels on the performance measures is thus seen primarily as a marketing opportunity. Despite this limited impact, health plans show no sign that they are starting to reduce their substantial investment in providing performance data.

Another problem facing both health plans and employers revolves around the nature of the performance measures themselves. Most performance measures focus either on processes of care or intermediate outcomes rather than on long-term outcomes. This focus is understandable, as care process and intermediate outcome data are easier to capture than long-term outcome data. For example, for diabetic patients, health plans can easily obtain blood sugar levels from lab databases and retinal exams from eye-care department procedure codes. In contrast, it would take many years to obtain data on such long-term adverse outcomes as limb amputations and retinopathy.

Like health plans, employers are often more interested in short-term outcomes. For employers whose workers typically stay only a few years, long-term outcome data may not be relevant to the bottom line. Likewise for health plans, because patients frequently switch insurance carriers, the assessment of long-term outcomes may not be feasible.

With access only to relatively short-term data such as care processes, employers are at a loss to determine how excellent health-plan performance can assist them in making health care investment decisions (assuming they have made the leap to considering health care an investment rather than a cost to contain). The case for health care cost savings can be made only in hypothetical terms. Although employers have had a role in suggesting current performance measures, these measures still do not include productivity, absenteeism, presenteeism, and disability—the largest cost drivers for employers and the ones for which they would like reliable and valid information.

However, even as labor outcomes become more widely used as a basis for demonstrating value to employers, one wonders whether current measures are sufficiently valid and reliable for employers to use in purchasing decisions. This question reveals a related gap between researchers who develop and validate measures of worker productivity and health plans and employers who represent potential users of such instruments. That is, as measures of outcomes more relevant to employers are developed, they are more technically complex than prior performance measures involving processes of care that are readily derived from administrative databases or chart review. Self-report productivity measures, the approach most feasible for health plans to implement in assessing value of treatment, require sophistication to interpret. For example, how much does a self-reported productivity change from 5 to 8 on a 10-point scale mean in terms of true productivity? How much confidence can employers place in the results of methods to monetize these changes—the very basis on which ROI can be calculated?

Several operational issues remain in order to narrow the gaps between health plans and employers in addressing questions of this type. Even if health plans and employers agreed upon a common language and set of performance measures, employers would logically prefer to have these data available for their own employees who are members of the health plans.

Employer-specific data allow for profiling health risks and disease burden and understanding areas of greatest health care need for targeting services. This information is very useful for employers' health care investment decisions. In contrast, health plans are more likely to view their members by the locations where they receive care (the clinic), their primary care physician, their demographic characteristics (e.g., age, gender), and their medical history (e.g., heart disease, asthma, diabetes). Such information is useful for service planning because it enables health plans to improve their ability to predict health-service utilization patterns (e.g., hospital days among Medicare members). Although the employer group to which health-plan members belong is also a variable that health plans capture, it is not as widely used as the others mentioned above. The net result of this gap is that health plans provide employers with data on characteristics of overall membership, only a subset of which is of interest to any individual employer. The effectiveness of health care services must then be extrapolated to the employer's own workforce, which may have a different risk profile than the average profile for all members of the plan.

Although some health plans have employer-specific prevention programs where health-risk appraisals are administered and health-risk patterns profiled for individual employers (e.g., Kaiser Permanente's Practicing Prevention Program, which is administered at employers' worksites), provision of employer-specific health-plan performance data is much less typical. Instead, health plans tend to adopt a proprietary stance on releasing health care utilization data in general and employer-level data in particular. Although it is possible to stratify health-plan performance measures by employer, the delivery of employer-tailored health care interventions within the health plan remains difficult.

USE OF WORKER-PRODUCTIVITY MEASURES BY HEALTH PLANS

Given that the development of self-report productivity measures has progressed significantly in the past several years, health plans now have an opportunity to incorporate productivity measures into their armamentarium of quality measures. By linking information about the characteristics of care-management programs to productivity outcomes, health plans could inform employers about which treatment approaches are likely to be associated with the greatest gains in these outcomes.

Feasibility concerns limit the use of some productivity measures by health plans. Among the assessment methods described in part 1 of this book, simulation for measurement of occupational performance and the Experience Sampling Method (ESM) are clearly more suited to research than to practical application in health plans. In addition, simulation methods are limited in generalizability to certain occupational groups, whereas health plans need global assessments that are suitable to the wide variation in occupations and employers represented by their membership.

Regarding archival methods, health plans do not have easy access to archival data on employer performance or workdays lost to which they can link health care treatments. Moreover, Health Insurance Portability and Accountability Act (HIPAA) regulations make the linking of such data sets challenging. Linked archival data are too complex for health plans to assemble on a routine basis. In addition, more detailed and accurate health care diagnostic and utilization data can be extracted from extant health-plan databases, with the missing link being work-performance data. It is also important to note that archival data do not measure the longitudinal change in illness status as a function of treatment, but provide only cross-sectional data. For these reasons, methods employing linked archival employer and health-claim data are impractical in routine use, although they are extremely informative for research purposes.

Likewise, the O*NET method described in chapter 6 is granular and better suited to research modeling the relationships between workers' underlying abilities, illness, and subsequent performance. As noted above, health plans typically need more global productivity measures that cut across occupations in order for them to be practical. But if measures of productivity are administered via health-risk appraisals at the work site, then the O*NET may have more practical applicability.

There are distinct advantages to health plans, in comparison, in using self-report measures of work performance to assess the relationship between these outcomes and processes of care. The Work Limitations Questionnaire (WLQ) and the Health and Work Performance Questionnaire (HPQ) now have data suggestive of their reliability and validity in comparison to objective and archival measures of work performance (Lerner et al. 2001; Kessler et al, 2003). These self-report measures are comparable to health and functional status measures that health plans are increasingly employing to assess patient-centered outcomes, such as general and disease-specific health-related quality of life. The global assessment approach used by the HPQ is more practical than the WLQ (which parses work function into several domains) for general comparisons of work performance across health-plan members varying in occupations and illnesses. In addition, incorporating questions about income range provides the necessary information with which to monetize changes in work performance associated with high-quality treatment.

REMOVING BARRIERS: ISSUES TO ADDRESS

The gaps in perspectives discussed above are not insurmountable, but they require concerted efforts in several areas. First, a more comprehensive set of stakeholders is required to participate in the dialogue about benefit design that employs value-based-purchasing or health-and-productivity-management (HPM) approaches (see chapter 9 for a discussion of HPM). Such approaches would help to reduce the silo mentality within large companies that purchase health care for their workers as well as in health plans. A richer and more productive dialogue would likely result from involving the executives (e.g., CFOs) responsible for organization-wide investment decisions and individuals from health-plan quality-management and research departments who can translate data on evidence-based treatments into ROI language for employers. Currently, it is unusual for these diverse sets of stakeholders to be at the same table, much less to engage in the discussion of the ROI of health care to employers.

Second, stakeholders, including health plans, employers, and researchers, must settle on a common language that incorporates evidence from the scientific literature and from health-plan and business operations, especially with regard to outcomes of importance to employers. This requires educating health care purchasing decision-makers about evidence-based treatments and their potential ROI to employers. It is particularly important for employers to understand the circumstances under which increasing investment in some care programs is a wise decision and those in which reducing benefits may yield increases in indirect costs associated with the medical condition (Rosenheck et al. 1999).

Third, employers and health plans would benefit from discussion on the respective value that each ascribes to current quality and performance measures, including HEDIS measures and newer decision-support tools such as the NCQA Quality Dividend Calculator (http://www.ncqacalculator.com/Index.asp). It is important for health plans to understand employers' views on the shortcomings of extant quality measures and to ascertain the interest of employers in obtaining work-performance data that are more employee-specific. As obtaining employee-specific data will require health plans to make significant investments in data collection and analysis infrastructure, employers need to communicate precisely what data they need and how the data are to be used.

Fourth, researchers should begin to educate employers on the state-of-the-art measurement tools of work performance. These efforts can help employers gain confidence in the validity and utility of these measures for assessing outcomes that are of the greatest importance to them.

Much of this discussion presupposes the need for stronger partnerships between stakeholders. For example, health-plan representatives must try to understand employers' needs for outcomes that inform their purchasing decisions. Researchers can benefit from partnerships with both health plans (especially individuals who design benefits) and employers (especially benefit managers and senior management, who make purchasing decisions) in order to understand the most useful approaches to translating their measures into practical applications. Both health plans and researchers need to take responsibility for translating the data into language that enables employers to view health care as an investment in their employees that yields a tangible benefit (Larson 1999).

What Researchers Need to Do

Because self-report work-performance measures are the most practical method for health plans to employ, researchers need to continue to validate these measures against objective and archival data and to develop large normative databases. The large-scale HPQ calibration study currently under way is an example of the direction needed to further instrument development and refinement (Kessler et al. 2003). This work will likely resemble the process of validating and developing norms for the most widely used health and functional status instrument currently in use in health care, the Short Form 36-item scale (SF-36) (Ware and Sherbourne 1992). Self-report measures of work performance must have sufficient validity to engender confidence among the health-plan and employer users of these data to enable them to make benefit-design and health care purchasing decisions.

Another role for researchers is to incorporate self-report work-performance measures into effectiveness trials of care-management programs in order to measure labor outcomes with more rigor than traditional prospective observational or cross-sectional research designs.

Approaches to Financing and Benefit Design

Next, there is a need to develop agreed-upon value-based or health-and-productivity-management (HPM) approaches to purchasing (Beauregard and Winston 1997). Several current efforts provide excellent examples of

such approaches (Midwest Business Group on Health 2002). These are discussed in more detail in chapter 9.

OPPORTUNITIES AND FUTURE DIRECTIONS FOR RESEARCH, BENEFIT DESIGN, AND VALUE-BASED PURCHASING

Health plans are increasingly able to provide evidence for treatment effectiveness by extracting and analyzing data from administrative databases and
electronic medical records (Kazmirski 1998). Even more significant, given
that health plans are in the unique position of being able to provide longitudinal data on processes of care and outcomes, including labor outcomes, they
also have the opportunity to demonstrate improvements in work performance resulting from effective treatment. This represents a critical link in
the ability to demonstrate how effective, evidence-based treatments associated with increases in work performance can be translated into cost savings
for employers. Health plans consequently have the opportunity to be on the
leading edge of productivity-based health outcome research. As Greenberg
and Birnbaum note in chapter 2, "by gathering information about changes in
clinical status, such prospective studies can both help to establish the impact
of treatment on productivity and provide more clinically accurate and detailed data than those obtained from retrospective claims." Recent studies
have begun to address this question, including a prospective observational
cohort study being conducted by our research team using the HPQ to assess
whether guideline-concordant depression care is associated with improved
work performance and employer cost savings.

Health plans also have the infrastructure, though it varies significantly
by plan, to routinely collect patient-centered outcome data, including self-
reported data on work productivity and absenteeism. This capacity is critical
to develop because the most feasible measures of labor outcomes are those
that can be obtained by self-report. As health plans decided to invest in primary data collection to track patient-centered outcomes, such as functional
status, symptoms of disease, and health-related quality of life, health plans
must also decide that it is worthwhile to invest significant resources into routinely collecting self-report productivity data. New technologies currently
available may lower the costs of such data collection and make the routine assessment and monitoring of patient-centered outcomes, including work performance, feasible. Examples include survey administration via interactive
voice response systems, the Internet, and electronic data-collection devices
administered at the point of care.

FUTURE DIRECTIONS FOR RESEARCH AND BENEFIT DESIGN: CAN RESEARCHERS HELP STAKEHOLDERS? AN EXAMPLE OF A NEW MODEL

We are currently conducting a research project funded by the Robert Wood Johnson Foundation entitled "Marketing Improved Depression Treatment to Employer Purchasers." The general goal is to translate recent research findings about the economic value of high-quality depression treatment into the design and marketing of a benefit option that employers can purchase. The project has five specific aims: (1) to estimate the ROI employers can realize from improved primary-care depression treatment delivered through the Quality Enhancement by Strategic Testing (QuEST) model (Rost et al. 2002; Smith et al. 2002); (2) to develop methods for delivering QuEST care through a partnering health plan that preserves its projected ROI for employers; (3) to develop and market a benefit option for health-plan provision of QuEST care; (4) to characterize the range and determinants of employer response to this benefit option; and (5) to conduct a pilot study evaluating the feasibility of recruiting companies across the country to a randomized trial evaluating an intervention for improved primary-care depression treatment.

This project is intended to serve as a prototype for a benefit design that incorporates evidence-based treatments for high-cost, high-morbidity conditions that yield a positive ROI to employers. We recognize that the benefit for a single condition such as depression may be too granular to drive health-plan selection or purchasing decisions. However, this prototype could be generalized to multiple conditions for purchasing or plan-selection decision-making on a larger scope (e.g., paying a greater proportion of the premium for the plan to provide incentives for employees to choose it). Or, it could be used to help motivate the expansion of specific disease-management programs that employers can purchase as part of a cafeteria approach to constructing employer-specific health care benefit packages. In terms of the latter possibility, depending on the findings of the depression study, we may expand a similar model of benefit design to other care-management programs and health care benefits. Specific components of this new benefit design prototype include the following:

- Ensuring fidelity of treatments delivered that are comparable to those delivered in effectiveness trials, and delivering these high-fidelity treatments to targeted employees.
- Using administrative databases to identify untreated or undertreated members who are good candidates for care-management programs, and providing this in-

formation to primary-care physicians and care managers via electronic medical records. A complementary strategy would involve administering health-risk appraisals at the worksite to determine employer-specific health risks and to target care-management programs to these individuals.

- Routinely monitoring clinical and work-performance outcomes of enrollees in these targeted care-management programs in order to assess whether outcome targets such as improvements in work performance as well as expected ROI projections were met.
- Accommodating variations among employers that influence their interest in a specific care-management benefit. Employers might select from several evidence-based care-management programs based on estimates of the prevalence of the condition among their workforce, the numbers of untreated employees, and even employee turnover rate, allowing an assessment of whether the ROI would accrue within the average tenure of eligible employees.

As noted in chapter 14, employers must ask the following key questions when attempting to choose care-management programs that will yield the greatest benefit to their workforce:

- What are the most commonly occurring health problems in my company?
- What are the effects of these health problems on work performance, sickness absence, industrial accidents, and disability?
- What is the financial impact of these workplace effects on the company's bottom line?
- How effective are available interventions in reducing these effects in my company?
- What is the ROI of these proposed interventions?

Although claim data can be extremely useful in answering the first of these questions, it is currently very difficult for employers to obtain data that can help them answer any of the last four questions. Initiatives like the Marketing Improved Depression Treatment to Employer Purchasers program have the potential to provide data to answer these questions. Employer interest in value-based purchasing requires availability of data of this sort.

CONCLUSIONS

The perspective of health plans is to focus on clinical outcomes, and because health plans are obligated to produce quality measures for accreditation and regulatory agencies, they face challenges and opportunities in attempting to incorporate measures of work outcomes into their performance measures.

The gaps between the perspectives of health plans and of employers constitute barriers to productive collaboration on health care purchasing decisions and benefit design. However, there are several ways to reduce these barriers.

Health plans can play a significant role in measuring labor outcomes and using these data to estimate the ROI that accrues from evidence-based medical care. Furthermore, new approaches are offered here to incorporate this information into benefit design and value-based purchasing decisions. The evidence for the validity and utility of self-report measures of performance, and the increasing ability of health plans to incorporate these measures into routine outcome assessment, hold out the promise of better methods for rationing health care on which health plans and employers can reach common ground.

REFERENCES

Beauregard, T. R., and K. R. Winston. 1997. Value-based formulas for purchasing: Employers shift to quality to evaluate and manage their health plans. *Managed Care Quarterly* 5:51–56.

Beyers, M. 2003. Viewpoint: Report cards are here to stay. *Patient Care Management* 19: 10–11.

Brown, M. L., J. Lipscomb, and C. Snyder. 2001. The burden of illness of cancer: Economic cost and quality of life. *Annual Review of Public Health* 22:91–113.

Chernew, M., and D. P. Scanlon. 1998. Health plan report cards and insurance choice. *Inquiry* 35:9–22.

Drummond, M. 1992. Cost-of-illness studies: A major headache? *PharmacoEconomics* 2:1–4.

Eckhart, J. 2003. Report cards—a willingness to change. *Clinical Leadership and Management Review* 17:99–102.

Goldfarb, N. I., V. Maio, C. T. Carter, L. Pizzi, and D. B. Nash. 2003. How does quality enter into health care purchasing decisions? *Issue Brief (The Commonwealth Fund)*, 1–8.

Hu, X. H., L. E. Markson, R. B. Lipton, W. F. Stewart, and M. L. Berger. 1999. Burden of migraine in the United States: Disability and economic costs. *Archives of Internal Medicine* 159:813–18.

Kazmirski, G. 1998. Marketing quality and value to the managed care market. *Topics in Health Information Management* 19:62–69.

Kessler, R. C., C. Barber, A. Beck, P. A. Berglund, P. D. Cleary, D. McKenas, N. Pronk, G. Simon, P. Stang, T. B. Üstün, and P. Wang. 2003. The World Health Organization Health and Work Performance Questionnaire (HPQ). *Journal of Occupational and Environmental Medicine* 45:156–74.

Larson, E. B. 1999. Evidence-based medicine: Is translating evidence into practice a solution to the cost-quality challenges facing medicine? *Joint Commission Journal on Quality Improvement* 25:480–85.

Lerner, D., B. C. Amick III, W. H. Rogers, S. Malspeis, K. Bungay, and D. Cynn. 2001. The Work Limitations Questionnaire. *Medical Care* 39:72–85.

Magid, D. J., T. D. Koepsell, N. R. Every, J. S. Martin, D. S. Siscovick, E. H. Wagner, and W. D. Weaver. 1997. Absence of association between insurance copayments and delays in seeking emergency care among patients with myocardial infarction. *New England Journal of Medicine* 336:1722–29.

Mainous, A. G., III, and J. Talbert. 1998. Assessing quality of care via HEDIS 3.0: Is there a better way? *Archives of Family Medicine* 7:410–13.

Mehrotra, A., T. Bodenheimer, and R. A. Dudley. 2003. Employers' efforts to measure and improve hospital quality: Determinants of success. *Health Affairs* 22: 60–71.

Merkesdal, S., J. Ruof, O. Schoffski, K. Bernitt, H. Zeidler, and W. Mau. 2001. Indirect medical costs in early rheumatoid arthritis: Composition of and changes in indirect costs within the first three years of disease. *Arthritis and Rheumatism* 44: 528–34.

Midwest Business Group on Health, Juran Institute Inc., and Severyn Group Inc. 2002. *Reducing the cost of poor-quality health care through responsible purchasing leadership.* Midwest Business Group on Health, http://www.mbgh.org/pdf/Cost%20of%20Poor%20Quality%20Report.pdf.

Mukamel, D. B., and A. I. Mushlin. 2001. The impact of quality report cards on choice of physicians, hospitals, and HMOs: A midcourse evaluation. *Joint Commission Journal on Quality Improvement* 27:20–27.

Mukamel, D. B., A. I. Mushlin, D. Weimer, J. Zwanziger, T. Parker, and I. Indridason. 2000. Do quality report cards play a role in HMOs' contracting practices? Evidence from New York State. *Health Services Research* 35:319–32.

Rosenheck, R. A., B. Druss, M. Stolar, D. Leslie, and W. Sledge. 1999. Effect of declining mental health service use on employees of a large corporation. *Health Affairs* 18:193–203.

Rost, K., J. L. Smith, C. E. Elliott, and M. Dickerson. 2002. Improving primary care depression management: Effects on employee work loss. Paper presented at the 15th Biennial International Conference on Mental Health Services Research, Washington, DC.

Scanlon, D. P., M. Chernew, C. McLaughlin, and G. Solon. 2002. The impact of health plan report cards on managed care enrollment. *Journal of Health Economics* 21:19–41.

Schultz, J., K. T. Call, R. Feldman, and J. Christianson. 2001. Do employees use report cards to assess health care provider systems? *Health Services Research* 36: 509–30.

Selby, J. V., B. H. Fireman, and B. E. Swain. 1996. Effect of a copayment on use of the emergency department in a health maintenance organization. *New England Journal of Medicine* 334:635–41.

Simon, L. P., and A. F. Monroe. 2001. California provider group report cards: What do they tell us? *American Journal of Medical Quality* 16:61–70.

Smith, J. L., K. M. Rost, P. A. Nutting, A. M. Libby, C. E. Elliott, and J. M. Pyne. 2002. Impact of primary care depression intervention on employment and workplace conflict outcomes: Is value added? *Journal of Mental Health Policy and Economics* 5:43–49.

Sorokin, R. 2000. Alternative explanations for poor report card performance. *Effective Clinical Practice* 3:25–30.

Thompson, B. L., and J. R. Harris. 2001. Performance measures: Are we measuring what matters? *American Journal of Preventive Medicine* 20:291–93.

Ware, J. E., Jr., and C. D. Sherbourne. 1992. The MOS 36-item short-form health survey (SF-36). I. Conceptual framework and item selection. *Medical Care* 30: 473–83.

Wedig, G. J., and M. Tai-Seale. 2002. The effect of report cards on consumer choice in the health insurance market. *Journal of Health Economics* 21:1031–48.

Young, D. W., D. Barrett, J. W. Kenagy, D. C. Pinakiewicz, and S. M. McCarthy. 2001. Value-based partnering in healthcare: A framework for analysis. *Journal of Healthcare Management* 46:112–32, discussion 133.

CHAPTER 11

The Pharmaceutical Industry and Productivity Research

CHRISTOPHER J. EVANS

INTRODUCTION

Interest in productivity research by pharmaceutical companies has built up slowly. At first, industry-sponsored research was directed at collecting productivity data for use in standard cost-effectiveness analyses and in cost-of-illness studies. These estimates of changes in productivity due to a disease were typically limited to absenteeism and excluded presenteeism (Andersson and Kartman 1995; Krahn et al. 1996; Koopmanschap and Rutten 1993). This oversight was significant, as researchers now realize that most of the economic loss for a particular condition comes from productivity declines while a worker is at work rather than during short absences.

Nevertheless, the industry saw this first wave of productivity research as a useful way to draw attention to a particular health problem and allow policymakers to rank diseases in terms of their economic importance. Unfortunately, in the absence of sound psychometric tools, these early studies were also particularly susceptible to methodological problems. For example, estimates of the cost of illness of any one disease often varied by enormous amounts (over seven-fold in the case of Alzheimer's disease) (Bloom et al. 2001). Pharmaceutical companies have since also deemphasized research on the direct and indirect costs of diseases because of the FDA's reluctance to permit the use of cost estimates in promotional materials (U.S. Food and Drug Administration 2000).

Today, the pharmaceutical industry is interested in work productivity data because it can help demonstrate the overall value of medicines. In an attempt to derail legislative initiatives designed to prevent pharmaceutical

companies from pricing their products according to market signals, the industry argues that price controls are likely to have a negative impact on both
the health of U.S. workers and the economy. As Alan Holmer, the former
president and chief executive officer of the Pharmaceutical Research and
Manufacturers of America, the representative and lobbying body for pharmaceutical and biotechnology companies, recently stated, "Prescription
medicines . . . bring value to the economy—in terms of worker productivity,
international competitiveness, and domestic employment. . . . [A] study
showed that prescription medicines netted average annual productivity savings of $276 per employee treated with high blood pressure medicines, $822
per employee treated with anti-depression medicines, and $1,475 per em-
ployee treated for diabetes" (Holmer 2003).

At the same time, pharmaceutical firms have also enlisted productivity
data in their efforts to improve market share or to justify a certain price to
managed-care organizations (MCOs) and other reimbursement authorities.
Thus, productivity assessment, along with quality of life and patient satisfaction, has become a mainstay in the armamentarium of a pharmaceutical
company's marketing department.

Pharmaceutical companies often make a case for a new treatment in
terms of cost offsets or cost savings. Take, for example, migraine treatment.
Figure 11.1 shows the cost for migraine treatment at $44 per employee per
month; however, this cost is more than offset by a reduction in labor costs and
a decrease in lost productivity (Legg et al. 1997).

The development of marketing materials based on productivity assessments is in its early stages. Currently, pharmaceutical companies often
lump information about productivity improvements with any changes in direct medical costs due to a treatment (e.g., the drug leads to a reduction in the
length of hospital stays). Although U.S. pharmaceutical companies tend to direct their message to MCOs (or pharmacy benefit-management companies if
the drug formulary is carved out), MCOs may have little interest in the data
because they do not pay for work absences or productivity declines. Thus, the
industry is gradually beginning to shift its attention to the direct stakeholders: patients, unions, and employers.

In this chapter I examine the issue of productivity research from the
perspective of the pharmaceutical industry. Explaining how productivity data
are used and communicated to various audiences, I review the different
methods that the industry may use to assess productivity in clinical trials. I
conclude with a discussion of the hurdles that must be overcome in order to
ensure that productivity assessment is viewed as a valid and reliable tool for
demonstrating the value of pharmaceutical interventions.

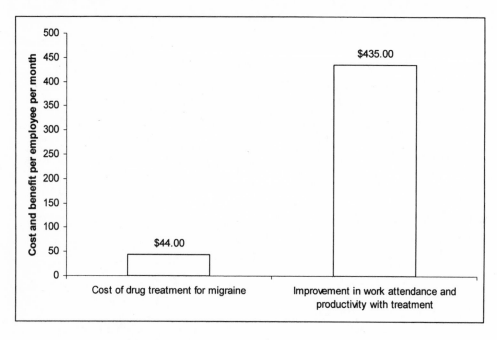

Figure 11.1. Cost of drug therapy for migraine versus benefits

MEASUREMENT OF WORK PRODUCTIVITY

The ideal method of measuring work productivity would rely on archival or objective data. However, as mentioned in chapter 4, such data may not be available, so most productivity assessments utilize self-report measures. These questionnaires are rooted in the methodology developed for patient-reported outcomes. The process involves item-generation based on interviews with experts and employees (suffering from a specific condition or a variety of conditions) and development of draft domains. Good questionnaire development also requires a commitment to the following practices: expression of items and instructions in a clear and comprehensive manner and the use of memory-retrieval aids, appropriate response items, and effective overall questionnaire structure.

In the next phase, psychometric testing is needed to address item-scaling and to aggregate items in domains (if warranted), as well as to demonstrate reliability, validity, and responsiveness (Chassany et al. 2002). Table 11.1 lists the main elements of psychometric tests.

Pharmaceutical companies typically use one of more of the following questionnaires in the assessment of work performance: the Endicott Work Productivity Scale (EWPS) (Endicott and Nee 1997), the Work Limitations

TABLE II.I.

SCALE LEVEL PSYCHOMETRIC TESTS AND CRITERIA

PSYCHOMETRIC TESTS	CRITERIA
ITEM DESCRIPTIVE STATISTICS	Item-level missing data (eliminate if > 10%) Item-level floor/ceiling effects (eliminate if > 70%)
CONSTRUCT VALIDITY	Factor analysis results (varimax and oblique rotations) Item convergent validity (eliminate if < 0.40) Item discriminant validity (eliminate if correlation with own scale < correlation with other scales) Item-level discriminative ability (eliminate if < 0.15) Item-level responsiveness
RELIABILITY	
INTERNAL CONSISTENCY	Cronbach's alpha coefficient ≥ 0.70
TEST-RETEST RELIABILITY	Intraclass correlation coefficient = 0.70
CONCURRENT VALIDITY	Correlations between productivity scales and similar scales for other questionnaires (e.g., another productivity questionnaire, SF-36, or EQ-5D) (≥0.3 and ≤ 0.9)
CRITERION VALIDITY	Correlation between productivity scales and objective productivity data (e.g., widgets produced or insurance claims processed)
KNOWN GROUPS VALIDITY	Baseline productivity scales' ability to discriminate between individuals with a chronic condition versus healthy individuals
CLINICAL VALIDITY	Correlation between clinician's assessment of the patient's health overall (poor–excellent) and the patient's report of productivity (low productivity–high productivity)
RESPONSIVENESS (LONGITUDINAL COHORT)	Differences in productivity scale scores between patients who reported improvement, deterioration or stability in health over a period of time Effect sizes calculated and defined as a small (effect size = 0.2), moderate (0.5), or large (0.8)

TABLE II.2.

PSYCHOMETRIC CHARACTERISTICS

AND RECALL PERIODS FOR WORK-PRODUCTIVITY

QUESTIONNAIRE	VALIDITY	RELIABILITY	RESPONSIVENESS	RETRIEVAL AIDS	RECALL (WEEKS)
EWPS	CcV	TR	X	X	1
HLQ	CoV	X	X	X	2
HPQ	CV	X	√	√	1
SPS	CoV, CcV	X	X	X	4
WHI	CoV, DV	X	X	√	2
WLQ	CV, CoV, CcV	IC	√	X	2 or 4
WPAI	CoV	TR	X	X	1

Notes: CV = criterion validity; CoV = construct validity; CcV = concurrent validity; DV = discriminative validity; TR = test-retest reliability; IC = internal consistency reliability; X = not tested or not present; √ = test conducted or presence of memory aids.

Questionnaire (WLQ) (Lerner et al. 2001), the Health and Labor Questionnaire (HLQ) (van Roijen et al. 1996; Hakkaart–van Roijen and Essink-Bot 2000), the Health and Performance Questionnaire (HPQ) (Kessler et al. 2003), the Stanford Presenteeism Scale (SPS) (Koopman et al. 2002), the Work and Health Interview (WHI) (Stewart et al. 2003), and the Work Productivity and Activity Impairment Questionnaire (WPAI) (Reilly, Zbrozek, and Dukes 1993). With the exception of the HLQ, all questionnaires have been developed by U.S. researchers.

A few disease-specific productivity measures are also available, such as the Angina-related Limitations at Work Questionnaire (ALWQ) (Lerner et al. 1998), the Migraine Work and Productivity Loss Questionnaire (MWPLQ) (Lerner et al. 1999), and the WL-26 in musculoskeletal disorders and occupational illnesses and injuries (Amick et al. 2000). In addition, developers of the general work-productivity questionnaires permit some adaptation of the questionnaires for specific disease areas. For instance, the WPAI has a form that may be altered to cover any specific health problem.

In the following section, the general productivity questionnaires are reviewed in terms of their content and psychometric properties. The main properties of the questionnaires are summarized in table 11.2.

Endicott Work Productivity Scale (EWPS)

The EWPS is a 25-item self-administered questionnaire that measures the degree to which a given medical condition affects work functioning. Designed to be used with various disorders and with various interventions, the instrument covers time spent on tasks, interaction with co-workers, mood, concentration, and memory. Work productivity is measured as the unweighted sum of all the items on the questionnaire. Information on the development phase of the questionnaire has not been published. The recall period is one week.

Test-retest reliability was tested in clinically stable depressed patients. The intraclass correlation coefficient of reliability for the total score was 0.92. Internal consistency reliability was 0.93, indicating that the items assessed the same dimension (α coefficient of 0.93). The total score on the EWPS has been compared to several measures of severity of illness: Hamilton rating scale for Depression total score, Global Clinical Index of Severity, and Symptom Checklist 90 to assess concurrent validity. Overall, the authors concluded that the EWPS total scores validly measure severity of illness and that patients with depression could be distinguished from a sample of the general population.

Work Limitations Questionnaire (WLQ)

The WLQ is a 25-item self-administered questionnaire that assesses the degree to which health problems interfere with the ability to perform aspects of paid work. The scope of the WLQ is broad, including both physical and emotional aspects of health. The questionnaire is divided into four work-limitation scales: time management (5 items), physical demands (6 items), mental-interpersonal (9 items), and output demands (5 items). A two-week recall was found to be more reliable when tested against a four-week recall version, although both versions are available.

In order to develop the initial items for the WLQ, the researchers reviewed the work-classification literature, convened four focus groups of employed patients with chronic conditions, conducted cognitive interviews with employed patients, and had a physician expert panel review candidate items. Initial items were reviewed by 40 chronically ill patients in terms of comprehensibility, redundancy, relevance, and ease of response. (For more information on the WLQ, see chapter 4.)

Health and Labor Questionnaire (HLQ)

The HLQ, developed by Dutch researchers, is a 17-item self-report questionnaire designed to collect data on the effects of a broad range of illnesses on paid and unpaid labor. The four modules of the HLQ are absence from paid work (3 items), reduced productivity while in paid activities (8 items), unpaid production (2 items), and impediments to paid and unpaid labor (1 item). The remaining items are skip or demographic questions. Certain items can be left out if not applicable to a particular study population (e.g., questions about paid activities for retired persons). The recall period is the past two weeks. Information on the development phase of the HLQ has not been reported publicly.

Reliability testing has not been reported on the HLQ. Construct validity of the first module was compared to general-population data and a previous migraine study conducted in the United Kingdom. This comparison found a high level of agreement with the absolute number of days lost and the difference between men and women. When the HLQ was compared to Dutch national-registry data for absence from work, the two were in close agreement (12.2 days for men for the HLQ compared to 12.9 days for men in the registry data).

The psychometric properties of the second module were tested by comparing the HLQ productivity question to a descriptive efficiency score. A low-to-moderate Pearson correlation coefficient ($r = 0.41$) was found between the two different approaches. Under the HLQ question, an average of 2.7 days per year was lost because of a decline in efficiency compared to 8.9 working days under the efficiency question.

The construct validity of time spent on unpaid work was estimated by comparing HLQ estimates to general-population data collected via a diary method. The average time spent on household production reported in a time-use survey was in accordance with the HLQ estimates except for child care. For example, the HLQ found that men spent an average of 7.3 hours per week on unpaid household work, as compared to 8.9 hours in a general-population survey.

The construct validity of the fourth module was tested based on the decrease of the experienced impediment as a result of micturition problems due to the implantation of an electro-stimulator in patients with spinal cord injuries. The impediment scores for paid and unpaid work discriminated highly between the two groups. In individuals who were absent from paid work, the impediment score was significantly higher than in those not absent from work (1.07 versus 0.28). For unpaid work, individuals who were not absent scored 0.12 versus 0.84 for those who were absent.

Health Performance Questionnaire (HPQ)

The HPQ was developed as part of the World Health Organization (WHO) Global Burden of Disease Initiative. The employee version of the HPQ consists of 91 questions in three sections: health (e.g., general health, presence of conditions, and consultation history in 59 items), work (e.g., job description, time missed from work, work performance, rating of job performance in 24 items), and demographics (8 items). A clinical-trial version has been developed and is currently undergoing revision by the developers. The recall period is the past four weeks for most questions.

The initial development of the HPQ included a review of existing scales and was augmented by pilot interviews. Initial items were evaluated and refined by experts in survey research methodology. Cognitive debriefing interviews were conducted to detect and remove any ambiguities in questionnaire wording.

Criterion validity of the HPQ has been demonstrated by comparing the HPQ to objective data on work performance. Four HPQ calibration surveys have been conducted (railroad engineers, customer service representatives, airline reservation agents, and executives); for these groups archival data (and a subsample of Experience Sample Method [ESM] evaluation) were available either on sickness absence, work performance, or both. Statistically significant relationships were found in logistic regression analyses between HPQ ratings and the odds of low archival/ESM performance in all occupations. There was also a significant relationship between HPQ ratings and the odds of high archival or ESM work performance for reservation agents and customer service representatives but not for executives. Pearson correlations coefficients indicate that self-reports of absences are associated with archival data. For reservation agents, this was .81 for hours missed and .87 for hours worked for a one-week recall and .79 and .71, respectively, for a four-week recall period. (For a review of recent survey initiatives using the HPQ, see the discussion in chapter 14).

Stanford Presenteeism Scale (SPS)

The SPS is a six-item questionnaire that measures the ability of workers to concentrate and accomplish work despite their medical condition. The questionnaire encompasses cognitive, emotional, and behavioral aspects of work tasks. The recall period is the past month.

The content of the SPS was determined by a review of the relevant literature and existing questionnaires. Items were generated by the developers (Stanford University researchers, Merck & Co. employees, Colombia University and University of Maryland researchers, one benefit manager, and one health and fitness coordinator). Prior to psychometric testing, 32 items were identified by the developers based on work and psychological focus in an iterative process.

Tests of reliability have not been performed on the SPS to date. High internal consistency was shown with a Cronbach's α of 0.80. Concurrent validity was tested by comparing scores on the SPS-32 with scores on the SPS-6 and documenting significant correlations in the expected direction. Known-groups validity was tested by comparing the scores on the SPS-6 with the presence of a physical disability. This test found that the mean total scores were significantly different ($p = 0.001$) for employees reporting a work- or non-work-related disability (mean 21.0) compared to employees with no disability (23.5). Discriminant validity was tested to determine if work productivity could be differentiated from job satisfaction and job stress. The tests demonstrated that the SPS-6 was only somewhat negatively correlated with job stress and only somewhat positively correlated with job satisfaction.

Work Health Interview (WHI)

The WHI is a computer-assisted telephone interview that collects work-absence and work-productivity data. The WHI consists of six modules. The first three modules collect data on employment status, usual work time, health problems, and informed consent. The fourth module includes items on activities at work, the time allotted to work tasks, and the importance of the tasks. The fifth module collects information on workdays missed and reduced performance while at work due to health problems. The sixth module captures demographic data. Data on the development of the WHI has not been published. The recall period is two weeks.

Psychometric testing of the WHI has been limited to tests of criterion and discriminant validity. The responses on the WHI have been compared to continuous performance data for customer service representatives at a northern California call center. Estimates of missed workdays based on the WHI correlated well with workplace data (0.85). A modest correlation (0.54) was found between the WHI and the diary measure of total productive time.

Work Productivity and Activity Impairment Questionnaire (WPAI)

The WPAI instrument was developed to measure the effect of general health and symptom severity on work productivity and regular activities (Reilly, Zbrozek, and Dukes 1993). The general-health version of the WPAI contains six questions on hours worked or missed, the impact of health problems on productivity while working, and impact on regular daily activities. The allergy-specific version of the questionnaire is similar and includes additional questions on the impact a person's allergies have on attendance at school and productivity while at school. Information on the development of the WPAI has not been published. The recall period for the WPAI is seven days.

Reliability testing of the WPAI has focused on reproducibility. Individuals completed a baseline self-administered questionnaire and were then assigned to one of two groups: self-administered retest or interviewer-administered retest. The within-group correlation coefficients for the self-administered sample were 0.71 for overall work productivity (health), 0.75 for overall work productivity (symptom), 0.77 for impairment of regular activities (health), and 0.86 for impairment of regular activities (symptom). The correlation coefficients for the interviewer-administered group were similar at 0.74, 0.72, 0.82, and 0.87, respectively. Overall, when comparisons between scores at baseline and the second assessment were made for both groups, the differences in scores were generally not statistically significant.

Construct validity was assessed by comparing the WPAI measures to several Medical Outcomes Study 36-Item Short-Form Health Survey (SF-36) concepts: general health perceptions, role limitations (physical), role limitations (emotional), and pain. The following qualitative measures were also compared with the WPAI: symptom severity, work interference, and regular-activity interference. The quantitative work-productivity and regular-activity impairment measures were positively correlated with the SF-36 dimensions and the symptom severity measures. For the SF-36 dimensions, the greatest differences between baseline and retest in the self-administered group were between the correlations of general health perceptions and overall work productivity (health) (0.52 versus 0.34, respectively), and between general health perceptions and work productivity (symptom) (0.49 versus 0.31, respectively). For the other qualitative measures, the largest differences between baseline and retest in the self-administered group were between symptom severity and overall work productivity (symptom) (0.36 versus 0.08, respectively) and regular activity interference and overall work productivity (symptom) (0.80 versus 0.60, respectively). For both groups at both time periods, the correlations were lower between the quantitative measures and role function (emotional), versus general health perceptions, role function (physical), and pain. Additionally, for most of the measures, interviewer administration was associated with higher correlation coefficients. The highest correlations were seen between impairment of regular activities (symptom) and the global measure of symptom interference in activities ($r = 0.81$).

VALUATION

Pharmaceutical companies interested in placing a dollar value on estimates of productivity changes typically rely on three methods (Rothermich and Pathak 1999): the human-capital approach (Weisbrod 1961), the friction-cost method (Koopmanschap and Rutten 1994), and the quality-adjusted life-years (QALYs) approach (Luce et al. 1996). The human-capital approach is the favored technique in the United States, and the friction-cost approach has had only limited use in Europe. As the QALY approach recommended by Luce and colleagues (1996) is applicable only to a specific type of study, a cost-utility study, details on its use are not reviewed here.

The human-capital approach typically assigns age-adjusted and sex-adjusted gross wage rates for any time absent from work. Although firmly rooted in economic theory, this approach has been criticized for ignoring some dimensions that may have economic value (e.g., the consumption value of any change in health status). In addition, the methods used by researchers to value forgone paid work often vary substantially (Berger et al. 2001).

The friction-costing method proposed by Koopmanschap and Rutten (1993, 1996), in contrast, takes into account real changes in production by incorporating information on the costs of short-term absences from work and reduced productivity while at work. Under friction costing, the situation within a firm and the labor market are examined directly, so collecting data is much more complicated than for studies using the human-capital approach. (For a microeconomic analysis of the effects of productivity losses on labor markets, see chapter 7 of this book).

The theoretical debate about the best way to value productivity and work absences continues to generate numerous commentaries (e.g., Koopmanschap et al. 1997; Johannesson and Karlsson 1997). Berger and colleagues (2001) find both the human-capital and friction-cost methods to be oversimplifications of the real work situation. For example, as Berger and his colleagues also argue in chapter 9 of this book, a firm that relies on team performance would require a different method of valuation than one relying on individual performance, because the impact of a productivity decline or work absence will be quite different. Further, companies with knowledge-based workers are different from companies with workers who perform rote tasks.

The problems identified by Berger have led researchers to consider the development of work or job multipliers (Baase and Sharda 2003). As a rule, productivity at the firm level is affected by three factors: the extent to which teamwork is involved, the time-sensitivity of the task, and the ease of labor substitution. In this framework, productivity losses will be highest when output is contingent upon team performance and the productivity of a team member is low. Furthermore, when the time-sensitivity of a task is high and an employee is ill or absent, the productivity loss to the firm will be greater than just the productivity of the ill worker. For instance, if it is necessary to meet a crucial deadline that will lead to a large sale for a company, and the person responsible for delivery of a piece of that work is absent, the entire sale can be jeopardized. This implies that the work/productivity multiplier is some number above one, indicating that the productivity loss is actually greater than that measured at the individual level.

ISSUES IN THE DESIGN AND MEASUREMENT OF PRODUCTIVITY IN CLINICAL TRIALS

As demonstrated above, several self-report questionnaires may be used to assess productivity in clinical trials. The content and ease of administration are perhaps the two most critical factors that pharmaceutical companies must weigh in selecting measures for clinical trials.

However, with regard to questionnaire development, several points should be reviewed carefully. First, did the item-generation process reflect concepts that employees and employers perceive as important (i.e., were employee and employer interviews, focus groups and cognitive debriefing conducted?)? Second, is the questionnaire understandable to subjects and are memory-retrieval aids embedded in the questionnaire? Third, what approach was taken for item deletion, weighting items, and defining scales? Fourth, was the questionnaire pilot-tested?

Some questionnaires fare better than others in response to the above questions. The reported development of the SPS indicates that the questionnaire was developed by the 10 authors of the publication. However, there is neither a report of employee or employer involvement in the development of the questionnaire nor any mention of a cognitive debriefing of items. Of the seven questionnaires reviewed, only two (the WHI and the HPQ) have memory-retrieval aids. As Kessler and co-workers (2003) note, responses to complex surveys may be improved with strategies that improve active memory search.

Once the development of a questionnaire has been reviewed, its validity needs to be examined. For validity, several areas should be considered (table 11.2): criterion, construct, discriminant, concurrent, and known-groups. In addition, it is important to look at the reliability and responsiveness of a questionnaire. As shown above, the extent of psychometric testing of the questionnaires varies considerably. For the WPAI, the psychometric testing was limited to reliability and construct validity.

While these properties are critical, the criterion validity of the questionnaire must also be established by comparing the questionnaire to some gold-standard measure. But though these data may be relatively easy to obtain for blue-collar or pink-collar workers (e.g., widgets produced or insurance claims processed), for white-collar workers the data may be nonexistent or of suspect quality (e.g., qualitative performance reviews). Of the questionnaires reviewed here, only three (the WLQ, the HPQ, and the WHI) conducted tests of criterion validity against gold-standard data, and only one (the HPQ) did so with data from white-collar workers.

Ultimately, selecting the best instrument for a trial is not purely a matter of scientific methodology, but requires finding a balance between what is practical and the requirements of the audience for information. Psychometric testing is an ongoing activity. The initial psychometric properties of a questionnaire are often tested many times over as the questionnaire is administered in subsequent trials. Thus, the reported properties of a questionnaire may change over time.

To explore the impact of a drug on productivity is not the same thing as to attempt to come up with an FDA-approved labeling claim based on productivity. If a pharmaceutical company wishes to measure the likely effect of a drug, then any of the questionnaires could be utilized (with an emphasis on choosing the measure that is likely to be most responsive). If, at a later date, a confirmation of the exploratory research results is desired, then a more indepth appraisal of options should occur.

In comparison, if the purpose of the research is to obtain a labeling claim from a regulatory body, then the questionnaires must be examined in great depth. As Stang and coauthors report in chapter 12 of this volume, though the FDA has yet to give firm guidance on productivity research, the future for productivity claims is potentially promising.

With regard to pharmaceutical companies that are interested in selecting an appropriate measure for productivity research, some lessons may be learned from the field of health-related quality-of-life assessment. The FDA has been reluctant to accept the claim of improved quality of life because few interventions affect all areas of life. Instead, the FDA is more likely to permit claims of a prespecified set of items (in a domain; e.g., physical functioning) (Burke 2001). Therefore, it may be anticipated that the FDA will also take a similar stance with productivity assessments. But researchers should proceed with caution. While some existing questionnaires essentially measure productivity as a single item, the FDA has cautioned that single items may not be sufficient to provide evidence of a benefit (Burke 2001).

In addition, the FDA may also require that the productivity questionnaire be field-tested in two well-controlled pivotal trials, with the productivity measure as a primary endpoint. This stipulation brings into question whether a pharmaceutical company will truly want to obtain a labeling claim. The easiest way to obtain the claim would be to piggyback the productivity assessment on a phase III trial that examines the efficacy of an agent. However, these trials represent a stylized world of clinical practice because of artificial inclusion and exclusion criteria as well as controls demanded by the protocol that can greatly hinder the generalizability of the trial results (Bombardier and Maetzel 1999). In other words, results based on such a stylized sample may fail to meet the needs of the industry's target audience, workplace decision-makers who want information particular to their situation. For example, a manufacturing labor union is unlikely to be interested in the results of a study conducted primarily on white-collar workers. This desire for situationally specific data creates a substantial challenge for the design of experimental treatment trials aimed at documenting effects on productivity.

Based on the above considerations, a naturalistic or effectiveness trial is likely to be a more appropriate trial design for demonstrating the value of an intervention based on improvements in worker productivity. A naturalistic study reflects real-world treatments by loosening the restriction on patient inclusion and exclusion criteria and by permitting routine medical practice (for instance, by permitting the titration or augmentation of medications). Although this study design would not, in most cases, reach the FDA's standards of "substantial evidence," it does have the considerable virtue of relevance to the decision-maker. Of course, the ability of a pharmaceutical company to promote productivity messages based on a trial becomes more limited. Strictly speaking, a company can cite only productivity information that was truly unsolicited and unprompted.

CONCLUSION

Pharmaceutical companies interested in measuring productivity data can choose among a variety of instruments. This chapter has highlighted some of the differences in the psychometric properties of self-report measures. The tools all have strengths and weaknesses. To cite some of the strengths: the development process was excellent for WLQ and HPQ; memory aids have been inserted in HPQ and WHI to improve responses; an attempt to establish clinical validity was made for HPQ, WHI, and WLQ; the multidimensional aspects of productivity are well covered in WLQ. However, none of the questionnaires have investigated whether productivity assessment in white-collar workers is truly feasible (although the HPQ makes a valiant initial attempt). As noted earlier, the development and testing of questionnaires is an ongoing process, and one may eventually emerge as a forerunner. Alternatively, perhaps limitations to the current methods will be revealed and researchers will have to develop a questionnaire from scratch.

For pharmaceutical companies interested in generating a productivity claim that will withstand FDA scrutiny, it is advisable to use instruments that have established criterion validity (WLQ, HPQ, and WHI). If the purpose is exploratory in nature or productivity is a tertiary endpoint, any of the tools could serve. Or, special considerations might come into play. For instance, the items in the EWPS have a depression focus, so this tool might be especially attractive in research on the effects of mental disease.

Productivity messages communicated by pharmaceutical companies need to be both simple and relevant. Benefit managers are not psychometricians. Nor are they health-service researchers or labor economists. The level of scrutiny they finally place on the underlying methodology of an instrument is low: reasonable measures that yield reasonable results are likely to be accepted by employers—if not by the FDA. Furthermore, employers are not interested in how a drug works under clinical-trial conditions, but how a drug works in real-world settings in which employees may, for example, not be compliant with their medication regimen and may also not have regular physician contact. As a result, naturalistic effectiveness trials are of greatest interest to employers.

If the measurement approach is to be incorporated into benefit design, pharmaceutical companies will have to overcome institutional inertia and keep their message focused and relevant. As researchers in pharmaceutical companies are well aware, managed-care organizations (MCOs) separate their drug budgets from other medical costs (Drummond et al. 2003). Thus, MCOs typically focus too narrowly on the acquisition cost of a medication and ignore savings in other areas of medical-resource use.

Likewise, as Scanlon notes in chapter 8 of this book, benefit managers are also narrowly focused on curtailing the cost of health programs (or shifting the cost of drugs to their employees) rather than examining the overall value of a program. This calculus prevents employers from making rational choices about how to allocate their health care dollars to maximize overall health outcomes.

The challenge for pharmaceutical companies interested in achieving optimal formulary pull-through is to overcome this silo mentality in employers. If this can be done, then employers will, in turn, encourage MCOs to provide the most cost-effective medications (especially those demonstrating value in terms of productivity). Although this development may sound like a pipe dream, there are reasons to hold out some optimism. For example, in recent years, the silo mentality in MCOs has become less entrenched through improvement in the educational qualifications of formulary committee members (Lyles 2001) and the development of a standardized method for submitting data to MCOs (Sullivan et al. 2001).

Given the staggering growth in employment-related health expenditures in recent years, employers can no longer afford to ignore the link between value-based investments in health care and improvements in work productivity. This opening may well allow pharmaceutical companies to benefit—to the extent that they can provide well-designed productivity studies that demonstrate the value of their products.

REFERENCES

Amick, B. C., III, D. Lerner, W. H. Rogers, T. Rooney, and J. N. Katz. 2000. A review of health-related work outcome measures and their uses, and recommended measures. *Spine* 25:3152–60.

Andersson, F., and B. Kartman. 1995. The cost of angina pectoris in Sweden. *Pharmaco-Economics* 8:233–44.

Baase, C., and C. Sharda. 2003. Defining and acting upon the total economic impact of chronic health conditions. Paper presented at the conference "Winning the Battle: HPM in the Trenches," Institute for Health and Productivity Management, October 8.

Berger, M. L., J. F. Murray, J. Xu, and M. Pauly. 2001. Alternative valuations of work loss and productivity. *Journal of Occupational and Environmental Medicine* 43: 18–24.

Bloom, B. S., D. J. Bruno, D. Y. Maman, and R. Jayadevappa. 2001. Usefulness of US cost-of-illness studies in healthcare decision making. *PharmacoEconomics* 19: 207–13.

Bombardier, C., and A. Maetzel. 1999. Pharmacoeconomic evaluation of new treatments: Efficacy versus effectiveness studies? *Annals of the Rheumatic Disease* 58 (Suppl. 1): 182–85.

Burke, L. B. 2001. US regulation of pharmaceutical outcomes research. *Value Health* 4:5–7.

Chassany, O., P. Sagnier, P. Marquis, S. Fullerton, and N. Aaronson. 2002. Patient-reported outcomes: The example of health-related quality of life—a European guidance document for the improved integration of health-related quality of life assessment in the drug regulatory process. *Drug Information Journal* 36: 209–38.

Drummond, M., R. Brown, A. M. Fendrick, P. Fullerton, P. Neumann, R. Taylor, and M. Barbieri. 2003. Use of pharmacoeconomics information—report of the ISPOR Task Force on use of pharmacoeconomic/health economic information in health-care decision making. *Value Health* 6:407–16.

Endicott, J., and J. Nee. 1997. Endicott Work Productivity Scale (EWPS): A new measure to assess treatment effects. *Psychopharmacology Bulletin* 33:13–16.

Hakkaart–van Roijen, L., and M. Essink-Bot. 2000. *Manual Health and Labour Questionnaire*. Rotterdam: Institute for Medical Technology Assessment.

Holmer, A. F. 2003. How can we not afford prescription drugs in America?—the value of new medicines for patients. Speech presented before University of Pennsylvania Leonard Davis Institute of Health Economics. www.phrma.org/publications/publications/24.01.2003.678.cfm.

Johannesson, M., and G. Karlsson. 1997. The friction cost method: A comment. *Journal of Health Economics* 16:249–55.

Kessler, R. C., C. Barber, A. Beck, P. A. Berglund, P. D. Cleary, D. McKenas, N. Pronk, G. Simon, P. Stang, T. B. Üstün, and P. Wang. 2003. The World Health Organization Health and Work Performance Questionnaire (HPQ). *Journal of Occupational and Environmental Medicine* 45:156–74.

Koopman, C., K. R. Pelletier, J. F. Murray, C. E. Sharda, M. L. Berger, R. S. Turpin, P. Hackleman, P. Gibson, D. M. Holmes, and T. Bendel. 2002. Stanford presenteeism scale: Health status and employee productivity. *Journal of Occupational and Environmental Medicine* 44:14–20.

Koopmanschap, M. A., and F. F. Rutten. 1993. Indirect costs in economic studies: Confronting the confusion. *PharmacoEconomics* 4:446–54.

———. 1994. The impact of indirect costs on outcomes of health care programs. *Health Economics* 3:385–93.

———. 1996. A practical guide for calculating indirect costs of disease. *PharmacoEconomics* 10:460–66.

Koopmanschap, M., F. Rutten, B. van Inevald, and L. van Roijen. 1997. Reply to Johanneson's and Karlsson's comment. *Journal of Health Economics* 16:257–59.

Krahn, M. D., C. Berka, P. Langlois, and A. Detsky. 1996. Direct and indirect costs of asthma in Canada, 1990. *Canadian Medical Association Journal* 154:821–31.

Legg, R., D. A. Sclar, N. L. Nemec, J. Tarnai, and J. I. Mackowiak. 1997. Cost benefit of sumatriptan to an employer. *Journal of Occupational and Environmental Medicine* 39:652–57.

Lerner, D., B. C. Amick III, J. C. Lee, T. Rooney, W. H. Rogers, H. Chang, and E. R. Berndt. 2003. Relationship of employee-reported work limitations to work productivity. *Medical Care* 41:649–59.

Lerner, D. J., B. C. Amick III, S. Malspeis, W. H. Rogers, D. R. Gomes, and D. N. Salem. 1998. The angina-related Limitations at Work Questionnaire. *Quality of Life Research* 7:23–32.

Lerner, D. J., B. C. Amick III, S. Malspeis, W. H. Rogers, N. C. Santanello, W. C. Gerth, and R. B. Lipton. 1999. The Migraine Work and Productivity Loss Questionnaire: Concepts and design. *Quality of Life Research* 8:699–710.

Lerner, D., B. C. Amick III, W. H. Rogers, S. Malspeis, K. Bungay, and D. Cynn. 2001. The Work Limitations Questionnaire. *Medical Care* 39:72–85.

Luce, B., W. Manning, J. Siegel, and J. Lipscomb. 1996. Estimating costs in cost-effectiveness analysis. In *Cost-effectiveness in health and medicine*, ed. M. R. Gold, J. E. Siegel, L. B. Russell, and M. C. Weinstein. New York: Oxford University Press.

Lyles, A. 2001. Decision-makers' use of pharmacoeconomics: What does the research tell us? *Expert Review of Pharmacoeconomics and Outcomes Research* 1:133–44.

Reilly, M. C., A. S. Zbrozek, and E. M. Dukes. 1993. The validity and reproducibility of a work productivity and activity impairment instrument. *PharmacoEconomics* 4:353–65.

Rothermich, E. A., and D. S. Pathak. 1999. Productivity-cost controversies in cost-effectiveness analysis: Review and research agenda. *Clinical Therapy* 21:255–67.

Stewart, W. F., J. A. Ricci, E. Chee, S. R. Hahn, and D. Morganstein. 2003. Cost of lost productivity work time among US workers with depression. *Journal of the American Medical Association* 289:3135–44.

Sullivan, S. D., A. Lyles, B. Luce, and J. Grigar. 2001. AMCP guidance for submission of clinical and economic evaluation data to support formulary listing in U.S. health plans and pharmacy benefits management organizations. *Journal of Managed Care Pharmacy* 7:272–82.

U.S. Food and Drug Administration. 2000. Lotronex warning letter. www.fda.gov/cder/warn/apr2000/dd042800.pdf.

Van Roijen, L., M. L. Essink-Bot, M. A. Koopmanschap, G. Bonsel, and F. F. Rutten. 1996. Labor and health status in economic evaluation of health care: The Health and Labor Questionnaire. *International Journal of Technology Assessment in Health Care* 12:405–15.

Weisbrod, B. A. 1961. The valuation of human capital. *Journal of Political Economy* 69:425–36.

CHAPTER 12

A Regulatory Perspective on Productivity Claims: Implications for Future Productivity Research

PAUL E. STANG, PAUL E. GREENBERG,
HOWARD G. BIRNBAUM, RONALD C. KESSLER,
LYNN HOFFMAN, AND MEI SHENG DUH

INTRODUCTION

The burgeoning field of productivity research has sparked the interest of numerous stakeholders. Understanding the impact of medical treatments on work performance is useful to patients, health-insurance companies, businesses, and society in general. As the primary health care purchasers in the U.S. economy, employers are looking for research tools that can help them assess their health care options. Unfortunately, employers have yet to come up with much hard evidence to support the business case for linking drug treatment and productivity management. The unmet needs of employers and other stakeholders should provide the impetus for researchers to develop standardized productivity instruments to measure job inputs and outputs.

In recent years, the various governmental agencies that regulate medical treatment, such as the Food and Drug Administration (FDA), have also emerged as stakeholders in productivity research. To increase the sales for their products in an increasingly competitive business environment, pharmaceutical manufacturers have begun to develop productivity-impact measures as components of established health outcomes and quality-of-life research methodologies. The goal is to use this information to differentiate products and appeal specifically to employers and payers. The wider the range of benefits that can be appropriately claimed for a given pharmaceutical product, the bigger the potential business opportunity. A new therapeutic agent that treats a given condition more effectively and with fewer side effects, while leading to increased patient compliance, can claim to have an effect beyond the positive economic benefits. Furthermore, even if the cost of a brand-name prescription drug is relatively high, companies may be able to argue that use of the drug both offsets other health care costs (e.g., inpatient care, physician office visits) and produces savings in indirect costs due to increases in workplace productivity.

Additionally, manufacturer interest in productivity-related outcomes and economic research reflects a societal trend that has resulted in a more activist role for individual participants in the health care sector. Today, patients typically evaluate health care interventions in terms of their ability to meet personal goals, including success in the workplace. Since career success itself may be affected by the choice of treatment paths, increasingly employees should be inclined to scrutinize the productivity outcomes that result from specific health interventions. Just as direct-to-consumer advertising of prescription drugs explicitly recognizes the voice of patients in treatment decisions, so too can productivity research enhance the voice of employees interested in minimizing the unfavorable effects of acute or chronic disease on their promotional tracks and salary trajectories.

As pharmaceutical researchers study the impact of treatment on work performance in response to both employer and employee interest, the FDA is responsible for evaluating these claims to ensure that they meet established standards of scientific rigor and validity. However, the FDA faces an additional burden when manufacturers seek to make formal claims in the product labeling regarding impact on productivity. The path for the FDA may turn out to be similar to the evolution of including patient-reported outcome claims, such as those relating to quality of life, in package inserts.

In this chapter we articulate the FDA perspective on productivity research related to prescription drugs. We offer it as a "case study" of the interactive relationship between a stakeholder and the research community. In its efforts to regulate productivity claims, the FDA is interested in new productivity measures. However, the FDA's particular concerns are pointing to gaps in current productivity models that need to be filled. In particular, there is still no widely accepted measurement approach that is generalizable across all jobs and diseases.

We begin by explaining how the FDA regulates productivity claims. We then discuss the evidentiary standards for the two types of productivity claims, those containing clinical information and those containing economic information. Given that the productivity-measurement literature has not yet advanced to the point where it can always meet these standards, we move on to a review of current productivity models and then conclude by asserting the need for a gold standard for productivity measurement.

HOW THE FDA REGULATES PRODUCTIVITY CLAIMS

The overarching mission of the FDA Office of Medical Policy's Division of Drug Marketing, Advertising, and Communications (DDMAC) is to protect public health by ensuring that prescription drug information is truthful, balanced, and accurately communicated. DDMAC achieves this goal by maintaining a surveillance, enforcement, and education program. DDMAC's primary role in assessing an increasing number of productivity-related claims about pharmaceutical products is to ensure that any promotional efforts are not false or misleading. In addition, DDMAC maintains close communication with other parts of the FDA's Center for Drug Evaluation and Research to maintain consistency in standards of evidence for product labeling and promotion.

DDMAC's productivity-specific responsibilities, performed in consultation with FDA medical-review divisions, include the following: review of protocols concerning productivity claims before studies are initiated, review of New Drug Applications with productivity endpoints, monitoring of productivity-related promotion activities, and input into productivity-research policy development. DDMAC's interactions outside of the FDA in the productivity-research field include participation in relevant meetings and workshops and other exchanges with members of the productivity-research community. These activities are designed to gain an in-depth understanding of evolving productivity standards in order to develop and implement FDA policy.

The FDA and DDMAC now confront the challenge of regulating increasing numbers of productivity claims for use in labeling and promotion, despite the fact that the scientific standards for such claims are still being developed. As with other claims, productivity-research claims must meet substantiation requirements (namely, either "substantial evidence" or "competent and reliable scientific evidence") in order to be considered by the FDA. Additionally, such claims may recommend a product for use as long as they are consistent with FDA-approved product labeling. Even if an intended productivity-related claim is submitted with sufficient supportive evidence from a clinical trial, for example, the appropriateness of the study design, the adequacy of statistical power to examine the productivity endpoints, the soundness of the methodologies used to generate the evidence, and the generalizability of the results must be demonstrated convincingly.

THE TWO EVIDENTIARY STANDARDS FOR PRODUCTIVITY CLAIMS

Productivity claims have two components: clinical information and economic information.[1] Productivity information that assesses possible clinical benefit involves performance endpoints, such as task speed, accuracy, and memory; rates of absenteeism; and levels of motor/functional performance. Productivity information that seeks to evaluate possible economic advantage includes data regarding the economic consequences of an illness or disorder, including the cost of absenteeism, the cost of presenteeism, the cost of work loss for caretakers, and the cost of underemployment or unemployment.

Evidentiary standards for labeling and promotion of pharmaceutical products require "substantial evidence . . . as demonstrated by adequate and well-controlled investigations" (Federal Food, Drug, and Cosmetic Act 1999) for claims of *clinical* benefit, and may be based on "competent and reliable scientific evidence," as described by the FDA Modernization Act of 1997, for claims of *economic* advantage (Food and Drug Administration Modernization Act 1997). The application of the "competent and reliable scientific evidence" standard is, however, restricted: it may be used only to substantiate health care economic information and to provide this health care economic information to formulary committees or other groups with training sufficient for its proper interpretation. Such economic information must also be *directly* related to the approved indication(s) of the product for which the claims are being made.

Marketing of prescription drugs and all related promotional activities are regulated by the FDA under the Federal Food, Drug, and Cosmetic Act ("the Act"). Section 505(d) [21 U.S.C. 355(d)] of the Act (as amended by the 1962 Drug Amendments to the Act) defines the concept of "substantial evidence," explicitly referring to "clinical" studies: "the term 'substantial evidence' means evidence consisting of adequate and well-controlled investigations [defined in 21 CFR 314.126], including clinical investigations, by experts qualified by scientific training and experience to evaluate the effectiveness of the drug involved, on the basis of which it could fairly and responsibly be concluded by such experts that the drug will have the effect it purports or is represented to have under the conditions of use prescribed, recommended, or suggested in the labeling or proposed labeling thereof" (*Federal Food, Drug,*

---

1. These standards are also discussed in Greenberg et al. 2001.

and Cosmetic Act 1999). This section, dating back to 1962, stipulates that scientific experts must plan and implement well-designed studies in order to assess the clinical effectiveness of drugs.

It was not until recently, with the Food and Drug Administration Modernization Act of 1997 (FDAMA), that any attempt was made to revise or augment this evidentiary requirement to facilitate the use of types of information other than that generated by primarily clinical investigations. FDAMA, in fact, marks the first time that the use of health care economic information has been discussed explicitly in the context of FDA regulation (Section 114), where this type of data is defined as follows: "[A]nalysis that identifies, measures, or compares the economic consequences, including the costs of the represented health outcomes, of the use of a drug to the use of another drug, to another health care intervention, or to no intervention" (*Food and Drug Administration Modernization Act* 1997). Section 114 of FDAMA goes on to make an important distinction about how economic information may be evaluated (as contrasted with clinical information, for which the "substantial evidence" requirement remains in effect):

> Health care economic information provided to a formulary committee, or other similar entity, in the course of the committee or the entity carrying out its responsibilities for the selection of drugs for managed care or other similar organizations, shall not be considered to be false or misleading under this paragraph if the health care economic information directly relates to an indication approved under section 505 or under section 351(a) of the Public Health Service Act for such drug and is based on competent and reliable scientific evidence. The requirements set forth in section 505(a) or in section 351(a) of the Public Health Service Act shall not apply to health care economic information provided to such a committee or entity in accordance with this paragraph.
> (*Food and Drug Administration Modernization Act* 1997)

The importance of this change in the regulatory environment is reflected in the fact that in the FDA Backgrounder summary of FDAMA (a very large and complex legislative work), the new guideline pertaining to the treatment of economic information is included in one of the seven document subheadings. This summary document reports that FDAMA "allows drug companies to provide economic information about their products to formulary committees, managed care organizations, and similar large-scale buyers of healthcare products" and provides these interpretive comments: "This provision is intended to provide such entities with dependable facts about the economic consequences of their procurement decisions. The law, however, does not permit the dissemination of economic information that could affect prescribing choices to individual medical practitioners" (Food and Drug Administration 1998). However, the availability of these data to employers, who are potentially both consumers of and payers for health care services, makes productivity claims so difficult to regulate that ultimately the position on the formulary will influence individual prescribing.

It is important to recognize that FDAMA urges that economic information (supported by the "competent and reliable" standard of scientific evidence) may be disseminated by manufacturers *only* to those who are likely to possess the skills necessary to interpret it properly. In addition, it is explicitly stated that, in order for economic information to be eligible for the application of this evidence standard when disseminated even to such sophisticated audiences, it must be directly related to the approved indication(s) for a product. The FDA would object, for example, to a claim that a drug approved for the lowering of cholesterol levels is cost-effective for preventing heart attacks unless the drug is also approved for the prevention of heart attacks.

MAY 1998 GUIDANCE FOR INDUSTRY: PROVIDING CLINICAL EVIDENCE OF EFFECTIVENESS FOR HUMAN DRUGS AND BIOLOGICAL PRODUCTS

In May of 1998, the FDA issued a guidance document describing its requirements for substantiating clinical evidence of effectiveness for drugs and biologics. This document discusses aspects of the longstanding "substantial evidence" standard regarding clinical effectiveness and notes changes that have taken place in both the U.S. health care marketplace as a whole and the health care research / clinical trials environment in particular. Of course, the changes required by FDAMA in 1997, as well as others commented on in this guidance, are relevant to intended productivity-related claims as well as claims about other kinds of effects. None of the regulatory shifts, however, reflect any kind of leniency in the current regulatory environment. In fact, the changes actually stem from increasingly rigorous standards in the research community as well as in government and industry.

The 1998 guidance states that the "science and practice of drug development and clinical evaluation have evolved significantly since the effectiveness requirement for drugs was established, and this evolution has implications for the amount and type of data needed to support effectiveness in certain cases. . . . [P]rogress in clinical evaluation and clinical pharmacology have resulted in more rigorously designed and conducted clinical efficacy trials, which are ordinarily conducted at more than one clinical site. This added rigor and scope has implications for a study's reliability, generalizability, and capacity to substantiate effectiveness" (U.S. Department of Health and Human Services 1998).

With regard to how many adequate and well-controlled investigations are required to substantiate claims, the FDA has generally conducted its reviews with the understanding that Congress intended to require at least two adequate and well-controlled studies to establish clinical effectiveness. The FDA has, however, exercised its discretion within the limits imposed by Congress and has broadly interpreted statutory requirements where possible when the data on a particular drug were very convincing: "[In some cases,] FDA has relied on only a single adequate and well-controlled efficacy study to support approval—generally only in cases in which a single multicenter study of excellent design provided highly reliable and statistically strong evidence of an important clinical benefit, such as an effect on survival, and a confirmatory study would have been difficult to conduct on ethical grounds" (U.S. Department of Health and Human Services 1998).

The more common situation, in which more than one adequate and well-controlled investigation is required for substantiation of evidence, reflects the need for "independent substantiation" of experimental results. Reasons for this include the possibility that unanticipated, undetected, systematic biases may affect a single trial's results; the possibility that positive trial results may be observed which are actually due to chance; the possibility that single-center results may be dependent on site- or investigator-specific factors; and, rarely, the possibility that favorable results may be due to scientific fraud (U.S. Department of Health and Human Services 1998).

Studies that may be acceptable on their own (depending, of course, on whether they meet high standards of scientific rigor and fitness of study design) will usually have at least some of the following characteristics: a large number of patients in a multicenter project; consistency across study subpopulations; an effect shown on multiple endpoints involving different events in a single study; and statistically persuasive findings (U.S. Department of Health and Human Services 1998).

Section 115(a) of FDAMA, in fact, codified observations discussed above, in amending Section 505(d) [21 U.S.C. 355(d)] as follows: "If the Secretary determines, based on relevant science, that data from one adequate and well-controlled clinical investigation and confirmatory evidence (obtained prior to or after such investigation) are sufficient to establish effectiveness, the Secretary may consider such data and evidence to constitute substantial evidence" (*Food and Drug Administration Modernization Act* 1997). These and other regulatory shifts, made in the context of the increasingly high scientific standards for research expected by government, industry, the medical profession, and consumers alike, form a part of the backdrop against which productivity investigators are attempting to further develop methodologies for the proper design and conduct of productivity research.

CURRENT PRODUCTIVITY MODELS AND THEIR SHORTCOMINGS

A major problem with the FDA's regulatory standards is that productivity research has not yet advanced to the point where the standards of evidence can always be met. For example, in the absence of any approach that can measure productivity across all jobs and diseases, the notion of "competent and reliable scientific evidence" may not be applicable. In this section we provide a brief overview of current approaches for measuring the impact of illness on productivity, highlighting new directions that could help fill in this gap.

The following equation encapsulates the key concepts involved in measuring productivity changes:

Cost of illness = $[(W + (X * Y)) * Z]$, where
W = number of work days missed over a given period (say a month or a year),
X = number of work-cutback days (or shortened workdays) during this period,
Y = 1 − percent average productivity on work-cutback days, and
Z = wage rate.

In other words, to measure the effect of an illness on productivity, researchers need to figure out how much time at work (and hence money) would have been saved if the person did not develop the illness.

Researchers typically use two types of measurement strategies to measure these variables: self-report instruments and archival-data assessment. (See chapter 4 in this volume for a discussion of self-report and chapter 2 for an overview of archival data.) Self-report methods may not always accurately capture W (work absences) or X (work-cutback days) because they may lead respondents to make a causal inference linking a health problem to missed work. Likewise, employer records regarding days or parts of days lost to sickness may not necessarily be accurate. For example, companies often do not track sporadic sick leave as carefully as long periods of work absence. In fact, in most instances, employees may be using sporadic sick-leave or "mental health" days to augment their vacation allotment.

In addition, neither the self-report nor archival-data methods may capture Y ($1 -$ percent average productivity on work-cutback days) and Z (wage rate) accurately. For example, workplace productivity sometimes operates according to a "winner-take-all" effect. Thus, even though one worker may be only slightly less productive on a given day, this drop-off can have potentially devastating effects. One worker's reduced productivity could cause a company to miss an important deadline, which might, in turn, mean failing to make a critical sale. Likewise, employees are not stand-alone entities: they affect one another. Thus, if one worker is unable to perform his usual tasks, the whole company's productivity may diminish significantly. These spillover effects also highlight the reason why the wage rate may not always be an accurate gauge of the cost of illness. The actual loss to the company may greatly exceed the wages lost by a given employee. (See chapter 9 for a more detailed discussion of this problem.)

At present, there appears to be a trade-off between the ability to measure productivity effects in a particular setting and the generalizability of the results. Studies evaluating a specific type of worker with a specific illness (say, asthma in customer-service representatives) may not carry over to other workers in other settings. Thus, research may not be able to meet the FDA standard of "component and reliable scientific evidence." This is particularly problematic when one considers the different potential ways to measure productivity in white-collar, pink-collar, and blue-collar workers. One way to address this problem might be to develop a gold standard for productivity measurement in which a self-report instrument could be validated using objective productivity data.

DEVELOPMENT OF A PRODUCTIVITY-MEASUREMENT GOLD STANDARD

Although researchers have developed self-report instruments and "validated" them without using external objective data, in the case of productivity measurement, it would be more desirable to assess whether a direct relationship exists between a self-report instrument and actual measures of worker performance. A tool that allows for such an assessment could be developed into a productivity-measurement gold standard.[2] This standard must draw on evidence of consistency between subjective and objective measures of workplace performance, which could eventually facilitate widespread use of a

---

2. This topic is also discussed in Greenberg et al. 2001.

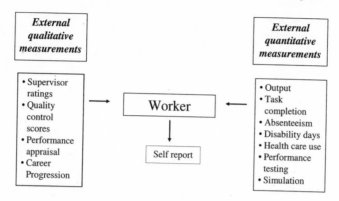

Figure 12.1. Inputs to a gold-standard self-report approach to productivity measurement

survey-based instrument as in quality-of-life research, even in situations where no objective measures of productivity can be accessed. In developing standardized instruments for measuring productivity, care must be taken to address the operational definition of productivity, the portability of definitions to different employer populations, and empirical verification of inter-population comparisons (see fig. 12.1).

A gold-standard self-report instrument would provide a basic productivity endpoint measurement tool to be incorporated into the appropriate design of clinical trials or field research. Ultimately, a productivity-measurement gold standard could provide stakeholders with a research tool that has some currency across occupational and organizational categories.

ADDITIONAL PRODUCTIVITY-RELATED REGULATORY ISSUES

At present, all stakeholders acknowledge the need for further development in several key elements of productivity-research design, methodology, and implementation. To support intended productivity claims of both clinical and economic benefit, researchers need to tackle the following problems:

- Determine the way in which claims may specifically reflect productivity;
- Define the interrelationship between clinical and economic information;
- Improve the ability to identify and use instruments for a particular project;
- Assess whether a given instrument has undergone the appropriate development and validation;
- Determine what study designs are appropriate in productivity research and what their relative strengths and weaknesses are;

- Determine what are the key methods for the analysis and interpretation of the data obtained from these efforts; and
- Decide how best to communicate the results either in publication or in product labeling and/or advertising.

CONCLUSION

Productivity measures have begun to appear in approved product labeling when evidence has been properly substantiated. Demand for productivity-related outcome information will no doubt continue to grow, so the FDA increasingly will review productivity-related promotional claims about pharmaceutical products and the evidence intended to support them. The FDA will have to determine which evidence standard applies to each intended claim, and then whether each claim is adequately supported; this will depend in part upon the promotional use(s) planned for the data in question. The more quickly the field of productivity research can advance, the better for all interested parties, including the FDA, drug manufacturers, health care professionals, consumers, and health-insurance providers. In the final analysis, investments both in furthering key elements of productivity-research methodology and in developing a gold-standard productivity measurement tool will be of great utility for all stakeholders.

ACKNOWLEDGMENT

We would like to thank Laurie Burke, RPh, MPH, at the Division of Drug Marketing, Advertising, and Communications, U.S. Food and Drug Administration, for her guidance and support in the preparation of this chapter.

REFERENCES

Federal Food, Drug, and Cosmetic Act. 1999. 21 U.S.C. 355(d).

Food and Drug Administration. 1998. *U.S. Food and Drug Administration Backgrounder.* http://www.fda.gov/opacom/backgrounders/modact.htm (cited 2002).

Food and Drug Administration Modernization Act of 1997. 1997. Public Law Number 105–115.

Greenberg, P. E., H. G. Birnbaum, R. C. Kessler, M. Morgan, and P. Stang. 2001. Impact of illness and its treatment on workplace costs: Regulatory and measurement issues. *Journal of Occupational and Environmental Medicine* 43:56–63.

U.S. Department of Health and Human Services. 1998. *Guidance for Industry: Providing clinical evidence of effectiveness for human drugs and biological products.* Rockville, MD: U.S. Food and Drug Administration.

CHAPTER 13

Investing in Health to Promote Human Capital in Developing Countries: The Importance of Productivity and Health to the World Bank

HARVEY WHITEFORD

INTRODUCTION

Policymakers often assume that improving the health status of people in developing countries simply requires sustained macroeconomic growth. According to this line of thinking, a higher gross national product (GNP) will automatically translate into improvements in the health of the population (although the rate at which this happens is subject to debate). However, considerable evidence challenges this widespread assumption. First, while macroeconomic growth does usually benefit both the poor and the better off (Dollar and Kraay 2001; Roemer and Gugerty 1997), it does not always lead to an equitable distribution of wealth and opportunity (U.N. Development Programme 1999). More important, successful macroeconomic policies are only part of the answer to promoting economic growth. Developing countries also need innovative policies that promote human development in order to achieve this growth (World Bank 1993). In other words, just as macroeconomic growth can improve the health of people in developing nations, public-health interventions can help spur economic growth. A recent study of 76 developing countries clearly demonstrated this interrelationship between economic growth and human development (Ranis, Stewart, and Ramirez 2000). Targeting human development, especially of people trapped

The opinions contained in this article are those of the author and do not necessarily represent the views of the World Bank, members of its Board of Executive Directors, or the countries they represent.

in poverty by poor health and education, can also help address inequities within societies (U.N. Development Programme 1999).

To clarify how investments in health can lead to economic growth in developing countries requires an explanation of the concept of human capital. Traditional capital theory arbitrarily divided productive factors (inputs) into three groups: natural resources, human labor, and man-made goods. The latter was called capital goods (or often just capital) and was defined as produced goods that could be used as inputs for further production. Over time, the other inputs, natural resources and human labor, began to be referred to as capital as well. In the early 1960s, economists such as Theodore Schultz and Gary Becker reintroduced Adam Smith's term *human capital* to refer to how educated and healthy workers productively utilized other capital inputs. Since that time there has been an explosion in the literature analyzing the contribution of human capital to economic growth.

It is increasingly recognized that impaired health and a lack of education and skills (poor human capital) are major restraints on economic growth in developing countries. More research has been done in the area of education than in that of health per se. Many research projects, such as one study of 98 countries (Barro 1991), have shown a strong association between school enrollment and economic growth rates. Furthermore, education and health are interrelated, with educated people more likely to be healthy and healthy children more likely to attend school (Psacharopoulos 1995). This link is evident even in established market economies such as the United States, where early-onset psychiatric disorders have been shown to result in higher rates of school dropout (Kessler et al. 1995). In developing countries, as in most established market economies, illness and disability are almost universally associated with increased poverty (World Bank 1993). The effect of ill health on social and occupational functioning is now a matter of serious policy debate (World Health Organization 1999).

Methods to evaluate the combination of various types of human functioning, including those attributable to health status and education, on individual productivity are being developed (Schultz 1995). In emerging market economies, nutritional status has been more commonly studied than illness or disability, although attention is now turning to health conditions. The abuse of drugs and alcohol has been shown to be an obstacle to the development of human capital (Cercone 1994). Controlling for factors such as tropical location, colonial history, and geographical isolation, Gallup and Sachs (2000) have shown that countries with intensive malaria had income levels in 1995 only one-third as high as countries without malaria (regardless of whether the countries were in Africa). However, to arrive at a comprehensive understanding of these relationships, we need to apply more sophisticated technologies to study the impact of common illness and disability on human development.

In contrast to the other chapters in this book, which focus on the link between health and productivity in industrialized nations, this chapter addresses the plight of developing nations. As numerous other chapter authors show, in countries such as the United States, judicious investments in health benefits make sense from both a microeconomic and a macroeconomic standpoint. Healthier workers can lead to both bigger profits for individual companies and greater economic and social well-being for the country as a whole. The situation in developing countries is different because so many people lack access to any health care at all. This chapter discusses how investments in health can dramatically improve the macroeconomic picture in developing nations.

The World Bank, which currently works in more than 100 developing countries, now sees better health care as a critical pathway to fulfilling its mission of eradicating global poverty. Since 1980, the percentage of lending for health, nutrition, education, and social protection has risen from 5% to 25% of the World Bank's total outlays—which amounted to about $17 billion in fiscal 2001. I begin by reviewing the considerable impact of illness on disability, work productivity, and social capital. I then discuss new intervention strategies for developing countries, highlighting the findings of the recent report compiled by the WHO Commission on Macroeconomics and Health. In my conclusion, I provide a brief overview of new directions in health investments in developing countries.

STATING THE PROBLEM: THE IMPACT OF ILLNESS ON DISABILITY, WORK PRODUCTIVITY, AND SOCIAL CAPITAL

Illness and Disability

Until recently, investment in health in developing countries has focused on conditions such as infectious diseases and infant mortality. However, as in industrialized nations, nonfatal, high-prevalence disorders that lead to chronic disability are typically more expensive to the health system than those with a fatal but short duration. The Global Burden of Disease study, with its more objective assessment of relative burden, the disability-adjusted life year (DALY), has helped "decouple epidemiology from advocacy" (Murray and Lopez 1996, 1). In conceptualizing nonfatal health outcomes, the DALY borrows from both disability and handicap as defined in the International Classification of Impairments, Disability, and Handicap (World Health Organization 1980) and combines years of life lost through premature mortality (YLL) and years lived with disability (YLD), weighted for the severity of the disability.

This research has demonstrated the previously underrecognized contribution of high-prevalence disabling conditions. Mental disorders are a case in point. In 2000, 12% of all DALYs lost and 31% of all disability were estimated to be due to neuropsychiatric conditions (World Health Organization, *World Health Report,* 2001). These disorders accounted for 47% of all disability in established market economies, such as the United States, and 18% in Africa. Four of the ten leading causes of disability worldwide are mental disorders: major depression, alcohol use, bipolar disorder, and schizophrenia. In 2000, depression was estimated to be second only to HIV/AIDS as a cause of DALYs lost in the world in the 15–44 age group and the leading cause of disability (YLD) for all ages (World Health Organization, *World Health Report,* 2001). Given the high prevalence of mental disorders, well documented in the Global Burden of Disease study and in specific epidemiological studies around the world (Andrews 2000), it would be surprising if they did not contribute to a substantial loss in human productivity and did not have large social as well as health costs.

Illness and Work Productivity

At the macroeconomic level, the effects of illness on lost productivity are substantial. The potential income loss from illness in eight developing countries has been calculated at 2.1% to 6.5% of yearly earnings, and the loss in the United States amounts to just under 2% (Psacharopoulos 1995). New research studies are quantifying the impact of illness on the national economies in the developing world. In Vietnam, for example, it is estimated that 1.1 billion workdays were lost to ill health in 1998 (Deolaliker 2000). The value of this lost work is equivalent to just over 7% of gross domestic product and approximately equal to the amount spent on health care in the country in that year.

The productivity loss associated with severe disability such as blindness or physical deformity is both visible and easy to quantify. However, even apparently less serious illness manifestations can have considerable economic consequences. A study in Ethiopia on the economic impact of non-ocular onchocerciasis (a nematode worm infection that affects the skin), which controlled for factors such as age, found that daily wage rates were 10% to 15% lower among those exhibiting the skin manifestations (Kim, Tandon, and Hailu 1997). A U.S. study of the workplace costs of allergic rhinitis showed that the annual national salary equivalent cost of work impairment due to high pollen and mold exposure among workers with allergic rhinitis was estimated to be between $5.4 billion and $7.7 billion (Kessler et al. 2001).

As would be expected, the burden of mental disorders shown in the Global Burden of Disease study has been complemented by impressive data, primarily from established market economies, on the impact of mental disorders in the workplace. Data from the U.S. National Comorbidity Survey has shown that work impairment is one of the major adverse consequences of psychiatric disorders, with approximately one billion lost days of productivity per year in the civilian workforce (Kessler and Frank 1997). Kessler and colleagues (1999) have shown that depressed workers had between 1.5 and 3.2 more short-term work disability days over a 30-day period than other workers, and these workplace costs were nearly as large as the direct costs of successful depression treatment. Depression has also been shown to have a greater length of disability and a higher incidence of disability relapse than comparable medical conditions (Conti and Burton 1994). This study showed that depression was the most common diagnosis encountered in the employee-assistance program studied. Berndt and colleagues (1998) have shown that for chronically depressed individuals, the level of perceived at-work performance is negatively related to the severity of the depressive illness and that a reduction in the severity of depression rapidly improves the patient's work performance.

When indirect costs such as workplace productivity are considered, the cost of more specialized interventions may be justified. The use of more expensive treatments, such as the new antidepressant medications called selective serotonin reuptake inhibitors (SSRIs), may be more cost-effective than the older antidepressant medication when their capacity to assist in reducing workplace absenteeism is taken into account (Claxton, Chawla, and Kennedy 1999). And, at least for established market economies, some evidence suggests that specialist mental health services can produce a greater net economic savings than services provided by primary health care providers (Zhang, Rost, and Fortney 1999).

Ill health, malnutrition, and disability can affect work productivity in at least three ways. First, illness can prevent participation in the workforce altogether (as evidenced by the data on disability enrollees collected by social security systems in numerous countries). Second, temporary absences, or work loss, arising from illness can be assessed where such records are held by employers and/or insurance companies. Perhaps even more important is the third impact, a reduction of work effort, or work cutback, which raises the effort price of labor (Chatterjee 1990). Work cutback tends to be a less visible form of lost productivity but is increasingly important for employers as countries strive for greater efficiency in the global marketplace. Studies by Berndt and colleagues (1997) have shown that productivity in the workplace is linked to the severity of particular disorders that affect both the amount of time spent at work and the performance while at work. Several studies have shown that the previously "hidden" disability of mental disorders causes more work cutback than work loss (Dewa and Lin 2000; Kessler and Frank 1997; Lim, Sanderson, and Andrews 2000).

Illness or disability can also reduce productivity by forcing workers to miss work to care for or support an ill family member. This cause of lost productivity is particularly common in developing countries where health and support services can be seriously deficient. The magnitude of such unpaid caring is enormous. The United Nations Development Programme estimated that US$16 trillion of unpaid caring work was missing from the 1995 global GDP of US$24 trillion (U.N. Development Programme 1995).

Illness and Social Capital

The papers in the first part of this book primarily describe measures for assessing the impact of illness and disability in remunerated (workplace) roles. The advances they outline are especially valuable for employers. However, governments and international development agencies such as the World Bank are, of course, also keenly interested in this perspective. The mounting evidence that investments in health and education result in greater productivity from more efficient workers has, as outlined above, resulted in greater investment in these areas. However, I believe this is only half the picture when we are trying to quantify the contribution of health to economic growth, particularly in developing countries. The contribution of better health to individuals and society goes beyond reduction in clinical symptoms and disability, greater workplace productivity, and the reduction of lost productivity of caregivers.

The ability of an individual to contribute productively in a nonremunerated social role can be as important as his or her ability to contribute in a remunerated role.[1] Fewer "days out of role" for individuals who do not have paid employment (that is, individuals in nonwage production) can both produce considerable social cost savings and promote economic development. Consider, for example, the household work traditionally carried out by women. In virtually all countries, women do the majority of unpaid work.

---

1. Remuneration is used here to mean identified payment for goods and services provided.

This gender differential is higher in developing as compared to developed countries, and there is some evidence that women in developing countries have poorer health than men (Chatterjee 1990). Thus, the extent of this type of lost productivity may be higher in these countries. According to a recent study covering four developing countries, common mental disorders (anxiety and depression) are associated with female gender, low education, and poverty (Patel et al. 1999). Noting that rapid economic change in these societies has been associated with rising income disparity and economic inequality, these authors advocate investments in health and education as a way to address these issues. Ignoring nonremunerated roles leads many policymakers to underestimate the social and economic impact of ill health and disability.

Further, more research is needed to measure the impact of improved health status not only on the wage and nonwage production of individuals but also on their social networks and society as a whole. The emphasis on improving human capital has been recently complemented by an emphasis on the economic benefits of cohesive social functioning. In fact, some scholars point to social capital as the "missing link" in economic development (Grootaert 1997). Since cohesive groups of individuals are considered to be more than just the sum of their human capital, social capital adds a critical element to sustainable development (Collier 1998; Knack and Keefer 1997). Economists are interested in social capital because it provides insight into community productivity and trade, especially the lowering of transaction costs. Communities that possess more social capital tend to have higher productivity as improvements in coordination and cooperation reduce the cost of doing business (Knack and Keefer 1997).

An extensive literature documents the health and social factors that determine health status both at an individual and at a population level. The socioeconomic determinants of health have been well studied, and there is good evidence that more socially isolated individuals have poorer health (House, Landis, and Umberson 1988) and that more socially cohesive societies are healthier and have lower mortality rates (Kawachi, Kennedy, and Glass 1999). For example, in his survey of how social-capital networks in Russia contribute to basic welfare such as income security, health, and food consumption, Rose (1999) concluded that measures of social integration explained almost 10% of the variance in "emotional health." The mechanisms by which social capital improves health are not entirely clear. It seems that social networks promote both better health education and better access to health services, which, in turn, lead to improved public health practices (regarding, for example, smoking, sanitation, and sexual behavior) (Baum

1999; Kawachi, Kennedy, and Glass 1999). The research examining how levels of social capital affect health status has suggested numerous ways to intervene at a population level to improve the health of individuals.

Much less work has been done on the reverse relationship—on improving mental and physical health to promote the development of social capital stocks. There are technical difficulties in measurement, given that social capital is inherent in the structure of social relationships (Henderson and Whiteford 2003). Some serious health problems clearly result in dramatic social decline due to impairments in physical, psychological, and social functioning. However, common mental disorders also have less dramatic effects on socialization and social productivity. In various studies, Kessler and his colleagues have demonstrated that mental disorders typically have several adverse consequences (not only for those who suffer from them, but also for their families and communities), including a breakdown in marital stability (Kessler, Walters, and Forthofer 1998), increased teenage parenthood (Kessler et al. 1997), and more distant social relationships (Mickelson, Kessler, and Shaver 1997). Research needs to be conducted to identify the precise contribution of high-burden illnesses, such as mental disorders, to deteriorated social capital. Combining such data with traditional productivity-loss data could produce better estimates of the economic impact of ill health.

Given that poor mental health depletes social capital, efforts to improve physical and mental health should have a considerable payoff. Specifically, individual and population-wide interventions that improve an individual's psychological functioning should be expected to help the individual engage in more constructive social interaction and assume a more productive social role. In the mental health sector, this transition has been referred to by a number of terms such as *social reintegration*. Studies carried out by the World Bank provide evidence that individual improvement also creates social capital. Research carried out in Rwanda and Cambodia demonstrated that improvements in interpersonal communication, trust, and resilience among individuals contributed to the rebuilding of social capital in the postconflict periods in both countries (Colletta and Cullen 2000).

WHAT IS NEEDED TO IMPLEMENT NEW INVESTMENTS IN HEALTH IN DEVELOPING COUNTRIES

Unfortunately, the knowledge that certain prevalent disorders are disabling, cause major losses in both lost work and nonwork productivity, and erode social capital does not automatically translate into more resources to target them. Even in established market economies, resources are not necessarily allocated rationally. Investments in health typically occur in response to the political pressure of advocacy groups, rather than from an understanding of their usefulness or expected effectiveness. Mental disorders are a case in point. Historically, governments and international agencies such as the World Bank have been cautious about investing in projects to reduce psychiatric disabilities despite their acknowledged burden. The list of essential health services proposed by authors from the Bank, following the release of the 1993 World Development Report, did not include any mental health interventions (Bobadilla et al. 1994), and country-level projects by the Bank often exclude mental health interventions (Jha, Ranson, and Bobadilla 1996). As Williams (1999) and others have argued, what is needed is evidence of the cost and magnitude of gains in health attributable to clinical interventions or preventive approaches.

Most health-economic research consists of cost-effectiveness studies, which compare one clinical intervention or mode of service delivery with another for the disorder being studied. While such data are useful, they provide limited information on the cost and health gain of interventions between different disorders. For example, very little work has been done comparing cost and outcome in a common dimension such as Quality Adjusted Life Years (QALYs) or Disability Adjusted Life Years (DALYs) for interventions across common health conditions. What is needed at this level is quantification of the health gain (e.g., in DALYs averted) for interventions that address conditions such as mental disorders, diabetes, cancer, and coronary heart disease. The methodology for this has been described (Cowley and Wyatt 1993), and the cost of treating serious mental disorders in developing countries is not dissimilar to the cost of treating other medical conditions (Suleiman et al. 1997). Once we have this quantification of health gain between different conditions, we will better understand where the best "buys" are— at least for clinical interventions.

In general, stakeholders such as businesses and governments also need evidence on how treatment of these disorders can lead to increased productivity at both the individual and the social level. Adding this lost productivity to the information contained in the DALY construct further enhances the information base for priority-setting with respect to clinical and health-service interventions. To assist here, a rank ordering of conditions with the biggest impacts on productivity would be particularly useful in deciding which conditions to invest in first. Lost productivity would be best disaggregated to identify inability to participate in the workforce, temporary absences from work, and reduction in productivity while at work (decrease per unit of work effort). This would allow programs to be targeted and the importance of their outcomes to be more readily seen by those with the financial responsibility for the impact of the disorders (e.g., employers, social security, etc.). Further, the identification of the reasons for the lost productivity in the workplace in terms of the impact of the illness or disability on areas such as cognitive or motor skills would provide information that would assist in a better skills / work role match for those with more chronic impairments.

As noted in part 1 of this book, researchers have developed several methods for collecting information to assess the magnitude of the impact of ill health on worker productivity in industrialized nations, notably employer records of work attendance (see chapter 2), employee self report (see chapter 4), and the Experience Sampling Method (ESM), which employs repeated assessments over time rather than a single assessment at a predetermined time (see chapter 5). Although using archival data is typically not an option in developing countries, because employers rarely maintain reliable records on employee health status and its relation to work performance, there is no reason why ESM and self-report could not be used. However, research based on these methods should assess the impact of illness and disability in both remunerated (workplace) roles and unremunerated (social or domestic) roles.

A further extension would be to examine the loss of vocational potential. Early-onset illnesses can have long-term effects on education and vocational achievement. Even in the research to date conducted in industrialized nations, the focus is typically on the productivity impact of illnesses that develop once a person is in the workplace, or on the impact, assessed cross-sectionally, on productivity of people in the workplace. Such assessment does not take into account any persistent diminution of vocational ability arising from childhood illness, for example. Early identification of (and interventions to treat) target psychiatric symptoms associated with this social and vocational decline is now possible (Hafner et al. 1999). The recent research on educational failure or early pregnancy as a result of mental illness (Kessler et al. 1997; Kessler, Walters, and Forthofer 1998) highlights the mismatch between pre-illness vocational potential and resultant employment. The individual and social cost of this unrealized potential is likely to be very significant for people in poor countries. Furthermore, as outlined earlier, we also need to better understand the ways in which improvement in physical and mental health status contributes to increasing the individual psychological attributes that enhance social and community participation. Economic modeling could then identify how this affects the productivity of social groups through improved social capital.

Finally, international agencies such as the World Bank and the World

Health Organization are particularly interested in health systems and macroeconomic outcomes. The WHO Commission on Macroeconomics and Health, launched in January 2000 (www.who.int/inf-pr-2000/en/pr2000-02 .html), has taken up the task of providing aggregate data for whole populations. In its report released in December of 2001, "Macroeconomics and Health: Investing in Health for Economic Development" (World Health Organization 2001), this commission has supplied the empirical data to back up the contention that better health is a necessary engine for economic growth in developing countries.

According to the report, allocating an additional $66 billion per year to health care for developing countries by 2015–20 would lead to a six-fold increase in economic benefits (about $360 billion) as people in poor countries would live longer and be more productive. Another way of looking at these figures is that an investment of $30 to $40 per person in developing countries (instead of the current level of $13) could prevent 8 million deaths or 330 million DALYs. By addressing communicable diseases such as HIV/AIDS and malaria and micronutrient deficiencies, the WHO commission hopes to reduce the incidence of premature death in developing countries. For example, life expectancy among the nearly 650 million people who live in sub-Saharan Africa is just 51, as opposed to 78 among the 900 million people in the most advanced industrial nations.

Even though the report does not specifically advocate investments in noncommunicable diseases such as mental illness and diabetes, it acknowledges the importance of addressing these health problems as well. The report makes a powerful case for greater health investments, but it is unclear whether donor nations will be willing to provide the additional $22 billion per year by 2007 and $31 billion per year by 2015 as is recommended. However, poverty is a key factor behind widespread discontent, creating an environment that can be exploited by radicals and organized crime. Perhaps in the wake of the tragic events of September 11, 2001, industrialized nations have become more sensitized to the need to eradicate poverty around the world.

Of course, beyond the economic argument for improving the health status of individuals in poor countries is the moral argument. Ultimately, economic growth and social development aim to improve human welfare. Good health is a fundamental component of human welfare, and the World Health Organization considers health a basic human right. Despite the reality of scarce resources and the vast unmet needs for health care in all countries, no priority-setting or resource allocation can be complete without considering the dimension of equity and human rights.

CONCLUSION

Including people with illness and disability in development strategies has historically been driven by equity and human rights concerns. Over the past 20 years, the acknowledgment that investments in health promote human development has resulted in increased attention and resources from governments and aid agencies. It is now accepted that better health contributes to the productive capacity of the economy by increasing the total supply of potential labor-hours and increased productivity in the form of output per employee. The World Bank has substantially increased its human-development lending and is now the single biggest source of external funding for health in developing countries.

The task of providing basic education and health for all those in the world who need it seems overwhelming. However, the cost of achieving this for the poor in both developed and developing countries is not insurmountable. The United Nations Development Report (U.N. Development Programme 1999) estimates that to provide water and sanitation to the one-third of the world's population (2 billion people) who have none would cost US$9 billion. To put this figure in perspective, Europeans spent US$11 billion on ice cream in 1998. To provide basic education to the 2 billion people in the world who do not receive it would cost US$6 billion. Americans spent US$8 billion on cosmetics in 1998. Likewise, to provide essential health care services in developing nations costs only about US$30 per person per year—which is quite modest, considering that industrialized nations typically spend about $2,000 per person per year (World Health Organization, Macroeconomics, 2001).

For agencies such as the World Bank, promoting economic growth and reducing poverty require a coordinated and balanced approach to the development of all forms of physical, natural, human, and social capital. Armed with more data (along the lines of the recent report by the WHO Commission on Macroeconomics and Health) demonstrating the likely productivity gains and improvements in social functioning from health investments, policymakers can begin to design and implement new programs that will vastly improve the welfare of people in developing nations.

REFERENCES

Andrews, G. 2000. Meeting the unmet need with disease management. In *Unmet need in psychiatry: Problems, resources, and responses,* ed. S. Henderson. Cambridge: Cambridge University Press.

Barro, R. J. 1991. Economic growth in a cross-section of countries. *Quarterly Journal of Economics* 106:407–43.

Baum, F. 1999. Social capital: Is it good for your health? Issues for a public health agenda. *Journal of Epidemiology and Community Health* 53:195–96.

Berndt, E. R., S. N. Finkelstein, P. E. Greenberg, R. H. Howland, A. Keith, A. J. Rush, J. Russell, and M. B. Keller. 1998. Workplace performance effects from chronic depression and its treatment. *Journal of Health Economics* 17:511–35.

Berndt, E. R., S. N. Finkelstein, P. E. Greenberg, A. Keith, and H. Bailit. 1997. Illness and productivity: Objective workplace evidence. Working Paper 42–97, MIT Program on the Pharmaceutical Industry, Cambridge, MA.

Bobadilla, J. L., P. Cowley, P. Musgrove, and H. Saxenian. 1994. Design, content, and financing of an essential package of health services. In *Global comparative assessments in the health sector: Disease burden, expenditures, and intervention packages,* ed. A. D. Lopez. Geneva: World Health Organization.

Cercone, J. 1994. Alcohol related problems as an obstacle to the development of human capital. Technical Paper no. 219, World Bank, Washington, DC.

Chatterjee, M. 1990. Indian women, health, and productivity. Policy, Research, and External Affairs Working Paper no. 442, World Bank, Washington, DC.

Claxton, A. J., A. J. Chawla, and S. Kennedy. 1999. Absenteeism among employees treated for depression. *Journal of Occupational and Environmental Medicine* 41: 605–11.

Colletta, M. L., and N. J. Cullen. 2000. *Violent conflict and the transformation of social capital: Lessons from Cambodia, Rwanda, Guatemala, and Somalia.* Washington, DC: World Bank.

Collier, P. 1998. Social capital and poverty. Social Capital Initiative Working Paper no. 4, World Bank, Washington, DC.

Conti, D. J., and W. N. Burton. 1994. The economic impact of depression in a workplace. *Journal of Occupational Medicine* 36:983–88.

Cowley, P., and R. J. Wyatt. 1993. Schizophrenia and manic depressive psychosis. In *Disease control priority in developing countries,* ed. J. L. Bobadilla. New York: Oxford University Press.

Deolaliker, A. 2000. Improving the health of Vietnam's poor: Analysis and recommendations from a health sector review. Paper presented at the Health, Nutrition, Population, and Poverty Seminar, World Bank, Washington, DC, February 1.

Dewa, C. S., and E. Lin. 2000. Chronic physical illness, psychiatric disorder, and disability in the workplace. *Social Science and Medicine* 51:41–50.

Dollar, D., and A. Kraay. 2001. Growth is good for the poor. Macroeconomics and Growth Working Paper no. 2587, World Bank, Washington, DC.

Gallup, J. L., and J. D. Sachs. 2000. The economic burden of malaria. Center for International Development Working Paper no. 52, Harvard University, Cambridge, MA.

Grootaert, C. 1997. Social capital: The missing link? Social Capital Initiative Working

Paper no. 3. World Bank, Washington, DC, http://www1.worldbank.org/prem/
poverty/scapital/wkrppr/sciwp3.pdf.

Hafner, H., W. Loffler, K. Maurer, M. Hambrecht, and W. van der Heiden. 1999. Depression, negative symptoms, social stagnation, and social decline in the early
course of schizophrenia. *Acta Psychiatrica Scandinavica* 100:105–18.

Henderson, S., and H. A. Whiteford. 2003. Social capital and mental health. *Lancet*
362:505–6.

House, J. S., K. R. Landis, and D. Umberson. 1988. Social relationships and health.
Science 241:540–45.

Jha, P., K. Ranson, and J. L. Bobadilla. 1996. Measuring the burden of disease and the
cost-effectiveness of health interventions. Technical Paper no. 333, World Bank,
Washington, DC.

Kawachi, I., B. P. Kennedy, and R. Glass. 1999. Social capital and self-rated health:
A contextual analysis. *American Journal of Public Health* 89:1187–93.

Kessler, R. C., D. M. Almeida, P. Berglund, and P. Stang. 2001. Pollen and mold exposure impairs the work performance of employees with allergic rhinitis. *Annals
of Allergy, Asthma, and Immunology* 87:289–95.

Kessler, R. C., C. B. Barber, H. G. Birnbaum, R. G. Frank, P. E. Greenberg, R. M. Rose,
G. E. Simon, and P. Wang. 1999. Depression in the workplace: Effects on short-
term disability. *Health Affairs* 18:163–71.

Kessler, R. C., P. A. Berglund, C. L. Foster, W. B. Saunders, P. E. Stang, and E. E. Walters. 1997. Social consequences of psychiatric disorders. II. Teenage parenthood. *American Journal of Psychiatry* 154:1405–11.

Kessler, R. C., C. L. Foster, W. B. Saunders, and P. E. Stang. 1995. Social consequences
of psychiatric disorders. I. Educational attainment. *American Journal of Psychiatry* 152:1026–32.

Kessler, R. C., and R. G. Frank. 1997. The impact of psychiatric disorders on work loss
days. *Psychological Medicine* 27:861–73.

Kessler, R. C., E. E. Walters, and M. S. Forthofer. 1998. The social consequences of
psychiatric disorders. III. Probability of marital stability. *American Journal
of Psychiatry* 155:1092–96.

Kim, A., A. Tandon, and A. Hailu. 1997. Health and labor productivity: The economic
impact of onchocercal skin disease. Policy Research Working Paper, World
Bank, Washington, DC.

Knack, S., and P. Keefer. 1997. Does social capital have an economic payoff? A cross-
country investigation. *Quarterly Journal of Economics* 112:251–88.

Lim, D., K. Sanderson, and G. Andrews. 2000. Lost productivity among full time
workers with mental disorders. *Journal of Mental Health Policy and Economics* 3:
139–46.

Mickelson, K. D., R. C. Kessler, and P. R. Shaver. 1997. Adult attachment in a nationally representative sample. *Journal of Personality and Social Psychology* 73:
1092–106.

Murray, C. J. L., and A. D. Lopez, eds. 1996. *The global burden of disease: A comprehen-*

sive assessment of mortality and disability from diseases, injuries, and risk factors in 1990 and projected to 2020. Cambridge, MA: Harvard University Press.

Patel, V., R. Araya, M. de Lima, A. Ludermir, and C. Todd. 1999. Women, poverty, and common mental disorders in four restructuring societies. *Social Science and Medicine* 49:1461–71.

Psacharopoulos, G. 1995. *Directions in development: Building human capital for better lives.* Washington, DC: World Bank.

Ranis, G., F. Stewart, and A. Ramirez. 2000. Economic growth and human development. *World Development* 28:197–219.

Roemer, M., and M. K. Gugerty. 1997. Does economic growth reduce poverty? CAER II Technical Paper no. 4, Harvard Institute for International Development, Cambridge, MA.

Rose, R. 1999. What does social capital add to individual welfare? An empirical analysis of Russia. Paper presented at the Social Capital and Poverty Reduction Conference, Washington, DC, June 22–24. http://www1.worldbank.org/prem/poverty/scapital/wkrppr/sciwp23.pdf.

Schultz, T. P. 1995. Evaluation of integrated human resource programs. Human Resources Development and Operations Policy Working Paper, World Bank, Washington, DC.

Suleiman, T. G., J. U. Ohaeri, R. A. Lawal, A. Y. Haruna, and O. B. Orija. 1997. Financial cost of treating out-patients with schizophrenia in Nigeria. *British Journal of Psychiatry* 171:364–68.

United Nations Development Programme. 1995. *Human development report.* New York: Oxford University Press.

———. 1999. *Human development report.* New York: Oxford University Press.

Williams, A. 1999. Calculating the global burden of disease: Time for a strategic reappraisal? *Health Economics* 8:1–8.

World Bank. 1993. *World development report 1993: Investing in health.* New York: Oxford University Press.

World Health Organization. 1980. *International classification of impairments, disability, and handicap.* Geneva: World Health Organization.

———. 1999. *The world health report.* Geneva: World Health Organization.

———. 2001. Macroeconomics and health: Investing in health for economic development. Report of the Commission on Macroeconomics and Health. Geneva: World Health Organization.

———. 2001. *The world health report.* Geneva: World Health Organization.

Zhang, M., K. M. Rost, and J. C. Fortney. 1999. Earnings changes for depressed individuals treated by mental health specialists. *American Journal of Psychiatry* 156:108–14.

PART THREE

Conclusion

CHAPTER 14

Future Directions in Health and Work Productivity Research

RONALD C. KESSLER AND PAUL E. STANG

As noted in chapter 1, cost-of-illness research suggests that the workplace costs of some illnesses substantially exceed the costs of their effective treatment. This means that expansion of employer-sponsored health care programs can, in some cases, be conceptualized as an investment opportunity for employers. Similarly, reallocation of existing employer health care investments to focus more on conditions that have indirect workplace costs that can be cost-effectively treated would represent a portfolio reallocation with a positive return. Finally, thoughtful targeting of reductions in employer-sponsored health care benefits to avoid reducing coverage for conditions where treatment has a positive ROI from the employer perspective would be a way to minimize the workplace costs of reducing health care benefits.

We also noted in chapter 1, though, that only a small minority of employers have been persuaded by this research. Indeed, the double-digit annual inflation of employer-sponsored health care in the United States over the past few years has had the effect of making most employers worry much more about how to hold down rising health care costs than about how to expand health care programs. As a result, enthusiasm for the notion of employer-sponsored health care as an investment opportunity is currently confined largely to providers (e.g., pharmaceutical companies, health plans, health care management consultants) and, indeed, is seen by many purchasers as nothing more than a marketing plot on the part of providers. The idea that targeted reductions in health care investments can be another way of investing wisely has been largely lost on employers.

A number of industry-sponsored organizations, such as the Institute for Health and Productivity Management (www.ihpm.org), the Integrated Benefits Institute (www.ibiweb.org), the National Business Coalition on Health (www.nbch.org), and the National Business Group on Health (www .wbgh.org) are working to change this state of affairs, but it's an uphill battle. Yet it is difficult to deny that employer health care investment decisions are consequential for the workplace. There is no doubt, for example, that sedating antihistamines cause cognitive and motor dulling that creates an increased risk of workplace accidents (Kay and Quig 2001). Therefore, any employer who restricts access to nonsedating antihistamines on the drug formulary available to employees increases the risk of workplace accidents. Whether this risk is so high and the likely cost of an accident is so great as to justify the added cost of adding nonsedating antihistamines to the formulary is a separate empirical question, but the decision about the role of sedating versus nonsedating antihistamines in promoting accidents is incontrovertible.

Health-and-productivity research has the potential to provide information that can help rationalize employer health care spending decisions. This is true, importantly, whether these decisions involve making new investments or cutting benefits. In order to be rational in health care decision-making, one needs information about the implications of these decisions, not only for direct health care costs, but also, and perhaps more importantly, for indirect workplace costs. It is impossible to gain this understanding without being able to measure the indirect workplace costs of illness. The absence of such measures impedes employer investments in health care (Hargraves and Trude 2002).

Employers are beginning to cooperate in the development of aggregate measures of this sort, but not yet in developing individual-level measures. With regard to aggregate measures, the NBGH Council on Employee Health and Productivity (CEHP) in collaboration with IBI, has launched the EMPAQ™ (Employer Measures of Productivity, Absence and Quality) initiative to develop standardized definitions, metrics, and benchmark aggregate databases on company-level workers' compensation, short-term disability, long-term disability, and family medical leave (www.empaq.org). The EMPAQ benchmark data promise to be of great value to employers in comparing aggregate health and productivity experiences with peer organizations. However, as the EMPAQ data are all collected in the aggregate, they cannot be used directly to target or evaluate fine-grained modifications in benefit designs or other employer interventions relevant to the health of workers. Individual-level data are needed to guide the latter kinds of efforts. The aim of this volume is to consider the options for obtaining such measures. Greenberg and Birnbaum (in chapter 2) and Howland, Mangione, and Laramie (in chapter 3) make it very clear that objective individual-level measures of work performance can be obtained for some workers in some situations either by focusing on special work units whose performance is easily measured or by creating simulations that allow us to measure subtle aspects of work performance that are usually difficult to assess. Yet, the information about health and productivity obtained using these methods has not been persuasive to employers. Why can't we simply focus on studies that evaluate the effects of health problems and health care solutions on workers in a small number of sentinel occupations who are employed by a small number of prototypical companies and extrapolate from these cases to all workers in all occupations in all companies?

The answer is easily obtained by talking with employers, who reply uniformly that they are unwilling to believe that the general case holds in their particular situation. This is not merely their stance on health care, but on quality assurance in general. Employers routinely monitor the quality of the raw materials they purchase and periodically reject certain batches of material because of quality flaws. They monitor the quality of outputs and periodically reject certain units because of quality flaws. If we want to engage employers in a serious conversation about employee health benefits as investments, then we have to accept that employers will approach their health care purchasing decisions in the same way. The reason employer-purchasers have generally not been as rigorous as this in evaluating health care purchasing decisions in the past is that health care has been seen as a benefit to be controlled rather than as an investment to be managed. As soon as we ask employers to start thinking of health care as an investment opportunity, though, the same standards of quality assurance that are used to evaluate other corporate investments will begin to be applied.

What should these quality assurance standards be? Up to now, the health care industry has attempted to focus purchasers on process quality-assurance standards rather than on outcome standards; that is, on things that are done by the provider organization (e.g., number of flu shots, procedures followed in managing hypertension) rather than on the results of these processes (e.g., mortality, role functioning, quality-of-life outcomes). This marketing strategy can clearly be seen by reviewing the quality-monitoring guidelines of health care accrediting bodies such as the National Committee on Quality Assurance (www.ncqa.org) and the Joint Commission on the Accreditation of Healthcare Organizations (www.jcaho.org) or the standards developed by the Society of Quality Assurance (Pomerleau and Benson 1994), all of which include a great variety of process standards and very few outcome standards. The reason is clear: providers have control over their processes, but they do not have control over the outcomes, because patients differ both in uncontrollable risk factors (e.g., genetic predisposition) and in adherence to required medical regimens (e.g., taking their medications, abstaining from contra-indicated behaviors). As a result, health care providers focus on the rationalization of processes and want to be held responsible for these processes rather than for outcomes.

Purchasers, in comparison, want the opposite. They want results. They generally do not care about the details of the process so long as the process leads to a cure. This is no less true for employer-purchasers than for individual patients. Up to now, because health care is considered a benefit to be managed rather than an investment to be optimized, employer-purchasers have largely been content to accept the process quality-assurance standards provided by the health care industry. In order for health care to be considered seriously as an investment opportunity, a shift will be required in which outcome quality-assurance standards are developed. This is where the assessment of health and work productivity comes into the picture, since the outcomes of most interest to employers have to do with performance at work, sickness absence, and work disability.

As demands for outcome quality assurance increase, health care providers will almost certainly protest that they do not have control over outcomes. However, this argument is much less true in the aggregate than in individual cases. It certainly is true that an individual patient can die despite the best efforts of the health care system. As shown clearly in the New York coronary artery bypass graft evaluation, though, it is nonetheless possible to make meaningful comparisons of mortality rates among patients with the same condition who are treated using the same treatment method across individual providers and health care systems (Chassin 2002). Accurate comparisons of this sort require thoughtful consideration, measurement, and case-mix adjustment for differences in the risk profiles of the patients seen by the providers and the systems being compared, but these things can be done using currently available statistical methods (Zaslavsky and Buntin 2002).

The same kind of valid aggregate comparisons can be made for the workplace consequences of health and health care if accurate measures are available. With appropriate adjustment for differences in demographics, occupations, and industries, valid conclusions can be drawn about the effects of various treated and untreated illnesses on work performance, sickness absence, and disability. Once these effects are transformed into monetary terms, before-after comparisons can be used to evaluate the cost-effectiveness of new health care interventions from the perspective of the employer. When these comparisons are made in a test-market framework, valid conclusions can be drawn about the return on investment (ROI) of the intervention. The comparisons can be made either across markets, among companies in a single market, or among health plans in a market. Ongoing monitoring of trends in rates of treatment and workplace outcomes, furthermore, can be used to provide outcome quality assurance comparable to the quality-assurance data employers require in order to monitor their other investments. Outcome evaluations of this sort should be seen as a legitimate requirement of rationalizing employer health care purchasing decisions.

THE KEY QUESTIONS FOR RATIONALIZING HEALTH CARE INVESTMENTS

Employers need to answer five key questions in order to make rational health care purchasing decisions:

- What are the most commonly occurring health problems in my company?
- What are the effects of these health problems on work performance, sickness absence, industrial accidents, and disability?
- What is the monetary value of these workplace effects on the company's bottom line?
- How effective are available interventions in reducing these effects in my company?
- What is the ROI of these proposed interventions?

Most employers lack answers to any of these questions. It is little wonder, then, that so little rationality exists in the employer-sponsored health care arena.

The companies that are leading in this regard are those with a large proportion of employees who carry out production work that can be easily measured. Some companies of this sort have very detailed information on quantity and quality of production that they combine with employee health survey data and medical claim data in order to pinpoint commonly occurring health problems that interfere with the speed and accuracy of productivity. They have been able to evaluate the cost-effectiveness of interventions that treat these health problems. And they have been able to use ongoing quality-control monitoring to make sure these health care interventions continue to be effective over time.

This same level of rationality in the organization and delivery of health care can be achieved by most companies even when they lack detailed individual-level assessments of worker performance, if they are able to find proxy measures that can be tracked over time. There are a number of ways to collect this kind of productivity-tracking data (e.g., 360 peer evaluations, annual performance reviews with supervisors, etc.), but the papers in part 2 of this volume make it clear that the approach that is the easiest to generalize is to carry out annual employee health surveys that use self-report measures of work productivity. Such surveys can also collect self-report data from employees about their health problems and rates of treatment for these problems. In cases where archival data, such as medical claim data or performance-review data, are available and can be linked to the employee surveys, all the better.

Once these surveys are carried out the first time, they can provide answers to the first three questions posed above: How many of my workers have health problems of various sorts? What are the effects of these problems on work performance? What are the costs to me of these health problems in terms of reduced worker performance, increased sickness absence, increased disability, and increased workplace accidents? If an intervention is put into place to improve the treatment of one or more conditions, changes in the tracking results obtained from annual replications of the surveys can be used to answer the last two questions: How effective is the intervention in reducing the bad outcomes that are costly to my company? What is the ROI of the intervention? The logic of these evaluations is identical to the logic of the test-market studies and market-tracking studies that are routinely carried out to track other investments by market research departments in most major corporations.

THE WHO HEALTH AND WORK PERFORMANCE QUESTIONNAIRE (HPQ)

As part of the work carried out to support the World Health Organization (WHO) Global Burden of Disease initiative, a short self-report questionnaire was created that includes a checklist of health problems, questions about treatment, and questions about workplace functioning (absenteeism, performance while on the job, and workplace accidents). This instrument, known as the WHO Health and Work Performance Questionnaire (HPQ), has been validated (Kessler et al. 2003) and is now being used by a number of large corporations to carry out the type of research described in the previous section of this chapter. It is instructive to consider the range of current HPQ initiatives to illustrate the various ways linked individual-level data on health and productivity can be used to guide employer health care purchasing decisions. Three main HPQ initiatives are highlighted here. These three involve HPQ survey data pooling, evaluation of interventions, and quality assurance.

Data Pooling

The first initiative is a series of large HPQ surveys that are being combined into a master data file to provide benchmark health-and-productivity comparisons for employers. Three sets of these surveys exist. The first set includes nationally representative general-population cost-of-illness surveys carried out by the WHO in 28 countries around the world, with a combined sample size of more than 200,000 respondents (Kessler and Üstün 2000). These surveys were administered face-to-face in the homes of respondents. The second set includes annual HPQ surveys being carried out in a number of large national corporations in the United States in order to track employee health and productivity. These surveys are being administered either as stand-alone annual employee Health-at-Work surveys, often using an inexpensive Web-based technology, or as part of larger annual employee Health Risk Appraisal surveys. The third set includes market-level annual HPQ tracking surveys being carried out by several regional business groups affiliated with the National Business Coalition on Health. These surveys use the same administration procedures as the national surveys, but they include respondents from a number of different companies in a single market rather than all the employees of a single company throughout the country.

The data from all these surveys are being combined in a master database under the auspices of a National HPQ Data Pooling Consortium in order to promote comparative analysis of HPQ survey data and to address the first three of the five questions posed in the previous section of the chapter. The first question (What are the most commonly occurring health problems in my company?) is addressed by examining variation in prevalence estimates across occupations and industries. The second question (What are the effects of these health problems on work performance, sickness absence, industrial accidents, and disability?) is addressed by carrying out multivariate analyses that estimate the effects of specific health problems and their comorbidities on the workplace productivity measures included in the HPQ (Kessler et al. 2001). The third question (What is the monetary value of these workplace effects on the company's bottom line?) is addressed by applying methods of the sort described in chapters 6 and 9 to the HPQ survey data in collaboration with a number of participating corporations.

In addition to providing answers, these HPQ data analyses are raising important new secondary questions. For example, an employer in the manufacturing sector who discovers that low back pain is a very common and costly health problem in his company will have an obvious question about whether this is typical of companies in the same sector of the economy. Comparative analysis in the master database can help answer this question and others involving cases where HPQ results are out of line with national norms either because of higher-than-average prevalence rates, lower-than-average treatment rates, or higher-than-average effects on work productivity.

In the case of higher-than-average prevalence rates, the employer will presumably want to know whether the company is doing something to increase risk of this health problem. Although the HPQ survey cannot answer this question directly, it can provide a good starting point for a more in-depth exploration by allowing the employer to see whether the source of the problem can be pinpointed. For example, HPQ data can be used to investigate whether the high prevalence is confined to certain divisions of the company, to employees who work at particular jobs, or to subsets of employees or settings that might give clues as to etiology. It is also possible to link HPQ data to employee records to investigate other correlates (e.g., whether the problem exists among employees of short tenure or only emerges after a number of years of employment). A subset of the companies participating in the National HPQ Data Pooling Consortium have developed coordinated linked administrative data files to allow these more in-depth analyses to be carried out. HPQ survey data are being merged here with health care claims and pharmacy data along with company data on disability and accidents and, where available, objective performance data of the sort discussed by Greenberg and Birnbaum in chapter 2 and Beck in chapter 10.

In the case where comparative analysis shows that a company has lower-than-average treatment rates for illnesses that are found to be associated with substantial lost productivity, it is important to determine whether untreated workers have significantly higher levels of work impairment than workers without the condition before becoming concerned about the low rate of treatment. Selection into treatment on the basis of impairment might be strong enough for some conditions of this sort that untreated workers would have no meaningful decrement in work productivity. Indeed, a low treatment rate in such cases might be desirable, at least from a short-term perspective. If substantial decrements in productivity are found to exist among untreated workers, though, then the employer will want to consider the cost-effectiveness of increasing the proportion of ill workers who receive treatment. The HPQ can provide no direct guidance about ways in which this care should be provided. However, analysis of HPQ survey data can sometimes offer useful hints in the same way it can regarding the reasons for high prevalence—by determining whether the low treatment rate is confined to certain divisions of the company, to employees with one particular health plan in companies that offer choice among health plans, or to other individual or organizational characteristics that might give clues about barriers to care.

In the case of higher-than-average productivity loss among workers with a particular condition, after differential treatment is taken into consideration, the employer has to consider the possibility that the quality of care provided by his health plan is at least partly responsible. It is important to recognize that thoughtful statistical case-mix adjustment is required before coming to this tentative conclusion, because the appearance of lower treatment adequacy can be created spuriously if treated workers in one setting are more seriously ill than those in another setting. In addition, even if they are not more ill, higher-than-average work impairment among treated workers in a particular setting can be due to distinctive patient factors (e.g., lower-than-average adherence to medical regimens) or environmental factors (e.g., special family or work conditions that exacerbate the condition) rather than to treatment inadequacies.

Despite this uncertainty, consistent evidence across a number of companies in a single market showing that workers treated for a particular condition in one specific health plan or provider group have substantially different levels of work impairment than those treated for the same condition in other plans or groups after case-mix adjustment can make a rather strong case for differential treatment adequacy. The same is true when national comparisons show that levels of work impairment associated with a particular treated condition are much lower in one market than others, or among patients treated in one model setting than others. In situations of this sort, where HPQ results are able to pinpoint best-of-class treatment settings, in-depth practice process analysis might provide insight into mechanisms responsible for these differences.

Evaluation of Interventions

With regard to the questions that are being raised and evaluated by the analysis of HPQ surveys, post hoc analysis of HPQ data can also play a part in arriving at tentative answers. However, definitive answers require intervention. For example, if a theory about the effects of poor workplace lighting in bringing about an especially high rate of tension headaches in a particular work setting is true, then the definitive test is to modify the lighting and see whether the rate of headaches decreases. Similar tests can be used to evaluate theories about barriers to treatment as well as about treatment effectiveness.

The second HPQ initiative is designed to facilitate such evaluations by using before-after HPQ case-control comparisons to determine the cost-effectiveness of interventions. The first evaluation of this sort that is currently in progress is a $5 million experiment funded by the National Institute of Mental Health to evaluate the cost-effectiveness of a model outreach and best-practices treatment program for workers suffering from clinical depression (Kessler et al. 1999; Simon et al. 2001; Wang, Simon, and Kessler 2003). A number of large national corporations are participating in this evaluation, which includes a screening sample of nearly 100,000 workers who are being randomized and followed for two years to evaluate the effects of the program on performance at work, sickness absence, disability, workplace accidents, and job retention. The ultimate goal is to calculate an ROI from the perspective of the employer.

An even more ambitious HPQ program was briefly mentioned in chapter 1: a collaboration with the Midwest Business Group on Health (MBGH) and the Georgia Healthcare Leadership Forum (GHLF), under the aegis of the Institute for Health and Productivity Management (IHPM), to carry out a large annual marketwide HPQ survey among employees of MBGH and GHLF participating employers that includes a number of embedded treatment experiments. This research program is linked to a separate initiative on the National Business Coalition on Health (NBCH) being piloted with the MBGH to develop materials—both data and data-interpretation tools—that can help employers evaluate the indirect workplace costs of illness and the cost-effectiveness of specific health care interventions in order to rationalize contracting for health care on the part of NBCH member companies.

The National HPQ Data Pooling Consortium is also considering a number of additional interventions that will target health problems associated with substantial productivity loss. These interventions will attempt to increase the proportion of ill workers who receive treatment, improve the quality of care, or, as in the depression intervention, both. Some of these interventions are planned for implementation in only one large corporation. For example, one participating corporation is interested in evaluating the cost-effectiveness of implementing novel disease-management programs for several commonly occurring health problems that have substantial effects on the productivity of its workers. This company employs more than 100,000 workers in approximately 20 facilities around the country, and the evaluations are being implemented by randomizing the disease-management programs to a number of test-market facilities. Before-after test-control market comparisons in the annual HPQ surveys are being used to assess the effects of the programs on performance at work, sickness absence, disability, workplace accidents, and retention. Other interventions are planned for implementation in a single market with test and control companies, or across markets with parallel test and control facilities in a number of different companies.

Quality Assurance

If the evaluations described just above show that a particular intervention has a consistently positive ROI in test markets, employers might be tempted to implement this intervention throughout their entire workforce. As they consider doing so, though, the employers will be aware that interventions that are effective in controlled test administration can sometimes degrade when they are disseminated more widely. This is especially true when, as will usually be the case, test-market interventions are based on designs in which the participating health plans know that the interventions are under close scrutiny and that positive results will lead to much wider dissemination of the interventions. Ongoing quality assurance as the interventions are disseminated and implemented more broadly is consequently of great importance, a sentiment echoed by Beck in chapter 10.

The third HPQ initiative is designed to facilitate this kind of quality assurance by providing benchmark expectations based on evaluations of interventions. For example, if before-after HPQ test-market evaluations find that a disease-management program leads to a 30% increase in treatment and a 17-day per-worker per-year decrease in excess sickness absence, then companies that implement this intervention should expect to find effects of this magnitude in their annual HPQ surveys the year after the program is implemented. The creation of such benchmarks can be of enormous value to employers in rationalizing their investments in health care. Indeed, it is not going too far to say that the absence of such evaluation standards in the past has been a key factor in limiting employer investments in health care. Success in finding that the same positive effects of the intervention exist in the company as a whole as in the test markets can definitively document the positive ROI of the intervention. Ongoing tracking of key parameters (e.g., percentage in treatment and various productivity measures) can be used to monitor continued quality of the intervention. Failure to find effects in the company as a whole comparable to those in the test markets after appropriate case-mix adjustment, in comparison, might mean that the positive ROI found in the test-market evaluation does not hold once the program is more widely disseminated and that the program should be discontinued. Alternatively, failure to meet these targets or documentation of slippage over the course of time could be a point of negotiation with the participating health plan about quality improvement or cost sharing.

FUTURE DIRECTIONS IN RESEARCH ON HEALTH AND WORK PRODUCTIVITY

Although the HPQ is only one of several approaches to self-report health-and-productivity assessment, the HPQ initiatives outlined above nicely illustrate the likely future directions of research on individual-level health-and-productivity assessment. The reviews in part 1 suggest that self-report measures like the HPQ are the most feasible means of assessing workplace functioning. However, as we noted in chapter 1, a blending of self-report measures administered to all workers with objective archival measures of the sort discussed by Greenberg and Birnbaum (chapter 2) can also be very useful in helping to confirm and calibrate self-reports. As a result, we anticipate that methodological data archives will be created in the future that include blended assessments and that refinements in self-report measures will occur based on analyses of the data in these archives.

An HPQ archive of this sort is currently under development. The core productivity measures will necessarily continue to be based on self-report, though, because the number of workers whose productivity is assessed in any other way is too small to be broadly useful in comparative studies. Comparative studies, in turn, are critical because they are needed to address the key benchmarking questions that employers must answer in order to rationalize their health care investments.

Important measurement issues also exist in the assessment of health problems, and these are likely to become the focus of attention in health-and-productivity research once methodological problems with productivity measures are resolved. We suspect that self-report measures will be central to the assessment of health, just as they will be to the assessment of productivity. We noted in the previous section of this chapter that the HPQ uses self-report measures of health problems rather than readily available treatment data from health claim records. The decision to rely on self-report was based on the concern that health claim data tell us nothing about the effects of un-treated health problems. In fact, the HPQ distinguishes never treated, previously treated, and currently treated health problems in order to track both failure to seek treatment and treatment dropout. Importantly, HPQ survey results consistently find that never treated and previously treated health problems sometimes have substantial effects on work productivity, justifying the decision not to base the assessment of health problems on treatment data.

Alternative methods of assessing untreated health problems will doubtlessly be explored in future expansions of health-and-productivity research. The ideal, of course, would be for employers to offer annual physical examinations to all employees. The data obtained from these examinations, if merged with HPQ work-productivity data, would provide much more rich information about untreated health problems than the simple self-report symptom-and-condition checklists in the HPQ. However, only a minority of employers both offer annual physicals to all their workers and capture the results of these examinations in a form that can be used for research. A much less expensive middle-ground approach would be to use computer-based expert systems self-report methods to generate diagnoses of untreated symptom-based conditions. A number of commercial systems of this sort are now available (Ware 1999), and some of these are already embedded in electronic Health Risk Appraisal surveys (e.g., www.wellmed.com). It is likely that future health-and-productivity studies will use systems of this sort to focus on conditions that have been found (in previous health-and-work surveys) to be important causes of lost work productivity.

In conjunction with refining measurement, there is a need to build a cumulative body of knowledge about the absolute and relative effects of a wide range of illnesses on standardized workplace productivity outcomes as well as replicated ROI evaluations of specific interventions. In order for this body of knowledge to develop, researchers need to agree on a standard set of evaluation models and procedures, including study designs (e.g., before-after test-control market designs), case-mix adjustment measures and procedures, and statistical methods for analyzing intervention effects in ways that adjust for incomplete data and the possibility of informative nonresponse. The accuracy of pooling across studies will increase as these various methods become more and more standardized.

Finally, as discussed in chapters 8, 9, and 10, corporations need to give more serious thought to the issue of monetizing health-and-productivity information if they want to obtain accurate ROI estimates of new health care programs. The sort of health-and-productivity studies described above in the discussion of the HPQ can estimate the number of sickness-absence days due to a particular illness and calculate the direct costs per illness-free day due to health care interventions. They can even calculate rough intervention cost-effectiveness ratios by assuming that each recovered illness-free day has a value to the employer equal to the salary of the worker or some other fixed value (e.g., salary plus fringe or salary plus fringe plus some profit multiplier). However, institutional knowledge that goes well beyond the information available in health-and-productivity studies is needed to estimate the true ROI of an intervention to the company. Is production organized in the company in such a way that a substantial rise in sickness absence for one month during the flu season would throw off the production schedule? If so, is the seasonality of sales in the industrial sector where the company operates such that a short-term perturbation in production capacity during the winter would pose serious problems for meeting production targets? If so, is the contracting environment in this industrial sector such that production target failure would create serious negative contracting ripple effects? Questions such as these need to be posed and answered by experts in the institutional arrangements of the company in order to arrive at an accurate estimate of the ROI of medical interventions.

Corporate decision-makers think in exactly these ways about other investment decisions, so it should not be difficult for them to integrate health-and-productivity information into their thought processes once reliable data on health and productivity become available. However, in order for them to include health care among the human-capital investment decision-making options they consider, they will also need to believe that their health plans are reliable coalition partners. This will occur only if health plans become more open to being evaluated on the basis of outcomes than they are currently. The substantial growth of medical demand-management companies over the past half-dozen years has been based, at least in part, on this kind of openness. We suspect that the emergence and early success of these companies will help motivate health plans to adopt a similar orientation.

The response of health plans to the outcome data generated by health-and-productivity studies is another matter. Outcome-based quality-assurance systems will provide no direct guidance about the process changes needed to effect these outcomes. However, there is good reason to believe that they will have a dramatic effect on quality-improvement efforts if their results are taken seriously by employer-purchasers and if these results are used to track changes in outcomes associated with health-plan quality-improvement initiatives. The best example we have of this process is the New York State Cardiac Surgery Reporting System (CSRS), which demonstrated that public reporting of medical-outcome evaluations can have dramatic effects on quality-improvement efforts (Chassin, Hannan, and DeBuono 1996), and that such efforts can have dramatic effects on important health outcomes (Hannan et al. 1994). Up to now, though, there has been surprisingly little dissemination of the CSRS system to other states and surprisingly little generalization of the CSRS approach to other illnesses. There are doubtlessly a number of reasons for this, since the impediments to quality improvement are many and varied (Fetterolf 2002). However, lack of organized and sustained demand for improvement on the part of purchasers is among the most important of these (Becher and Chassin 2001). Our hope is that the development of productivity-and-health evaluations will help address this issue and that the resulting increase in organized and sustained purchaser demand for improved outcomes will become an important element in broader efforts (Institute of Medicine 2001) to improve the quality of health care.

REFERENCES

Becher, E. C., and M. R. Chassin. 2001. Improving the quality of health care: Who will lead? *Health Affairs* 20:164–79.

Chassin, M. R. 2002. Achieving and sustaining improved quality: Lessons from New York State and cardiac surgery. *Health Affairs* 21:40–51.

Chassin, M. R., E. L. Hannan, and B. A. DeBuono. 1996. Benefits and hazards of reporting medical outcomes publicly. *New England Journal of Medicine* 334: 394–98.

Fetterolf, D. E. 2002. Why do multi-organizational quality initiatives usually fail? *American Journal of Medical Quality* 17:43–46.

Hannan, E. L., D. Kumar, M. Racz, A. L. Siu, and M. R. Chassin. 1994. New York State's Cardiac Surgery Reporting System: Four years later. *Annals of Thoracic Surgery* 58:1852–57.

Hargraves, J. L., and S. Trude. 2002. Obstacles to employers' pursuit of health care quality. *Health Affairs* 21:194–200.

Institute of Medicine. 2001. *Crossing the quality chasm: A new health system for the 21st century.* Washington, DC: National Academy Press.

Kay, G. G., and M. E. Quig. 2001. Impact of sedating antihistamines on safety and productivity. *Allergy and Asthma Proceedings* 22:281–83.

Kessler, R. C., C. Barber, A. Beck, P. A. Berglund, P. D. Cleary, D. McKenas, N. Pronk, G. Simon, P. Stang, T. B. Üstün, and P. Wang. 2003. The World Health Organization Health and Work Performance Questionnaire (HPQ). *Journal of Occupational and Environmental Medicine* 45:156–74.

Kessler, R. C., C. B. Barber, H. G. Birnbaum, R. G. Frank, P. E. Greenberg, R. M. Rose, G. E. Simon, and P. S. Wang. 1999. Depression in the workplace: Effects on short-term work disability. *Health Affairs* 18:163–71.

Kessler, R. C., P. E. Greenberg, K. D. Mickelson, L. M. Meneades, and P. S. Wang. 2001. The effects of chronic medical conditions on work loss and work cutback. *Journal of Occupational and Environmental Medicine* 43 (Suppl. 3): 218–25.

Kessler, R. C., and T. B. Üstün. 2000. The World Health Organization World Mental Health 2000 Initiative. *Hospital Management International,* 195–96.

Pomerleau, P. O., and B. W. Benson. 1994. Looking back—a history of progress: Society of Quality Assurance. *Quality Assurance* 3:110–16.

Simon, G. E., C. Barber, H. G. Birnbaum, R. G. Frank, P. E. Greenberg, R. M. Rose, P. Wang, and R. C. Kessler. 2001. Depression and work productivity: The comparative costs of treatment versus nontreatment. *Journal of Occupational and Environmental Medicine* 43:2–9.

Wang, P. S., G. Simon, and R. C. Kessler. 2003. The economic burden of depression and the cost-effectiveness of treatment. *International Journal of Methods in Psychiatric Research* 12:22–33.

Ware, J. E., Jr. 1999. John E. Ware Jr. on health status and quality of life assessment and the next generation of outcomes measurement. Interview by M. Stevic and K. Berry. *Journal of Healthcare Quality* 21:12–17.

Zaslavsky, A. M., and M. J. Buntin. 2002. Using survey measures to assess risk selection among Medicare managed care plans. *Inquiry* 39:138–51.

About the Contributors

LANCE ANDERSON, managing associate, Caliber Associates, Fairfax, Virginia

ARNE BECK, director of research, Kaiser Permanente Colorado Clinical Research Unit

MARC L. BERGER, vice president, Outcomes Research and Management, Merck & Co., Inc., West Point, Pennsylvania

HOWARD G. BIRNBAUM, codirector, Health Economics Practice, Analysis Group, Inc., Boston

THOMAS DELEIRE, assistant professor, Department of Economics, Michigan State University, and senior analyst, Health and Human Resources Division, Congressional Budget Office

MEI-SHENG DUH, vice president, Analysis Group, Inc., Boston

CHRISTOPHER J. EVANS, director of economics and outcomes, Mapi Values, Boston

PAUL E. GREENBERG, managing principal, Health Economics Practice, Analysis Group, Inc., Boston

LYNN HOFFMAN, research associate, Galt Associates, Inc.

JONATHAN HOWLAND, professor, Boston University School of Public Health, Center to Prevent Alcohol Problems among Young People

RONALD C. KESSLER, professor, Department of Health Care Policy, Harvard Medical School

ANGELA LARAMIE, Occupational Health Surveillance Program, Massachusetts Department of Public Health, Boston

JENNIFER LEE, Biostatistics, Tyco Healthcare/Mallinckrodt, St. Louis

DEBRA J. LERNER, research scientist and associate professor, Tufts–New England Medical Center, Boston

THOMAS W. MANGIONE, senior research scientist, John Snow, Inc., Boston

WILLARD G. MANNING, professor, Harris Graduate School of Public Policy Studies and Department of Health Studies, Biological Science Division / Medical School, University of Chicago

JAMES F. MURRAY, senior director, Human Resources Decision Support, Merck & Co., Inc., Whitehouse Station, New Jersey

SEAN NICHOLSON, assistant professor, Department of Policy Analysis and Management, Cornell University

NANCY A. NICOLSON, assistant professor, Department of Psychiatry and Neuropsychology, Maastricht University, Netherlands

SCOTT H. OPPLER, American Institutes for Research, Washington, D.C.

MARK PAULY, professor, Health Care Systems and Economics, Wharton School, University of Pennsylvania

ANDREW ROSE, chief scientist, American Institutes for Research, Washington, D.C.

DENNIS P. SCANLON, associate professor, Health Policy and Administration, Pennsylvania State University

PAUL E. STANG, associate professor, Department of Health, West Chester University, and executive vice president, Galt Associates, Inc.

PHILIP S. WANG, assistant professor, Department of Health Care Policy, Harvard Medical School, and Department of Psychiatry and Division of Pharmacoepidemiology and Pharmacoeconomics, Brigham and Women's Hospital

HARVEY WHITEFORD, Kratzmann Professor of Psychiatry and Population Health, University of Queensland, Australia

Author Index

Abbott, T. A., 37
Affleck, G., 92, 103, 107, 109
Allen, H. M., 79
Alliger, G. M., 98
Almeida, D. M., 1
Almond, S., 160
Amick, B. C., III, 79, 228
Anderson, L., 14, 15
Anderson, R. T., 68
Andersson, F., 224
Andrews, G., 256, 258
Appels, A., 102
Asmussen, L., 102
Atcheson, S. G., 2
Auerbach, B., 49

Baase, C., 234
Barber, C. B., 1, 36
Barge-Schaapveld, D. Q., 102, 105, 108, 110, 111, 112
Barrett, P. R., 64
Barro, R. J., 254
Barton, J., 100, 106
Barton, M., 38, 44
Baum, F., 259
Beauregard, T. R., 217
Becher, E. C., 284
Beck, A., 18, 19, 20, 207, 278, 280
Becker, G., 254
Becker, M., 56
Benson, B. W., 273
Berger, M. L., 17, 158, 185, 191, 202, 234
Bergner, M., 77

Berkhof, J., 97, 99, 104, 112
Berndt, E. R., 38, 45, 47, 76, 192, 257, 258
Bertera, R. L., 37, 47
Beyers, M., 212
Birnbaum, H. G., 5, 6, 7, 9, 12, 21, 29, 31, 38, 44, 45, 200, 218, 242, 272, 278, 281
Bobadilla, J. L., 261
Bodenheimer, T., 212
Bolger, N., 101
Bombardier, C., 237
Boonen, A., 1
Bradburn, N. M., 10, 71, 72, 73, 88
Brandstätter, H., 99, 101, 105
Brandt-Rauf, P., 2, 78
Brazier, J. E., 198
Brinkerhoff, R. O., 81, 82
Broadhead, W. E., 36, 74, 75
Brouwer, W. B., 158, 160
Brown, G. W., 93
Brown, M. L., 200, 210
Bunn, W. B., III, 79
Buntin, M. J., 274
Burke, L., 252
Burke, L. B., 236
Burton, W. N., 2, 39, 42, 46, 47, 198, 199, 200, 257

Cannell, C. F., 69
Carli, M., 96
Carney, M. A., 103, 109
Carter, T., 2
Cercone, J., 254
Chassany, O., 226

Chassin, M. R., 274, 284
Chatterjee, M., 257, 259
Chawla, A. J., 40, 44, 200, 257
Chen, C. Y., 198, 199
Chernew, M., 212
Claffey, R., 107
Clark, H. H., 10
Clarke, B. C., 101
Claxton, A. J., 40, 44, 200, 257
Cochran, W. G., 92
Cockburn, I. M., 40, 45, 47, 192
Colditz, G. A., 198
Coleman, P., 198
Colletta, M. L., 260
Collier, P., 259
Collins, R. L., 103
Collins, W. E., 61
Conti, D. J., 39, 42, 200, 257
Cooney, N. L., 103, 108
Coulehan, J. L., 1
Cowley, P., 261
Coyte, P. C., 200
Cremieux, P. Y., 31, 45
Cruise, C. E., 103, 109
Csikszentmihalyi, M., 89, 90, 92, 93,
    94, 96, 97, 98, 101, 103, 104, 105, 106
Cullen, N. J., 260
Currie, J., 152, 159

Davis, R. B., 1
Deaton, A., 152
Deb, P., 36
DeBuono, B. A., 284
DeJong, A., 77
DeLeire, T., 15, 16, 142
Delespaul, P. A. E. G., 92, 101, 104, 105,
    108, 111
Delle Fave, A., 109, 111
DeMeuse, K. P., 2
Demo, D. H., 93
Deolaliker, A., 256
DeVries, M. W., 89, 90, 105, 107, 108
Dewa, C. S., 258
Dijkman-Caes, C. I. M., 102, 108, 109, 111

Dolhert, N., 61
Donner, E., 105
Dressler, D. E., 81, 82
Drummond, M., 190, 195, 210, 238
Dudley, R. A., 212
Duh, M. S., 21, 242
Dukes, E. M., 76, 228, 232
Dworkin, S. F., 49

Eaton, W. W., 36
Eckhart, J., 212
Edington, D. W., 47
Eisenhower, D., 88
Endicott, J., 78, 226
Erickson, P., 1, 12, 67
Essink-Bot, M., 228
Ettner, S. L., 159
Evans, C. J., 20, 21, 224
Evans, S., 98

Farchaus-Stein, K., 102, 112
Fassbender, K., 189
Feeny, D. H., 111
Fetterolf, D. E., 284
Figurski, T. J., 93
Finkelstein, S. N., 76
Fiore, M. C., 199
Fireman, B. H., 210
Fitz-Enz, J., 3
Folkard, S., 99, 100, 101, 105, 106
Forthofer, M. S., 260, 262
Fortney, J. C., 257
Fowler, F. J., Jr., 68, 69
Frank, R. G., 36, 75, 159, 257, 258
Franklin, J., 199
Freeman, S., 103
French, M. T., 36
Fries, J. F., 66, 77

Gable, S. L., 89, 90
Gabriel, L. H., 63
Galer, B. S., 36
Galinsky, T. L., 14
Gallup, J. L., 254

Garber, A., 160

Gaubatz, S., 99, 101, 105

Glass, R., 259, 260

Godaert, G. L. R., 103, 109, 112

Gold, M. R., 1, 185, 188

Goldfarb, N. I., 212

Goldstein, I. B., 105

Gorin, A. A., 110

Gower, C. G., 101

Grabowski, H. G., 66

Greenberg, P. E., 1, 5, 6, 7, 9, 12, 21, 29, 30, 38, 40, 42, 43, 44, 45, 48, 200, 218, 242, 245, 250, 272, 278, 281

Grootaert, C., 259

Gruber, J., 159

Gugerty, M. K., 253

Guico-Pabia, C. J., 189, 200

Gustafsson, A., 8

Gutterman, D. L., 36, 76, 189

Guyatt, G. H., 111

Hafner, H., 262

Hailu, A., 256

Hakkaart-van Roijen, L., 228

Hannan, E. L., 284

Hansen, R. W., 66

Harbour, J. L., 9

Hargraves, J. L., 272

Harris, J. R., 212

Harris, T., 93

Harwood, R. H., 77

Hatziandreu, E. I., 198, 200

Haworth, J. T., 98, 99, 105

Hays, R. D., 68, 111

Haythornthwaite, J. A., 89, 90, 93, 94

Hedricks, C. A., 109

Hemp, P., 78

Henderson, S., 260

Henson, L. C., 57

Herrin, J., 200

Hillbrand, M., 107

Hoffman, L., 21, 242

Holloway, J., 13

Holmer, A. F., 225

Honkoop, P. C., 103, 109, 110, 112

Hormuth, S. E., 91, 92, 94, 95

Horne, J. A., 64

House, J. S., 259

Howard, K., 78

Howland, J., 7, 13, 54, 62, 272

Hu, X. H., 200, 211

Huban, S. P., 3

Huse, D. M., 200

Jackson T., 49

Jacobs, P., 189, 200

Jamner, L. D., 105

Jarman, M., 99, 105

Jha, P., 261

Johannesson, M., 234

Johns, G., 37, 75

Johnson, C., 102, 112

Johnson, J. A., 200

Johnson, M. D., 8

Jungkind, K., 202

Kaplan, C. D., 103, 107, 112

Kaplan, R. M., 77

Karlsson, G., 234

Kartman, B., 224

Katon, W., 36

Katzelnick, D. J., 36

Kawachi, I., 259, 260

Kay, G. G., 272

Kazdin, A. E., 109

Kazmirski, G., 218

Keefe, F., 49

Keefer, P., 259

Keller, S. D., 69

Kennedy, B. P., 259, 260

Kennedy, S., 40, 44, 200, 257

Kessler, R. C., 1, 2, 3, 9, 11, 21, 30, 34, 35, 36, 72, 75, 89, 90, 93, 94, 110, 159, 215, 217, 228, 235, 242, 254, 257, 258, 260, 262, 271, 276, 277, 279

Khaltaev, N. G., 1

Kihlstrom, J. F., 71

Kiiskinen, U., 200

Kim, A., 256
Knack, S., 259
Knauth, P., 100, 106
Koopman, C., 228
Koopmanschap, M. A., 30, 158, 190, 224, 233, 234
Koplan, J. P., 200
Kouzis, A. C., 36
Kraan, H. F., 102, 108, 110
Kraay, A., 253
Krahn, M. D., 224
Kubey, R., 98, 105

Landis, K. R., 259
Laramie, A. K., 7, 54, 272
Larson, E. B., 217
Larson, R., 89, 90, 92, 94, 97, 98, 101, 102, 103, 104, 106, 112
Laurell, H, 61
Lawrie, S. M., 8
Lee, A. C., 57
Lee, J., 9, 10, 12, 13, 32, 66
Lee, S., 99, 106
LeFevre, J., 97, 98, 105, 106
Legg, R. F., 36, 189, 225
Leigh, J. P., 200
Leirer, V., 61
Leistikow, B., 200
Leon, A. C., 77
Leopold, C., 103, 110, 112
Lerner, D. J., 9, 10, 12, 13, 32, 66, 78, 79, 215, 228
Lewins, J., 56
Lewis, J., 13
Liguori, A., 61
Lim, D., 258
Lin, E. H., 36, 258
Lipscomb, J., 200, 210
Lipton, R. B., 36
Litt, M. D., 103, 108
Little, R. J. A., 94
Loeppke, R., 3, 78
Lopez, A. D., 255

Lousberg, R., 102, 110
Lucas, B., 49
Lucas, D. O., 2
Luce, B., 234
Lydick, E., 200
Lyles, A., 238
Lynch, W., 3, 78

Madrian, B., 152, 159
Maetzel, A., 237
Magid, D. J., 210
Mainous, A. G., III, 212
Mallory, G., 13
Mangione, T. W., 7, 54, 61, 272
Manning, W. G., 15, 16, 142
Marcus, S. C., 74, 75
Marks, M. L., 2
Massimini, A., 109, 111
Massimini, F., 96
Mathieu, M. A., 108
Mathiowetz, N. A., 88
Mayfield, J. A., 36
Mayne, T. J., 78
McCunney, R. J., 2
McGrail, M. P., Jr., 3
Mehrotra, A., 212
Melhorn, J. M., 200
Merkesdal, S., 200, 211
Merrick, W. A., 102, 110
Mickelson, K. D., 260
Miller, A. R., 15
Miller, W., 3
Mintz, J., 76
Moneta, G. B., 96
Monroe, A. F., 212
Moore, M. J., 159
Morgado, A., 95
Morganstein, D., 88
Morrow, D., 61
Morse, P., 103, 108
Muellbauer, J., 152
Mukamel, D. B., 212
Mumenthaler, M. S., 61

Mundt, J. C., 61
Murray, C. J. L., 255
Murray, J. F., 17, 18, 158, 185
Mushlin, A. I., 212

Neale, J. M., 93
Nebenfuhr, P., 202
Nee, J., 78, 226
Nelson, R. O., 109
Ng, Y. C., 200
Nicholl, J. P., 198
Nicholson, S., 17, 158, 185
Nicolson, N. A., 11, 13, 88, 97, 99, 104, 105, 110, 112
Norman, G. R., 68

O'Hanlon, J. F., 62
Oppler, S., 14
Orenstein, W. A., 200
Ormel, J., 36, 49, 77
Osterhaus, J. T., 36, 76, 189
Oyserman, D., 11

Parker, S. K., 100
Parsons, C., 8
Pashko, S., 37
Patel, V., 259
Pathak, D. S., 233
Patrick, D. L., 1, 12, 67, 111
Patrick, J., 8
Pauly, M. V., 1, 17, 74, 158, 185, 191
Plachetka, J. R., 36, 76, 189
Pomerleau, P. O., 273
Pope, A. M., 66
Prescott, S., 90
Price, K. L., 36
Psacharopoulos, G., 254, 256

Quig, M. E., 272

Ramirez, A., 253
Ramsey, S., 44
Ranis, G., 253

Ranson, K., 261
Rasinski, K., 10
Rasmussen, B. K., 36
Reginster, J. Y., 1
Reilly, M. C., 76, 228, 232
Reis, H. T., 89, 90
Revecki, D. A., 9, 14, 37, 68, 75
Rice, D. P., 29
Richards, M., 98, 106
Riedel, J. E., 3, 78
Riggs, J. D., 200
Rips, L. J., 10, 88
Rizzo, J. A., 37
Robinson, J., 93
Roemer, M., 253
Rose, A., 14
Rose, R. M., 259
Rosenheck, R. A., 41, 45, 216
Ross, L. E., 61
Ross, M., 88
Rost, K. M., 219, 257
Rothermich, E. A., 233
Rubin, D. B., 94
Rutten, F. F., 30, 158, 190, 224, 233, 234

Sachs, J. D., 254
Sanderson, K., 258
Savon-Williams, R. C., 93
Scanlon, D. P., 16, 17, 19, 165, 212, 238
Schandry, R., 103, 110, 112
Schober, M. F., 10
Schultz, J., 212
Schultz, T. P., 254
Schwartz, J. E., 89, 92
Schwarz, N., 10
Seavey, W., 200
Selby, J. V., 210
Serxner, S., 2
Shapiro, D., 105
Sharda, C. E., 234
Shaver, P. R., 260
Sherbourne, C. D., 77, 217
Shiffman, S. S., 89, 90, 91, 103, 107

Shinkman, R., 48
Shiu, A. T., 99, 106
Simon, G. E., 279
Simon, L. P., 212
Simonson, D. S., 36
Sloan, F. A., 1
Smith, A., 29, 254
Smith, J. L., 219
Smith, L., 100, 105, 106
Smith, S. S., 199
Smyth, J. M., 103, 110, 112
Snyder, C., 200, 210
Solomon, G. D., 36
Songer, T. J., 200
Sorbi, M. J., 103, 109, 112
Sorokin, R., 212
Spelten, E., 100, 105, 106
Spingh, G., 66
Spitz, P. W., 77
Stang, P. E., 1, 21, 22, 36, 236, 242, 271
Steiger, H., 102
Stewart, F., 253
Stewart, W. F., 36, 228
Stone, A. A., 89, 90, 92, 93, 94, 102, 103, 107, 109, 112
Stoudemire, A., 30, 73
Streiner, D. L., 68
Sudman, S., 10, 72, 73
Suleiman, T. G., 261
Sullivan, S. D., 200, 238
Swain, B. E., 210
Szalai, A., 93

Taffinder, N. J., 61
Tai-Seale, M., 212
Talbert, J., 212
Tandon, A., 256
Tarlov, A. R., 1, 66
Taylor, J. L., 61
Testa, M. A., 36
Teuchmann, K., 100
Thompson, B. L., 212
Tighe, S., 194

Tornos, J., 61
Toth-Fejel, G. E., 109
Totterdell, P., 99, 100, 101, 105, 106
Tourangeau, R., 10, 70
Trude, S., 272
Turner, C. F., 10

Umberson, D., 259
Ungar, W. J., 200
Ustun, T. B., 276

van Diest, R., 102
van Eck, M., 97, 99, 102, 104, 105, 106, 108, 110, 111, 112
van Roijen, L., 36, 78, 228
Vendrig, L., 102
Vermeeren, A., 62
Viscusi, W. K., 159
Voelkl, J. E., 108
Von Korff, M., 36, 49

Waite, B. M., 107
Walters, E. E., 260, 262
Wang, P. S., 11, 13, 88, 279
Ware, J. E., Jr., 69, 77, 217, 282
Warner, K. E., 37, 199
Warr, P., 105
Watson, R. M., 3
Wedig, G. J., 212
Weiler, J. M., 62
Weisbrod, B. A., 233
Weiss, K. B., 200
Wells, K. B., 1
White, C. C., 200
Whitecotton, L., 36
Whiteford, H. A., 22, 253, 260
Wiersma, D., 77
Wilkinson, L., 200
Williams, A., 261
Williams, A. F., 199
Williams, K. J., 96, 98, 101, 106
Williamson, A. M., 101
Wilson, K. C. M., 107, 108

Winston, K. R., 217
Witting, P., 47
Wong, M. M., 96
Wyatt, R. J., 261

Yawn, B. P., 200
Yawn, R. A., 200
Yen, L. T., 47
Yesavage, J. A., 61

Young, D. W., 211
Young, D. Y., 77

Zarkin, G. A., 36
Zaslavsky, A. M., 274
Zbrozek, A. S., 76, 228, 232
Zhang, M., 257
Zhao, S., 1, 30

Subject Index

Page numbers in italics refer to tables and figures

absenteeism: calculation of, 189; depression and, *1*, 159; productivity and, 31–32; self-report and, 14; wellness programs and, 197
administrative claims data, 29–30, 33, 45, 49
allergies: costs and, 200; treatment of, 6, *39*; WPAI and, 232
ALWQ (Angina-related Limitations at Work Questionnaire), 228
Alzheimer's disease, 224
American Heart Association: indirect cost estimates of heart disease, 188–89
Angina-related Limitations at Work Questionnaire (ALWQ), 228
antihistamines: increased productivity and, 6, 45, 47; sedating vs. nonsedating, 272; simulation and, 58, 60, 62, 64
antidepressants. *See* depression: care; depression treatment
anxiety: ESM and, *102*, *111*; in developing countries, 259
archival data: approach to gathering productivity data, 30–32, *33*; comprehensiveness of, 81–83; corporate benefit design and, 48–50; in developing countries, 262; health plans and, 215, 217; HPQ and, 231, 249–50; as in vivo equivalents of simulations, 9; retrospective studies and, 37, *38–41*, 42, 44,

45, *46*; vs. self-report data, 3, 249–50; work performance and, 5–7
archival measures: ESM and, 11; linked data sets and, 31, 38, 46, 48. *See also* archival data
arthritis: ESM studies of, 110, 112; HAQ and, 77; impact of on costs, 200; rheumatoid, *38*, 200; work impairment and, 34, *35*, 44
asthma: costs of, 200; ESM and, 89, 92, 110; work absences and, *39*, 42
auto-immune diseases, 34

back pain, 40, 42, 43, 203, 277
benefit, health care as, 2–3, 273
benefit design: archival data and, 34, 36–37, 42, 45, 48–49; health plans and, 176–80, 183–85, 207–11; HPM approaches and, 216–18; impact of on costs of disease, 201; new model of, 219–21, 238; productivity and, 29–31, 34; value-based purchasing and, 18–19
benefit manager, 165, 172, 196–98, 231, 238. *See also* human resource personnel; Human Resources; human resources manager
benefits: calculator, 201; disability, 152; health, 195–204; health promotion programs and, 198–204; human resources and, 16–17, 54; information systems

benefits (*continued*)
and, 178; investments and, 1, 185–90,
255, 271–73; IRR and, 172; management, 3–6, 167–75, 178–80; mental
health, 45; pharmaceutical claims and,
242; prevention programs and, 199–
200; rationalization of, 272; sickness,
189–91; staff dedicated to, 167
bias: definition, 69; ESM and, 94–95,
97, 104; supervisor ratings and, 82
Bridges to Excellence, 179

cancer: costs of, 200; work absences
and, *39*, 42, *43*, 45
Centers for Medicare and Medicaid Services, 180
chronic care model (CCM), 171
clinical trials: evidence in, 247–49; gold
standard self-report instrument and,
251; methods to assess productivity in,
225–26, *227*, 228–34; O*NET and, 136,
139; questionnaire design in, 235–37;
sickness absence and, 74
Committee on Quality of Health Care,
179
cost-effectiveness: analyses of, 143, 160,
224; clinical depression and, 279; disease management programs and, 202;
employers and, 274–75, 278, 280;
health-care interventions and, 2, 17–18,
23, 54, 156; health plans and, 19, 21, 54;
ratios of, 283; studies of, 261
cost of illness: analyses, 143; calculation
of, 249–50; estimates for, 160, 224;
research, 271
cost-of-illness (COI) literature, 15, 29,
142, 159
cost-of-illness perspective, measures
and, 12–13
costs: benefit, 185, 201; benefit managers and computing, 33; of chronic
conditions, 210; development, 194; of
depression, 44; direct, 172, 210, 272;

direct medical, 225; disability, 42, 44,
201; disease-related, 224; disease-
specific, 44; employer and social, 143;
ESM and, 96–97; health care, 17, 20,
49, 165, 182, 271; health plans and,
207–12, 218; health problems and, 275;
health-related programs and, 166, 171–
73, 176, 196; health-sector, 159; hidden, 47; of hiring, 157; of illness, 1, 19,
120, 142, 158; impact of diseases on,
200; input, 145; labor, 225; medical
and disability, 42; non-wage, 188, 211;
O*NET and, 131; other medical, 238;
out-of-pocket, 179–80; prevention programs and, 199; production, 193;
productivity, 36, 73, 78, 120, 139; productivity losses and, 139; replacement,
201; of rhinitis, 256; sickness-absence,
42; simulation and, 8, 55; social, 16,
142, 148, 160; societal, 190–91; total
health care, 66, 199; transaction, 259;
treatment, 36, 45; wage, 190; of
worker injuries, 142; worker's compensation and, 168; work loss, 191,
211; workplace, 21, 23, 37, 256–57,
271

Department of Labor, information system for describing occupations, 123–
24. *See also* O*NET
depression: care, 218; change in, 159;
clinical, 279; cognitive impairment in,
108; costs of, 44, 200–201; disability
claims for, *38–40*, 44; disease management and, 219; economic impact of,
42; effects on productivity, 95; eliminating, 159; ESM and, 108, 110–11;
geriatric, 108; intervention, 280;
major, 34, 36–37, 44–45, 256; marketing programs and, 220; pilot studies
on, 108; prevalence among women,
159; recidivism and, 42; self report
and, 30, 74, 76; simulators and, 64;

treatment of, 36–37, 45–46, 219, 257; treatment-resistant, 44; work absenteeism and, 1; work performance and, 11, 159–60, 257; workplace burden of, 38–40, 45

depression treatment: cost-effectiveness and, 1; employer-purchasers and, 219–20; specialist mental health services and, 257

developing countries: health and work productivity in, 22; health status of people in, 253–56; human capital and, 5; illness and work productivity in, 256–60; new investments in health and, 260–64

diabetes: costs of, 200–203; ESM and, 103, 110; offsets from treatment and, 36–37; productivity savings of treatment for, 225; workplace burden of, 39, 44, 47

digestive disorders, 39, 46, 47

direct costs: benefit design and, 201; depression treatment and, 257; health plans and, 210; HPM and, 172; migraine and, 36

disability: absenteeism and, 31, 200; average duration per claimant, 42, 43; benefits, 181; chronic, 255; claims, 44–45; costs, 42, 49, 201; depression and, 36; in developing countries, 254–59, 262, 264; employer's perspective and, 209, 213; employers and, 168, 169; health-care investments and, 274–80; health plans and, 211; insurance, 167; labor-demand model and, 147, 150, 158; lost income due to, 181; management, 2, 181, 182; mental disorders and, 258; noncash benefits, 152; nonoccupational, 181; occupational, 182; O*NET and, 124; payments, 45; periods of, 74; prevention, 181; productivity loss and, 256; programs, 202; records, 44; scales, 77–78; self-reported, 75;

short-term, 44, 201, 204; SPS and, 232; work productivity and, 66, 202–3

disability-adjusted life year (DALY), 255–56, 261

disease management programs: chronic diseases and, 202–4; evaluation of, 173; HPQ and, 281; productivity and, 17; relative cost per employee and, 198, 199

EMPAQ (Employer Measures of Productivity, Absence and Quality), 272

employee assistance program (EAP), 169, 172

employee perspective, 5

Employer Measures of Productivity, Absence and Quality (EMPAQ™), 272

employer perspective: costs of illness and, 19; health benefits and, 271; health plans and, 210–11, 214, 219–20; vs. individual and societal perspective, 187, 189, 203

employer-purchaser: as stakeholder, 4–5, 7; health and productivity and, 16, 17, 19–20; health benefits and, 284; health-care organizations and, 23; quality assurance and, 273

Endicott Work Productivity Scale (EWPS), 226, 228–29, 238

epidemiological surveys, 2, 32, 34

error: measurement, 129–30, 132–34, 135; productivity research and, 49, 73–76, 138; random, 68–69; recall, 70–72, 75, 81; sampling, 134; sources of in self-report, 10, 69

ESM (Experience Sampling Method): compliance with, 94, 101, 104, 108, 109; data collected with, 93; definition, 89; participants in, 92; recall bias and, 11, 113; schedule for recording information and, 90–91; signaling and data-collection instruments and, 91–92;

ESM (Experience Sampling Method)
(*continued*)
  strength of, 13–14; studies of chronic
  illness and, 102–3, 107–12; studies of
  work performance and, 96–97, 98–
  100, 101, 104–6; types of nonresponse
  in, 94–95
eValue8 group, 173
EWPS (Endicott Work Productivity
  Scale), 226, 228–29, 238
Experience Sampling Method. *See* ESM

Food and Drug Administration (FDA):
  productivity assessments and, 236–38;
  productivity claims and, 244–49; productivity-related outcome information
  and, 252; regulatory perspective of, 21–
  22, 242–44
frictional costs of illness: friction cost
  method, 233; health impairment and,
  158

Georgia Healthcare Leadership Forum,
  279
gold standard: archival data and, 81, 93;
  criterion validity and, 68, 236; development of, 250–52; related to productivity measurement, 22, 244; self-report
  and, 67; simulators as, 56; validation
  of, 48
Groningen Disability Schedule, 77

HAQ (Health Assessment Questionnaire), 77
headache. *See* migraine
Health and Labor Questionnaire (HLQ),
  78, 228–29
Health and Productivity Management.
  See HPM
Health Assessment Questionnaire
  (HAQ), 77
health care organization perspective, 18,
  20

health impairment: effects of, 142–43;
  frictional costs of illness and, 158–60;
  labor market consequences of, 142;
  labor market effects of, 143–50; models
  for, 152–58; social loss and, 144–47,
  150–52, 155. *See also* illness; impairment
Health Insurance Portability and Accountability Act (HIPAA), 174, 215
health plans: archival data and, 216; as
  stakeholder, 5, 18–21, 208–14; benefit
  design and, 218–21; employer data
  and, 215; evaluation of, 284; eValue8
  group and, 174; General Motors and,
  179–80; HEDIS and, 212–13, 216;
  HPM approach and, 217; HPQ and,
  281; self-report measures and, 214,
  216, 218; worker-productivity measures and, 214–16
Health Plan Employer Data and Information Set. *See* HEDIS
Health Savings Accounts (HSAs), 166
health utilization data, 42
health-risk appraisals, 214–15, 220
health-risk assessments, 32, 47
heart disease: benefit from pharmaceutical intervention, 37; costs of, 43, 189,
  200–201; disability days and, 43
HEDIS (Health Plan Employer Data and
  Information Set), 19, 174, 180, 202,
  212–13, 217
HIV/AIDS, 256, 263
HLQ (Health and Labor Questionnaire),
  78, 228–29
HPM (Health and Productivity Management): definition, 23, 166; effectiveness of, 175; IRR and, 172; barriers to,
  167–68, 171, 173–74; solutions for minimizing the barriers to, 176–82; value-
  based purchasing and, 216–17
HPQ (WHO Health and Work Performance Questionnaire): ESM and, 11,
  17; future directions in research on

health and productivity and, 281–84; health plans and, 217–18; initiatives, 276–81; pharmaceutical companies and, 230–31, 237–39

human capital: approach, 233–34; developing countries and, 254, 259; firm-specific, 153, 156–57, 191, 203; investment, 3, 5, 64; investment of, 5, 22, 283; method, 189,198, 202. *See also* lost-wages method

human resource personnel, 54

Human Resources, 165, 167, 171

human resources manager, 16

hypertension, 37, 39, 42, 200–201, 273

ICD-9 (International Classification of Diseases, 9th ed.), 44

IHMP (Institute for Health and Productivity Management), 23, 279

illness: abilities and, 121, 123, 132–36; absences due to, 197; annual costs of burden of, 138; burden of, 45, 135, 136, 137, 139; childhood, 262; chronic, 107, 110, 112, 173; confidentiality of, 95; consequences of, 31, 49; costs of, 19, 42; developing countries and, 254–64; disability burden of, 44; dollar impact of, 131; economic burden of, 37, 66; economic consequences of, 245, 256; effect on daily performance, 111; effect on productivity, 89, 122, 147, 171, 249, 257; effect on social functioning, 254; effects of, 11, 12, 48, 82, 94; effects on productivity, 81, 122, 139, 256; employee, 29; ESM and, 107, 109; EWPS and, 229; frictional costs of, 158; hidden costs of, 47; health plans and measurement of, 214–16; how to manage, 36; impact of, 122, 160, 211, 249, 262; impact of change in, 150; impact on abilities, 123, 132, 136; impact on labor market, 142; impact on productivity, 38–41, 123, 132; impairment due to, 48;

influence on skills, 125; influence on time use, 110; labor demand model and, 15, 145, 150–59; labor market consequences of, 159; labor supply and, 16; longitudinal change in, 215; long-term impact of, 49; lost productivity due to, 78; measuring impact of, 37; non-workplace, 181; objective measures of, 33; occupational performance and, 133, 136, 137–38; O*NET examination of, 128–31, 138; performance and, 6, 61, 89, 111, 113; prevalence rates of, 34; productivity and, 47, 74, 121, 192, 256; productivity consequences of, 73; productivity costs and, 120, 138, 139; productivity impact of, 31, 32, *33*, 34, 37; psychosomatic, 108; quality-of-life perspective and, 12; self-report of, 30, 34, 77–81; sick days due to, 30; social consequences of, 1; social cost of, 16, 142; societal costs of, 190; symptoms of, 45, 112; treatment and, 31; untreated, 6; wage rate and, 250; wage loss associated with, 151; work cutback during, 31; work absences due to, 74, 195; worker absences per, 42; work loss due to, 198; workplace costs of, 16, 18, 21, 272, 280; workplace impact of, 36. *See also* health impairment; impairment

impairment: aggregate cost of, 48; cognitive, 108, 278–79; days, 34, 37; work, 16, 36, 257, 278–79. *See also* health impairment; illness

indirect costs: depression and, 257; health-care investment and, 271–72, 280; health plans and, 210, 216; HPM program and, 172; labor market consequences and, 159; prescription drug use and, 243; three perspectives and, 187–91, 195, 198–99, 202–3

Institute of Medicine, 174, 177, 179, 284

Institute for Health and Productivity Management (IHPM), 23, 271–72, 279

Integrated Benefits Institute, 17, 23, 272
integrated benefits management strategies, 4
internal rate of return (IRR), 172
International Classification of Diseases, 9th ed. *See* ICD-9
International Labor Organization, 5
International Maritime Organization, 56, 63
investment: approach to health, 17–18, 185–86, 283; business case for, 19; developing countries and, 255, 258, 263; eValue8group and, 173; health care as, 1–2, 203, 217, 271–74; health plans and, 20, 208, 212–14, 216; HR programs and, 17, 171–72; human capital, 5, 19, 64; perspective, 210–11; portfolio of choices in health-related productivity, 198–203; quantification of, 12, 187; rationalization of, 22; return on (ROI), 23, 186, 196, 200, 204

John D. and Catherine T. MacArthur Foundation, 4, 23
Joint Commission on Accreditation of Health Care Organizations (JCAHO), 207, 273
Juran Institute, 166

labor demand model, 147, 151–52
Leapfrog Group, 180
London Handicap Scale, 77
lost-wages method, 189–91. *See also* human capital

managed care organizations (MCOs), 17. *See also* health plans
measurement approaches, 4–5, 12, 54
measures: absenteeism, 201; aggregate, 12; clinical, 48; clinical status, 32; clinical trials and, 235–37; consumer-oriented, 212; development of, 54, 68–69; disaggregated, 15; disease-specific

productivity, 228; employers and, 190–91, 202–3; ESM and, 93–94, 104–6, 109–10; FDA and, 21–22, 242–43, 250–52; gold-standard, 48, 250–51; health plans and, 174, 177, 207–17, 220–21; health status, 48; illness-specific, 110; indirect cost, 195; individual-level, 18; integrated benefit management and, 3–6; investments in health care and, 272–83; job performance and, 134; labor-market outcomes and, 142–43, 156, 218; occupational performance and, 54; O*NET and, 15,125, 132–37, 139; pharmaceutical industry and, 226–35, 237–38; physiological, 105; quality, 19, 179, 207, 212–16, 220; self-report, 9, 67–68, 73–81, 83–84; sickness absence, 75; teamwork and productivity, 49; treatment-process, 23; validity associated with any, 62–63; value/benefit, 180; WLQ, 78; work productivity, 9–15, 18–23, 30–34, 49; World Bank and, 258–59; WPAI, 233
medication, 20, 212, 238, 257
mental disorders, 47, 72, 256, 257–61
mental illness, 42, 47, 95, 262–63
Merck & Co., Inc., 201–2, 231
meta-analysis, 123, 129
MGBH. *See* Midwest Business Group on Health
MHP (Minnesota Health Partnership and Coordinated Health Care and Disability Prevention Program), 181–82
MIDUS (Midlife Development in the United States Survey), 34, 36
Midwest Business Group on Health (MBGH), 17, 166–67, 218, 279
migraine: costs of, 200; ESM and, *103*, 109, 112; HLQ and, 230; self-report and, 30; treatment of, 225–26
Migraine Work and Productivity Loss Questionnaire (MWPLQ), 228

Minnesota Health Partnership and Coordinated Health Care and Disability Prevention Program (MHP), 181–82
MOS 36-item Short-Form Health Survey. *See* SF-36
MWPLQ (Migraine Work and Productivity Loss Questionnaire), 228
mystery customer method, 8

National Business Coalition on Health (NBCH), 17, 272, 276, 280
National Business Group on Health (NBGH), 272
National Committee for Quality Assurance (NCQA), 23, 273
National Comorbidity Survey (NCS), 36, 257
National Health Interview Survey (NHIS), 74
National Highway Traffic Safety Administration, 56, 63
National Institute of Mental Health (NIMH), 279
National Institute for Occupational Safety and Health (NIOSH), 5
National Medical Expenditure Survey (NMES), 37
NBGH (National Business Group on Health), 272
New York State Cardiac Surgery Reporting System (CSRS), 284

O*NET (Occupational Information Network of the Department of Labor): abilities domain and, 128–29; content model of, 124–26; data collection and, 127–28; definition, 123; meta-analysis and validity generalization and, 129–30; micro approach and, 55; overall work performance and, 14–15; practicality of, 215; productivity research and, 139; research plan and, 131–39; utility analysis and, 131

panic disorder, 34
PAQ (Position Analysis Questionnaire), 125
performance: abilities and, 15, 128–39; archival data and, 7, 32, 215, 262; assessment, 14, 207, 226; assessment using the WLQ, 78; audits, 3, 9, 11, 13; bias in reports of, 95; component vs. aggregate, 12; consistency, 58; criteria, 68; depression and, 257; disaggregated assessment of, 13; effects of alcohol on, 62; effects of chronic disease on, 88; effect of illness on, 111–12; effect of treatment on, 62; effects on, 5, 277, 279, 280; employee, 33, 64, 82; employee well-being and, 105; endpoints, 245; ESM and, 11, 89–107, 113; evaluation, 8, 56; formula, 131; gold standard measure, 48, 56, 250; health and, 2–3; health plan, 207, 210; health plans and assessment of, 208–9, 211–20; HPM programs and, 166, 174, 178–79; HPQ and, 231–32, 276–79; impact of diseases on, 47; impact of treatment on, 242–43; impairment, 36, 76; internal validity and, 63; investment decisions and, 213, 272–76; job, 71; measure of, 59, 134, 221; measurement of occupational, 54, 211; measurement tools and, 217; measures, 14, 19, 177; multiple task loading, 59; O*NET and, 120–22, 131; objective data and, 278; objective measures of, 272; objectivity, 58; occupational, 123, 131, 133, 136, 215; on-the-job, 45; paying for, 178–79; perspective, 12; pharmaceutical claims and, 21; predicting, 132, 135–37; and productivity, 258; ratings, 82; records, 31; self report and, 30, 67, 88, 215; sensitivity, 72; simulation and, 4, 7–9, 54–63; skills, 125; social loss and, 151; standard deviation of, 138; supervisor ratings of, 7; team, 191, 234; tests, 105; vendor pay-

performance (*continued*)
ment based on, 17; and well-being, 105, 106; work cutback and, 31; workplace, 250; work productivity scales and, 78–81
pharmaceutical companies, 5, 21–22, 224–25, 235–39, 271
pharmaceutical industry, 20–21, 194, 224–25
pharmacoeconomic investigation, 31
pharmacoepidemiological perspective, 13
Position Analysis Questionnaire (PAQ), 125
presenteeism: employer's perspective and, 209, 213; health investments and, 185, 187, 197, 200, 202–3; HPM and, 180; population health approach and, 168; productivity claims and, 245. *See also* work cutback
prevention programs, 198–200, 203, 214
productivity: archival data and, 9–10, 32, 45, 47–49; archival measures of, 37, 38–41, 42, 44; assessment of, 4, 235, 273, 281–84; benefit management and, 29–31, 165–72, 178–83, 211; clinical trials and, 235–37; depression and, 95, 159; developing countries and, 256–64; effects, 30, 36; employer data and, 81–83; employer perspective and, 17–20, 29–31, 178, 185–204; ESM and, 89, 92–97, 105–6, 113; FDA perspective on, 242–52; generalizability and, 139; global measures of, 11, 215; gold standard measurement, 22, 244, 250–52; health and, 17, 272–76; health insurance and, 200–201; health outcome research and, 47–50; health payments, 174; health plan perspective, 18–19, 207–8, 211–16; health programs and, 17, 199; HLQ, 229–30; HPQ and, 276–83; human resources perspective, 16; industrialized nations and, 255; labor demand model and, 15–16,142–58;

management, 10, 19, 175–76, 217; measurement approaches, 4–16, 66; measurement of, 226, 227, 228–33; migraine and, 36; O*NET model of, 120–23, 128–29, 132, 138–39; objective data on, 6; paid work and, 81; perceived effectiveness and, 76; pharmaceutical industry and, 224–25, 233–39; poor health and, 2; prevention programs and, 199–200; research, challenges of, 21; ROI and, 196; self-report measures and, 7, 34, 81–84, 214; self-report tracking surveys, 23; self-reports of, 11, 67, 71–74, 88; shift work and, 106; sickness absences and, 74–76; simulation and, 9, 54–55, 63–64; social, 260; social costs of, 148; social-role disability scales and, 78; strategies to examine, 31–47; study approach categories, 57; study designs, 251; temp employees and, 158; tracking data, 275; types of, 143; valuation, 233–35; value-based purchasing and, 173; WHI and, 232; WLQ and, 78–80; work-productivity scales, 78–81; World Bank and, 253; WPAI, 232–33
productivity claims, 17, 22, 236, 243–44, 251
productivity offset, 36, 49
prospective studies, 48, 218
psychiatric disorders, 107, 110–11, 254, 257

quality-adjusted life-years (QALYs), 233–34, 261
quality assurance: companies and, 6, 272–74; HPQ and, 276, 280–81; outcome-based, 284; programs, 207; targets, 23
Quality Dividend Calculator, 201, 216
Quality Enhancement by Strategic Testing (QuEST), 219
Quality of Well-Being Scale, 77
quasi-simulation, 7–8

recall accuracy, 37, 71, 75, 81, 230. *See also* recall bias

recall bias: ESM and, 11, 14, 88–89, 113; options for reducing, 75; simulation and, 58. *See also* recall accuracy; error: recall

report cards, 19, 201, 207. *See also* HEDIS

retrospective reports, 10, 14. *See also* administrative claims data

Robert Wood Johnson Foundation, 181, 219

sampling: approaches, 90; ESM and, 101, 109; theory, 13

self report, 32, 249, 262. *See also* measures: self-report

self-report data, 3, 7, 67, 70, 275

self-report methods, 66, 249

self-report surveys, 10, 88, 113

SF-36 (The MOS 36-item Short-Form Health Survey), 77, 217

Sheehan Disability Scale, 77

Short Form 36-item scale (SF-36). *See* SF-36

sick leave: administrative claims data and, 31–32, 34, 37, 44; employer records and, 249; labor demand model and, 143n1, 144n2, 153, 158

sickness absence: employers and, 3, 6, 18, 273–75; HPQ and, 277, 279–81, 283; self-report and, 9, 74–76

Sickness Impact Profile, 77

simulation: advantages of, 57–61; definition of, 54–55; exercise and, 199; health plans and, 215; history of, 56–57; performance assessment and, 4, 7–9, 13, 15, 59; regulation and, 63

simulator: aircraft, 56; automobile and truck, 61; bridge, 56; cargo-loading, 56; cost-effectiveness of, 59; definition of, 55; dental, 57; driving, 63; engine, 56; electrical, 56; flight, 58, 60, 61–62;

gunnery, 57; maritime, 62; medical conditions and, 64; NHTSA's national driving, 63; ship, 62; surgery, 57; training, 56; ultrasound, 57; workplace context and, 60

sleep problems, 34

social losses, 153, 160

social role-disability scales, 76–78

Social Security Administration (SSA), 124

Society of Quality Assurance, 273

SSA (Social Security Administration), 124

Stanford Presenteeism Scale (SPS), 228, 231

stroke, 42

substance abuse, *40, 43, 61, 168*

telescoping, 71

treatment: archival data and, *30–32, 33, 34, 36–37, 47–48*; of chronic illness, 173; disease management programs and, 202; drug, 110, 225, *226, 242–46*; employer databases and, 81; ESM and, 110–11; generalizable indicators and, 82; health plans and, 19, 171–73, 213–18; HPM and, 167, 178, 181–82; HPQ and, 276–82; investment in, 1–3, 16–19, 23, 271–75, 283–84; labor demand model and gains from, 143, 145, 151, 159; O*NET and, 128–29; performance and, 62, 243; productivity offset and, 49; role functioning and, 1; ROI evaluations of, 23; self-report and, 67, 73–74, 77, 81, 275

ulcers, *34, 39, 42*

utility analysis, 123, 131

validity: assessment of work performance and, 14, 77, 79; clinical, 237; concurrent, 229, 232, 235; construct, 79, 110, 230, 233, 235; content, 75; criterion, 76, 80, 231, 235–36, 238; discrimi-

validity (*continued*)
nant, 232, 235; definition of, 62–63, 68; ecological, 60; ESM and, 92–93, 113; external, 7, 63; face, 58, 62, 63, 202; generalization, 129–30; internal, 63; known-groups and, 232, 235; mean-corrected, 130; O*NET and, 129–30, 132–36, 138; responsiveness and, 68; self-report questionnaires and, 83, 215, 217, 221, 226; unproven, 190

value-based purchasing (VBP): benefit design and, 19–20; health plans and, 207–8, 210–11, 216, 220–21; large firms and, 173

war games, 8. *See also* simulation

WHO (World Health Organization): Commission on Macroeconomics and Health, 255, 263–64; Global Burden of Disease Initiative, 230, 276

WHO Health and Work Performance Questionnaire. *See* HPQ

WLQ. *See* Work Limitations Questionnaire

work absence, 32, 45, 75, 181, 234. *See also* absenteeism

Work and Health Interview (WHI), 228

work cutback, 31–32, 34, 249–50, 257–58. *See also* presenteeism

Work Limitations Questionnaire (WLQ), 78, 80, 215, 229

work performance: assessments, 9, 14; audits of, 11, 13; data, 7; depression and, 257; ESM and, 88–89, 105–6; health and 2–3, 6, 29; health plans and, 215–18, 220; O*NET and, 15, 120; objective measures and, 272; pharmaceutical companies and, 2, 231; self-report and, 12; simulation and, 61–62, 64, 113

Work Productivity and Activity Impairment Questionnaire (WPAI), 228, 232

worker's compensation, 31

World Bank, 5, 22, 253–55, 258, 261–64